STEAMING THROUGH THE
CHEDDAR VALLEY

It is hard to believe this was once a typical, everyday scene at Yatton. No 1463 (82A) on the left, releases steam from her safety valves while awaiting departure with the 2.43pm to Clevedon on 19 August 1957. Prairie 2-6-2T No 5565 (82A) stands in the Cheddar Valley bay to the right before hauling the 2.52pm to Witham. *H. B. Priestley*

Above: The last through train to Witham, the 6.15pm from Yatton hauled by 0-6-0 No 2268 crossing its westbound counterpart at Wells Tucker Street on 7 September 1963. *Hugh Ballantyne*

Below: It's not all strawberries and sunshine in the Cheddar Valley as seen here on 4 January 1963 with '22xx' 0-6-0 No 2277 firmly stuck in snowdrifts between Cheddar and Draycott. *Mike Horwood*

STEAMING THROUGH THE
CHEDDAR VALLEY

Recollections of the East Somerset and Cheddar Valley Branch Lines including the Wrington Vale Line

Derek Phillips

Oxford Publishing Co

Above: BR Standard 2-6-2T No 82039 (82E) hauls the 3.28pm Witham-Yatton, formed of a two-coach 'B' set, away from Shepton Mallet High Street on 27 July 1963. The goods shed to the left once housed the broad-gauge locomotives of the GWR when Shepton Mallet opened as a temporary terminus before the opening of the extension to Wells. *Hugh Ballantyne*

First published 2001

ISBN 0 86093 551 5

© Derek Phillips 2001

Published by Oxford Publishing Co

an imprint of Ian Allan Publishing Ltd, Hersham, Surrey KT12 4RG.
Printed by Ian Allan Printing Ltd, Hersham, Surrey KT12 4RG.

Code: 0103/A2

Front cover: The broad gauge origins of Brunel's 1870 Bristol & Exeter Railway train shed are evident as Class 2MT 2-6-2T No 41245 heads the 3.28pm Witham to Yatton away from Cheddar on 17 August 1963. Three weeks later, on Saturday 7 September, this engine worked the same duty on the last day of passenger services. *Hugh Ballantyne*

Back cover, above: Class 5700 0-6-0PT No 3702 waits at the Cheddar Valley line bay at Yatton before heading the 2.45pm Yatton to Witham on 17 August 1963. A dmu sits in the Clevedon bay and intending passengers await a service from Bristol. *Hugh Ballantyne*

Back cover, below: Leaving Shepton Mallet behind, BR Standard 2-6-2T No 82035 hauls the 11.12am from Yatton towards Witham on 21 July 1962. In the distance, above the engine's bunker, can be seen the goods shed of Charlton Road station on the Somerset & Dorset line, which runs in a cutting in front of the new houses in the left background.

Contents

Acknowledgements   5

Bibliography   5

Introduction   7

History   9

> The Wilts, Somerset & Weymouth Railway, The East Somerset Railway, The Somerset Central, The Cheddar Valley & Yatton, Wrington Vale Light Railway, Projected Lines, The Gauge Conversion

Signalling and Services   16

> Signalling on the Great Western, Signalling on the Somerset Central, Services

Witham-Dulcote Quarry   19

> Witham, Wanstrow, Merehead Quarry-East Cranmore, Cranmore, Doulting Siding, Kilver Street Level Crossing, Shepton Mallet (High Street), Dulcote Quarry Siding

Wells   76

> East Somerset Station and Yard, GWR Locomotive Shed, Wells Shed Diagrams 1944 and 1963, Locomotives shedded overnight, Unusual Locomotive workings over the line, Other workings of interest, Enthusiast Specials over the line, Goods services 1948-62, Summer 1962 and from September 1963, Locomotives used during the last week of Passenger services, Staff at Wells Locomotive Shed, Priory Road Station, Tucker Street Station

Wookey-Cheddar   117

> Wookey, Lodge Hill, Draycott, Cheddar

Axbridge-Yatton   157

> Axbridge, Winscombe, Sandford and Banwell, Congresbury, Wrington Vale Light Railway, Wrington, Langford, Burrington, Blagdon, Yatton and the Clevedon Branch

Index   216

Acknowledgements

I am extremely grateful to the following for their photographic contributions or for providing expert detailed knowledge of the lines described in the book. Thank you to: Andy Viles, Harry Viles, John Reakes, Paul Fry, Terry Morgan, Brian Pike, Robin Jacob, Mendip Rail, Foster Yeoman Ltd, Joe Moss, Roger Carpenter, R. C. Riley, Hugh Ballantyne, R. E. Toop, Ian Allan Library, Peter Nicholson, Henry Esain, Mark Bailey, Paul Boddy, Peter Woods, Andrew Linham, Yeovil Library, Don Flook, Ben Ashworth, Signalling Record Society, Mr Freak, HMRS, Ken Nunn Collection LCGB, Ron Lacey, H. B. Priestley, Mid Somerset Newspapers, Wells Journal and Weston Mercury, The Engine Shed Society, Richard Harman and Mike Horwood.

Bibliography

The Somerset & Dorset Railway by Robin Atthill (Pan Books)
Cheddar Railway Station by Mark Bailey
The Somerset & Dorset Railway by D. S. Barrie and C. R. Clinker (Oakwood Press)
The Newbury Railway by C. G. Down and A. J. Warrington (Industrial Railway Society)
GWR Service Timetable Appendices 1945 (GWR)
GWR Country Stations by Chris Leigh (Ian Allan Publishing Ltd)
Branch Lines of Somerset by Colin Maggs (Alan Sutton)
Branch Line to Cheddar by Vic Mitchell and Keith Smith (Middleton Press)
The Story of the Westbury to Weymouth Line by Derek Phillips (OPC)
Foster Yeoman. The Rail Album by Hugh Searle and Robin Jacob (Foster Yeoman Ltd)
West Country Railway History by David St John Thomas (David & Charles)

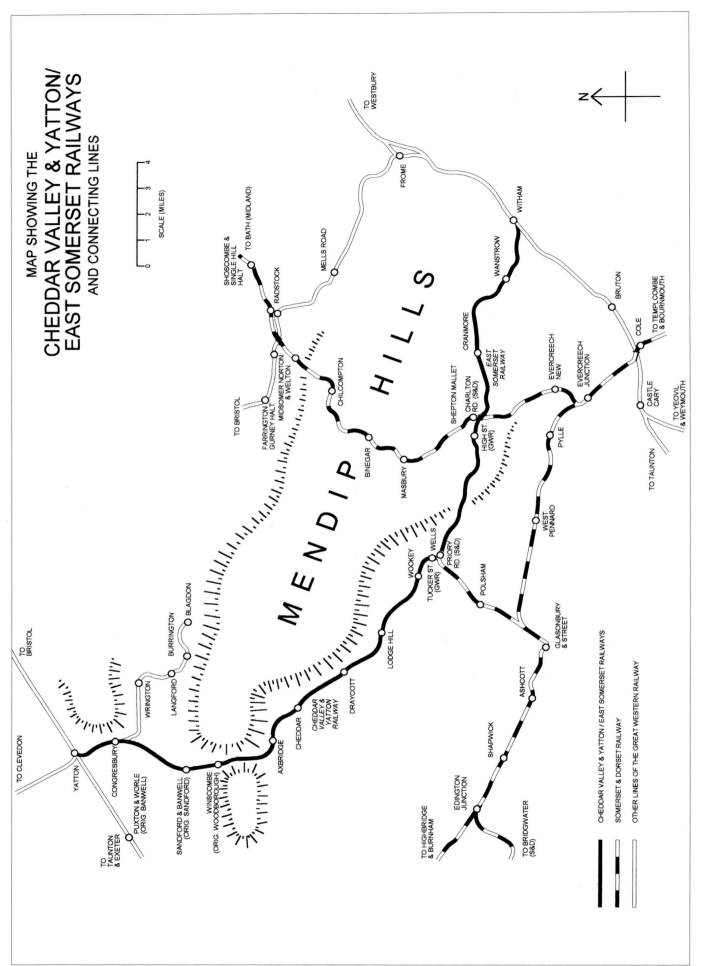

MAP SHOWING THE
CHEDDAR VALLEY & YATTON/
EAST SOMERSET RAILWAYS
AND CONNECTING LINES

SCALE (MILES)
0 1 2 3 4

N

TO WESTBURY

TO BATH (MIDLAND)

SHOSCOMBE &
SINGLE HILL HALT

RADSTOCK

FROME

MELLS ROAD

MIDSOMER NORTON
& WELTON

FARRINGTON
GURNEY HALT

TO BRISTOL

CHILCOMPTON

WITHAM

WANSTROW

CRANMORE

EAST
SOMERSET
RAILWAY

M E N D I P   H I L L S

BINEGAR

MASBURY

SHEPTON MALLET

CHARLTON
RD. (S&D)

HIGH ST.
(GWR)

EVERCREECH
NEW

EVERCREECH
JUNCTION

PYLLE

BRUTON

COLE

CASTLE
CARY

TO TEMPLCOMBE
& BOURNMOUTH

TO YEOVIL
& WEYMOUTH

TO TAUNTON

WEST
PENNARD

WELLS

TUCKER ST.
(GWR)

PRIORY
RD. (S&D)

WOOKEY

POLSHAM

GLASTONBURY
& STREET

ASHCOTT

LODGE HILL

DRAYCOTT

CHEDDAR

CHEDDAR
VALLEY &
YATTON
RAILWAY

AXBRIDGE

SHAPWICK

EDINGTON
JUNCTION

TO HIGHBRIDGE
& BURNHAM

TO BRIDGWATER
(S&D)

BLAGDON

BURRINGTON

LANGFORD

WRINGTON

WINSCOMBE
(ORIG. WOODBOROUGH)

SANDFORD & BANWELL
(ORIG. SANDFORD)

PUXTON & WORLE
(ORIG. BANWELL)

CONGRESBURY

YATTON

TO CLEVEDON

TO BRISTOL

TO TAUNTON
& EXETER

CHEDDAR VALLEY & YATTON / EAST SOMERSET RAILWAYS

SOMERSET & DORSET RAILWAY

OTHER LINES OF THE GREAT WESTERN RAILWAY

The route diagram of the East Somerset and Cheddar Valley lines with both routes merging at Wells.
Richard Harman

Introduction

Many years have now passed since GWR tank engines departed from the junction stations at Witham and Yatton, heading along the East Somerset and Cheddar Valley branch lines, trailing a two-coach 'B' set to Wells and Cheddar. The slap of the vacuum pump, the shriek of the whistle echoing around the sylvan Somerset countryside — the clatter of lower quadrant signals clearing the way ahead as trains approached the stations, have all gone now. Through the pages of this book the stations are open and alive again including Congresbury and the meandering line to Blagdon, and Cheddar with its imposing and grand Brunellian overall roof, so befitting for visitors alighting to visit the famous caves in the nearby picturesque gorge. The city of Wells with its beautiful cathedral had, at one time, to endure the complexities of the visitations of not one, but three railway companies, each with its own station, staff, and engine sheds. Country people who, in those days, had no transport other than the railway, remember Axbridge, Cheddar, Draycott, and Wookey with fondness. Shepton Mallet station at the end of the High Street was more convenient for the townsfolk than the Somerset & Dorset station at Charlton Road.

An historical point, which must be taken into consideration, is that the 'Cheddar Valley' was the GWR branch which extended from Yatton to Wells; the section that ran from Wells to Witham via Shepton Mallet was never regarded by the Great Western Railway as the Cheddar Valley but was known as the East Somerset. Reference to timetables makes it clear that the two parts were worked as separate lines. There were never any tabled trains that went right through without at least a 10-minute stop at Wells. A down train from Witham became an up train when continuing from Wells to Yatton. In fact, the whole of the line from Yatton to Witham was always referred to as the 'Wells Branch' by the GWR.

Strawberries, the most delicious of summer fruits, and none better than grown on the fertile slopes of the Cheddar Valley, were loaded daily when in season, and delivered by train to destinations far and wide, as was the famous and tasty Cheddar cheese. Limestone from the quarries on the brooding and majestic Mendips was hauled away by the railway, for use in roadmaking schemes, far away from Somerset. The former station buildings standing empty today, alongside the Axbridge bypass, remind us of our folly in destroying the rural railway system.

Cranmore has been reopened under the auspices of artist David Shepherd and the East Somerset Railway and steam trains now ply over a very small section of the old branch line, giving tourists nearly, but not quite, the impression of what the real thing was like. Recollections of the old line come to life at times, when one is in a reflective mood: a grimy pannier tank bound for Witham dragging a heavy mineral train over the main road at Kilver Street Crossing, smoking engines standing under the echoing overall roof at Cheddar, the slam of signal levers, and the ringing of block bells from the open signalbox windows at Congresbury. Of such things are dreams and memories made, never forgotten.

Derek Phillips
Yeovil, October 2000

Below: The signalman, staff and passengers pose for posterity in this splendid view of Cranmore as an up train of six-wheeled coaches headed by a pannier tank approaches the station. The brand new brickwork of the signalbox opened in 1904 can be seen to good effect, as can be the new surface of the down platform on the left. The imposing stationmaster's house can be seen to the far right. The large building in the background is the crushing and loading plant of the Mendip Granite Works which was supplied with limestone from Waterlip Quarry in tubs made of elm wood, running on a 2ft gauge track. These were worked by gravity from the quarry in trains of 12 wagons at a time. The empty tubs were hauled back to the quarry by a team of shire horses. *John Reakes collection*

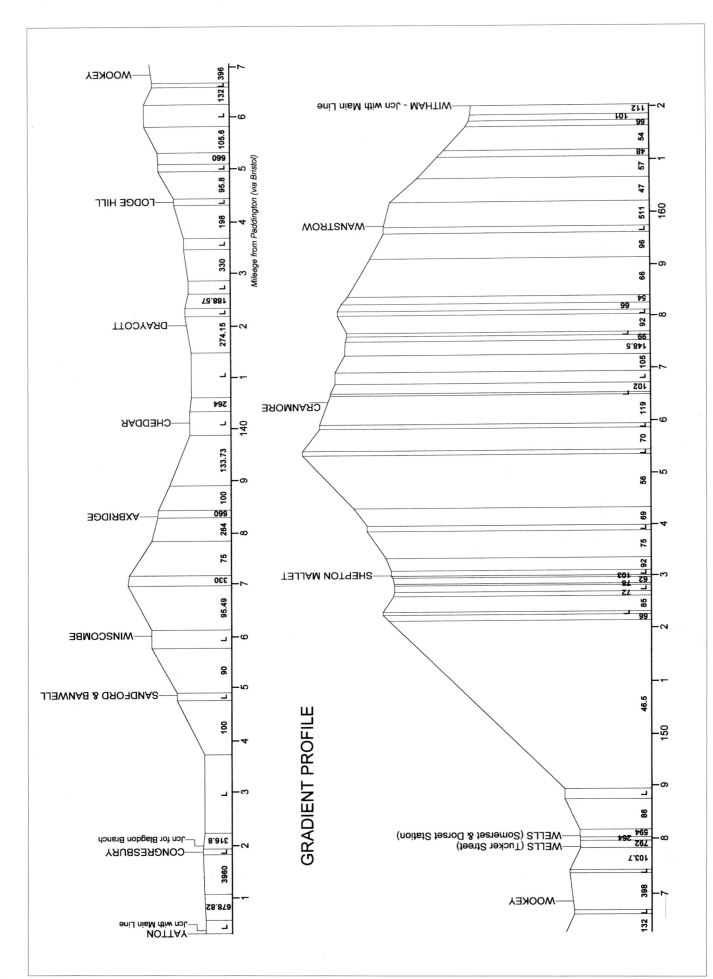

The gradient profile shows the severity of the East Somerset branch compared with the Cheddar Valley line.

Richard Harman

History

The Wilts, Somerset & Weymouth Railway

As with all schemes in the heady days of the Railway Mania, we have to look elsewhere for the beginnings of the line in question. In 1844, southern Somerset and Dorset found themselves in the front line of the 'Battle of the Gauges' and the arrival of the railway at Westbury in 1848 was the direct result of the gauge war between the standard gauge London & South Western Railway and the GWR. The LSWR (in 1844) had proposed a line from Basingstoke to Swindon — thus striking into what the GWR considered to be the heart of its territory. The GWR retaliated by proposing lines from Reading to Basingstoke and Newbury (known as the Berks & Hants) and from Corsham to Salisbury with branch lines to Devizes, Bradford-on-Avon and Frome with a coal line to Radstock, the whole to be known as the Wilts & Somerset Railway.

The GWR had formulated the Wilts & Somerset at a meeting held at the Bath Arms in Warminster on 9 July 1844. Brunel, in company with other officers of the company was present, and he presented his scheme for a line from Thingley Junction to Salisbury via Trowbridge and the Wylye Valley, with branches to Bradford-on-Avon and Frome, and from Melksham to Devizes. The Bristol & Exeter meanwhile was striking out from the west, with proposals for a line from Durston to Yeovil and onwards to Weymouth. The plans of the GWR were altered in the autumn of the same year, with the Newbury branch of the Berks & Hants being extended to Hungerford. However at a meeting held in the George Inn, Frome, on 23 October 1844, Saunders, the Secretary of the GWR, announced to the provisional committee meeting, that the Bristol & Exeter had said it would prefer to carry the line from Durston through Crewkerne, Beaminster and Bridport to Dorchester, with a branch to Yeovil, instead of a direct Yeovil-Dorchester-Weymouth line as previously sanctioned by the Board of Trade. Following this alteration, the GWR and the B&E suggested and obtained the sanction of the Board of Trade, that the Wilts & Somerset be extended the 27½ miles from Yeovil to Weymouth and a branch added from Maiden Newton to Bridport. Yeovil to Sherborne was never completed, the B&E constructing a line from Durston to Yeovil but not extending towards the south in competition with the Weymouth and Bridport lines. The branch from Trowbridge to Bradford-on-Avon was also extended through the Avon Valley to make another junction with the GWR at Bathampton. The name of the undertaking was amended to the Wilts, Somerset & Weymouth Railway.

The Wilts, Somerset & Weymouth Act was passed on 30 June 1845 authorising a railway to be built from the GWR at Thingley to Salisbury with branches to Weymouth, Devizes, Bradford, Radstock, Sherborne and Bridport, the gauge to be that of the GWR, and powers given to lease the line to that company. Authorised capital was £1½ million with borrowing powers of £½ million and powers allowing the GWR to subscribe and guarantee interest up to 5%. The WSWR was to have 12 directors, of whom four were to be appointed by the GWR. The line from Thingley Junction to Westbury opened on 5 September 1848; this section, the only one completed by the independent WS&W, happened to coincide with the financial depression at that time and all further work was suspended and the contractors dismissed. Some of the land was re-let, much of it to the previous owners, and the countryside for many miles along the route was punctuated with stretches of half-completed earthworks and bridges.

The GWR absorbed the now-defunct WS&W which, although nominally independent, was always a creature of the GWR, the hope being entertained that a seemingly local company would make better progress with raising subscriptions. Transfer of the former company to the GWR was confirmed by Parliament in the Great Western Railway Act of 3 July 1851. The erstwhile Wilts, Somerset & Weymouth company was now dissolved. Westbury to Frome opened on 7 October 1850 and Westbury to Warminster on 9 September the following year. Frome to Radstock came into operation on 14 November 1854, but progress was painfully slow on the Weymouth branch with the line from Frome to Yeovil opening as a single line on 1 September 1856, almost eight years bar a few days since the opening to Westbury in 1848. The final section from Yeovil to Weymouth opened on 20 January 1857. However, this is beyond the remit of our book; more expanded details of the WS&W and the line from Westbury to Weymouth can be found in the author's *The Story of the Westbury to Weymouth Line* (OPC).

The East Somerset Railway

It is not surprising that Shepton Mallet and the neighbouring cathedral city of Wells, both places of considerable local importance, were early candidates for connection to the railway system. Shepton Mallet was the scene of the inaugural meeting of the East Somerset Railway on 29 September 1855 in the offices of local solicitors Phipps & Mackay, when it was planned to construct a line from Frome to Shepton. At the meeting it was formally agreed that subject to the approval of the ESR's Engineer, Isambard Kingdom Brunel, to the proposed route of the new line, a prospectus would be issued and public meetings held in order to raise financial capital. A letter from Charles Saunders, the Secretary of the GWR, to the directors of the ESR stated that the shareholders of the GWR 'regard with much interest and favour the promotion of a broad gauge line of railway between Frome and Wells provided it is established in direct connection with this railway at or near Frome but without seeking pecuniary assistance of any form from this company.' The GWR was heavily committed to other areas of its empire at the time, and although agreeing in principle to the proposed line, would not be forthcoming with any financial assistance, and the ESR would be on its own, a situation from which the GWR would benefit at the gauge conversion.

Brunel proceeded to survey the route of the new line. Faced with a choice of two routes, through Stoke Lane to Doulting, or from Witham, the latter was chosen as it would be cheaper to build, and enough land was set aside for double track, although as was often the case, the initial earthworks were set out for a single route of railway, laid to the broad gauge. The directors of the ESR, in a letter sent by Brunel in December

1855, were informed that if they were able to raise £30,000 a contractor — Rowland Brotherhood of Chippenham — would subscribe the sum of £25,000, the intent being that Parliament would realise that the public envisaged the scheme as a viable concern and therefore would look at the application in its favour. The relevant Act of Parliament was passed on 5 June 1856 allowing a capital of £75,000 to be raised in shares of £10 each, plus additional borrowing powers of £25,000. The citizens of Wells, disappointed with the slow progress of the Somerset Central from Glastonbury, and to bring pressure on the directors of the SCR, asked the directors of the ESR to apply to the next Parliamentary session for an extension of the East Somerset line to their city. This was agreed by the board of the ESR, the proviso being that the Wells deputation would subscribe the sum of £12,500. A subscription list for £12,090 appeared from Wells in October of the same year and this urged the directors of the ESR to apply for the necessary powers. The relevant extension Act was passed on 25 July the following year, 1857, this allowing the East Somerset Railway to raise an additional £40,000 with further borrowing powers of £13,000.

Rowland Brotherhood, the contractor, signed the £64,500 contract for building the 9-mile-long line between Witham and Shepton Mallet on 6 February 1857, a junction to be made connecting the ESR with the WS&W Weymouth branch at Witham. It was announced at the general meeting of the ESR on 31 March the same year, that work would proceed in a few days with completion expected in 18 months. The contractor's workmen started work on 1 April by fencing the intended route of the railway. From Witham the line climbed steeply and was laid mainly on clay subsoil until reaching the southern border of the Mendip Hills where limestone was reached. The broad gauge permanent way, formed of bridge rail, was laid on longitudinal sleepers with transoms spaced at intervals of 11 feet. The estimated cost of the permanent way was £1,900 per mile with the contractor maintaining the trackwork for 12 months, at a cost of £900; the GWR would then maintain the trackwork after the first year. The annual general meeting held the following year announced that the contractor, although having been delayed by various landowners haggling over the price of land, would shortly complete the line. A length of approximately 1½ miles had been ballasted between Cranmore and Doulting and was ready for rails to be laid; track laying was moving ahead rapidly during the following month.

The ESR gave notice to the Board of Trade on 28 September, 1855, were informed that if they were able to raise £30,000 a ber of the intention of opening the line within four weeks. The Inspecting Officer — Captain Yolland — duly arrived and although partially satisfied with the state of the new works, discovered a number of things that needed immediate attention, including distant signals being required at Witham and Shepton Mallet, the lack of a crossing keeper's cottage at Kilver Street and a ramp being needed at Shepton Mallet station. However, it was the arrangement of working between the single-line ESR and the WSWR single line at Witham that gave rise to concern for the Inspecting Officer. In his view, if the branch was to be worked separately, a turntable would be required at Witham or the turntable at Shepton Mallet would be useless, but if trains worked through to Frome the turntable there would suffice. Captain Yolland therefore did not sanction the opening of the line in view of the absence of an undertaking showing how the line was to be worked, plus the state of incompleteness. In order to put things right, the secretary and deputy chairman of the ESR signed an undertaking that the line would be worked by tank engines, therefore making the requirement for a turntable at Witham unnecessary.

The strong personage of Isambard Kingdom Brunel personally negotiated with the Board of Trade which, in its wisdom, granted permission for the line to open, which it did on 9 November 1858 with an intermediate station at Cranmore. Services on the branch were to be worked by the GWR which would also supply locomotives and rolling stock, all to a price of course, and before the working totals were debited from gross receipts a debenture debt not exceeding £1,250 would be paid to the GWR annually, and any deficiency charged to the ESR. The small station at Wanstrow opened two years later in 1860.

The Somerset Central Railway branch from Glastonbury to Wells opened at last on 15 March 1859 and the directors of the SCR felt the extension of the ESR to Wells would threaten its monopoly of the Wells traffic. In a letter to the ESR dated 23 November 1859 George Warry, the Chairman of the Somerset Central put forward the following proposals: 'The ESR should abandon its line to Wells and build instead a line from Shepton to Street to link up with the SCR, the proposed line to be built jointly by the two companies, the line when made, to be worked as part of the ESR and leased to the GWR on the same terms as the line to Wells.'

The GWR and the ESR soundly rejected the proposals of the Somerset Central. Brunel had submitted further plans for the extension from Shepton to Wells in 1857 and he envisaged a line running immediately below the villages of Croscombe and Dinder. A station was to have been constructed at Croscombe with the line proceeding in the valley fronting Dinder House. However, the owner of the estate, J. C. Somerville, did not wish to see trains from his house, and would only support the line if it was out of sight behind Dulcote Hill. This presented the ESR with a new Act of Parliament having to be drawn up, as well as a new route for the railway. Plans were submitted

EAST SOMERSET RAILWAY.	Stations.	1 2 class a m	1 2 class a m	1 2 3 class a m	1 2 class p m	1 2 class p m	Stations.	1 2 class a m	1 2 3 class a m	1 2 class p m	1 2 class p m	NO SUNDAY TRAINS.
	Wells .. dep	6 55	10 25	10 25	1 45	6 30	Paddington..dep			6 0	11 45	4 50
	Shepton Mallet	7 10	10 40	10 40	2 0	6 45	Didcot			8 0		6. 5
	Cranmore	7 20	10 50	10 50	2 10	6 55	Swindon			9 15	1 30	6 50
	Wanstrow	7 30	11 0	11 0		7 5	Chippenham			10 0	2 10	7 20
	Witham	7 35	11 5	11 5	1 50	7 10	Bristol	6 45	8 50	1 40	6 25	
	Frome	7 53	11 30	11 30	2 40	7 28	Bath	7 20	9 20	2 0	7 0	
		1,2,3										
	Yeovil ..	9 35	12 5	12 5	1 10	9 5	Salisbury	6 55		1 40	6 25	
	Dorchester	10 30	12 55	12 55	5 0	9 45	Warminster	7 48		2 35	7 18	
	Weymouth	10 50	1 15	1 15	5 20	10 0	Westbury	8 22		2 57	8 2	
	Westbury ..	8 25	12 27	12 27	3 0	8 5	Weymouth	6 10	9 0	1 0	5 45	
	Warminster	8 40	12 40	12 40	3 15	8 20	Dorchester	6 25	9 17	1 15	6 0	
	Salisbury	9 35	1 35	1 35	4 10	9 15	Yeovil	7 0	10 10	1 50	6 35	
		1 2 cl.						1,2,3				
	Bath ..	9 0	12 50	12 50	3 50	8 35	Frome	8 35	11 0	3 10	8 15	
	Bristol ..	9 35	1 15	1 15	4 25	9 0	Witham	8 55	11 20	3 30	8 30	
	Chippenham ..	8 45	12 35	12 35	3 30	8 18	Wanstrow	9 2		3 37	8 37	
	Swindon	9 20	1 30	2 35	4 5	8 55	Cranmore	9 15	11 35	3 50	8 50	
	Didcot ..	10 0		3 25	4 45	9 40	Shepton Mallet	9 25	11 45	4 0	9 0	
	Paddington..arr	11 15	3 0	5 6	6 0	11 0	Wells ..arr	9 40	12 0	4 15	9 15	

Left:
The East Somerset Railway timetable for March 1862.

in 1859 by R. J. Ward, the ESR Engineer, proposing the line would run south of the two villages mentioned to avoid the additional expense of cutting a 286yd-long tunnel under the turnpike road at Church Hill, Dinder. This was the route whose deviation was finally adopted by an Act of 14 June 1860 and this act seems to have cancelled a proposed connection with the SCR at Wells; the connection was not realised until some considerable time after. Work started on the extension in December 1860 with D. Baldwin as the contractor. The East Somerset Railway subscribed £20 for the services of a chaplain to the navvies engaged on the construction of the railway. The contract for the terminus station at Wells was awarded to a George Beaven of Wells for the princely sum of £2,411 14s 8d. The contractors are reported as working by night and day in September 1861 despite delays caused by bad weather. As with the original line, the permanent way was laid with bridge rail on longitudinal sleepers and was ready for inspection by February 1862.

However, the redoubtable Colonel Yolland did not pass the line for opening due to its incompleteness; the question of turntables arose again, when he required that one be installed at Wells, and proposed that the Shepton Mallet turntable be moved to Witham as it was almost useless because of the lack of one at the junction. The colonel also suggested that a clock was needed at Wells to be seen from the platform. The Board of Trade withdrew its prohibition when the Secretary of the ESR, G. W. Mackay, gave an undertaking that only one engine in steam, or two coupled together, would be operated and that a turntable would be installed at Wells if the traffic warranted it. An agreeable proposal was also made to the GWR by the ESR that it would put in a turntable at Wells. The Spagnoletti electric telegraph would also be installed, if the GWR would lose no time in installing a turntable at Witham. The electric telegraph was installed by 1 May the same year. The ceremonial opening of the extension had taken place on 28 February 1862 with a special train conveying Lord Bath, the directors and the well-heeled, and was greeted at Wells by the Mayor and the Civic Corporation with the band playing 'God Save the Queen'. The usual celebrations for this type of event, attended by the wealthy and the upper crust, were held at the Swan Inn. Public services on the extension began the following day, 1 March. However, the Somerset Central had opened its station on 15 March 1859 and for 16 years the two termini would confront each other across Priory Road.

Although constructed with hope and optimism, the financial fortunes of the East Somerset Railway did not flourish according to expectations, and in December 1872, it was proposed that the GWR would purchase the ESR for the sum of £86,680. However, the accountants did not have their sums right, and the figure was adjusted to £87,138 due to the oversight of some re-issued share stock. The GWR by comparison, looking for a bargain, offered Great Western Consolidation 5% Stock at 80 for every £100 ESR, and ordinary shareholders, Great Western Consolidated 5% Preference Stock at 40 for every £100 of ESR stock. Talks broke down in June 1863 as the GWR refused to offer more than £2 10s 0d for ordinary shares instead of £5. But darker clouds lay on the horizon for the East Somerset Railway. The days of the broad gauge on the WS&W and its branches were drawing to a close, and in January 1874 the secretary of the GWR informed the ESR of the intention to convert the Wilts, Somerset & Weymouth (from Thingley Junction to Dorchester Junction) to standard gauge, in May of the same year. The cost of converting similarly from Witham to Wells, including junction and signalling alterations at Witham, altering sidings and platforms at Shepton Mallet and Wells, totalled £7,390. The East Somerset was in no position to pay

this vast amount, so to sell to the GWR now was not an option but a necessity, and it was recommended that its shareholders seek £67,499 of GWR Consolidated Preference Stock. The terms of the proposed transfer of the East Somerset to the GWR were accepted on 19 June 1874 although the total of preference stock was reduced to £67,442. Amalgamation with the GWR took effect on 30 June. A special meeting of the ESR approved the transfer on 22 September 1874, but this was only a rubber-stamp job, as by this time the broad gauge had disappeared from the Wilts & Somerset, with the GWR eventually purchasing the line on 2 December the same year.

The Somerset Central Railway

The area of land between the Mendip and the Polden hills, which run east to west, comprised mostly marshland until the 1770s, when attempts were made to drain it and enclosure began. An Act of 1801 was granted to extend the drainage and the North and South drains were built to connect with a tidal sluice at Highbridge. The Glastonbury Canal, authorised by an Act of 1827, had opened on 15 August 1833, the route from a tidal lock at Highbridge following the River Brue as far as Bason Bridge where a lock was constructed. From there, the canal proper was cut to travel by Shapwick, and then straight across the moor to Glastonbury. The canal was purchased by the Bristol & Exeter Railway in 1848, as always, eager to snap up a bargain, the proviso being that the canal was to be maintained in a navigable condition. It was the course of the canal from Shapwick that the line from Highbridge followed when it was built.

The Somerset Central was an independent company incorporated on 17 June 1852 with the intention of constructing a line from Highbridge Wharf as far as Glastonbury with an

24. It shall be lawful for the Company, on default of the *Somerset* Company so to do within Six Months after being required by the Company, on that Portion of the *Somerset* Company's Railway which lies between the authorized Junction of the *Cheddar Valley* Railway with the *Somerset and Dorset* Railway and the Broad Gauge Rails of the *East Somerset* Railway, at the Turnpike Road or Street separating the Station of the *Somerset* Company from the *East Somerset* Railway at *Wells*, to lay down additional Rails for the Broad Gauge so as to give to the Company a free and unrestricted Communication for the Purposes of all Traffic whatsoever between the *Cheddar Valley* Railway and the *East Somerset* Railway; and it shall be lawful for the Company to enter into and upon the Railway and Station of the *Somerset* Company for the Purpose of executing and to execute such Works, doing as little Damage as may be in the Alterations necessary for the Purpose of providing such Communication, and interfering with the Traffic and Use of the *Somerset and Dorset* Railway only so far as may be needful for executing such Works, and, except as is otherwise provided by the Agreement set forth in the Schedule to this Act annexed, making the *Somerset* Company full Compensation for all such Damage.

25. The Company may pass over and use, for the Purposes of Traffic of all Kinds whatsoever, and with their Engines, Carriages, and Servants, the Portion of Railway aforesaid which lies between the authorized Junction of the *Cheddar Valley* Railway with the *Somerset and Dorset* Railway, and the Broad Gauge Rails of the *East Somerset* Railway Company, and all Works and Conveniences connected therewith, including the Passenger Station of the *Somerset* Company at *Wells*, upon such Terms and Conditions and under such Regulations as are expressed in the Agreement set forth in the Schedule to this Act annexed.

Above: Articles 24 and 25 in the schedule of the B&E Additional Powers Act of 1865 giving the company passage over the Somerset Central metals; the Board of Trade however had other ideas.

eastward extension contemplated, the exact route of which was a bone of contentiæ, but it was generally directed towards the Wilts, Somerset & Weymouth line. This was to be either through Shepton Mallet to Frome, or southwards to Castle Cary. The Bristol & Exeter Railway managed to acquire a considerable proportion of the capital of the Somerset Central and the ownership of the Glastonbury Canal was transferred to the Somerset Central at the same time.

The first sod of the Somerset Central Railway was cut on Monday, 18 April 1853 by the Hon P. P. Bouverie in a field in the immediate vicinity of the Highbridge station of the Bristol & Exeter Railway. The 12 mile 38 chain single broad gauge line from Highbridge Wharf to Glastonbury was formally opened on 17 August 1854 and opening to the public on 28 August. The Bristol & Exeter worked the line on a seven-year lease for a guaranteed 4% on the capital. The canal was closed on 1 July the same year. James and Cyrus Clark of Street, founders of the famous shoe-making firm, had been prominent amongst local business people from Glastonbury wanting the line, and both gentlemen became directors of the line in its early days.

Two other projected schemes for the eastward extension were now brought forward. The first proposed a line through Wells and Shepton Mallet to join the Wilts, Somerset & Weymouth at or near Frome. The second proposal followed the route as described, with the difference of striking out in a southerly direction to Wyke Champflower (instead of east-

ANNO VICESIMO OCTAVO

VICTORIÆ REGINÆ.

****

Cap. xcvii.

An Act to transfer to the *Bristol and Exeter* Railway Company the Powers of constructing and working the *Cheddar Valley and Yatton* Railway; to extend the Time for purchasing Lands; to authorize the Purchase of additional Lands; and for other Purposes.   [19th *June* 1865.]

WHEREAS by "The *Cheddar Valley and Yatton* Railway Act, 1864," (in this Act called "the *Cheddar* Act,") the *Somerset and Dorset* Railway Company (in this Act called "the *Somerset* Company") were authorized to make Three Railways (in this Act called "the *Cheddar Valley* Railway") from *Wells* to the *Bristol and Exeter* Railway at *Yatton*, and were authorized to raise for such Purpose by Share Capital One hundred and seventy thousand Pounds, and by borrowing Fifty-six thousand Pounds, and the *Bristol and Exeter* Railway Company (in this Act called "the Company") were empowered to subscribe towards that Share Capital One hundred thousand Pounds: And whereas by Articles of Agreement set forth in the Schedule to the *Cheddar* Act, and by such Act confirmed, the Company and the *Somerset* Company

27 & 28 Vict. c. clxxxi.

[*Local.*]   14 Q   respectively

Above: The Act for the transfer of powers to the Bristol & Exeter for constructing and working the Cheddar Valley & Yatton Railway.

wards to Frome) and making a junction with the WS&W at Cole (Bruton). Both plans were seen as directing expected traffic to Southampton via Westbury and Salisbury. The second plan gave rise to a possible connection with a proposed route from Poole (referring to what was to become the Dorset Central Railway). After much deliberation in committee, the SCR adopted the Bruton plan, which was authorised by the Act of 21 July 1856. This action now aggravated the inhabitants of Wells as the eastward extension was now planned from Glastonbury, and not Wells, leaving it instead at the end of a branch line. It was this action that led the citizens of the city to persuade the East Somerset to extend its line westwards from Shepton Mallet to Wells, and used their cause to try to put pressure on the Somerset Central to get a move on with its line to Wells before its powers lapsed.

The SCR was spurred on by this action; £17,000 of additional capital was issued in the form of 5% preference shares, and the broad gauge, 5 mile 33 chain line from Glastonbury to Wells was completed at a cost of £48,000, opening formally on 3 March 1859 with public services commencing on 15 March. An intermediate station at Polsham was opened in 1861. The line was worked by the Bristol & Exeter for a rent of £3,950 per year (including the Burnham extension) until its original lease of the SCR expired on 28 August 1861. The line from Highbridge to Burnham had opened the previous year on 3 May.

The Somerset Central had originally planned to make a junction with the East Somerset at its terminus, but this was never carried out. The SCR was the first company to arrive at the aforesaid city and thus began the very complicated railway history of the area. We will not digress with the Somerset Central, and its intention of a continuous rail route from Highbridge or Burnham on the Bristol Channel, and the eastwards extension to link up with the standard gauge Dorset Central and thus enter Poole on the English Channel, as this has been chronicled elsewhere. Suffice to say, that by 1862, the SCR had mixed the gauge throughout its system, constructed locomotive shops at Highbridge, and provided standard gauge engines and stock for working its own and the Dorset Central services. Due to the financial state of the SCR — between the expiry of the Bristol & Exeter lease (28 August 1861) and the opening to Cole — the B&E provided locomotives and rolling stock on hire for a further five months to maintain the broad gauge service between Burnham and Wells. August 1862 witnessed the amalgamation of the two Central companies, to form the Somerset & Dorset Railway. By this time, the only broad gauge train running on the Somerset Central was a daily Bristol & Exeter goods (also carrying passengers), which the B&E ran by arrangement between Bristol and Wells via Highbridge until the end of October 1868. This train, also in the first year or so, made an occasional return trip from Glastonbury to Evercreech. The broad gauge rail was finally lifted from the Somerset Central by 1870.

The Cheddar Valley & Yatton

The Cheddar Valley line was originally a Somerset & Dorset project promoted in 1863 for a line to Bristol via Wells and Yatton for which an Act was authorised on 14 July 1864, the Cheddar Valley & Yatton Railway. The Bristol & Exeter by way of contrast was planning a route from Bleadon (south of Weston-super-Mare) to Wells. A settlement was reached between the two companies, which agreed that the B&E would build the line from Yatton to Wells — providing the whole capital might be subscribed

Above: After arrival with the 12.50pm from Glastonbury, 0-4-4T No 54 has now reversed out of Priory Road station so as to free the line for GWR services, and having run round its stock, stands in the loop by the S&D signalbox before propelling back into the station for the next run to Glastonbury. The locomotive and its train of six-wheeled carriages are in immaculate condition. *Ken Nunn Collection/LCGB*

by the B&E, and the line be constructed to the broad gauge — and abandon its proposed route from Bleadon. Both companies agreed they would then abandon any further intentions to encroach upon each other's territory. The original powers under the Act of 14 July 1864 were transferred to the B&E by the Bristol & Exeter Railway (Additional Powers) Act of 19 June 1865 (Section 140).

The Somerset & Dorset's 1863 proposals for the Cheddar Valley & Yatton line — which it had surrendered to the B&E — had included a western spur at Wells to allow through running between Glastonbury and Bristol, and also an extension to the East Somerset station. After a dinner for 250 held in the market place at Axbridge, which was full of people from far and wide with the stables of the inns being full causing congestion in the square, a procession was formed. Headed by the Weare Band and with Mayor Oliver Coathupe flanked by two Aldermen and Corporation plus many dignitaries including the Lord Bishop of Newfoundland, Mr Fox (Engineer to the Bristol & Exeter), various clerical figures and the well heeled, it made for Shute Shelve for the ceremony of cutting the first sod. This was a very wet Tuesday, 26 February 1867 with the Axbridge Union Fife and Drum Band blowing lustily at the rear in company with hundreds of spectators and many schoolchildren present. A huge crowd had gathered for the ceremony which was performed by Mrs Yateman, wife of the Reverend Yateman of Winscombe, using a small silver spade and wheelbarrow. The *Weston Mercury* also informs us that 'good order' was maintained by Police Superintendent Gillbanks and a large number of officers, and that 'the only liberty that appeared to be taken with any of the dignitaries in the procession being some mirthful ejaculations from the street urchins at the quaint appearance of the mace-bearers, who certainly had a comical and not altogether imposing aspect.' The newspaper also reported: 'Axbridge streets had been decorated by means of a public subscription. In the market place several trees were planted, evergreens and flags were prominently displayed, and at various points triumphal arches were displayed.'

J. P. Sturge & Co, the Bristol & Exeter solicitors, negotiated the agreed route of the line. It would depart from a bay

on the downside platform at Yatton with intermediate stations at Congresbury, Sandford (Sandford & Banwell from 1869), Woodborough (becoming Winscombe in 1869), Axbridge, and Cheddar. This section to Cheddar opened on 3 August 1869. The remainder of the line with stations at Draycott and Lodge Hill opened to Wells on 5 April 1870, Wookey opening in 1871. The line had a total length of 17 miles 55 chains, terminating at the Somerset & Dorset station. This arrangement, as officially set out in the 1865 Transfer Act, clearly gave running powers for the B&E trains over mixed-gauge track, through the Somerset & Dorset station to a connection with the broad gauge rails of the East Somerset company. The idea was for the B&E to share the ESR station. Provision was also to be made at the S&D station for the presence of both companies' staff (S&D and B&E). However, the Board of Trade inspector would have other ideas, resulting at the 11th hour in the B&E having to provide its own terminus at the bottom of Tucker Street in Wells, construction beginning in March 1867.

The contractors for the permanent way were Messrs John and William Pickering of 14 Blackfriars, London with a bid of £100,000, excluding rails and sleepers. The track was to be broad gauge, but in contrast to the accepted Brunellian method of longitudinal baulk timbers, was to be laid on conventional cross sleepers, this being done with an eye to a future easier conversion to the 'narrow' or standard gauge, which was then increasingly invading broad gauge territory.

Although there were no insurmountable difficulties during construction of the line, the works involved could not be called 'light'. The main problem was breaching the Mendip Hills and this was achieved by excavating a 180yd-long tunnel through the lowest point at Shute Shelve. The natural rock was found to be stable enough to leave it unlined, apart from the openings, which were of brick masonry. The other major works included a solid rock cutting at Easton and substantial earthworks at various points along the route. Subsidiary works such as the station buildings were to be carried out by William Brock, a Bristol contractor, who resided in Totterdown; his house 'Bellevue' was perched on Pylle Hill overlooking Temple Meads station. The buildings he erected were

Above: Although this well-known view of a B&E broad gauge mixed train is purported in several books to be the opening day at Cheddar, this is in fact, not the case. When the line from Yatton was opened to the temporary terminus at Cheddar on 3 August 1869 it is recorded that the station was incomplete, and passengers were accommodated in the goods shed until completion of the station in May 1870. Newspaper reports on Saturday 7 May the same year state: 'The new station will be opened in the early part of next week.' Therefore the photograph can be dated approximately as 9 or 10 May 1870. The view for all that, is a very interesting record of the broad gauge, with the footplate crew and their locomotive waiting patiently at the Axbridge end of the down platform for the photographer to compose his portrait. Staff and passengers pose for posterity and evergreens and flags adorn the building. Without a doubt a station such as this should have graced the fair city of Wells.
Ian Allan Library

solid and pleasing to the eye, with chimney pots of castellated terracotta, decorative bargeboards, earthenware tiles, and walls of Mendip limestone which reflected in some places, the pinkish hue of Westbury Quarry. All lighting and metal-work was supplied by Thomas Hale & Sons, brass and bell founders of Bristol. The new works between Yatton and Cheddar were inspected by Colonel Yolland on 30 July 1869 and opened to the temporary terminus on 3 August.

The Chief Engineer of the Bristol & Exeter Railway, Francis Fox, was the resident engineer of the Cheddar Valley at the time of its inception. A 48-year-old Quaker, and a staunch Liberal, he was born in Plymouth during the reign of King George III and he was to live under six monarchs before dying at the age of 96 in Teignmouth on 13 March 1914. Coincidentally, the new railway would pass close to the Friends School at Sidcot where he had been a pupil between 1829 and 1835. Upon leaving there, he studied engineering under Edwin Tregellis at the Neath Iron Works and on various projects with which he was involved, including the Central Cornwall Railway. He joined the staff of Isambard Kingdom Brunel as assistant engineer on the Glamorgan section of the South Wales Railway. When this arrangement expired in 1851, he remained as the contractor's engineer until the final completion of the Carmarthen part of the line. Returning briefly to the Cornwall Railway he engineered the Falmouth branch before becoming Chief Engineer to the Bristol & Exeter in 1854. The stations and their respective buildings on the Cheddar Valley were to bear the individual stamp of Francis Fox, the overall-roofed station at Cheddar bearing a family resemblance to the old St David's at Exeter, and in particular to Weston's second station at Locking Road (now the site of a Tesco store). The current Weston-super-Mare station is also his creation, as is the present-day Bristol Temple Meads. Moving into the district during the construction of the Cheddar Valley, he took up temporary residence at Sidcot, and appointed his younger brother, John Hingston Fox, as

assistant engineer. He had previously worked with Francis on a number of projects including the Taunton to Chard branch.

The 13 mile 45 chain East Somerset line from Witham, in common with other lines of the Wilts, Somerset & Weymouth, was converted to standard gauge between 18 and 22 June 1874, by which time the company had been acquired by the GWR. As previously stated, through running between the ESR and B&E stations upon the arrival of the line from Yatton was impossible because the distance — some 9 chains — was owned by the Somerset & Dorset, passing through its Priory Road station. Although an agreement was reached to mix the gauge over this short section to facilitate broad gauge running, the Board of Trade objected to passenger trains running over part of the S&D goods yard on the level. An attempt, made by means of a clause in a Bill of 1871 to get Parliament to override the Board of Trade's edict, failed. The two lines were therefore worked as separate units until 1 January 1878 when through running was made possible. By this time, both lines had been absorbed by the GWR and the gauge converted. Passenger traffic was now concentrated at Tucker Street, leaving the former East Somerset station to be relegated to goods traffic. GWR trains passed through the S&D station without stopping, this practice continuing until 1 October 1934.

Wrington Vale Light Railway

It was not long before the rich farming valley of the River Chew, lying to the east of Congresbury, was brought into the railway age. A railway was proposed to serve the area in 1880 and in 1881 a company was formed to promote a single standard gauge line between Farrington Gurney on the Bristol-Frome line (the North Somerset) and Congresbury by way of Wrington. The GWR agreed on 11 May 1882 to work the line for 50% of the gross profits, and the Act was obtained on 18 August 1882 for the Radstock, Wrington & Congresbury Junction Railway. However, little financial support was obtained, and the scheme was abandoned with an Act of 4 June 1896 putting an end to this venture. Proposals to make a less ambitious railway scheme were still fostered amongst the local landowners and farmers. The Light Railways Act of 1896 afforded minor railways in rural areas to be built on the cheap, and at this time, powers were sought for a line from Congresbury to Blagdon. Support also came from another body, namely the Bristol Waterworks Co, which was on the verge of constructing a large pumping station and reservoir at Blagdon. The GWR had been given its shareholders' approval in 1898 to finance, construct and work the line. A Light Railway Order was applied for at the Board of Trade and the Wrington Vale Light Railway Order was granted on 18 March 1898. Construction began, and the 6 mile 41 chain line was opened on Monday, 4 December 1901. Stations were opened at Wrington, Langford, Burrington and Blagdon. Extensive alterations and rebuilding of the layout at Congresbury also occurred. Initially the service on the Wrington Vale line consisted of four trains per day each way (with one running mixed), trains running direct to and from Yatton.

Projected Lines That Did Not Materialise

The directors of the ESR concluded in 1864 that a broad gauge line running from Doulting to Radstock would keep the 'narrow gauge' out. Plans for the East Somerset Extension Railway were deposited with Parliament in November the same year. The line would have comprised a 7-mile broad gauge connection from a proposed junction with the ESR at Doulting, thence running through Coleford and Vobster to a junction adjacent to Mells Road station on the WS&WR branch between Frome and Radstock. A 5-mile branch would have headed westwards from Coleford along the Nettlebridge Valley, terminating near Old Down. The object was to transport coal and mineral traffic from the local collieries and quarries, but unfortunately, this project was thrown out by Parliament. It was revived in 1868 however, as the Mendip Mineral Railway, and this time the ESR directors did support the project, and although backed by the Somerset & Dorset, the bill was withdrawn in April 1869. A mineral line known as the Newbury Railway (and to the GWR as the Vobster branch) serving Vobster Quarry, Bilboa Quarry and Newbury Colliery was eventually constructed from Mells Road station on the Radstock branch.

Plans to rival the ESR's proposal emerged in 1866 with the Bristol & North Somerset Southern Extension Bill promoting a line from the Bristol to Radstock branch near Farrington Gurney ascending the Mendip Hills and descending to Shepton Mallet, making a junction with the ESR and joining with the Somerset & Dorset south of Evercreech. As with the previous proposals, Old Down was mentioned with a branch tracking through the Nettlebridge Valley connecting with the Radstock to Frome line near Mells Road; here again the intention was to connect with the collieries and quarries.

The Gauge Conversion

The gauge conversion of the Wilts, Somerset & Weymouth main and branch lines by the GWR was a magnificent engineering achievement which entailed a virtual masterpiece of planning, combined with the knowledge and manual skills of the 1,800 railway navvies employed on the project who were drafted in from far and wide. Even the much-vaunted final conversion of 1892 pales into insignificance when compared with the gauge conversion of the 131 miles of the WS&W in June 1874. The cost of carrying out the alterations and additions to the permanent way, stations and works on the project was estimated at £290,000. As well as the gauge conversion, this sum included laying the third rail on the main line between Swindon and Thingley Junction beyond Chippenham, and between Bristol and Bathampton plus doubling the line between Frome and Witham and between Westbury and Warminster. An outlay of £70,000 covered the cost of locomotive, carriage and wagon stock necessary to work the district. The lines in the Wilts & Somerset area to be converted consisted of Thingley Junction to the junction with the London & South Western Railway at Dorchester, from Bathampton to Bradford Junction, Westbury to Salisbury, the mineral branch from Frome to Radstock, Witham to Wells, the goods branch from Yeovil to Clifton Maybank, and the branch from Maiden Newton to Bridport. All the lines were single except between Thingley Junction and Frome, Bradford and Bradford Junction, Yeovil to Evershot and Dorchester station to Dorchester Junction.

The conversion was to be carried out in June to give the engineers the benefit of working in better weather and longer daylight hours. Much preparation work was done beforehand following the lessons of earlier conversions. Work started early on Tuesday, 16 June, with Thursday, the 18th being the final day for broad gauge working south of Frome and on all the branch lines. When the last down trains had finished their journeys on that fateful Thursday, they were then despatched as empty stock from Weymouth, the Bridport and Wells branches, and Salisbury. A special engine left Weymouth at 11pm with an inspector aboard checking that all rolling stock had been cleared from all sidings etc. The single lines were then handed over to the civil engineer and traffic was suspended. The final broad gauge train departed from Frome on Sunday, 21 June. Strict timing was adhered to, with trains of the new 'narrow gauge' stock now being despatched from Swindon to Weymouth, Wells, Bridport, Salisbury and to Bristol via Bathampton. The stock arrived at Wells on Sunday, 21 June formed of six-wheeled carriages with five compartments each. It is reported that the first train with the new stock from Wells was poorly patronised, and was half an hour late in arriving at Frome. Some delay to services was to be expected as the final remnants of the previous gauge were removed and the double line sections were duly completed by the following Thursday. The normal service of passenger and freight trains was then restored, although some restrictions applied to freight services until the last sidings were finally converted. The broad gauge was now extinct from the Wilts, Somerset & Weymouth and its branch lines. The line from Yatton to Wells was converted in 1875, the only portion of its system that was actually regauged from broad to standard by the B&E. With the directors disapproving of Sunday labour, work started on Monday, 15 November, and was completed on time by the following Thursday. The broad gauge track had originally been laid on cross sleepers, in which state it had lasted for less than six years. Amalgamation with the GWR occurred on 1 January 1876.

Right: Wells East Somerset signalbox c1936 showing the original position of the external stairway, which was moved to the west end of the building due to the construction of the new turntable in 1948. *Scrimgeour Collection-Signalling Record Society*

Signalling and Services

Signalling on the Great Western

The Wilts, Somerset & Weymouth lines pre-dated block working and signalling as understood today. The single lines were controlled by double-needle telegraph instruments installed in the station offices; interlocking between points and signals was unknown. The fixed signals at the time were very basic, and at most places consisted of just two signals for each direction of travel, a 'stop' signal immediately at the approach to a station, and the 'auxiliary' some distance to the rear of it. Most signals were of the disc and crossbar pattern (WS&W) which were revolved by means of a handle on the post by the policeman. There were no 'starting' signals; a written train order and a hand signal by the policeman gave permission for a train to proceed into the section ahead. By means of the telegraph, trains were signalled forward from station to station, but not 'blocked back', meaning there was no 'out of section' message. In 1863 the GWR decided to replace the double-needle instruments with the single-needle version, and this was accomplished by 1865.

Somewhat surprisingly, the GWR was not very enthusiastic with regard to the electric train staff (ETS), claiming that it would interfere with the ready working of traffic and cause heavy delays, and continued to control its single lines by the disc block. The Board of Trade, meanwhile, carried out an inspection of the WS&W lines in 1877, upon the completion of the new signalboxes that were being brought into use at that time, and pressed for the implementation of the ETS, but the GWR refused to accept the recommendation. A threat by the Board of Trade to withdraw sanction for the

operation of a passenger service over the lines failed to persuade the company, and after various heated exchanges, the General Manager's report of 1880 indicates that the Board of Trade had become tired of the argument, and left the GWR to carry on as it thought fit. By the time of the aforesaid report, ETS working had been introduced on various sections of the line, including the Radstock branch. When the Bristol & Exeter opened the line from Yatton to Wells, it was worked by train staff and ticket, the block posts being Yatton, Congresbury, Woodborough, Axbridge, Cheddar, Draycott, Lodge Hill and Wells. The 'train staff and ticket' procedure for working trains over single lines was introduced by the GWR on 18 January 1864 and entailed having a wooden 'staff' for each section of the line, and an engine driver could not enter any section unless he was in possession of the correct staff — and was going forward under the authority of a correctly printed 'ticket'. As many tickets could be issued as were required, but trains could only go in the single direction indicated by the printing on it. The last train requiring to pass through in that direction carried the train staff to the opposite end of the section when the traffic flow was reversed — thus ensuring that only one train at a time entered the single-track section. The electric train staff was installed from Yatton through Wells and onwards to Witham in 1896, and to cut down on the expense of installing the ETS at locations at which it was not necessary, such as the places without crossing loops — Congresbury, Winscombe, Draycott, Dulcote Siding, and Doulting Siding — signals were removed, and the ground frames controlling the points had to be unlocked by the Annett's key fitted on the end of the train staff.

Draycott had a level crossing and the fixed distant signals were retained under the Board of Trade regulations with targets and lamps fitted to the gates. The ETS was in full operation on the branch from Monday, 11 May 1896 following alterations and removal of the redundant signalling on the previous Sunday. The new sections under the ETS regulations were: Yatton to Sandford, Sandford to Axbridge, Axbridge to Cheddar, Cheddar to Lodge Hill, Lodge Hill to Wookey, Wookey to Wells (Tucker Street), Wells (East Somerset) to Shepton Mallet, Shepton Mallet to Cranmore, and Cranmore to Witham. The short section between Wells East Somerset, Wells A (S&D) and Wells Tucker Street signalboxes was worked as a 'no staff' arrangement using GWR block instruments. The GWR used its standard type of signals comprising lower quadrant arms supported on wooden posts although some, but not all, of the wooden posts between Witham and Yatton were replaced by tubular steel versions under Nationalisation. Ground signals on the GWR would originally have been of the miniature semaphore type, but these were replaced in time by the white disc version.

The Wrington Vale Light Railway when opened in 1901 was worked on the 'one engine in steam' principle, the train staff having an Annett's key fitted to unlock the ground frames etc. As the Wrington Vale was built to light railway standards, conventional signalling was not therefore used, the only requirement being fixed distant signals. Congresbury regained its signalling (and more) when the Wrington Vale line opened. Eventually the ETS system was replaced by the electric key token (EKT) with Yatton to Congresbury worked by this system by 1948, Lodge Hill ceasing to operate as a block post from 21 September 1952, and Cheddar to Wells being converted to the EKT system when Wookey closed as a block post on 29 August 1954. The GWR service timetable appendices for 1945 give the following speed restrictions over the branch and through junctions etc:

between Witham and Wells the speed at any point in
    either direction was not to exceed 35mph (passenger
    trains) and 20mph (goods trains).
Witham: to and from Wells line — 10mph.
Cranmore: through up and down loop trailing
    junctions — 15mph.
Shepton Mallet: through down loop facing and trailing
    junction — 15mph.
Wells S&D: all trains 5mph.
Cheddar: through up loop facing junction — 20mph.
Cheddar: through up loop trailing junction — 15mph.
Axbridge: through up loop facing junction — 20mph.
Axbridge: through up loop trailing junction — 15mph.
Congresbury: through up loop trailing junction
    — 15mph.
Congresbury: through down loop trailing junction
    — 20mph.
Yatton Junction: main line to Wells branch — 15mph.
Yatton Junction: when passing from Cheddar Valley
    single line to up Cheddar Valley line at the single
    line junction near Milepost 31½ — 15mph.

Signalling on the Somerset Central

Signalling on the Somerset Central at origination consisted of disc and crossbar signals exactly as on the Bristol & Exeter and GWR lines, which was not surprising as the route was worked by the B&E with the confidence that the SCR would eventually form part of the GWR empire, although history would prove otherwise. The signals themselves

Above: The block bell used by signalmen to communicate with their counterpart in the S&D box is seen here in the East Somerset signalbox c1936. The inscription on the brass plate reads 'Wells S&D box'. *Scrimgeour Collection-Signalling Record Society*

Below: The interior of the East Somerset box c1936 showing the electric train staff instrument as used for the Wells East Somerset-Shepton Mallet section. This system which came into operation on the line from Monday, 11 May 1896, was eventually superseded by the electric key token system. *Scrimgeour Collection-Signalling Record Society*

would be worked by 'policemen'; there were no 'starting' signals so a written train order and a handsignal gave permission for a train to proceed into the section ahead by the policeman. By means of the telegraph, trains were signalled forward from station to station, but not 'blocked back'; in other words there was no 'out of section' message. A red disc displayed towards a train was the order to proceed, and the apparatus would be turned at a right angle placing the

YATTON, CHEDDAR, WELLS AND WITHAM

	Week Days									Sundays	
	a.m.	a.m.	a.m.	p.m.	p.m.	p.m.	p.m.	p.m.	p.m.	p.m.	p.m.
Bristol (Temple Meads) dep.	.	7 25	9 0	12 40	2 15	5 50	5 50	.	7 35	2 10	
Yatton .... dep	7 0	7 58	10 0	1 5	2 45	5 45	6 10	8 8		2 30	
Congresbury .... "	7 5	8 3	10 4	1 9	2 49	5 49	6 14	8 12		2 34	
Sandford & Banwell ... "	7 11	8 9	10 10	1 18	2 55	5 55	6 20	8 18		2 40	
Winscombe (Somerset) ... "	7 15	8 13	10 14	1 22	2 59	5 59	6 24	8 22		2 44	
Axbridge .... "	7 20	8 20	10 19	1 28	3 5	6 5	6 29	8 27		2 49	
Cheddar .... "	7 25	8 26	10 24	1 35	3 10	6 10	6 34	8 32		2 54	
Draycott .... "	7 32	8 31	10 28	1 38	3 15	6 14	6 39	8 37		2 58	
Lodge Hill .... "	7 37	8 36	10 33	1 43	3 20	6 19	6 44	8 42		3 3	
Wookey .... "	7 42	8 41	10 38	1 48	3 25	6 24	6 49	8 47		3 10	
Wells { Tucker Street arr./dep.	7 45	8 44	10 41	1 51	3 28	6 28	6 52	8 50			
{ Priory Road (*) ... "		9 5		12 7	3 49		7 2			3 17	
		9 7		12 8	3 50		7 3			3 18	
Shepton Mallet (†) ...... "		9 23		12 23	4 7		7 16			3 31	
Cranmore .... "		9 31		12 30	4 18		7 24			3 30	
Wanstrow .... "		9 38		12 38	4 25		7 31			3 46	
Witham .... arr.		9 44		12 44	4 31		7 36			3 51	

X—Third class only (limited accommodation).
a—Shepton Mallet arrive 4.1 p.m. ᵈ—Third class only.
‡—Langport West Station. §—For additional trains, see page 50.
¶—Bradford Peverell and Stratton Halt.
*—Somerset and Dorset Railway Station.
†—High Street Station; about 1 mile from Somerset and Dorset Railway (Charlton Road) Station.

X—Third class only (limited accommodation).
ᵈ—Third class only.
*—Somerset and Dorset Railway Station.
†—High Street Station; about 1 mile from Somerset and Dorset Railway (Charlton Road) Station.
¶—Bradford Peverell and Stratton Halt.

WITHAM, WELLS, CHEDDAR AND YATTON.

	Week Days										Sundays	
	a.m.	a.m.	a.m.	a.m.	p.m.	p.m.	p.m.	p.m.	p.m.	p.m.	p.m.	p.m.
Witham .... dep	8 25	10 20	1 20	3 37	6 50	9 20	5 30					
Wanstrow .... "	8 32	10 27	1 27	3 45	6 57	9 28	5 37					
Cranmore .... "	8 39	10 37	1 34	3 53	7 7	9 38	5 43					
Shepton Mallet (†) ... "	8 47	10 44	1 42	4 3	7 16	9 46	5 51					
Wells { Priory Road (*) "	8 57	10 54	1 51	4 16	7 25	9 56						
{ Tucker Street arr./dep.	8 58	10 55	1 52	4 17	7 26	9 57	6 2					
Wookey .... "	7 13	8 3	9 18	11 13	2 3	2 45	4 25	7 3	8 18	7 23		
Lodge Hill .... "	7 17	8 8	9 23	11 18	2 8	2 48	4 30	7 8	8 23	7 29		
Draycott .... "	7 21	8 12	9 27	11 22	2 12	2 52	4 34	7 13	8 29	7 33		
Cheddar .... "	7 25	8 16	9 31	11 26	2 16	2 57	4 40	7 18	8 32	7 38		
Axbridge .... "	7 29	8 22	9 36	11 30	2 21	3 7	4 44	7 23	8 36	7 43		
Winscombe (Somerset) ... "	7 34	8 27	9 41	11 37	2 26	3 7	4 49	7 29	8 41	7 49		
Sandford & Banwell ... "	7 37	8 30	9 44	11 40	2 29	3 10	4 52	7 33	8 44	7 54		
Congresbury .... "	7 42	8 35	9 50	11 46	2 34	3 15	4 58	7 40	8 50	8 0		
Yatton .... arr.	7 47	8 39	9 55	11 50	2 38	3 19	5 2	7 44	8 54	8 4		
Bristol (Temple Meads) arr.	8 18	9 11	10 13	12 11	3 5	4 16	5 36	8 19	9 51	8 25		

Above: The GWR passenger timetable between Yatton-Wells-Witham for 6 October 1947.

disc edge-on with the crossbar at right angles to the track to indicate 'stop'.

The S&D rule book for 1864 shows the disk and crossbar signals in use at the time. This type of signal was used on the SCR from Burnham to Cole including the Wells branch. At the leasing of the S&D by the Midland Railway and the London & South Western Railway under the Act of 13 July 1876, it was the LSWR which undertook responsibility for the signalling as well as the civil engineering, and lower quadrant LSW semaphore signals soon became established on that company's pattern lattice masts, although many original wooden posts remained at least until the Grouping, whereupon the Southern Railway replaced many of the older wooden posts with a version developed by itself of two rails bolted together. Upper quadrant signal arms replaced some of the lower quadrants under Nationalisation. The S&D originally used the Stevens 'flap type' ground signals, with the standard Westinghouse replacing them, and then being themselves replaced by the white half-disc pattern. The section between Wells and Glastonbury was worked as a single block section 5½ miles long with the branch trains arriving and departing from the outer face of the down island platform at Glastonbury. Originally the line was worked by block telegraph, but this was changed to 'train staff and ticket' working c1886, and thence to electric train staff using Tyers No 1 instruments from 1895.

Services

Four passenger trains per day were operated by the East Somerset Railway when it arrived at Wells in 1862, the Bristol & Exeter providing six passenger trains each way on weekdays and this service was perpetuated into GWR and BR days. Services consisted of direct trains between Yatton and Witham, plus trains in either direction starting or terminating at Wells. The 1910 *Bradshaw* shows a through service between Yatton and Witham of four weekday trains plus four Yatton to Wells services, and two Wells to Witham trains. Although the GWR provided trains for commuters to Bristol, there was a long gap between trains during the day. The GWR timetable for 1947 shows the same level of service, including one Sunday train in each direction of which the 5.30pm Witham to Yatton arrived at Wells at 6.2pm and departed at 7.20pm. (Sunday services were introduced west of Wells in 1886 and east of there in 1900.) The Sunday service under BR had the same number of trains, the difference being that one train at Wells stopped for 46min in one direction and 56min in the other. All trains to Wells from either Witham or Yatton were treated as down trains, becoming up on leaving the station. The section from Wells (Tucker Street) to Yatton was always the busier for passenger traffic, including excursion trains from Bristol to Cheddar and Wookey. The arch-enemy of the rural railway system, the motor omnibus appeared in the 1920s and began to poach passenger traffic from the railways. An early casualty was the Wrington Vale branch, when passenger services were withdrawn on 14 September 1931, and the line was cut back from Blagdon to Wrington on 1 November 1950. The Somerset & Dorset branch from Glastonbury to Wells (Priory Road) closed to all traffic on 29 October 1951. Passenger services between Yatton and Witham were withdrawn as from 7 September 1963, and freight trains to Wells (East Somerset) were withdrawn on 13 July 1964, freight traffic continuing until the section from Yatton to Cheddar closed completely on 1 October 1964, but a private siding remained in use at Cheddar until 28 March 1969. The eastern end of the line is still open, with steam trains at Cranmore and limestone traffic from the giant Merehead Quarry of Foster Yeoman & Co.

Witham–Dulcote Quarry

Witham

The station, five miles southwest of Frome, situated near the small village of Witham Friary, opened as a passing loop on the then broad gauge single line branch between Frome and Yeovil of the Wilts, Somerset & Weymouth Railway, on 1 September 1856. A daily service of five passenger trains, with two on Sundays, was provided. The line was doubled from Frome to Witham in 1875, and onwards to Castle Cary in 1880, the station being rebuilt at the same time. The station layout consisted of two platforms with the main buildings, including the slate-hung stationmaster's house, situated on the up platform. Branch line services for the East Somerset line to Wells used the bay platform at the rear of the up platform. The bay was unique in having a wooden overall-roof train shed with an extended canopy over part of the main line platform. The train shed only covered one carriage and was in situ from 1870 until removal in the 1960s.

Branch services also started from Frome, with Frome and Bristol crews working the 'circuit' using the East and North Somerset branch lines on a circular journey. One of the regular workings was the 3.30pm Frome-Yatton. The train, after connecting with the 12.30pm from Paddington, arrived at Frome at 3pm, would depart for Witham, thence via the branch to Yatton, and after arrival at Bristol Temple Meads would then form the 5.20pm to Frome via Radstock with a booked arrival at Frome of 6.30pm.

The early years of the 20th century were to witness part of the WS&W transformed from a sluggish backwater into a first class main line, with alterations to the Berks & Hants, and the opening of the Castle Cary cut-off route to Taunton. However, this was to no avail to Witham as West of England trains did not stop there as the station was served by Weymouth line trains, local services and the Wells branch trains. Due to a shortage of '45xx' class 2-6-2T engines, the 3.30pm Witham-Wells became a pannier tank working in 1944, remaining fairly consistent to at least 1949 with only the later or modified cab design locomotives appearing. The other Westbury diagram on the branch, the 8.25am from Witham, was formerly in the hands of 'Bulldog' 4-4-0s and when they were transferred it became a Mogul duty, these being the largest locomotives at work on the line.

There was a fair amount of passenger exchange during the summer months as this was the quickest route from Wells and Shepton Mallet to Weymouth, and on some Saturdays in 1952 the 2.50pm Yatton-Frome, usually worked by a railcar, had to be replaced, as the traffic was too heavy for this particular mode of transport. Also in the same year, the 3.27pm Frome to Frome, worked via Wells and Bristol, arriving in Temple Meads at 5.36pm, drew to the end of

Below: Class 4300 2-6-0 No 7305 heads towards Westbury on the West of England main line near Witham with a freight from Weymouth on the last day of the GWR, 31 December 1947. Part of the load consists of fitted vans containing potatoes from the Channel Islands. *LRGP*

Above: Witham up platform and branch bay, looking towards Frome during a quiet moment while the stationmaster hurries along the down platform in May 1948. *J. H. Moss*

Below: The 1903 survey for Witham shows the turntable located in the vee created by the main line in the bottom left and the branch to Wells. The station was relatively close to the village of Witham Friary. *Crown Copyright Reserved*

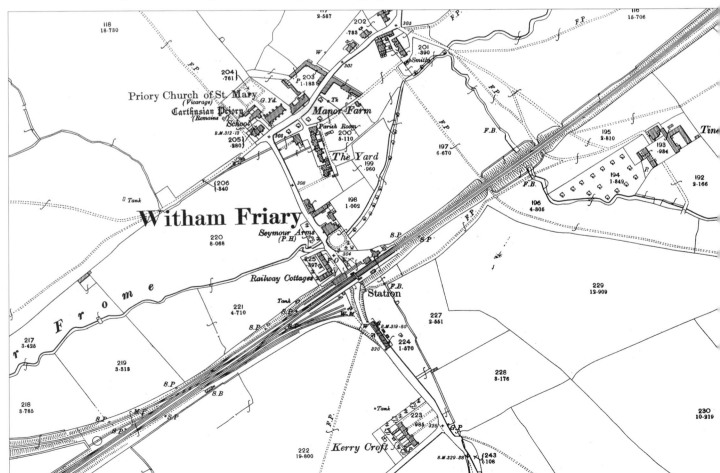

Right: A view of the approaches to Witham, taken from an arriving service running in from the East Somerset branch behind No 5512 in May 1948. *J. H. Moss*

Below: Freight wagons await collection in the down yard at Witham in May 1948, as seen from an arriving branch train. The station can be seen in the distance with the down main line starter in the off position. *J. H. Moss*

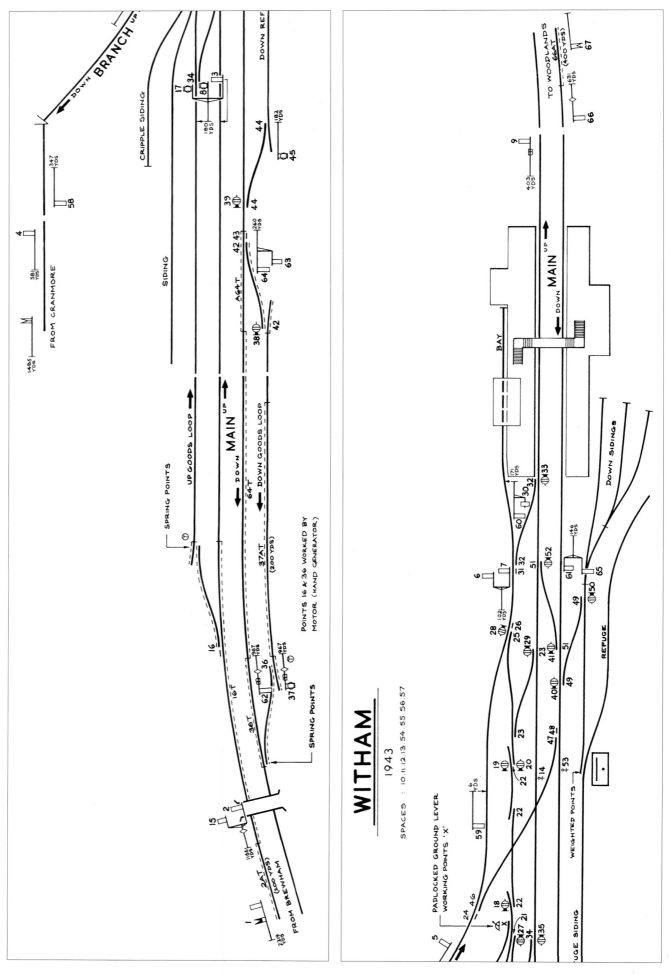

WITHAM

1943

SPACES : 10.11.12.13.54.55.56.57

The 1943 signalbox diagram for Witham showing the vast operating layout including the branch to Wells. *Signalling Record Society*

Above: A down West of England express headed by Old Oak Common-allocated 'Castle' class 4-6-0 No 5004 *Llanstephan Castle* thunders through Witham in 1948. *J. H. Moss*

Platform 7 and formed the 6.15pm to Frome via Radstock. Motive power for this service was a '45xx' or pannier tank from Westbury shed, but the motive power on 20 May 1952 was Class 4300 2-6-0 No 7300, also from 82D shed. The same year, a Westbury Mogul also worked the 8.3am Westbury-Bristol via Frome and Wells, the locomotive returning to its home shed on the 12.45pm via Bath. On 7 August 1952 the various Sunday schools of Axbridge and Cheddar had their annual outing to Weymouth, the special train hauled by Nos 4563 and 5506 (both 82A) working empty to Axbridge, leaving at 8.40am and after calling at Cheddar, running nonstop to Wells, where a stop was made for water, before continuing nonstop to Witham. There, the train reversed and 'Hall' class 4-6-0 No 5975 *Winslow Hall* took the train onwards to Weymouth including two extra coaches put on at Witham, which had been brought forward by the 7.25am Bristol-Frome via Wells, making the load up to 278 tons. The Sunday school special returned from Weymouth to Witham hauled by No 5975, where Nos 4563 and 5506 took over, hauling the train along the branch to Cheddar and Axbridge before returning it as empty stock to Bristol.

The 8.25am Witham-Wells was still being worked by Westbury Moguls in 1954 with No 4377 being the usual performer, and the 3.30pm from Witham was normally in the hands of a pannier tank, although '45xx' tanks did appear for as long as several weeks at a time. The down platform contained the original stone-built Brunellian waiting shelter which lasted until closure, when it was demolished. Branch passenger services were withdrawn on 9 September 1963, the final trains running on the previous Saturday, 7 September. The last through train, the 2.45pm Yatton-Witham, was worked by 0-6-0 No 3218.

At Witham, a 34ft 6in-diameter turntable for turning tank engines was situated between the ESR branch and the up

sidings, but this facility was removed in 1936. The track layout was vast: a fan of four sidings for local traffic ran to the rear of the down platform, plus sidings on the up side, and crossovers for trains to gain access to the branch from the down main line. Loop lines were installed alongside both main lines during August 1943, thus increasing the layout further. The suffix 'Somerset' was added to the station nameboards from 9 June 1958, to distinguish the station from another with the same name in East Anglia. The signalbox, dating from c1877, stood between the down sidings and the down main line west of the station. It was originally equipped with 30 levers, this being increased to 47 with rebuilding in 1896, and in 1942 the frame was further enlarged to 67 levers. The station closed to goods on 30 December 1963 and to passengers on 3 October 1966. With the demolition of the station, a modification of the track layout was brought into use on 25 June 1972 to cope with the increasing number and length of limestone trains from Merehead Quarry on the former East Somerset branch. The former branch bay line was extended eastwards over the site of the former up main platform to serve a new connection with the main line while other improvements have since been made to the track system. The signalbox closed on 26 November 1984 and today the layout is known as East Somerset Junction and comes under the control of Westbury power box. Trains arriving from Westbury for Merehead Quarry use a facing crossover in the down main line, and can be signalled either into the up main or the up branch loop; both are signalled for bi-directional working from the facing crossover to the facing point on the branch giving two loops for limestone trains, and providing flexibility of working. The goods loop extends around the bend of the branch to the foot of the incline and the single-track, 3 mile 45 chain branch to Merehead Quarry Junction.

Above: Prairie tank No 5512, in unlined GWR livery, standing in the branch bay at Witham before departing for the East Somerset and Cheddar Valley branch lines in May 1948, forms the backdrop to a pleasing group photograph including the driver and fireman standing either side of the guard. The station staff includes the stationmaster, on the far right. *J. H. Moss*

Below: In this view looking towards Bruton, taken from a train departing on the East Somerset branch, we see the main line and associated loops and sidings at Witham. The down loop signal in the distance has been lowered, suggesting that a freight train is being 'looped' allowing a faster down service to overtake. *J. H. Moss*

Above: Witham from the down platform in May 1948 with the starting and advanced starting branch signals to the right having been lowered in preparation for a Wells-bound service to depart from the bay platform. The East Somerset branch can be seen curving to the right in the mid-distance. The two GWR wooden-armed lower quadrant signals at the end of the down platform are the down main starter (left) and down main to down branch (right). The roof of the signalbox can be seen behind the truck in the left distance. *J. H. Moss*

Below: Witham from the station footbridge in 1959 showing the vast layout then in operation with the East Somerset branch line to Wells curving to the right in mid-distance. Concrete sleepers have been laid on the down main line, and WR pressed-steel signal arms have replaced the GWR wooden versions. Wagons stand in the down yard to the left awaiting the next pick-up goods. *J. H. Moss*

WEEKDAYS   **WITHAM, WELLS AND YATTON**

Above: A hot 20 June 1959: signal wires rustle, lower quadrant signal arms drop with a metallic clang, and the trackwork trembles as No 7004 *Eastnor Castle* (81A) slams through Witham with the 1.35pm Paddington-Penzance. This fine locomotive, built at Swindon in June 1946, was finally withdrawn in January 1964 and disposed of at Swindon Works after having attained a mileage of 876,349 miles. *R. E. Toop*

Left: A pannier-tank 'sandwiched' and propelling auto-coach No 9 with a local service on the main line near Witham. The former steam railmotor services between Frome, Castle Cary and Taunton were worked under the jurisdiction of Frome and Westbury locomotive sheds. *LGRP*

Inset: The 1956 weekday summer freight timetable between Witham, Wells and Yatton.

Steam escapes from the safety valves of '57xx' 0-6-0PT No 3773 standing in the branch bay before heading towards Wells with the 1.10pm Witham-Bristol after connecting with the 11.12am Weymouth-Paddington which is arriving behind No 4924 *Eydon Hall*, on 20 June 1959. Platform staff prepare to meet the incoming train, the guard of the branch train begins to walk back to the end of his train, and the footplatemen wander back to the pannier tank. *R. E. Toop*

Lower quadrant signals abound in this view of the west end of Witham station on 20 June 1959. North British Type 4 No D604 *Cossack* (83D) approaches at speed with the 8.15am Perranporth-Paddington. The signalbox in the left distance dating from c1877 closed on 26 November 1984. Signalling is now controlled from Westbury Power Box. *R. E. Toop*

Above: The timber overall roof at Witham bay platform had been in existence since 1870 and was used by services on the East Somerset branch but could only cover one carriage. It survived intact until the early 1960s and while a small timber awning gave passengers a brief respite from the ravages of the weather on the up platform, branch passengers had plenty of shelter. Passenger services to Shepton Mallet began on 9 November 1858. *H. B. Priestley*

Below: The original Brunellian stone-built waiting shelter on the down platform at Witham was unfortunately destroyed with the closure of the station in 1966. Witham was served by Weymouth trains and the local stopping services. The track was doubled between Frome and Witham in 1875 and between Witham and Castle Cary in 1880. *Author's collection*

Above: Ivatt '2MT' class 2-6-2T No 41203, dating from 1946 and originally based at Abergavenny (4D), had been allocated to Bristol Bath Road (82A) in 1959. It is pictured here after arrival at Witham from Frome. The crew now wait for the station staff to finish unloading and loading parcels etc, before departing for the East Somerset branch. Note the overall timber train shed has been removed from the branch bay. The running-in board on the up platform proclaims 'Witham Somerset junction for Shepton Mallet & Wells'. The station received the suffix 'Somerset' from 9 June 1958 so as not to be confused with a station bearing the same name in East Anglia. *Courtesy of John Reakes*

Above: A solitary passenger awaits the arrival of the 10.10am Witham-Yatton headed by No 5540 at Wanstrow on 2 July 1955. The station opened in January 1860 and was paid for by the local inhabitants as the East Somerset Railway could not afford to build one. The station served the nearby village of the same name situated on the Frome-Bruton road. *R. C. Riley*

Class 4575 2-6-2T No 5540, complete with an 82C shedplate, having picked up its solitary passenger pulls away from Wanstrow with the 10.10am Witham–Yatton on 2 July 1955. No 5540 was allocated to Gloucester in July 1928, also serving at Plymouth Laira (83D) in 1950 before being withdrawn from Oswestry (89A) in August 1960. The short goods loop holding 10 wagons was added in January 1927. Two sleeper-built cattle pens were also provided, and traffic dealt with included coal, cattle feed and livestock. The Annett's key on the end of the single-line token unlocked the loop ground frame. Closure to goods traffic came on 10 June 1963, with the station closing to passenger traffic on 9 September of the same year. The station approach road can be seen to the right leading down to the Frome–Bruton road. *R. C. Riley*

Above: Wanstrow station complete with milk churns, platform barrows and a solitary bicycle in the early years of the 20th century. Part of the station has been rebuilt in timber, this view also showing the paraffin lamps and platform fencing. Note the bridge rails secured to longitudinal timbers. The station was unstaffed until 1 April 1909 when a stationmaster was appointed, this being Grade 6, the lowest for that rank. This was a single-handed job and he had to perform all the working tasks himself, from issuing tickets to paperwork, handling milk churns and cleaning etc. *Author's collection*

Wanstrow

Situated 2¼ miles from Witham, and serving the village of the same name, Wanstrow, with its small station building upon a single platform, was opened in January 1860, and was paid for by the local inhabitants as the ESR could not afford to build one. With the opening of the station, the first up and last down trains stopped, and as Shepton Mallet held its market day on Fridays the first down, and last up train called to pick up and set down villagers on that particular day, but no extra time was allowed in the timetable for the extra stop at Wanstrow. The journey from Witham to Shepton Mallet took 35min. Three up services, but only one down train, served the station in 1874.

A severe snowstorm accompanied by a gale in March 1891 swept the county, and on Monday the 9th, because of the severe conditions, a pilot locomotive was attached to assist the 8.35pm Wells to Chippenham goods train. On its return to Witham at 1.15am on the following morning, it was snowed in at Wanstrow; assistance in the form of two locomotives was sent from Witham, but to no avail, and they returned to Witham. The shed at Wells then sent two locomotives to rescue the one at Wanstrow, but they only managed to get as far as a mile from Shepton Mallet, and after being stopped for an hour and a half were eventually

dug out and returned to Wells. The locomotive at Wanstrow was still stuck there on the Wednesday; the line reopened on the following day, although trouble was still forthcoming with one train being delayed for two hours, forcing the cancellation of the following service.

Lit by the customary oil lamps, the station was unstaffed until 1 April 1909 when a stationmaster was appointed. Accommodation for the stationmaster was provided in the form of a timber-built office on the platform. It is interesting to note that the position of stationmaster at Wanstrow was Grade 6, the lowest class of that rank. This was a single-handed job as he had to perform all the working tasks himself, from issuing tickets, handling milk churns, doing the paperwork and returns, filling and lighting the oil lamps, to assisting with the shunting and attending to traders' requirements, and keeping the premises clean and tidy. A short goods loop that could hold 10 wagons was added in January 1927 at the western end of the station; two sleeper-built cattle pens were also provided. Traffic dealt with in the siding included coal, cattle and cattle feed. The Annett's key on the end of the single-line staff unlocked the ground frame. Closure to goods traffic came on 10 June 1963, the station closing completely with the cessation of passenger traffic in the same year. The station building and platform edging had been removed by April 1965.

Above: Wanstrow, looking towards Cranmore in 1956. A solitary wagon can be seen standing on the short goods loop in the distance. *J. H. Moss*

Below: A view from the platform at Wanstrow in 1956 shows the track curving away in the direction of Cranmore. The cattle pens are in the left distance past the wagon standing on the goods loop. The difference in construction styles and materials of the station can be seen to good effect. *J. H. Moss*

Above: A rear view of the station building at Wanstrow in 1956 showing the substantial construction needed due to the undulating nature of the ground. The original stone-built portion of the station is to the far right with the various extensions built in timber standing on brick foundations. *J. H. Moss*

Left: A glance back towards Wanstrow from a Witham-bound train in May 1948; the train has just passed the bridge carrying the line over the Frome-Bruton road. *J. H. Moss*

Above: Class 59/1 No 59104 *Village of Great Elm* in Hanson livery breasts the summit from White's Crossing and heads towards East Somerset Junction with a train of loaded Foster Yeoman hoppers. These locomotives are quite impressive and tackle the short but sharp climb with ease at this spot with just a faint whine from the power output. The twisting line to the right is used by empty trains to gain access to the Merehead terminal. *Brian Pike*

Left: Foster Yeoman used a pair of ex-BR Class 08 diesel shunters to work trains between the loading area and the sidings. Here, No 11 *Dulcote* (ex-No D3002) and No 33 *Mendip* (ex-No D3044) are seen at the Torr Works terminal on 8 July 1980. No 11 is now preserved in Devon by the Plym Valley Railway while No 33 is still part of the Mendip Rail fleet and was to receive a major overhaul in late 2000 when its TOPS number, 08032, was due to be reinstated. *Peter Nicholson*

Merehead Quarry–East Cranmore

The quarry, owned by Foster Yeoman Ltd since 1958, was originally served by a siding operated by a ground frame, from 14 March 1948 until 30 April 1970. The construction boom of the late 1960s demanded large quantities of limestone to be moved by rail, with the result that a rail complex was started in late 1969. A new line from the Wells-Witham branch was laid north to the mechanised loading installation serving the extensive quarry at this point. A loop with a siding leading from it was laid ¾ mile to the west at Whites Crossing, this being the transfer point between the quarry sidings and BR, and was brought into use on 31 May 1970. A new road bridge was constructed in order for the new line to pass under the A361 and into the rail loading terminal in the quarry, which was named Torr Works after its designer, Ronald Torr. Test trains were utilised in the summer of 1970 with the new site officially

opened by the Chairman of British Rail, Sir Henry Johnson, on 19 August. Initially, all rail traffic was moved by BR locomotives, and such was the volume of traffic, that the 1,000th train headed by No D1000 *Western Enterprise* departed from the complex on 26 March 1971. Many Class 52 'Westerns' appeared on limestone trains, as did members of the 'Hymek', 'Warship' and '47' classes. Rail capacity was increased with a new chord line which opened on 16 September 1973, forming a triangular layout, with empty trains running from Quarry Junction, where there was a ground frame that lasted until 24 November 1984 (nowadays under the control of Westbury), into the reception sidings at the quarry. Loaded trains are propelled from the departure sidings into the reversing siding at Whites Crossing and thence on the original formation of the branch towards Witham. A total of three arrival and three departure sidings are provided at the terminal. A new maintenance facility for wagons and locomotives was built in 1980, and

Above: No 59104 stands coupled to a rake of loaded 102-tonne Foster Yeoman hoppers in the departure sidings at Merehead Quarry on 12 June 2000. The hopper wagons built by Orenstein & Koppel in Germany have a payload of 79 tonnes. Loaded trains reverse to White's Crossing and then gain the East Somerset branch proper before heading for East Somerset Junction (Witham) and the main line. *Brian Pike*

Below: The massive bulk of EWS Class 66/0 No 66225 is seen to good effect in this view taken at Merehead TMD on 12 June 2000. EWS has introduced a total of 250 of the Class 66s built by General Motors for its heavy haul freight operations in the UK. *Brian Pike*

Above: Class 59/1 No 59104 *Village of Great Elm* and EWS Class 66/0 No 66225 stand outside the Merehead Traction Maintenance Depot on 12 June 2000. *Brian Pike*

later expanded for the new Class 59 locomotives. A pair of Class 08 diesel shunters was purchased from BR in 1972 and subsequently repainted into the colours of Foster Yeoman: Nos 11 *Dulcote* and 22 *Merehead*.

New ground was broken in 1980 when Foster Yeoman accepted delivery of a massive 1,000hp General Motors-built switcher for shunting operations; the new locomotive was numbered 44 and named *Western Yeoman II*. The arrival of the 3,250hp Brush Type 5, Class 56 locomotives allowed trains in excess of 3,000 tons to be run for the first time. No 56031 was named *Merehead* in a ceremony at the complex on 16 September 1983 to mark the 30 millionth ton of stone removed by rail from Torr Works since 1969. It then set off in tandem with No 56032 hauling a 43-wagon train of 4,600 tonnes — the heaviest ever worked in Britain at that time. With increasing payloads, the BR locomotives, although at a peak in development with the Class 56 design, were not satisfactory, and Foster Yeoman, impressed with the performance and reliability of the GM switcher, took the then unprecedented step of providing its own main line locomotives. An order for four locomotives was placed with General Motors, Electro-Motive Division, construction taking place at La Grange workshops in Chicago. The locomotives were unloaded at Southampton on 22/23 January 1986, and becoming Class 59, they were unique in being the

first privately owned main-line production locomotives to enter traffic in Great Britain. The locomotives, looking superb in the silver and blue livery of Foster Yeoman, were named: No 59001 *Yeoman Endeavour*, No 59002 *Yeoman Enterprise* (renamed *Alan J. Day* 21 June 1996), No 59003 *Yeoman Highlander* (currently at work in Germany) and No 59004 *Yeoman Challenger* (renamed *Paul A. Hammond* on 21 June 1996). Such was the success of the original locomotives that another was ordered, arriving in the UK in 1989, becoming No 59005 *Kenneth J. Painter*.

Trains in size of up to a maximum of 5,000 tons could now be handled with ease by the Class 59s. The rail operations of Foster Yeoman and ARC combined in 1993 to form Mendip Rail, by pooling both companies' locomotives and freight wagons to incorporate operating flexibility and costs. The ARC Class 59/1 locomotives, work out of the massive Whatley Quarry, which is rail-served from the North Somerset branch near Frome. Revised liveries for both fleets of locomotives occurred in 1998-9 with the ARC fleet painted in Hanson colours. The latter are named after local villages: No 59101 *Village of Whatley*, No 59102 *Village of Chantry*, No 59103 *Village of Mells* and No 59104 *Village of Great Elm*. Foster Yeoman celebrated its 75th anniversary at Merehead in June 1998 with a three-day rail gala with visiting locomotives ranging from the steam era to the modern diesel age.

Above: Foster Yeoman took delivery of an 'SW1001' class locomotive from GM-EMD in Chicago for shunting and marshalling operations at the Merehead terminal in 1980. Numbered 44 and named *Western Yeoman II*, the switcher is seen here at work in the Merehead sidings on 12 June 2000. *Brian Pike*

Above: The private sidings at Cranmore for the Mendip Mountain Quarries, showing the vast amount of traffic handled at the station for the limestone quarries, with loaded wagons standing on the branch as far as the station in the distance. *John Reakes collection*

Above: The stationmaster and staff pose for the camera at Cranmore in the early 1900s. The station opened to traffic on 9 November 1858 with a single platform. A signalbox was a later addition, located to the eastern end of the ticket office until replaced by a new box standing off the end of the down platform which came into use in 1904. The wooden structure to the left of the picture is the gentlemen's toilet, replaced in later years by a cast-iron structure, which is still in place, as is the original station building, under the auspices of the present-day East Somerset Railway. *John Reakes collection*

Cranmore

Opened as a single-platform station at the beginning of services on the line, the single-storey station building, which is still in situ, held the usual station offices etc; a signalbox used for operating the quarry sidings to the west of the station was a later addition, situated to the eastern end of the ticket office. Goods sidings were laid in February 1863, and a siding was opened in 1880 running alongside the through line, opposite the platform. This was subsequently formed into a loop by installing points at the eastern edge of the station, and a down platform with a wooden waiting shelter came into use in 1904 when the original signalbox was replaced by a new box, measuring 29ft x 12ft and elevated 8ft, standing off the down platform at the Shepton Mallet end. This was brought into use on 11 September. A ground frame was also installed at the Shepton Mallet end of the layout, enabling access to the quarry sidings. The up platform was extended eastwards at the same time in connection with the construction of new sidings to the rear of the station, and a stationmaster's house was also provided.

A total of six passenger trains was run each way between Yatton and Witham in 1910, with some of the services terminating or starting at Wells. Trains between Shepton Mallet and Cranmore were limited to 20mph through the up and down loop trailing junctions. The signalbox was open during weekdays for the first train, and closed after the final evening train, and opened as required on Sundays. Passenger services calling at Cranmore in 1947 consisted of the 7.58am ex-Yatton, 12.7pm ex-Wells, 2.45pm ex-Yatton

and 6.10pm ex-Yatton. Return services from Witham to Yatton were 8.25am, 10.20am (GWR diesel railcar, described as third class only), 1.20pm, and 3.37pm. The 6.50pm from Witham had a booked arrival at Wells of 7.26pm and then formed the 8.15pm to Yatton. The last train from Witham, the 9.20pm, terminated at Wells. Single-line tokens were exchanged at Cranmore, breaking the long section between Shepton Mallet and Witham. Passenger traffic from Cranmore was never prolific, although freight traffic from the local quarries, up until 1946, was heavy. Staff at the station consisted of a stationmaster, porter, clerk, shunter and two signalmen.

The late Reg Seviour, who lived at Dean near Cranmore, has left a fascinating account of his working days at the station during the 1920s.

'I spent the first 20 years of my life at Cranmore and the station was in those far off days part of the daily scene. Not that it was ever bustling with people, far from it. For few of the local folk in the years up until 1923 had either the money or the time for more than necessary rail travel. I recall that the return fare to Shepton Mallet being one shilling, yet quite often, people going shopping would walk to town, and use the train for the return journey when loaded with their purchases. Then on occasions during the summer, there would be excursion tickets available at cheap rates to Weston-super-Mare or Weymouth but even these concessions attracted only a small number, say half a dozen or so. As a boy and later as a youth the station was something that one was aware of, but not vitally interested

41

Waterlip Quarry

Above: Waterlip Quarry was opened in 1899 with the narrow gauge line being horse-worked. The 2ft gauge tramway was extended c1907 for a distance of three miles to the Somerset Basalt Quarry at Downhead with a branch diverging at Long Cross serving Moons Hill Quarry of John Wainwright & Co. The new extension was worked by steam locomotives including *Gamecock,* Peckett 0-4-0 saddle tank No 1030 dating from 1904 and scrapped in 1927. This view was taken at Waterlip in c1913. The steam locomotives only worked as far as Waterlip (where an engine shed was provided), not being able to proceed to Cranmore due to the low bridge under the main road, leaving the loaded tubs to travel by gravity. *John Reakes collection*

Below: In connection with the development of Waterlip Quarry, the former horse-worked 2ft gauge tramway between Waterlip and Cranmore was converted to standard gauge in 1926. This view shows the newly completed works, with the 2ft gauge still extant inside the formation of the new trackwork with a narrow gauge tub in the background. The works involved in rebuilding the bridge underneath the Frome-Shepton Mallet road are also to be seen. Note the rock-lined cutting, which is typical of the limestone Mendip area. *Brian Pike collection*

in. There was the whistle of the engines, an occasional stranger arrived in the village, and far more noticeable the daily passage of farm carts from almost all of the surrounding farms, taking the day's milk for conveyance to some distant town. It was in the summer of 1923 that I acquired a greater knowledge of the functions of the station, for it was then that I started work there as a relief porter for two months while the regular staff were on holiday and one recovering from illness. In total they numbered five. There was the stationmaster, Mr Lee, two signalmen and two porters.

'It was not passenger traffic that kept the station busy, but freight, and this was mainly of two kinds. It was the conveyance of milk and the despatch of road stone from quarries situated at Stoke, Downhead and Waterlip. Before I relate the workings of the stone traffic, it is interesting to dwell for a moment on the despatch of milk. It was a far different procedure than is the case today when all milk is collected at the farm. In those days, all milk not made into cheese on the farm was sent by rail, mainly to Bristol and London. Later, a collecting point was set up in the village for Prideaux's milk factory,

but it was many years before all farmers forsook the railway. Each farmer had his own churns identified by his name on a brass plate, and each held 17 gallons. When full they weighed near on two hundredweight and were more than one man could lift. In my short time as a porter, the trade was considerable with something like 60 churns a day sent off and received. It can therefore be seen how important this commodity was to the railway and in particular to the work of the station. Every morning, a succession of carts in their many forms made their way from farm to station where they off-loaded the churns on to platform trolleys and then picked up their empty ones. Fortunately most of the churns were despatched in the direction of Witham and had in consequence not to be wheeled across the line. The returned ones came in on the down platform and it was my daily task to carry these on my back across the rails to the side where the farmers could collect them.

'The second item of freight was the despatch of roadstone, and every afternoon, the trucks, of which there were many, were shunted on to the main line and coupled to the goods train. A particularly interesting feature in connection with

Below: At one time, entire farms were moved by rail — animals, equipment and tractors, furniture, hay and straw, farmers and their families, in fact the whole lock, stock and barrel were moved in a trainload. In this remarkable picture taken at Cranmore, one such farm special of 31 wagons has arrived, conveying Mr R. S. Creed from Crewkerne, near Yeovil. Mr Creed, seen to the left foreground, is supervising the unloading of the dairy cattle before travelling to his new abode at Manor Farm, Doulting. Points of interest in the photograph include a farm cart on the rest of the train in the station to the left and the pannier tank on the cattle wagons to the right, with the railway staff keeping a good distance from the livestock. *John Reakes*

— CRANMORE —

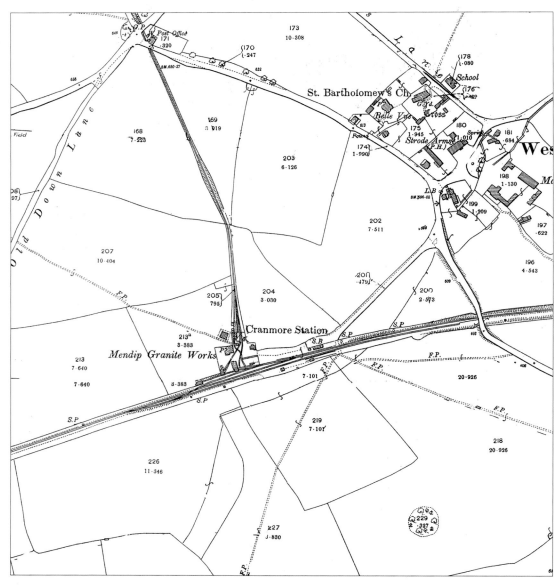

Above: Cranmore as surveyed in 1903. The Mendip Granite Works is prominent, as is the 2ft gauge tramway (converted to standard gauge in 1926), extending from the works and tunnelling under the main Shepton Mallet-Frome road towards Waterlip Quarry. *Crown Copyright Reserved*

Attractive Regular EXCURSIONS

from

CLEVEDON, CRANMORE, HIGHBRIDGE for BURNHAM-on-SEA, NAILSEA SHEPTON MALLET (High Street), **WANSTROW, WELLS, WESTON-SUPER-MARE** and **YATTON**

18th JUNE to 9th SEPTEMBER, 1962
(INCLUSIVE)
(or until further notice)

The Train Services in this pamphlet are subject to alteration or cancellation at short notice and do not necessarily apply at Bank or Public Holidays. Passengers should confirm beforehand the service on which they intend to travel.

BRITISH RAILWAYS

Above: Ivatt 2-6-2T No 41203 (82A) arrives and enters the down loop at Cranmore during the 1960s with a train for Yatton. The single-line token will be exchanged here for the next section to Shepton Mallet High Street station. *John Reakes collection*

Above: Cranmore from the up platform looking towards Shepton Mallet in 1933. The attractive timber-built waiting shelter stands on the down platform to the left, with the signalbox off the end of the platform. Part of the stone crushing plant can be seen in the distance. Paraffin lamps and 'spear' fencing complete the branch line scene. *Ian Allan Library*

Below: The station at Cranmore viewed from the Batcombe road overbridge in 1948. Goods wagons stand in the up sidings to the far right but the stone crushing and loading plant has totally disappeared. *Ian Allan Library*

Above: Viewed from the signalbox, GWR railcar No 24 approaches Cranmore hauling a single coach on a Bristol-Witham service in 1948. The building housing Marcroft's wagon works can be seen in the distance beyond the sheeted wagons. *J. H. Moss*

this stone was the method used in getting it to Cranmore from where it was won. The crushing plant was adjacent to the railway and connected to the several quarries by a light railway. Waterlip was a collecting point for the small trucks called "tubs" and to this point were hauled by steam locomotives. It was the summit of the light railway and from there to Cranmore it was downhill all of the way. The tubs were assembled into what were referred to as "journeys", that is into trains of a dozen, and were given an initial push by an engine and sent off to Cranmore energised only by gravity. Each journey was in charge of a man who rode on projecting steps of the last tub. In order to check the speed when it became too fast, as it did in places, he then jumped off and pushed what were called "sprags" through the perforated wheels. These were pieces of steel approximately 1in in diameter and 18in long, and getting these through the small wheels whilst running at speed needed some skill. The tubs were constructed of elm wood and held about one ton of block stone as loaded in the quarry. Horsepower was used for the return trip to Waterlip, and a fine team of shire horses was kept for this purpose. The narrow-gauge line between Cranmore and Waterlip was replaced in later years by standard gauge with wagons of that gauge being used. The crushing plant was then removed from Cranmore station. I write this in detail, because, as far as I know, it was a unique method of transport from such a long distance.

'From the station there was a daily despatch of stone in some 20 to 30 truckloads of broken stone to various destinations. These two main commodities, milk and stone, entailed more work for porters than all else the station handled. Each individual consignment had to be accompanied by the rail consignment note made out in triplicate and there was a certain amount of shunting to be

done. But as the junior porter, it fell on me to do the more menial jobs, of which there were many. Signal lamps had to be replenished with oil, cattle pens and all cattle trucks had to be kept in an unsullied condition with plentiful applications of limewash. The floors of the lavatories and the waiting room were given a daily scrub with disinfectant, and of course, the numerous milk churns had to be marshalled like soldiers along the edge of the platform, and then carried on one's back across the line to the other side. But to a young man, I was 19 at the time, it was stimulating physical work and never dull.'

Waterlip (also known as Cranmore) Limestone Quarry, situated approximately 1 mile from Cranmore station, was worked as early as 1889 under the ownership of W. B. Beauchamp and John Hamblin and connected with the ESR at Cranmore. Due to a low bridge under the Shepton Mallet to Frome road this was a horse-worked narrow gauge line, and the sidings originally were laid to the north of the station. The 2ft-gauge Waterlip line was extended c1907 for a distance of three miles to the Somerset Basalt Quarry Co at Downhead Quarry with a branch diverging at Long Cross to serve Moons Hill Quarry under the ownership of John Wainwright & Co. It is known that narrow gauge locomotives worked the lines of the new extension and one of the earliest was *Gamecock*, a Peckett 0-4-0 saddle tank, while other locomotives included *Tattoo*, *Keighley* and *Horwich*, with the engine shed at Waterlip. The narrow gauge locomotives did not work the main line between Waterlip and Cranmore as the loaded tubs were worked by gravity, with the returns being horse-worked. Limestone was conveyed to Cranmore via the narrow gauge and loaded into GWR wagons through the crushing plant at Cranmore station, which was eventually relocated to Waterlip with the abandonment of the narrow gauge line.

Right: The Cranmore stationmaster standing outside the large and impressive station house poses for the camera of Joe Moss in 1949. *J. H. Moss*

Below: The sidings, crossing loop and semaphore signals at Cranmore as viewed from the end of the up platform looking towards Shepton Mallet in 1950. The remnants of the former stone crushing/loading plant are seen to the right. Railwaymen applied the nickname 'Siberia' to the station, due to the inclement weather that the southern slope of the Mendip Hills can throw at mere humans. Freight wagons standing in the sidings at Westbury, destined for Cranmore, invariably had the word 'Siberia' chalked on their sides. *J. H. Moss*

Above: Cranmore as viewed from the up platform looking towards the timber-built waiting room standing on the down platform in 1949. Wooden sleepers on the platform and lengths of rail lying alongside the track suggest that relaying is imminent. *J. H. Moss*

The narrow gauge trackwork and points of the former quarry at Downhead, although closed as long ago as 1925, were recorded as still extant in 1993 with trees and bushes growing through. Throughout the history of quarrying in the Mendips, company names changed quite frequently. Waterlip came under the ownership of the Mendip Granite & Asphalt Co Ltd in 1894, and in 1923 was leased by Mendip Mountain Quarries Ltd, and taken over again in the following year by Roads Reconstruction Ltd which became Roads Reconstruction (1934) Ltd from 22 February 1934. The RR, as it was always known, had extensive quarrying operations in the Mendips and had a large fleet of standard and narrow gauge locomotives at various locations. Upon the takeover by the RR, Waterlip Quarry was expanded, including the first large-scale use of electric power in the area, the former horse-worked line to Cranmore was converted to standard gauge by 1926 with the rebuilding of the former low bridge, Downhead Quarry was closed c1925, and the line north of Waterlip lifted.

The New Works of the Mendip Mountain Quarries at Waterlip, now under its new owners, Messrs Roads Reconstruction, were formally opened by the Director General of Roads, Brigadier General Sir Henry Maybury, on 29 September 1927. The quarry, which had been in use for some 60 years, was now fitted with the latest equipment to deal with an expected output of 10,000 tons per week. Compressed air tools were brought in, pneumatic drills replaced the old method of hand drilling into the quarry face, and the entire plant of the original owners was scrapped and replaced. New primary and secondary crushing plants, storage bins, screening sheds, power house and workshops, and an asphaltic tarmacadam mixing plant were provided, the capacity of the tar plant being 1,250 tons per 48-hour week, which could be double-shifted when necessary, all of this placing Waterlip into the super-quarry league. Two electrically operated navvies mounted on caterpillar tracks with buckets of $2\frac{1}{4}$cu yd capacity operating on a 500/550V ac supply loaded stone from the quarry face into five specially constructed standard gauge steel trucks of 15 tons capacity supplied by English Electric, each equipped with its own electric motor of 15hp. The remotely controlled wagons operated on a live, third-rail system of 230V direct supply between the quarry face and the primary crusher, and were the state of the art at the time. The track consisted of two loops, each serving a particular navvy, and divided into a number of sections, controlled by an operator, positioned in a control tower on the roof of the quarry sub-station. Electricity was supplied by the North Somerset Electric Supply Co and delivered at 11,000V and transformed to 400V by the transformers located in the quarry power house. Sentinel geared steam locomotives (shedded at the quarry) worked the standard gauge line between Waterlip and the exchange sidings at Cranmore, hauling trains of eight wagons at a time. An average of 100 wagons per day were handled here between 1926 and 1946 when the quarry closed, bringing to an end the stone traffic from Waterlip. Mineral traffic from

Above: Class 25s Nos 25319 and 25296 head a train of bitumen tank wagons out from the sidings at Cranmore station on 8 July 1980. Other tank wagons are in the platform, right, the station tracks not being available for use by the East Somerset Railway at that time. *Peter Nicholson*

Below: A down passenger train headed by 2-6-2T No 4573 awaits departure from Cranmore towards Shepton Mallet in 1949 while a member of the station staff chats to the guard at the rear of the train. *J. H. Moss*

Dulcote Quarry was also marshalled here before despatch to Witham and the main line.

Cranmore was never known under its real name by railwaymen, due to the harsh weather that the southern border of the Mendip Hills can throw at mere humans. Icy winds and rain, fog, harsh frosts and snow can make working life very uncomfortable, and no joke, especially when engaged in shunting movements at the station, or on an unprotected footplate. Peter Woods, former fireman at Wells shed, recalls that the nickname 'Siberia' was applied to Cranmore. Freight wagons standing in the sidings at Westbury invariably had 'Siberia' chalked on the sides, and in fact Cranmore was one of the most disliked places that local railwaymen had to

work, especially in inclement weather. Quarrying having ceased at Waterlip in 1946, the site was then used by RR as a central plant depot and repair workshops for its locomotives from all over the Mendip area. In addition to repairing locomotives, the site was well known as an area of decaying industrial locomotives of both gauges until closure in the 1960s. The well-known firm of Marcroft Wagons Ltd had a repair siding and depot at Cranmore until it moved to larger premises in the former GWR yard at Radstock. Brian Pike, who was employed at the works in the late 1950s, recalls the following staff at Marcroft's: Edgar West (foreman), Den Neate, Tom Langley, John Mitchell, Jim Major and Norman Mullins. The job involved working on wooden five- and seven-plank wagons during a 5½-day week. The work was hard and mostly involved heavy general repairs including changing axles and wheelsets, headstocks and solebars, plus painting, with at least four wagons at a time being in the workshop at various stages of repair with plenty more outside the works awaiting their turn to come in.

Twenty finished wagons per week emerged from the works; the headstocks and solebars arrived complete from the suppliers, but had to be drilled out, and mortised and tenoned. The solebars were made from American redwood, headstocks from oak, facing boards in elm and the planking in pine. Completed wagons were conveyed to Westbury via the local goods service. Brian Pike remembers the following incident: 'There was trouble with a wagon that had its brakes stuck on in a goods train at the station, so we set out to burn the brake blocks off. This we did, and only then did we realise that it was a loaded gunpowder wagon being conveyed to Cheddar for the local quarries.'

Staff at Cranmore over the years has included stationmasters Mr Lush, Mr Bartram, Mr Ball and Mr Greenslade; signalmen, T. Baber, J. Hares, C. Oddy and E. Lay; platform staff G. Bennett, G. Padfield and L. Hodges; permanent way J. Mason, F. Warren, G. Edwards, H. Bennett, P. Padfield and H. Selway.

Top: Signalman Ted Lay comes to grips with a signal lever in Cranmore box. Opened on 11 September 1904, the signalbox closed on 19 May 1968 with the branch from Witham to Cranmore then being operated as 'one engine in steam'. *J. H. Moss*

Above: Dating from 1904 the former GWR signalbox at Cranmore, pictured here on 10 June 2000, is now used for art exhibition purposes and as a museum. *Brian Pike*

Above: This view of 'old' Cranmore epitomises the rural branch line station. A Witham-Yatton train headed by No 9668 (82D) stands alongside the down platform on 15 August 1958 without a passenger or member of staff in sight, smoke drifting lazily from the chimney, before resuming the journey to Shepton Mallet. Haymaking has been taking place in the field to the left, and no doubt the workers are availing themselves of a refreshing glass of 'scrumpy' in a shady corner of the field in order to escape the hot summer sunshine. With no disrespect to the volunteers of the modern-day Cranmore, in my view, the buildings should have been left in their original state, as the additional building on the platform does little to preserve the branch line atmosphere. But of course, commercial reasons dictate otherwise in the hard financial world in which preserved railways now find themselves. *H. B. Priestley*

Below: A look back at Cranmore in 1950 from a passenger train leaving the down loop and joining the branch line proper. Quarry sidings to the left, including the remaining masonry of the former stone crushing/loading plant can be seen alongside the far siding. *J. H. Moss*

Above: The original station building at Cranmore has hardly altered with the passage of time, as seen in this view taken on 10 June 2000. Unfortunately, other buildings have encroached upon the former up platform, the station house on the right dating from 1974. *Brian Pike*

The ground frame connection to the Roads Reconstruction sidings was abolished on 30 April 1963, with the signalbox closing on 19 May 1968. The branch now was being operated as 'one engine in steam' from Witham to Cranmore and as a long siding to Cheddar. Signals were removed on the branch, apart from Witham, although various fixed distant signals remained; the layout at Cranmore was still more or less complete, with the pointwork being operated by hand throws. Goods traffic was withdrawn on 17 January 1966, except for bitumen traffic, which ironically became the saviour of the station before preservation. With the closing of the passenger service, a goods service was run from Westbury to Wells on Mondays to Fridays, plus a service to Cranmore on Saturdays, the goods trains to Wells running until 1964. The bitumen traffic originated in Essex and was hauled from the railhead at Westbury by a variety of diesel locomotives, including 'Hymeks' and Class 25s, 33s and 47s. The tankers were stabled and unloaded in the 1904 sidings behind the station, and bitumen was loaded into road tankers and delivered to the local quarries where it was used in the tarmacadam-making process. The loaded bitumen tank wagons were heated by gas burners to allow the contents to flow more easily; the roaring of the gas jets would wake many a villager in the early hours of the morning. The daily Monday-Saturday bitumen trains continued running until the late 1970s when they were reduced to four per week, and by 1985 a service of two days per week was running until rail tank traffic was discontinued in September the same year.

International wildlife and railway artist, David Shepherd OBE, FRSA, discovered the area as a home for his two ex-BR steam locomotives, No 92203 *Black Prince* and No 75029 *The Green Knight*, during a visit on a wet winter's day in 1971. The Cranmore Railway Co was formed to trade under the title of the East Somerset Railway, and a splendid two-road locomotive shed and workshop designed in the Victorian style by Robin Butterell was constructed. In addition to David Shepherd's, other locomotives, including ex-SR 'Schools' class No 928 *Stowe*, plus an assorted variety of

rolling stock, were moved into the new site from storage at Eastleigh on 18 November 1973, but all three of these locomotives have since left the railway. A station house was constructed on the platform in 1974 and Prince Bernhard of the Netherlands officially opened the new railway in 1975. At first, operations were confined to the shed yard, but with the cessation of the bitumen traffic, the ESR trains were able to use the station from 23 June 1985. The rather sparse original station building has been complemented by the addition of a new building completed in 1991, containing a buffet, shop, art gallery and offices. Visitors gain entrance to the platform and shop via a wide stairway, and other artefacts are to be found on the platform, including a bookstall from Salisbury station, a rare telephone/postbox from Bristol, and a GWR cast iron gents' toilet. It is interesting to note that much of the material for the main building came from other locations on the Cheddar Valley branch, namely Lodge Hill station and Wells (S&D) Priory Road goods shed. Also on display in the car park at one time on a short stretch of track were an ex-Zambezi Sawmills Railway 4-8-0 built in Glasgow in 1896 and a former Rhodesian Railway sleeping car dating from 1927, but these have since been moved to Bristol.

The line from Cranmore today runs for two miles through the sylvan Somerset countryside. A halt, named Cranmore West, is situated near the locomotive shed; the materials for the concrete prefabricated platform were recovered by ESR volunteers from Ilton Halt on the ex-GWR Taunton-Chard branch. Operations were extended to Merryfield Lane, near the former Doulting stone siding on 4 April 1980, and at first this was just a run-round loop, but a platform was completed in 1981, this being the terminus of the line from April 1980 until June 1985, when the loop was then converted into a siding for storage of freight wagons. The present-day terminus of Mendip Vale, two miles from Cranmore, was opened as a run-round loop only on 23 June 1985. The single platform, which has no public access other than by train, was completed in 1993 and can accommodate five coaches. A ground frame operates the points for the loop.

Westbury-allocated pannier tank No 8744 arrives with the 3.28pm Witham–Yatton on 21 August 1958.

The locomotive, dating from June 1931, was built by W. G. Bagnall & Co to Lot 272 for the GWR. At Witham, before the start of the journey, the fire would have been built right up to the firehole door in a saucer fashion, and the strong climb from Witham to Wanstrow would lift the fire, enabling the fireman to tend to the injector only, giving a comfortable ride to Wells without lifting the shovel. *Hugh Ballantyne*

With steam issuing from the safety valves, '5600' class 0-6-2T No 5637 arrives at Cranmore on 14 June 2000. The former stationmaster's house can be glimpsed in the background behind the original station building. *Brian Pike*

BR Standard '3MT' class 2-6-2T No 82009 (82A) is seen here going well at the top of the 1 in 75 rise out of Cranmore to the line summit (one mile west of Cranmore) with the 3.28pm Witham–Yatton on 23 April 1960. The second coach is a chocolate and cream liveried slip coach, one of a number displaced to working on branch lines in the 1960s with the slip gear removed. The Cranmore up distant signal can be seen to the left of the rear coach. *Hugh Ballantyne*

Ivatt 2-6-2T No 41202 (82A) climbing east of Shepton Mallet towards the summit west of Cranmore with the 2.45pm Yatton–Witham on 23 April 1960. This point is about one third of a mile east of the present Mendip Vale station. *Hugh Ballantyne*

Doulting Siding

From Cranmore the line towards Shepton Mallet rises at 1 in 70/119 for over a mile to Doulting Siding. The siding, situated at the highest point of the line, one mile from Cranmore near Merryfield Lane bridge, was first discussed in 1866. However, the GWR was not happy with the extreme gradients on either side, and the levels were eased in 1868, enabling the siding to be laid, the owner of Chelynch Quarry sharing the costs with the GWR and ESR. The siding was opened on 10 July 1868; a horse tramway which crossed the Frome-Shepton Mallet road, connecting the quarry with the siding, conveyed large blocks of Doulting stone to it. Being open-ended, this could be entered by either up or down trains, making the task of shunting easier for the pick-up goods. For a short time, between 1866 and 1874, a small goods station was extant at Maesdown Bridge near Doulting serving the beautifully named Bramble Ditch Quarry. However by c1882 the quarry was using a narrow gauge tramway along Doulting Cutting via an overbridge to the Doulting Stone Works. The signalbox and running signals protecting the siding were removed on Sunday, 10 May 1896 and a ground frame installed which was unlocked by the Annett's key on the single-line staff. Shunting was carried out under the jurisdiction of the Cranmore porter, the station of Cranmore being the local railhead. Traffic came to an end in 1948; the present-day station of Merryfield Lane has been built in the proximity of the siding, adjacent to which the original Doulting Stone Works can be seen, part of which is a listed building. The Doulting Stone Quarry near the Shepton Mallet-Frome road, which at one time supplied dressed stone for Wells Cathedral, is still in operation today.

All down mineral trains had to stop and screw down brakes before descending from the summit of the line, which ran through the deep limestone cutting at Doulting. From here, during the construction of the line, stone was recovered and used in the building of bridges at Cranmore and Shepton Mallet, and the station at Cranmore. The gradient drops at 1 in 56 here, before levelling out and crossing Fosse Lane by an overbridge, then crossing over the S&D main line at Charlton Road by two overbridges, one of which survived until July 1999, before approaching Kilver Street level crossing on the outskirts of Shepton Mallet.

Left: Chelynch Quarry (Doulting Quarry) seen here in this early view was connected by a horse tramway that crossed the Frome-Shepton Mallet road to Doulting siding, which had opened on 10 July 1868. Small wagons, known as 'tubs' are seen being lowered down to the working face in order to be loaded with blocks of Doulting stone, raised on to the track to the left and taken to the siding. *John Reakes collection*

Below: The 1903 survey for Doulting Stone Works siding, situated alongside the up part of the line between Cranmore and Shepton Mallet with the horse-drawn tramway extending towards Chelynch Quarry. The small signalbox converted to a ground frame on Sunday, 10 May 1896 is marked SB alongside the down part of the branch. *Crown Copyright Reserved*

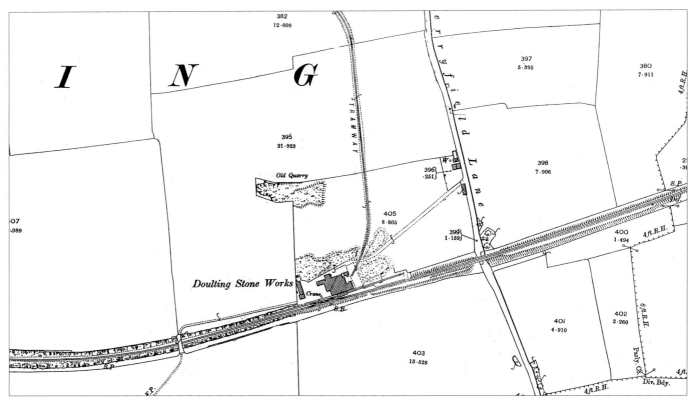

On the outskirts of Shepton Mallet, the East Somerset branch crossed over the Somerset & Dorset main line via two overbridges.
Having just passed under the ESR branch, one of the stalwarts of the S&D, 2-8-0 No 53808 (71G), now preserved, pulls away from Shepton Mallet (Charlton Road)
and heads towards Evercreech Junction with an unfitted coal train in July 1954. *Don Flook*

Above: BR Standard '3MT' class 2-6-2T No 82043 (82A) rattles past the gatekeeper's cabin at Kilver Street crossing with the 2.52pm Yatton-Witham on 23 May 1957. *Hugh Ballantyne*

Kilver Street Level Crossing

The gatekeeper's cabin was situated on the Cranmore side of the gates, on the up side of the line, practically opposite the gatekeeper's house. The crossing was not a block post; the keeper was in telephone contact with the signalmen at Cranmore and Shepton Mallet, and bell signals from the boxes were repeated in a small box near the gate locking levers; a train indicator was also provided. The gates were worked by hand, and the crossing was protected by two distant signals, one positioned 1,021yd from the cabin on the Cranmore side for down trains, and another for up trains sited at 502yd towards Shepton Mallet. The crossing keeper postwar was Bert Sandford, an ex-Swindon locomotive driver. Don Flook from Bristol recalls his railway days and the level crossing at Kilver Street:

'During the late 1940s until the late to mid-1950s I was employed as a fitter/turner by BR with responsibilities for the examination and maintenance of cranes, pumps, turntables and other ancillary outdoor machinery. I was based at a workshop/depot located adjacent to the Bristol Midland Road goods depot. Our area or district covered all of the former LMS stations and installations. The boundaries of the area extended to Charfield on the Bristol-Gloucester main line, Avonmouth of former

MR/GWR ownership, and Bath Green Park and Shepton Mallet on the S&D section. In those days, all of our journeys were by train (however infrequent or inconvenient) as access by road transport was unheard of then. This is why, on a particular day in July 1954 my mate (fitters' assistant) and I were at Shepton Mallet Charlton Road, carrying out the three- to six-monthly examination and service to the 5-ton hand crane located in the goods yard and the 30cwt crane on the goods shed dock.

'Having completed our work we found that we were too late to catch our usual train back to Bristol via Bath Green Park. If we were late back, no overtime would be paid, so we decided to walk down the line to High Street station for a trip through the Cheddar Valley to Bristol Temple Meads. And it was whilst we were walking past the crossing at Kilver Street, we were politely challenged by the crossing keeper who probably thought of us as unlawful trespassers! This of course he was perfectly entitled to do, as part of his duties. On establishing we were bona fide railwaymen, he invited us into his cabin, of which he was extremely and justly proud. An incredible scene met my eyes when I entered the cabin: there was a highly polished (black-leaded) cabin stove, various artefacts adorned the walls including the GWR coat of arms, decorated plates and a framed certificate

Above: This is the interesting scene inside the gatekeeper's cabin at Kilver Street that Don Flook recorded for posterity in July 1954. Attention is immediately drawn to the nameplate of *Fawley Court* above the fireplace. Other items listed by Don included a Railway Convalescent Home calendar (July/August 1954), highly polished (black-leaded) cabin stove, gloss-painted fire surround, wall-hung Tilley lamp, framed and unframed GWR coats of arms, toasting fork and shoe horn, signalbox mantel clock, bunch of keys hanging by a chain, notice board with a GWR route map, operating instructions for Tilley lamps, working instructions for level crossings, framed certificate for Best Garden Competition, two small coloured lanterns operated by a tumbler switch (visible over the shoe horn), a selection of decorated plates, candlesticks, aircraft cannon shell cases, bellows and various knick-knacks. *Don Flook*

Top: Mr Bert Sandford and his dog Ben pose for the camera of Don Flook on the lawn of the crossing keeper's cottage at Kilver Street in July 1954. The immaculate garden is worthy of the Best Garden Certificate seen inside the gatekeeper's cabin in the previous photograph. My good friend, railway editor Peter Nicholson, now resides in the former crossing keeper's house. *Don Flook*

for the best-kept garden competition, but taking pride of place above the gloss-painted fire surround was a nameplate from *Fawley Court*, a "Saint" class locomotive built in May 1912, numbered 2942 and withdrawn from service in December 1949. Its last depot is shown as Bristol Bath Road, so it was a fairly local engine, but too large to have worked over the crossing! By chance I was carrying my camera, and asked permission to photograph the cabin interior. He readily agreed, and requested that I photograph him and his pet dog. These pleasantries were halted by the sound of the signal bell, to which he immediately responded, closed the level crossing gates to road traffic, and I then photographed pannier tank No 7727 as it passed over

the crossing from Shepton Mallet with a pick-up freight. The photographs, viewed again after an interval of 46 years, clearly show a vanished way of life, most certainly in Somerset. I well remember that day in Shepton Mallet. Unfortunately I never knew the name of the crossing keeper (or his dog!) and on subsequent visits our paths did not cross, and our return journeys were made by the officially recognised route. This latter was in case we were required for emergency work at Bath loco shed or Bath goods on our homeward trip.'

When the passenger service was withdrawn, the gatekeeper's position was dispensed with and the cabin demolished, leaving the gates to be operated by the train crews.

Above: Crossing keeper Bert Sandford keeps his hand firmly on the frame lever as No 7727 (82D) steams across the level crossing at Kilver Street with a pick-up goods in July 1954. Note the 'bull's-eye' lantern on the crossing gate to the left and the signal repeaters for Cranmore and Shepton Mallet signalboxes in the box on the right. Upon the passenger service being withdrawn in 1963, the gatekeeper's position was dispensed with and the gate cabin demolished, leaving the gates to be operated by the train crews. *Don Flook*

Above: The GWR station at Shepton Mallet seen here c1900, gives a fascinating glimpse into the past as people dressed in the fashions of the day walk towards the station building, which was situated on the up platform. A horse carriage awaits custom, and a train formed of six- and four-wheeled carriages stands alongside the down platform before departing for Wells. The signalbox and goods shed can also be seen. Advertisements for Player's cigarettes, Pears soap and Bass beer can be seen on the left-hand side of the building. *Author's collection*

Shepton Mallet (High Street)

Shepton Mallet, nestling at the foot of the Mendip Hills, was an important wool-producing centre in the 17th century, and 30 mills were working at one time, using the resources of the River Sheppey. The first part of the town's name is derived from the old English 'scaep tun' — an enclosure into which sheep were driven for safety. 'Mallet' comes from the family name of the post-Conquest Lords of the Manor. The aftermath of the 1685 rebellion was felt in the town, with 12 of the Duke of Monmouth's followers being executed here on the orders of Judge Jefferies.

The opening of the line was met with the usual celebrations, the first train arriving at Shepton Mallet on 9 November 1858, hauled by *Homer*, a 4-4-0 bogie saddle tank, driven by the line's engineer, R. J. Ward. The locomotive was covered in flowers, and the town band played 'See the Conquering Hero' as the train approached the station. A day of great excitement and rejoicing was held in the town, processions and sports events were held, with banners and flags adorning the streets. The directors, as usual in this type of proceedings, had their customary celebrations, and the day ended with a firework display. The initial service consisted of five trains each way on weekdays, but this was reduced to four trains from 1 December 1858. Locomotive facilities and a turntable were provided, the locomotive shed being constructed for the sum of £50. Water for the station and engine shed was supplied by the Shepton Mallet Waterworks Co for an annual figure of £25, but this was later reduced to £4 for supplying the station only. The locomotive provided for the opening train was built in 1854 by R. & W.

Hawthorn of Newcastle upon Tyne and was housed in the temporary engine shed which had opened with the line. *Thunderer*, an 0-6-0 tender engine of the 'Caesar' class, built at Swindon in July 1851 and previously allocated to Westbury, was brought to Shepton Mallet and used on the construction of the ESR extension to Wells. Passengers to Wells used a horsebus before the opening of the extension to the city; the temporary engine shed was then used as a goods shed.

The main stone-built station building was of a similar style to Cranmore but larger and was situated on the up platform and had a large canopy. The down platform was opened on 8 January 1895 and this was furnished with a stone-built waiting shelter complete with an attractive small awning. A footbridge was provided to link the platforms and the station became a passing place from the same date. The down siding, which ran behind the down platform, was also provided with cattle pens at the Cranmore end. Two sidings, a goods shed, loading dock, weighing machine and a crane of 3-ton lifting capacity were situated on the up side of the layout. The goods yard dealt with coal, timber, agricultural implements and feedstuffs, limestone, beer and general traffic for the local traders. Wagons to and from Dulcote Quarry were also dealt with. As with all branch lines, traffic declined with the advent of road transport, the tonnage of coal and coke received at the station, which reached a peak of 9,378 in 1903, reducing to a total of 1,536 tons in 1933. General goods forwarded totalled 16,580 tons in 1903, reducing to 462 tons in 1933.

Above: Another early view of the GWR station frontage at Shepton Mallet with at least six horses harnessed to various forms of transport, an abundant supply of freight wagons standing on the siding to the right, and wagons are also being unloaded in the goods shed. *Courtesy V. Freak*

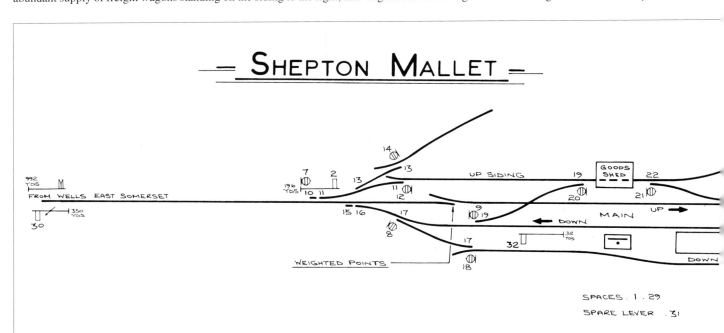

— SHEPTON MALLET —

FROM WELLS EAST SOMERSET

UP SIDING

GOODS SHED

MAIN

WEIGHTED POINTS

SPACES . 1 . 29

SPARE LEVER . 31

Above: A well-known view of Shepton Mallet c1905 which is included for its interest. Staff and passengers pose for the camera on the down platform as a '517' class 0-4-2T approaches with a Witham-Yatton train. The down platform was opened on 8 January 1895 complete with a footbridge linking the platforms; the brick-built waiting shelter and small awning are seen to good effect in this view. The shunter and a member of the footplate crew stand alongside a '2721' class 0-6-0 saddle tank, No 2729, on the up loop. Built in May 1898, this locomotive was fitted with pannier tanks in September 1920 and withdrawn from service in March 1946. Most of the class members were used in South Wales and used only sparingly in the south. Shed allocations for No 2729 included Pontypool in 1922 while her last GWR shed was Tondu at the time of withdrawal.
J. A. Sommerfield collection

Passenger tickets issued from the station in 1903 totalled 29,631, reducing to 18,584 in 1923 and 6,308 in 1933. The signalbox, situated off the end of the down platform, opened in 1894 and controlled the passing loop and associated signalling of the station layout. The box opening times, like those of all the signalboxes between Cranmore and Congresbury, are stated in the GWR service timetable appendices for 1945 as: '. . . for first train on week days and closed after last train, and only open during the train service on Sundays.' Trains to Witham could be signalled away from either the up or down platforms. The close proximity of the station to the High Street of the town was in its favour — compared with the Somerset & Dorset station opened in 1874 situated almost one mile away to the east. Staff consisted of a stationmaster, chief booking clerk, two booking clerks, three porters plus a porter/shunter and two signalmen. The *ABC Railway Guide* for 1953 shows the two alternative routes to London from Shepton Mallet. The ex-GWR

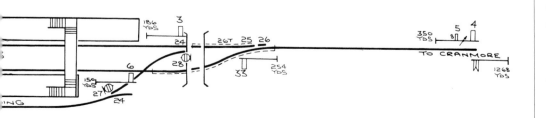

Left: Shepton Mallet (High Street) signalbox diagram showing the unique down siding which ran behind the platform virtually acting as a goods loop. The goods shed was on the up side of the layout.
Signalling Record Society

Above: Shepton Mallet looking towards Wells in September 1933. A raft of cattle wagons stand on the siding behind the down platform and shunting seems to be in progress near the goods shed and signalbox. The attractive station building on the up platform is seen to the right. *Ian Allan Library*

Below: Looking east from Shepton Mallet towards Kilver Street level crossing on a wet 14 August 1958. Up trains could be signalled away from either platform, which was useful as a goods train could be shunted out of the way in order to allow a Witham-bound passenger train to pass. The cattle pens were situated alongside the down siding at the Cranmore end of the station. The pointwork is interesting as it shows the access from the down siding to the up branch, and from the branch to the down platform loop. *H. B. Priestley*

Above: The rear coaches of the 3.28pm Witham-Yatton snake over the points behind '57xx' 0-6-0PT No 5757 into the down platform loop at Shepton Mallet (High Street) station on 23 May 1957. The locomotive emerged from Swindon Works in May 1929 and was withdrawn from its home shed at Westbury in December 1960. The 'High Street' suffix was applied to the station from 26 September 1949. *Hugh Ballantyne*

route, with changes at Witham and Westbury, gives a departure from Shepton Mallet High Street at 9.20am and arrival at Paddington at 1.15pm; other departures being from Shepton at 12.20pm and 4.7pm, arriving in the capital at 5.50pm and 7.15pm respectively — all three services to Paddington had refreshment cars. Travellers to Shepton Mallet from Paddington via Westbury and Witham could catch the 5.30am arriving, eventually, at 10.44. The 10.30am from the capital was advertised as 'By Slip Carriage to Westbury' and intrepid travellers would arrive at 1.53pm. Three other services left Paddington at 12.30, 3.30 and 6pm, arriving at 4.1, 7.16 and 9.46pm, all three trains having refreshment cars, and the 3.30 down was also advertised as a slip carriage to Westbury. The fares in 1953 from Paddington to Shepton Mallet were: first class single 25s 5d, return 50s 10d; third class single 16s 11d, return 33s 10d.

The alternative route from Shepton to London was via the S&D station at Charlton Road and involved changing at Templecombe, departing at 8am, 10.50am, 2.15pm, 5.15pm, 5.42 and 8.7pm, arriving in Waterloo at 11.8am, 2.15pm, 6.33pm, 8.25pm, 10.8pm and 3.53am respectively. Travellers from the capital could leave Waterloo at 1.25am, 5.40am, 9am, 11am, 1pm, 3pm and 6pm to arrive in Shepton at 7.43am, 11.17am, 12.42pm, 3.25pm, 5.1pm, 6.10pm and 9.37pm respectively. The fares from Waterloo in 1953 were, first class 28s single, 56s return; third class single 18s 8d and return 37s 4d.

The GWR timetable for October 1947 had six down services from Witham, one of which, the 10.20am from Witham, was a GWR diesel railcar advertised as third class only with limited accommodation, with a booked arrival at Bristol Temple Meads of 12.11pm. The last evening train departed from Witham at 9.20pm and terminated at Wells. The up weekday service from Yatton comprised three services only, plus the 12.7pm, which started from Wells. The 2.15pm from Bristol (dep Yatton 2.45pm) was also worked by a GWR diesel railcar. The Sunday service departed at 2.30pm from Yatton, calling at all stations to Witham and arriving at 3.51pm. Departure from Witham was at 5.30pm with a booked arrival at Wells of 6.2pm where a lengthy wait occurred before the train departed for Yatton at 7.20pm, this train arriving at 8.4pm with Bristol being reached at 8.25pm — nearly three hours after leaving Witham. Sunday services were withdrawn in the late 1950s.

The station received the suffix 'High Street' from 26 September 1949 (the S&D station then being renamed Charlton Road). Signalmen in the 1950s included Len Gauger and Ted Hardcastle and a ganger postwar was Fred Snook. At this time, a water column on the up platform was supplied from a tank in the embankment of the road that crossed the line and was on a meter, coming from the town mains supply. Therefore, loco crews were not encouraged to refill at the station. Goods traffic was withdrawn on 13 July 1964, almost a year after closure to passenger traffic, although mineral trains from Dulcote Quarry continued to travel through the rapidly decaying station until October 1969, the signalbox having closed on 3 March 1965. The station building at Shepton Mallet still survives and is in use as commercial premises.

Trains crossed at Shepton Mallet on a regular basis as seen here on Saturday 1 September 1962, with 0-6-0 pannier tank No 9651 arriving with the 2.40pm (SO) Yatton-Witham while No 82039 (82E) stands alongside the down platform waiting to haul the 3.17pm (SO) Frome-Yatton to its next stop at Wells Tucker Street. *R. E. Toop*

BR Class 3MT 2-6-2T No 82040 (82A) runs into Shepton Mallet with the 3.17pm (SO) Frome-Yatton on 6 April 1963.
The water column on the up platform was supplied from the tank seen on the embankment to the left of the overbridge. The water was on a meter supplied by the town mains supply, and therefore, footplate crews were not encouraged to refill their locomotives at the station. *R. E. Toop*

Right: A final look at Shepton Mallet (High Street) during its working years, taken from a Wells-bound train in 1948. The down platform starter and advanced starting signals clear the way ahead, as the train swings on to the single line from the down platform loop. The goods shed stands in the background with stacks of coal for the local traders plus a goods wagon standing alongside the 3-ton-capacity yard crane to the far left in the up yard. Point rodding, ground signals and the open catch point in the up line, protecting the train in accordance with signalling regulations, can also be seen. The goods yard dealt with coal, timber, agricultural implements, limestone, beer and general traffic for the local traders. *J. H. Moss*

Below: The down siding can be seen curving away behind the platform at Shepton Mallet in 1949. Staff consisted of a stationmaster, chief booking clerk, three porters plus a porter/shunter and two signalmen. The close proximity of the station to the High Street was in its favour, compared with the S&D station at Charlton Road on the outskirts of the town. *J. H. Moss*

Above: The former East Somerset station building at Shepton Mallet is still extant and under private ownership as Mid-Somerset Cleaning Supplies. It is seen here on 12 June 2000. *Brian Pike*

Dulcote Quarry Siding

The quarry siding, approximately three miles from Shepton Mallet and two miles from Wells, lay alongside the up side of the branch line at Dulcote Hill. (When Brunel was surveying the route that was proposed to run from Shepton Mallet to Wells via Croscombe and Dinder, he reported the limestone would be suitable for use as ballast.) From there the branch descended at 1 in 47 to Wells. The GWR obtained a 14-year lease on the site from 25 March 1873 for the extraction of limestone for use as ballast and was in pursuance of the formal inspection by informing the Board of Trade on 13 November the same year. The inspection was carried out by Colonel Rich of the Royal Engineers who had some doubts regarding the siding which he considered as very dangerous. He was concerned that freight wagons left on the main line might break away and run down the incline towards Wells and its level crossing while an engine was pulling them from the siding. A home signal interlocked with points and a catch point had been provided by the GWR, but the inspector recommended: 'A second home signal and distant signals in each direction are required, a catch siding to hold a portion of a train, and the brake van should be taken off the junction between the siding and the passenger line whilst wagons are got out of, or put into a siding.' A further inspection by Colonel Rich occurred in April 1875 when he reported: 'The locking arrangements are satisfactory, but the down distant signal cannot be seen by the person who locked it owing to an intervening hill. A repeater signal should be provided.'

Above: An 0-6-0 saddle tank with plenty of steam to spare pulls away from Dulcote Quarry and heads towards Cranmore with a train for remarshalling, prior to World War 1. The GWR obtained a 14-year lease for the extraction of limestone for use as ballast from the site on 25 March 1873. The crushing and loading plant can be seen behind the locomotive and the first four wagons. The quarry was never directly worked by the GWR as this was achieved by a contractor for the company. The East Somerset yard at Wells was the railhead for empty wagons destined for Dulcote. *T. Phillips courtesy Henry Esain*

Dulcote Quarry Siding is seen here c1905. The branch line is nearest the camera with the quarry sidings beyond. The ground frame standing in the distance alongside the down side of the branch-controlled entrance to the sidings. Due to the undulating nature of the ground, the rear of the ground frame was constructed on stilts. Items of interest in this view include a ballast wagon being loaded, the brick-built explosives magazine and the timber-clad crushing and grading plant. One of the narrow gauge 'tubs' can be glimpsed to the right of the main building. *Courtesy of Foster Yeoman Ltd*

Above: The main working face of the GWR quarry at Dulcote taken in the early years of the 20th century showing the primitive conditions and methods used at the time to extract limestone. Narrow gauge trackwork of 2ft gauge ran from the quarry face to the crusher using tubs propelled by hand. One of the tubs can be seen to the right of the rock face. This was work of the hardest kind in all winds and weathers performed by only the strongest and fittest, with the hand-excavated stone taken by barrow to the narrow gauge tubs. Drilling was at first by hand, then at a later date, by using steam-powered drills, the infamous 'widow makers', so called because of the dust generated by the drilling process causing health problems to the quarry workers. *T. Phillips courtesy Henry Esain*

The GWR objected to having to provide a repeater, stating that the siding would never be worked unless the engine was the possession of the staff for the section between Wells and Shepton Mallet. The quarry was never worked directly by the GWR, this was undertaken by a contractor for the company. A ground frame controlling access to the sidings was situated alongside the down side of the branch, the rear of which was built on stilts to cope with the undulating nature of the ground. A fatal accident occurred on 14 March 1904 when a young man was knocked down and killed outright by the locomotive of the 1.30pm from Shepton Mallet when he attempted to cross the line with a bag of coal on his back while returning from the engine house at the quarry. Two men unloading a truck at the quarry had in fact shouted a warning which went unheeded. Another fatal accident occurred in April of the same year, when sadly, a 12-year-old boy was knocked down and killed by a train near Dulcote Bridge.

A run-round loop was installed in the sidings in the early 1900s. Trackwork of 2ft gauge ran from the quarry face to the rock crusher using tubs propelled by hand. Blasting, as at all quarries, was held at specified times but Dulcote was unique in having a railwayman arrive from Wells at the appointed time of blasting, complete with a 'blasting disc' and the single-line staff, to ensure this section of the branch was closed to traffic. The firing of the detonators could not go ahead without the presence of the railwayman. Prior to World War 1 an empty ballast train would depart at 7.20am from the East Somerset yard at Wells and proceed to Dulcote Quarry. Upon arrival the empty wagons would be shunted for loading purposes, and loaded wagons coupled to the locomotive. A flexible timetable, depending where the ballast was required, either in the London or Bristol Divisions of the GWR, allowed a departure from the sidings at 7.48am for Witham or 7.52am for Wells from whence the train would work onwards

Left: Another old view of the GWR quarry at Dulcote showing the narrow gauge tramway used to transport limestone from the quarry face to the crushing plant, the tubs being hand-propelled. *Henry Esain*

to Yatton as required. Loaded wagons were also despatched to Cranmore for remarshalling.

Foster Yeoman opened a second quarry at Dulcote in 1923. The son of a West Hartlepool ship builder, he moved to Somerset after World War 1 in which he himself served. It was his concern for the blight of unemployment among ex-servicemen that led directly to the employment of approximately 100 former servicemen at the quarry. The quarry, known as Dulcote Hill, dated from the 1860s and although near to the branch line, had never been rail-connected and was situated immediately west of the GWR quarry. However, this was soon to change and under the control of Foster Yeoman it was renamed Dulcote New. This quarry rapidly expanded and an agreement with the GWR was made to provide a junction and sidings west of its sidings, which was to cost £4,075 with all the earthworks to be carried out by Foster Yeoman. The latter company also laid its own sidings inside the quarry and installed a rock crusher and weighbridge. Production of limestone in the first year was 24,018 tons, rising to 75,457 tons in 1926-7, output during the 1930s varying between 30,000 and 78,000 tons per annum, most of which was transported by rail. Crushed rock, scalpings, graded limestone and tarmacadam were despatched to civil authorities in London and the Home Counties in a fleet of 140 wagons purchased from the Gloucester Railway Carriage & Wagon Co. The 12-ton wagons varied between four- and five-plank types and were painted black with the owner's name, Foster Yeoman, in white lettering and branded as 'Return empty to Dulcote. Wells. Somerset. GWR'. The wagons were sold when rail operations ceased at Dulcote in December 1949 although some were buried in a disused part of the quarry. A locomotive was hired by the GWR to Foster Yeoman in 1923 at 20 shillings an hour for the marshalling of wagons prior to despatch.

Works for the new junction involved slewing the two

Above: Foster Yeoman opened the second quarry at Dulcote in 1923 which was previously known as Dulcote Hill Quarry and dated from the 1860s and renamed Dulcote New Quarry. Although never originally rail-connected, this was soon to change, with a junction and sidings being laid to the west of the GWR sidings. A fleet of 140 wagons was purchased by Foster Yeoman from the Gloucester Railway Carriage & Wagon Co. The 12-ton wagons varied between four- and five-plank versions. The wagons, as pictured here in an official picture of No 36 taken by the makers in September 1923, were painted black with white lettering and branded 'Return empty to Dulcote, Wells, Somerset'. *HMRS ACG933*

Below: A four-plank wagon, No 126, in the livery of Foster Yeoman Ltd as photographed by the GRC&W in January 1925 showing the differing lettering style as compared with the five-plank version. *HMRS ACG936*

Above: A member of the most prolific class on the GWR (the '57xx' locomotives had reached a total of 863 engines in 20 years between 1929 and 1950) 0-6-0 pannier tank No 3748 tackles the 1 in 47 climb to Dulcote near Parkwood with a Yatton-Witham train in April 1959. The locomotive, allocated to Bristol Bath Road (82A) when this photograph was taken, had previously been Swindon (82C)-based. The maximum loading for a '57xx' locomotive from Wells to Shepton Mallet was 176 tons. *RAS Marketing*

sidings at the western end of the GWR layout away from the branch. The sidings for Foster Yeoman were extended again in 1927 for a further 300yd into the quarry. Shunting at the two rail-connected quarries was made awkward as the two connections to the branch line faced in opposite directions — the connection into Foster Yeoman's quarry faced Witham and the GWR quarry opened towards Wells. With the incline running down at 1 in 47 to Wells, great care had to be taken when shunting wagons out on to the branch from the quarry sidings, and this was not allowed unless a locomotive was positioned at the Wells end of the wagons during shunting movements. Another unusual movement allowed a locomotive to propel an empty ballast train with the brake van leading, from East Somerset yard to Dulcote. The regulations also allowed two trains to be worked in tandem this way to the quarry sidings, and when required, a locomotive would be despatched from Wells to bank a loaded train departing from Dulcote towards Shepton Mallet. Operations ceased at the GWR quarry sometime during 1936 with the sidings lifted by 1938. However, the Foster Yeoman quarry was expanding; rail traffic was prolific and locomotives handling the mineral traffic at this time were '57xx' 0-6-0 pannier tanks with a 2-6-2 Prairie tank appearing on occasions. A Westbury crew would arrive at Shepton Mallet with a freight from Westbury, then proceed to East Somerset yard at Wells, whereupon they changed over with a Wells crew who then worked an empty ballast train to Dulcote. The load would average 20 or so wagons, and after stabling the empty wagons at the quarry, the locomotive

coupled to 13 loaded wagons (the maximum permitted) and then worked to Cranmore. The locomotive and brake van would return to Dulcote in the early afternoon and haul a second loaded train to Shepton Mallet where the train would be stabled. The permitted load for a '57xx' pannier tank from Wells to Shepton Mallet was 176 tons, Shepton Mallet to Cranmore 220 tons and Cranmore to Witham 420 tons. The maximum loading for the same class of locomotive in the opposite direction was Witham to Cranmore 176 tons, Cranmore to Wells 308 tons and Wells to Yatton 264 tons.

The quarry sidings of 2ft gauge running from the quarry face to the primary crusher were worked by a Ruston & Hornsby four-wheeled diesel-mechanical locomotive, builder's No 237909, which was delivered new to the quarry in 1946 and operated until March 1955 when narrow gauge workings were discontinued. The locomotive was dismantled in 1959 and scrapped by 1962. The closure of passenger services in 1963 and the severance of the section between Congresbury and Cheddar a year later meant that rail traffic from the quarry was now worked to and from Witham. The section between Cheddar and Dulcote was closed on 19 April 1969 with the ground frame at Dulcote closing in October. The siding was effectively closed from 20 August 1975 when the legal agreement between British Railways and Foster Yeoman ceased. Lorries now haul quarry materials from Dulcote Quarry instead of straining pannier tank engines throwing out steam and smoke struggling up the bank through Shepton Mallet en route to Cranmore.

Wells

East Somerset Station and Yard

Following the opening train carrying Lord Bath and the directors, which arrived in Wells on 28 February 1862 the public opening of the ESR extension from Shepton Mallet took place on the following day, 1 March. A service of four trains ran daily between Witham and the terminus at Wells. The populace was now offered an alternative route to London via Witham, Frome, Westbury, Thingley Junction and Swindon, to compete with the S&D which also ran services to London via Templecombe and the LSWR, or the B&E via Highbridge and Bristol. Third class passengers would depart from Wells at 10.25am, arriving in London at 5.5pm.

The East Somerset station at Wells was constructed in the Brunel style with a single platform and overall roof, described in contemporary writings as 'a light and neat structure' with a glass awning; a single-storey building, complete with booking office, waiting rooms and station offices. The station, although standing a few chains from the Somerset Central terminus, which had opened on 15 March 1859, would not see passenger trains passing between the two until 1878. The stationmaster and goods manager in 1875 was Mr Isaac Welch. The ESR also opened a single-road engine shed situated east of the station. Opened at the same time as the station, the shed measured 50ft by 20ft and housed *Virgil*, a 4-4-0 saddle tank dating from September 1854 built by R. & W. Hawthorn of Newcastle. A water tank with dimensions of 20ft by 10ft, coal platform 12ft by 15ft and a 40ft turntable were also installed. The turntable was situated at the rear (Shepton Mallet end) of the shed. Broad

Above: Photographs of the East Somerset station at Wells are rare indeed. This view was taken when, unfortunately, the building then in use as a cheese store, was destroyed by fire on Friday, 21 September 1929. Smoke billows out from the doomed building as railway staff assist the fire brigade. The right-hand gable formerly abutted the overall roof, which was removed when the station closed in 1878. The gabled portion of the building to the left was previously the main entrance to the station. *Andrew Linham collection*

Above: The attention of the spectators is drawn to the trackside beside the former ESR station where the fire brigade is fighting the conflagration. Flames can be seen licking amongst the rafters, and the corrugated lean-to seems to be in imminent danger of collapse. Despite valiant efforts, the building was destroyed within an hour. A Dean Goods 0-6-0 was brought along the yard at the height of the blaze, water from the tender being used to extinguish fires that had broken out on several sleepers and a telegraph pole. The wooden signal posts were believed at one time to have been in danger, but in the end came to no harm. The gasworks served by the railway can be seen in the background. *Andrew Linham collection*

gauge 4-4-0s and 0-6-0 saddle tanks were used in the early days — *Homer* and *Seneca* are also known to have been used. The ESR laid sidings and constructed a goods shed to deal with the expected traffic for local traders, of whom the Wells Gas Light Co, established in 1832, was consuming 1,873 tons of coal per annum by 1899. A siding from the goods shed served the gasworks.

Passenger services totalled six return services running between Witham and the ESR station at Wells by 1874 with journey times taking 40min, a similar time being taken for the return trip to Witham. At least two of the services to Wells ran as mixed and an interesting development was a separate goods train running from Oxford to Wells and return. This train was booked to accomplish the journey along the branch from Witham in 55min. Three of the six services to Witham were run as mixed trains.

With the opening of the Bristol & Exeter station at Tucker Street in 1870, some of the services left something to be desired, with one of the ESR trains only allowing one minute for passengers, complete with luggage etc, to walk from the B&E premises along Bull Lane to the East Somerset station. Complaints came from passengers who had missed their connections and it was wisely decided to allow five minutes for the transfer of passengers between the two stations. A signalbox with a frame of 28 levers was opened in 1877. The complexities and vexations of having three stations at Wells with no physical link between them are best described in extracts from a memorandum to the chairman of the GWR written by Sir Alex Wood (Deputy Chairman of the GWR) following a visit in 1876.

'On the 2nd ultimo, being on a visit near Nailsea, and not having ever been over the Cheddar Line, I took the opportunity of visiting it, travelling by the 9.10 from Swindon and reaching Wells at 12.45. I asked the B&E stationmaster to accompany me over his station, and also the Somerset & Dorset station as far as the Great Western Railway station on the Witham branch. The B&E accommodation and particularly the cattle pens, which are well made, and paved, and the nearest of any to the cattle market, seemed to be all that could be desired, for this description of traffic.

'Proceeding through the Somerset & Dorset station I had pointed out to me what had already been done to form a physical connection with the B&E lines, so that, by arrangement, vehicles could then pass from one of our

77

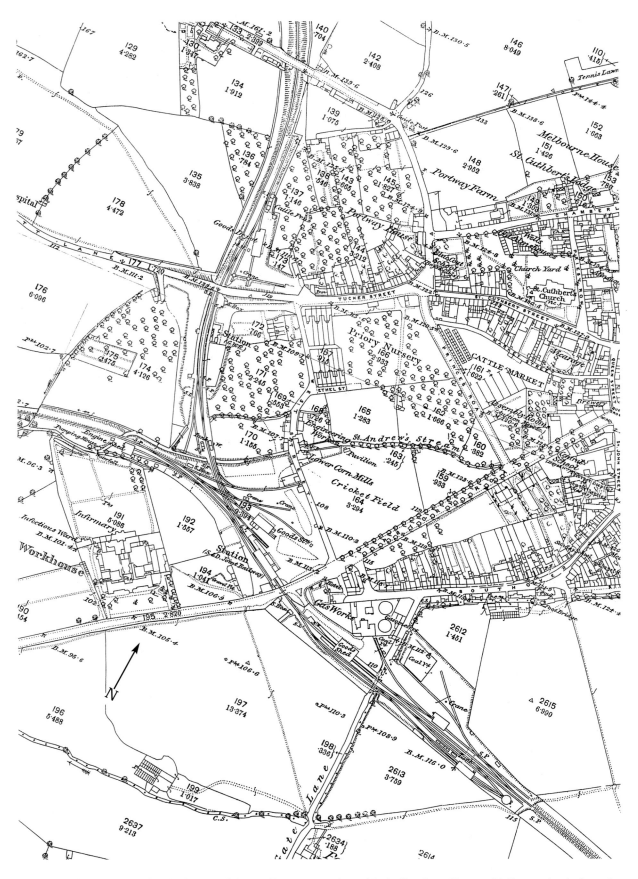

The survey for Wells showing the legacy of three railway companies, with the line from Shepton Mallet coming in from the bottom right through the East Somerset yard; the S&D line from Glastonbury coming in from the left and the Cheddar Valley line going into Tucker Street station. *Crown Copyright Reserved*

stations to the other. Proceeding to the Great Western Railway station, as our 1.10 train for London was being made up I requested the stationmaster to join me in the yard as soon as his train was despatched. The first thing which attracted my attention was a new first class coach, sent from Swindon upon the order of Mr Stevenson. I subsequently learned that at Wells there was no advice of this vehicle's arrival, and that being destined to relieve a B&E coach, it had been sent to the wrong station at Wells and to reach the right one, it had to do so via Bristol. I merely mention this as a forcible illustration of the very great importance of connecting our two Wells stations, at the earliest moment. The next thing in the yard that attracted my notice was the cattle pens. They evidently had been disused for some time, and the gates were closed by a chain and padlock. On the stationmaster joining me, he explained that as much as four months previously the Government inspector, in consequence of the pens not being paved, had condemned them and prohibited their use, that Mr Humphrey had dealt with the matter and that it was thought the B&E pens would very shortly be used, and then there would be no need of the others; upon which I enquired whether any arrangements, in the meantime, had been made to send London cattle via Bristol? I was told not and that the only cattle passing to or from the Great Western Railway system at Wells station on the Witham branch had been loaded or unloaded, as the case might be, at the passenger station, and on the passenger platform. I was shown how this was done, and it certainly seemed to be, for many reasons, a most objectionable arrangement, and I am not surprised that it has not been largely used. As regards the general goods, there also was a sufficient reason, namely, that while the South Western and Midland goods were delivered regularly between 9 and 10am, ours remained undelivered till between 2 and 3pm. As regards the passenger traffic I was told that our best train [to London] is the 1.10 timed to run in 4hr and 40min, but that our morning train runs from Swindon at express fares. Passengers are on the road upwards of five hours, while if they do not pay express fares from Swindon, upwards of six. Seeing that the South Western convey their passengers from Wells to London, starting at a more convenient time in the morning than ours, accomplish the journey without express fares, at a very little over four hours, they naturally get the best of the Wells passenger traffic.'

The relevant points in the above letter speak for themselves; the coach for example delivered to the wrong station at Wells, due to the lack of a physical connection between the stations, would have to travel many miles via Westbury, Bristol and Yatton to reach a position only a few chains from where it was standing in the East Somerset yard! The goods traffic for Wells ESR was conveyed to Witham via the 11.35pm London to Weymouth goods which was due in at 8am, the branch goods train departing from Witham at 8.35am (due in Wells at 9.20am). However, if the London train was late, and this seemed to be a regular occurrence, then the goods traffic would not leave Witham until 12 noon arriving in Wells at 12.40pm. The problem with the main line train was that it had formerly left the capital at 11.15pm thus arriving at Witham at 7.30am, but had been retimed in order that a new and important 'narrow gauge' train from London to Exeter should start at 11.15pm. However as it could not be guaranteed that the London train would not reach Witham in time for the branch goods, alterations were made to the timetable allowing the branch goods to start its journey from Witham later.

With the opening of through services the former East Somerset station was closed and used as a cheese store. The goods shed was removed in 1914 and in photographs of the yard taken from the gates, a stone building with a hipped roof can be seen on the left. This was the shunters' and guards' cabin, known as 'Long John's' cabin, after a shunter at East Somerset yard (John Gould), and this is believed to have been the original goods office. All the GWR passenger traffic was now handled at Tucker Street. The name East Somerset yard continued until closure, a fan of four sidings serving the goods yard which also had an 8-ton crane for unloading agricultural machinery and other heavy goods, while another siding ran to the rear of the former ESR station. General goods traffic was handled and there was accommodation for petrol tank wagons. Wagons were marshalled in the East Somerset sidings that ran alongside the branch line coming in from Shepton Mallet. Trip working to and from the S&D and Tucker Street goods yards was handled, plus the making up of empty mineral wagons destined for Dulcote Quarry. Freight wagons, empty coal trucks and loaded wagons from Dulcote Quarry were dealt with before despatch onwards to Yatton and the main line. The standard load for a '43xx' 2-6-0 from Yatton to Wells was 330 tons, while from Wells to Shepton Mallet, the loading reduced to 220 tons. An 0-4-2T of the '517' class could handle 154 tons and 95 tons respectively from Yatton to Wells and onwards to Shepton Mallet. Sidings were constructed for a Ministry of Food cold store situated east of the yard and south of the branch line in 1942. At one time, turkeys as well as other food supplies for the United States Army based in the UK during the war, were kept in chilled storage at the depot for Thanksgiving Day celebrations. The refrigerated articulated lorries of the US Army were kept at Priory Road Garage.

The original signalbox was replaced on 3 July 1912 by a GWR timber-built box known as East Somerset box, containing a 21-lever frame and placed adjacent to the level crossing on the down side of the running line at the Shepton Mallet side of the level crossing. The gates were operated by a wheel inside the box, the wickets being worked by a small two-lever frame.

The former ESR station building caught fire on Friday, 21 September 1929, the fire brigade being alerted by the signalman in East Somerset box, and despite valiant efforts to save the building, it was reduced to a smoking, blackened ruin within an hour. Due to the conflagration, all train services were stopped between Wells and Shepton Mallet and passengers transferred by bus. At the height of the blaze, a Dean Goods 0-6-0 was brought along the yard, with water from the tender being used on several sleepers and a telegraph pole that had caught fire. For a while, the wooden signal posts were believed to have been in danger, but in the end came to no harm.

The signalbox frame was replaced in December 1955 by a 27-lever version fitted with BR (Western Region) vertical tappet interlocking. The box was fitted with an external stairway at its east end leading into an internal porch. However, with the construction of a new turntable in 1948 the stairway was moved to the west end of the box, complete with an external porch to prevent a signalman falling into the turntable pit when coming down the stairway. The three signalboxes at Wells were at one time designated Wells 'A' (Priory Road), Wells 'B' (East Somerset) and Wells 'C' (Tucker St). The 'B' box was eventually renamed Wells East Somerset and 'C' became Wells Tucker Street. The signalbox at Priory Road was always known as 'A' although at one time it is reported to have carried the name Wells Priory Road but in any case, the S&DJR referred to its box simply

Class 2MT 2-6-0 No 46525 (82B) stands under the roofless part of Wells shed on 17 March 1962. This locomotive, plus class members 46526 and 46527, was allocated to St Philips Marsh shed in 1953 with No 46527 working the afternoon goods from Bristol along the Cheddar Valley line on 15 April the same year. A popular class of engine and ideal for tender-first working due to their tender-cab, members of the class worked passenger trains along the Cheddar Valley at times from 1955. *R. E. Toop*

Class 3MT 2-6-2T No 82039 rattles through East Somerset yard past the ex-GWR locomotive shed on 17 March 1962 with the 1.30pm (SO) Witham–Yatton. *R. E. Toop*

as Wells. The East Somerset box closed on 23 May 1965. East Somerset yard staff included goods guards Stan Webb (1930s), Jack Davies, George Lock, Reg White and Ernie Ross. Signalmen were Walt Bolter (1940s), Reg Garland (1950s and also at Tucker Street), and Harold Francis (1960s). Shunters included Brindley Difford and John Gould.

GWR Locomotive Shed

The former ESR locomotive shed was found to be inadequate and was demolished and replaced in September 1879 by a brick-built, two-road shed with a slate northlight pattern roof erected on the same spot as the original, the building measuring 75ft by 30ft. A water crane was situated between the two lines at the Priory Road end of the shed and a water tank with a capacity of 13,650 gallons stood between the shed and the brick-built shed offices. The tank was refilled from a local stream by a stationary engine housed in a wooden hut and was operated by connecting a steam heating pipe on a locomotive standing on the No 1 road of the shed. During the big freeze of January 1963 the pipe taking water up to the tank burst, and after this, water was no longer pumped. The coal stage was under the water tank and had a small crane. Coal was loaded from a wagon into a drum on the crane and swung around and tipped into a locomotive's tender or bunker. Apparently the bunkers of the BR 2-6-2 tanks and their Ivatt equivalents were too high, and the coal had to be tipped on to the coal stage and shovelled from there. The usual facilities for a shed of this size were supplied including a locomen's cabin, shed office, sand furnace and oil house. Most of the shed roof was

removed c1960, with the shed closing on 7 September 1963 at the end of passenger working and not November 1963, as usually stated. Driver Harry Viles and a fireman, after the closure of passenger services, worked on for two weeks loading the sand into a wagon, and shed artefacts and other oddments into a box van for transportation to Bristol. The tracks through the shed were removed in 1964, although a short spur from the turntable towards the shed was retained for a while, with the building demolished in April 1965. 'Metro' tanks, 0-6-0 saddle tanks and the main classes of GWR locomotives for branch line work were used on the route including 0-6-0 pannier tanks, '45xx' and '55xx' 2-6-2 tanks, Dean Goods, 'Bulldogs', '43xx' Moguls, Collett '2251' class and steam railmotors. GWR diesel railcars appeared in 1946 and BR introduced Ivatt Class 2MT 2-6-0s and Ivatt and BR Standard 2-6-2 tanks, although pannier tanks were the mainstay of freight traffic until the abolition of steam. In July 1926, there were seven sets of men, plus four engine cleaners and two shedmen (one day and one on nights); 1941, six sets of men, plus two cleaners and two shedmen; and in 1963, three sets of men and one night shedman. For around two months of the shed's life the shedman had left and one of the drivers was transferred, with two of the firemen taking it in turns doing the shedman's work, leaving the other two drivers to cover the transferred driver's work. The usual occupants of the shed were a Collett 0-6-0 and a 2-6-2 Prairie tank. Shed allocations for 1921 were: Class 1016 0-6-0T Nos 1042 and 1051, Class 1076 0-6-0T No 1297, 'Metro' class 2-4-0T No 1456 and Dean Goods 0-6-0 Nos 2353 and 2443. Allocations for 1934: Dean Goods 0-6-0 No 2400, Class 4575 2-6-2T No 5564. The allocation for December 1947 was Collett 0-6-0 No 2258 and 2-6-2T No 5506. Nos 2225, 2340 and 5572 were reported as being on

Below: Two occupants await their next turn of duty at Wells shed on 1 September 1961. Coal wagons for the depot's use stand on the left, a gas lamp being the sole source of illumination near the points in the foreground. The water tower standing above the coal stage can be seen to the left and part of the Government cold store opened in 1942 to the east of the yard is to the far right.. Two locomotives were shedded overnight from the 1930s, one passenger, one goods, and up until the 1950s the passenger engine was always a '45xx' or '55xx' Prairie tank. *R. S. Carpenter*

Above: A view along the East Somerset yard looking towards the level crossing on 1 September 1961. A 'Toad' brake van branded as 'Wells R.U. Not in common use' stands on the left. A Class 2MT 2-6-0 Mogul can be seen in the shed. The shed, dating from 1879, replaced the former broad gauge premises that stood on the same spot. The water tank had a capacity of 13,650gal. Most of the shed roof was removed c1960. Staff in July 1926 had comprised seven sets of men plus four engine cleaners and two shedmen. *R. S. Carpenter*

shed on 15 April 1951. The turntable was sited at the rear of the shed but was later moved in 1948 to the opposite end of the yard, near the signalbox. With the closure of the line to passenger trains, a freight train worked by a '57xx' 0-6-0 pannier tank was diagrammed to run from Westbury to East Somerset yard on Mondays to Fridays and on Saturdays to Cranmore only. With the abolition of steam, 'Hymek' Type 3 diesels began working a Monday to Friday freight train from Westbury to Cheddar in 1965 with an added train to Cranmore on Tuesdays, Thursdays and Fridays.

Wells Shed Diagrams 1944 (Six Turns)

Turn 1: '45xx' or '55xx' Wells engine. Book on 6am. Work 7.10am Wells-Yatton passenger, leave coaches at Yatton. Light engine (LE) to Bath Road shed. Return to Yatton on cushions. Then '45xx'/'55xx' Yatton engine 10.20am Yatton-Witham passenger. Then 1.30pm Witham-Yatton passenger as far as Wells Priory Road. (Turn 2) 2pm relief from another set of Wells men who worked train on to Yatton, then 4.5pm passenger to Clevedon, return to Yatton with mixed train. Engine to Yatton shed, then relieve men on 2.35pm Paddington-Weston-super-Mare (WSM) (at Yatton) at 5.15pm. (The locomotive on this train was generally the same engine left at Bath Road by the other Wells crew in the morning, and would have been used on local Bristol workings during the day.) Then LE back to Yatton, and at times would pick up milk tanks at Puxton and drop off at Yatton. (Turn 5) Relief from another Wells set of men who had worked the 5.10pm East Somerset-St Philips Marsh (SPM) goods, then working the 8.47pm Yatton-Wells passenger with the same engine that had come up from WSM, the

5.10pm goods being taken on from Yatton by Bristol men. The crew (Turn 2) who had worked up from WSM would return on the 8.47 ex-Yatton to Wells travelling on the cushions and upon arrival at Wells, the coaches were dropped off at Tucker Street, the loco was turned and put on shed overnight, working the 7.10am passenger to Yatton the following morning.

Turn 2: Book on 1.37pm to relieve Wells set at Priory Road at 2pm as above.

Turn 3: Pannier tank, '45xx', '55xx', or '43xx', '53xx', '63xx', '73xx'. Book on at 8.40am, relieve Westbury men at Wells and work 9.30am goods to Cranmore, sometimes on to Witham then goods back to Wells. Relief from another Westbury set, off duty at 4.25pm.

Turn 4: '22xx' or Dean Goods. Book on 7am, work 7.55am Bristol goods with engine that was shedded overnight, change footplates at Axbridge or sometimes at Sandford with Bristol men who had worked the 9.30am goods from Bristol with a Dean Goods or an LMS '2F', train worked back to Wells and locomotive back to shed for servicing etc.

Turn 5: Book on 3.55pm, work 5.10 goods to Bristol SPM as far as Yatton with engine from 9.30am goods from Bristol. Relieved by Bristol men at Yatton and work 8.47pm back to Wells (as above).

Turn 6: '22xx' or Dean Goods (Ivatt 2-6-0s were used from 1953). Book on at 1.45pm, shunt yard with engine that had arrived with the first goods from Bristol (3.55am Bristol West Depot-Wells), which had been used during the morning to pump water into the shed tank, then work engine and brake van to Wookey at 5pm, pick up the paper van left just inside the mill siding, then work 5.20pm Wookey-Witham goods tender-first. (From the summer of 1948 this train left Wells at 2.45pm and worked to Cheddar, shunted yard, picked up stone traffic, and worked 4.45pm to Witham; this working was SX. The Saturday working would work just to Wookey departing from Wells at 5pm.) Then work 9.17pm Witham-Wells passenger (later 9.20pm), leave coaches at Tucker Street, engine to shed to be stabled overnight and work 7.55am Bristol goods in morning.

Wells Shed Diagrams Summer 1963 (Three Turns)

Turn 1 Weekdays: Book on 5.50am, off shed 6.35am to Tucker Street. Pick up two sets of coaches and work 7.5am Wells-Yatton passenger, then work 9.38am Yatton-Wells passenger (two coaches), return to Yatton at 10.35am, work 11.35am Yatton-Witham, then 1.30pm ECS to Tucker Street. Stable coaches, engine to shed and stabled overnight for same turn next day, off duty 2.50pm.

Turn 1 Saturdays: Book on and work 7.5am as above, work 11.12am Yatton-Witham, then 1.10pm Witham-Yatton as far as Wells, relieved by Wells men on Turn 3 at 1.47pm, book off at 3.30pm.

Turn 2 Weekdays: Book on 7am, off shed 8.40am with engine that had arrived with 3.30am Bristol West Depot-Wells goods, work 10am Wells-West Depot as far as Axbridge or Sandford, change footplates with Bristol men on 9.45am West Depot-Wells, work train back to Wells, engine to shed, book off duty 3.25pm.

Turn 2 Saturdays: As above, but timed to leave Wells 9.45am, work through to Yatton, relieved by Bristol men, ride back on cushions to Wells on 2.45pm Yatton-Frome, book off at 3.30pm.

Turn 3 Weekdays: Book on 11am. Day shedmen's duties shunt with engine off 9.45am from West Depot, make up the 3.35pm Wells-West Depot and take it over to Tucker Street and get relief from Bristol men, shedmen's duties off duty at 7pm.

Turn 3 Saturdays: Book on 1.47pm, relieve Wells men on Turn 1 at Tucker Street. Work train to Yatton, then 2.45pm Yatton-Frome passenger, leave Frome 4.50pm ECS to Witham, then 6.20pm Witham-Wells, wait at Tucker Street. Then 8.15pm Wells-Yatton as far as Axbridge, change footplates with Bristol men who had worked 8.20pm Yatton-Wells, work train back to Wells, leave coaches at Tucker Street, turn engine and engine to shed, book off at 10pm.

Locomotives Shedded Overnight at Wells

Passenger Engines

From the 1930s, two locomotives were shedded overnight, one passenger, one goods, and up until the 1950s the passenger engine was always a '45xx' or '55xx' 2-6-2T. Pannier tanks started to appear from the 1950s and Ivatt Class 2MT 2-6-2Ts from 1955. Ivatt 2-6-0s worked passenger trains at times and Class 3MT 2-6-2Ts began to be seen in 1958. After Bristol Bath Road shed closed to steam during 1960, the '45xx' and '55xx' Prairie tanks were no longer stabled overnight at Wells, although they did appear over the line at times on workings from Westbury and Frome. During 1962, Bristol Barrow Road shed started supplying locos for Wells, and in 1963, Collett '2251' class 0-6-0s were often used on

the 7.5 passenger, with Nos 2217 and 2251 being the main contenders. No 2277 appeared on a few occasions and when used on passenger trains, usually worked chimney-first to Yatton. No 3218 was used during the last week of passenger working in 1963 and was especially asked for because of its clean condition, and was given an extra special polish during its brief stay at Wells.

Goods Engines

During the 1940s and early '50s, '22xx' and Dean Goods 0-6-0s were shedded overnight for the goods services. Because of the way the loco diagrams worked, the goods engine stabled overnight was different from day to day. During 1953, Ivatt 2-6-0s Nos 46525-7 were allocated to St Philips Marsh, and No 46527 was noted working the afternoon goods from Bristol along the Cheddar Valley line on 15 April although this was normally a '22xx' working. All three Moguls appeared regularly on the branch up to and including early 1963 when they were reallocated (Nos 46526/7 went before this, having been replaced by 46506 and 46517). No 46507 also appeared on the line, and because of their tender cabs, they were ideal for any tender-first workings, such as the 4.45pm Cheddar-Witham goods. From January 1963, after water was no longer pumped at Wells shed, only the passenger engine was stabled overnight. The first goods locomotive down from Bristol in the morning would work straight back on the first Wells-Bristol goods. During the winter timetable, the passenger engine was changed as required, and during the summer the Wells engine worked the 8.15pm SO Wells-Yatton; at Axbridge it would cross the 8.20pm SO Yatton-Wells where the loco crews changed footplates and the Wells set would bring this loco back to shed, therefore it was changed weekly. But if they had a rough engine they would change it during the week with one of the goods locomotives.

Unusual Locomotives Working Over the Line

'Bulldog' 4-4-0 No 3455 *Starling* worked the 7.55am Wells-West Depot goods on Saturday, 24 June 1944. Harry Viles also recalls that before the war, 'Bulldogs' worked over the line from Westbury with No 3364 *Frank Bibby* being among them. Prairie tank No 4103 worked the 7.5am Wells-Yatton passenger on Monday, 21 January 1963, and on Monday, 8 July ex-LMS '4F' class 0-6-0 No 44226 (21A) was reported as working a strawberry special to Draycott. On at least two occasions during August 1963, '8100' class 2-6-2T No 8102 worked the 9.30am West Depot-Wells goods. Another unusual visitor during the 1950s was '9400' class 0-6-0PT No 8492 working the 9.30am West Depot-Wells goods, even though members of this class were not allowed over the line. Type 3 diesel-hydraulic No D7004 (82A) worked a snowplough over the line on 1 January 1963 and then hauled the 3.17pm Frome-Yatton.

Other Workings of Interest

Former Midland & South Western Junction Railway Beyer Peacock 0-6-0 goods engines Nos 1008/11/3 were transferred to Bristol early in 1936 and worked over the line on goods trains, but did not last long as the three locomotives were withdrawn in December 1936, May and June 1937 respectively. The LMS '2F' 0-6-0s mentioned in Turn 4 of the 1944 diagrams were borrowed by the GWR as

Above: Wells East Somerset yard, looking towards Shepton Mallet in 1957 from beside the signalbox, the locomotive shed in the distance with the wartime cold store to its right. Part of the turntable pit can be seen in the foreground and the platform edgings of the former East Somerset station stand alongside the branch line to the left. Today, the Wells relief road cuts through the former East Somerset yard and is known as East Somerset Way. *J. H. Moss*

replacements for the Dean Goods loaned to the War Department and Harry Viles recalls the engines were rough, and probably all the examples shedded at SPM appeared on the line, with Nos 3071, 3078, 3094, 3103 and 3603 being recorded as working the second goods down from Bristol. They were not able to work the first goods because that engine was required later for working the last passenger train back from Witham and they were not vacuum-fitted. During the 1940s and '50s, members of the 0-4-2T '1400' and '5800' classes worked some of the Yatton-Wells and return workings. The loco on the 8.12am Frome-Bristol passenger worked back down from Bristol LE during the afternoon and shunted at Yatton before working the 6.15pm Yatton-Frome, with No 2268 being a main contender during 1963. North British Type 2 diesel-hydraulic No D6357 (82A) made its debut on the branch for this class on Saturday, 8 December 1962 working the 9.55am SO Westbury-Yatton. The 'D63xxs' worked this train up until the end of passenger services.

Enthusiast Specials Over the Line

On Sunday, 28 April 1957, the 'North Somerset Railtour', organised by the RCTS, was worked from Yatton-Wrington by 2-6-2Ts Nos 41202 and 41203. Saturday, 15 September 1962 saw a three-car DMU working from Bristol over the Radstock branch, thence over the East Somerset and Cheddar Valley, organised by the Bristol & District Railway Society and on Sunday, 6 October 1963 Home Counties Railtours worked a train over the branch hauled by GWR 2-6-2Ts Nos 4103 and 6148. On Saturday,

16 November 1968 a three-car DMU organised by the LCGB Bath branch ran through to Cheddar, this train having departed from the closed Bath Green Park. On Saturday, 31 May 1969 an RCTS railtour worked from Paddington to Cheddar with a four-car DMU and this was the last passenger train to work as far as Cheddar.

Goods Services 1948-62

1. West Depot 3.55am — Wells East Somerset arr 7.23am.
2. SX Yatton 6.55am — Sandford empties arr 7.37am, dep 8.10am EBV arr Yatton 8.26am.
3. West Depot 8am — Cheddar, return from Cheddar 11.40am — Stoke Gifford.
4. SX Yatton 8.40am — Blagdon, engine coupled to 8am goods West Depot-Cheddar, return to Yatton from Blagdon 11.41am.
5. West Depot 9.30am — Wells East Somerset arr 1.59pm.
6. 5.20am Westbury-Wells arr 8.32am, dep Wells 10.25am — Witham arr 1.17pm, dep Witham 1.40pm — Wells arr 3.49pm, dep Wells 4.25pm arr Witham 6.41pm.
7. Wells dep 7.55am — West Depot arr Yatton 1.50pm.
8. Wells dep 4.40pm — SPM arr Yatton 8.21pm.
9. Wells dep 2.45pm EBV — Cheddar arr 3.9pm, shunt dep 4.45pm — Witham arr 8.15pm. (This only went as far as Wookey on Saturdays at a later time — 5pm from Wells.)

Goods 3 had finished by 1951; Goods 9 ceased in 1959; Goods 6 only worked one trip between Witham-Wells by 1956.

Goods Services Summer 1962

1. West Depot dep 3.30am — Wells East Somerset arr 6.59am.
2. West Depot dep 9.45 SX — Wells East Somerset arr 2.50pm.
3. Wells — West Depot dep 10am, arr Yatton 1.28pm (dep 9.45am SO).
4. Wells — SPM SX dep 3.35pm, arr Yatton 6.30pm.
5. Yatton dep 9.10am — Sandford empties, then work back to Congresbury and Wrington goods, arr back at Yatton 12.1pm.
6. (Tuesdays and Thursdays-only working) Westbury dep 9.35am — Wells arr 12.55pm, dep from Wells 1.30pm, arr Witham 3.17pm.

Goods Services from 9 September 1963

Bristol Turn 800: 'D63xx' SX Winter 1963/64. Bath Rd 6.10am, West Depot 6.35, Yatton 7.20, Cheddar 8.15, Wookey R, Wells arr 8.40; dep 10.15, Wookey R, Cheddar 11.10, Sandford 11.45, Yatton arr 12.3 work to West Depot, dep from West Depot 2.30, Yatton 3.20, Congresbury 3.38, Sandford 4.5, Cheddar arr 4.38 dep 5.25, Sandford 6.10, Yatton 7.20 then return to West Depot.

Bristol Turn 945: Westbury men. Pannier tank SX. Shed 8.15am, Westbury dep 8.35, Witham 9.40, Cranmore 10.30, Shepton 11.10, Wells East Somerset arr 11.38, shunt dep 1.30, Shepton 2.5, Cranmore 2.35, Witham 3.30, on shed Westbury 4.35pm.

Summer 1964, Bristol Turn 800 same, Bristol Turn 945 same but an SO working with pannier tank Westbury-Cranmore, shed 8.10, Cranmore arr 10.15, shunt dep 11.30, shed 1.30pm.

Summer 1965, 'D70xx' working from Westbury-Cheddar and return SX, and working SO as far as Cranmore. This working came in when Yatton-Cheddar section closed in Autumn 1964.

Abbreviations: EBV — engine and brake van; ECS — empty coaching stock; LE — light engine; SO — Saturdays only; SX — Saturdays excepted; SPM — St Philips Marsh.

Locomotives Used During the Last Week of Passenger Services

The first loco listed for each day was the engine stabled overnight at Wells which worked the 7.5am passenger etc, the other two locos working the two goods from Bristol and return (only one goods on Saturday).

2.9.63 Nos 3218, 2217 and 2277.
3.9.63 Nos 3218, 2251 and 2277.
4.9.63 Nos 3218, 2217 and 2251.
5.9.63 Nos 3218, 2251 and 2217.
6.9.63 Nos 3218, 2251 and 2217.

Other locomotives working on 6 September included No 41208 on the 7.58am Yatton-Frome and 3.17pm Frome-Bristol; No 2268 working the 8.12am Frome-Bristol and 6.13pm Yatton-Frome; No 82040 2.45pm Yatton-Frome, 6.20pm Witham-Wells then LE to Bristol Barrow Road; and No 82037 5.20pm Bristol-Wells and return.

7.9.63 Nos 3218 and 2277.

Other locomotives working on the final Saturday were No 82037 on the 7.58am Yatton-Frome and 3.17pm Frome-

Bristol; No 2268 on the 8.12am Frome-Bristol and 6.13pm Yatton-Frome; No D6353 9.57am Westbury-Bristol; No 41245 1.45pm Yatton-Wells and return, and No 3696 8.20pm Yatton-Wells.

On the last day of passenger working Saturday, 7 September 1963, the final passenger service was the 8.20pm from Yatton to Wells hauled by No 3696. A Bristol driver and fireman came down on the cushions and worked the train back to Bristol as empty stock. At Wells, the fireman wanted the engine to be turned, and therefore the locomotive went down to the turntable at Wells East Somerset and was probably one of the last to use the turntable. As there was no locomotive available to work the first goods down from Bristol on 5 September, No 2251 went down to Yatton later in the morning and double-headed the 9.35am Yatton-Wells with No 3218.

Staff at Wells Locomotive Shed

A notebook found in the locomotive shed at the time of closure gives details of prewar staff and provides a fascinating glimpse into the past, showing how footplatemen were moved from shed to shed in order to achieve their grade.

July 1926. Drivers: W. Knight (Bill), driver in charge; G. I. Basley; J. Morgan (Jimmy); W. H. Coleman (Bill); G. P. Offer (George), returned from Severn Tunnel Junction 5.8.19; H. W. Coleman (Wilf) and P. R. Upton (Phil). Firemen: E. R. Mapstone (Reg); F. Western (Fred); W. G. Allen, to Pontypool Road pre-1926 and returned to Wells; W. A. Vernon; F. W. Knight; F. B. Cooper and W. H. Woodburn (Bill) to Coke Ovens pre 1926 and returned to Wells. Cleaners: G. Giblett; C. E. Osmond (Charlie); R. C. Woodburn (Bob) and H. H. Ford.

Other names mentioned in the notebook from Wells Loco: W. E. Phipps, removed to Pontypool Road 1.11.16, killed 13.7.18; A. S. Fairley, removed to Bristol; W. G. Collins, removed to Tondu; S. W. Slowman; W. K. Standard, removed to Bristol; T. J. S. Knight, removed to Neath 13.1.20, returned to Wells 2.7.23; S. Johnson, resigned 8.6.18; E. R. Harcross; J. M. Mactravers; G. N. Browne; E. H. Symes; S. Talbot, removed to Bristol; N. L. Williams; A. E. Sharman, removed to Treherbert; A. Western; P. P. Gould; J. House, removed to Bristol; A. A. West, killed 13.10.16; E. J. Abbot, removed to Swindon 1.11.19; H. J. Cockiage and A. H. J. Crabb, removed to Bristol.

Notes on above: Alfred Augustus West, a married man aged 28 living in Silver Street, Wells, was killed at Wells, East Somerset by the engine of a Bristol goods travelling tender-first with 11 trucks and a brake van. The driver, John Talbot, said that he saw the deceased about 25yd away, and before West crossed the metals, he put his hand up, which was taken as the usual salutation between one railwayman and another, and he was only two steps from the rail. Talbot continued driving until he heard another witness shouting, and felt that he had gone over something. He reversed his engine and stopped as soon as he could. He found that the rear wheels had gone over the deceased's legs and arm. Dr Manning was sent for, but nothing could be done. West died within a few minutes of the arrival of the doctor. A verdict of accidental death was returned by the coroner, although he did state that there was a certain amount of mystery as to why a healthy 28-year-old man with good hearing and of sober habit, and an experienced railwayman, should take it into his head to cross the line just in front of a train. Shedman Sidney Slowman said that West was employed

Above: The turntable in East Somerset yard, dating from 1948, replaced an earlier table located at the Shepton Mallet end of the GWR locomotive shed and is seen here a year after closure of the line to passenger traffic. Note the extra window installed in the signalbox after removal of the doorway and staircase in 1948. *Terry Morgan*

pumping water at Tucker Street, and may have been coming over to the shed to get firelighters as he sometimes did.

J. Morgan retired 1941/2; H. W. Coleman retired through ill health; E. R. Mapstone, removed to Neath, returned to Wells and retired from there in 1960; F. Western, removed to Tondu, returned to Wells 1941/2 replacing J. Morgan, and W. H. Woodburn made driver at Bristol.

Staff at Wells Loco as at 3 June 1940. Drivers: J. Morgan, driver in charge; Bill Coleman; George Offer; Wilf Coleman; Reg Mapstone and Bill Wyatt. Firemen: Fred Cyrill; Bob Woodburn; Bill Woodburn; Charlie Osmond; Les Parsons and Ron Snook. Engine cleaners: Harry Viles and Ron Goulping. Shedmen: Harold Goulping and Ned House.

Notes on above: Reg Mapstone became driver in charge when J. Morgan retired, and retired himself in 1960; B. Wyatt arrived from Salisbury via Pontypool Road; Ron Snook and F. Cyrill made drivers at Bristol; Bob Woodburn made driver at Oxford; Bill Woodburn made driver at Bristol; C. Osmond made driver at Gloucester and returned to

Wells; L. Parsons made driver at Taunton, returned to Wells then moved to Old Oak Common; H. Viles made fireman at Swindon 1941, returned to Wells 1941 and transferred to Bath Road 1963.

Other Wells loco staff 1940-63: Fred Western, Bill Heather, Joe Knott, Les Grist, Ivor Payne, Denny Payne, Eric Hall, Jack Bazeley, Dave Sheppard, George Whittaker, Herbie Hallet, Roy Parsons, Graham Granville, Joe Hudd, T. Collins, Gerry Boulton, Stan Western, Paul Boddy, Alex Western, Ken Mapstone, Walt (Bill) Fowler — driver from Wells S&D shed 1951, when it closed he was near to retirement so made out his time at Wells Loco driving in the yard etc, Bill Rawles — fireman from Wells S&D shed; when it closed came to Wells Loco before going to Bath Green Park — Ron Nation, Tony Rossitor, Peter Wood and Will Griffiths.

Staff as at 1963: Drivers: Harry Viles (driver in charge), Eric Hall and Will Griffiths. Firemen: George Whittaker, Dave Sheppard and Peter Woods. Night shedman: Ivor Payne. Harry Viles recalls that after he went to Bristol Bath

Above: Wells East Somerset box standing adjacent to the level crossing opened on 3 July 1912, replacing an earlier box which was situated nearer the ESR station. The frame was replaced in December 1955 with a 27-lever version. The stairway was moved to the west end of the box to prevent a signalman falling into the turntable pit when this was installed in 1948, as seen here complete with an external porch.
J. H. Moss

Road shed, the only time he ever worked on the Cheddar Valley line again was on a strawberry special to Draycott with a Class 3MT 2-6-2T in 1963.

Paul Boddy now recalls his footplate days at Wells.

'I started as an engine cleaner at Wells shed in 1950 and on my first day met Ned House, the day shift shedman, a friendly pleasant man who chain-smoked Woodbines and chuckled a lot. Around midday he bet me that I could not climb the water column chain, so I did, but when I was level with the leather water bag, he turned the water on full, washing me off the chain and on to the floor, wringing wet. He laughed then sent me home, telling me to come back the next day and we would start again. After that, Ned took me under his wing. I liked him, was very happy and keen to learn, and work at every job involved in the daily running of the shed. Once I had got the bug I could not get enough of it, always early for work and often staying late in my own time, sometimes having a trip with the afternoon men to Axbridge. Wells was a two-road shed; on the right of No 1 was the drivers' cabin and oil store, and on the left of No 2 were the offices and the coal stage. Then on the other side of the offices and coal stage were the two back roads and the main line to Shepton Mallet, then the mileage yard with shunters' cabin, and the Brooke Bond tea hut on stilts with a Trojan van for deliveries. The day started with cleaning the fire on a "22xx" engine, which had been brought to the shed earlier by a set of St Philips Marsh men. The clinker from the firebox was thrown on to a large steel plate, and when watered down and cold it was thrown up into a wagon which was placed on the back road

at the opposite end of the steel plate. Next the engine was moved back to the coal stage, soon to become a drive for me! Coaling was achieved by filling a 1-ton bucket from a wagon on the back road and winding it up on a crane, which was swung around to the opposite side of the coal stage over the tender. The bucket was top heavy so that when the catch was released the bucket tipped over. We had two engines allocated from St Philips Marsh, a "55xx" and a "22xx".

'After breakfast, it was time to clean the engine with cotton waste and oil. About the same time as I started work, the S&D shed at Wells closed down. Bill Fowler, the Somerset & Dorset driver, came over to our shed in order to finish his time out before retiring. Bill was a lovely old man with a grey walrus moustache. He used to help me clean the engine, and taught me a lot about locomotives. He gave me his engineman's book; it was old and a bit worse for wear, and I still have that book to this day. Included in my duties was keeping the drivers' cabin clean, and woe betide if it wasn't kept spick and span. The floor was made up of red brick, which I used to scrub, and the table was scrubbed with sand until it was white. Once a week I used to walk to Tucker Street station to collect the tea and sugar rations from the signalbox. But I was only allowed as far as the doorway. A grubby little engine cleaner was not allowed inside the box! I used to stand in awe at the sight of the shiny coloured levers and gleaming brass bells. The linoleum on the floor was so highly polished that the signalman used to walk about with dusters tied to his slippers so that the floor was continually

Above: A Witham to Yatton service is signalled towards Tucker Street from the S&D station at Wells Priory Road. The station came into use on 15 March 1859 with the opening of the Somerset Central branch from Glastonbury which was the first railway to open to the city of Wells. Opened as Wells, the station became Priory Road from October 1883. GWR services did not stop at Priory Road until 1 October 1934. The East Somerset signalbox can be glimpsed in the distance. *Ian Allan Library*

polished. His outside shoes were always by the door on a piece of newspaper. My first firing turn was on a Saturday morning with Fred Western. Fred was a very clean and tidy man with polished John White toe-capped shoes, so the footplate had to be dust-free and dry. What I remember most was breakfast time. We had a "55xx" engine at Witham, and out of Fred's box came a gadget made of quarter-inch copper pipe with a gland nut at one end, and shaped down to a coil and back up to a bend. He screwed the nut on to the steam lance cock on the smokebox, and held the coil down into the can of water, and turned on the cock. I was amazed how quickly the water came to the boil, in a matter of seconds, and the tea was put straight into the boiling water. Fred then fried his egg and bacon on the shovel, and when he had finished, I fried my jam sandwich in the hot bacon fat. Boy was that gorgeous! — especially when washed down with Fred's special brew.

'Another turn I remember was my first passenger train with Bill Wyatt. We had an hour or so to wait before departure from Witham. Bill told me to drop the dampers and build up a haycock fire with fist-size lumps of coal on a "22xx" engine. He kept on saying more and more, until the fire was black, and no more coal would go under the deflector plate. I was a bit worried, but Bill's experience and wisdom triumphed and by the time we had the "right away" the fire had burnt through, with the boiler full and 200lb of steam on the gauge. There was very little firing to do to Wells because the fire had to be run down, to go to the shed for engine requirements etc. I used to stand on the footplate at Witham and Yatton watching the "Kings" and

"Castles" etc going through and thinking, that one day, that will be me. I well remember the shedmen, Ned House and Alex Western, and drivers Reg Mapstone, Fred Western, Bill Wyatt, Wilf Coleman and Les Taylor. Firemen were Jack Beasley, George Whittaker, Dave Shepherd and Joe Knott. When fireman George Whittaker returned to Wells shed from Old Oak Common, I obviously did not want to return to engine cleaning, so I transferred to Gloucester (85B) as a fireman. I have very fond memories regarding my early footplate days at Wells, especially the men that I worked with, and the line between Witham and Yatton. Unfortunately, it will never be seen again, but the memories will never fade. Happy days.'

The Wells relief road now cuts through the former East Somerset yard which is known today as East Somerset Way and traces of its past are virtually impossible to identify although the former cold store erected in 1942 is still standing.

Priory Road Station

Construction of the 5 mile 33 chain Wells branch involved the Somerset Central Railway in some heavy gradients, mostly rising from the Glastonbury direction towards Wells with a final ascent at 1 in 105. It is reported that Messrs J. & C. Rigby, the contractors, had 300 men and 80 horses at work on the line by August 1858 with the heaviest works being near Glastonbury, the cutting constructed through solid rock at Coxley, and the layout of Wells station. The directors met at Glastonbury and 'went over the Wells

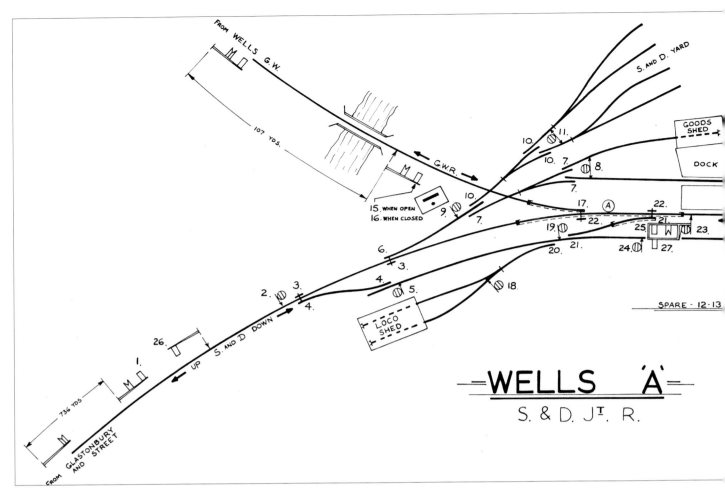

Above: An overall view of the S&D yard and goods shed in May 1959. The track from Tucker Street station, emerging from the left and cutting across the throat of the goods yard which gave the Board of Trade some concern, is seen to good effect. The goods shed, measuring 80ft long, was constructed in Mendip stone, as was the station. The stationmaster's house, seen to the left of the now-roofless station, was built in red brick. The sidings were taken out of use on 12 October and subsequently lifted, with the goods shed being dismantled in December 1988 and most of the materials transported to Cranmore for the construction of a new shop and restaurant at the ESR station. The level crossing gates can be seen closed to rail traffic in the distance. The corrugated iron building to the far right of the picture is the former Anglo American oil depot.
RAS Marketing

To WELLS EAST SOMERSET

DOWN UP

LAY-BY SIDING

28.

28.

370 YDS.

SLOTTED BY WELLS EAST SOMERSET.

CLOSING SWITCH PULLED HALF-WAY RELEASES 16.
16 PULLED RELEASES SECOND HALF OF CLOSING SWITCH.

line with an engine and carriage' on 7 January 1859 to review progress on the new line that was constructed to the broad gauge at an estimated cost of £48,000. This figure included a junction with the East Somerset Railway. However, this was cancelled before the arrival of the ESR at Wells, and as soon as the SCR branch was opened the contractor, Rigby, lost no time and had 470 men and 50 horses at work on the extension from Glastonbury to Cole, increasing to 600 men and 70 horses by February the following year. At last the city of Wells was connected to the railway and mass transport was available to the populace who celebrated in fine style for the formal opening on Thursday, 3 March 1859 with bands, processions, a triumphal arch in Sadler Street proclaiming 'The triumph of the 19th century' and the inevitable wining and dining for the fortunate few. There was even an old Russian gun, one of a number captured at Sebastopol during the Crimean War (1854-6) and stored in Woolwich Arsenal, before being located in towns and cities, including Wells, which had provided men for the campaign. It was hauled to the top of Park Hill by a local team of Crimean veterans, from which place a 24-gun salute was fired as the train arrived. Public services started on 15 March and for three years, until the arrival of the East Somerset Railway, the SCR had the monopoly of rail services. The Bristol & Exeter undertook to work the Wells branch as well as the Burnham extension for an annual rent of £3,950 until 28 August 1861 when the original lease of the SCR expired. An intermediate station at Polsham was opened in December 1861. From 1859 until 1862 the Wells branch was the terminus of the SCR from Highbridge, before the extension to Cole was opened on 3 February 1862. Originally, a single line ran from Glastonbury to

Wells Branch Junction signalbox where the line to Evercreech wandered away eastwards following a path as straight as an arrow for four miles to West Pennard. The line to Wells diverged north-easterly from the junction across the edge of Sedgemoor before reaching Polsham, located three miles from Glastonbury. It then meandered nprth-easterly over Coxley Crossing from where it climbed for a mile at 1 in 106 before curving east in order to reach Wells. The S&D rule book for 1864 contains the following instructions for enginemen when approaching Wells Branch Junction: 'All trains approaching this junction from Wells, or from West Pennard, are to stop fifty yards short of the points. No train, under any circumstance, must pass the junction from either end, unless accompanied by the Pilotman appointed for that purpose, and who is distinguished by a broad red badge on the right arm.' The junction between the Wells branch and the Evercreech line was removed together with the signalbox on 2 December 1878 when a second set of rails was laid from Glastonbury to the site of the former junction; all physical connection between the lines was then moved to Glastonbury. From there the two single lines ran side by side for approximately one mile before diverging their separate ways.

The line from Glastonbury ran into Wells under a road bridge before running past the two-road stone-built locomotive shed to the right and the brick-built signalbox on the left. A fan of sidings serving the goods shed and yard spread dead ahead as the running line, curving right, entered the single-platform terminus. Of the three railway stations constructed in the cathedral city, that of the Somerset Central was the most imposing, constructed in Mendip stone with a part-timber overall roof. The single platform was situated on the down side nearest the town, but like most all-over roofed stations, was often described as gloomy. Facilities, all positioned on the down side of the terminal building, consisted of a stationmaster's office, booking office, waiting room, ladies' waiting room, toilets and a porters' room. The platform was 180ft long. The goods shed, 80ft in length, was also built in Mendip stone, while the stationmaster's house was constructed in red brick. Cattle pens were also provided in the spacious goods yard, which covered four acres. Opened as Wells, the station became Priory Road from October 1883. Services on the broad gauge line were worked by the Bristol & Exeter with seven trains a day running each way between Wells and Highbridge in 1861, the quickest train being the 6am from Wells, stopping only at Glastonbury and running to Highbridge in 35min. Trains for Glastonbury and Wells used a platform at the Highbridge B&E station until the Somerset Central station was opened in May 1862. Sunday services consisted of two trains only, although in October 1862 it was decided to discontinue Sunday trains over the winter, only running during the summer in 1863 and 1864, and withdrawn altogether by 1874.

The Somerset Central, having completed the link from Glastonbury to Cole in order to meet the Dorset Central line from Templecombe, and also laying the third rail to its

broad gauge track, began working its own 'narrow gauge' trains on 3 February 1862 between Burnham and Wells and also to Templecombe, pending amalgamation with the Dorset Central in August of the same year by an Act of Parliament of 1 September, thus forming the Somerset & Dorset Railway. The Bristol & Exeter meanwhile continued to run a daily broad gauge passenger train from Bristol to Wells via Highbridge plus daily goods to Cole, the B&E continuing to work the line until October 1868. The B&E working timetables show the goods train running to Wells and thence back to Glastonbury and onwards to Evercreech, this portion of the trip ceasing after February 1864. During 1864-5 the train departed from Bristol for Wells at 10.30pm, but was later retimed to leave Bristol at 3.30am. By 1863, there were five through trains from Wells to Highbridge or Burnham with cross-channel trips to Cardiff. Cheap fares to Glastonbury and Wells could be obtained from Cardiff in 1882 for three shillings, travelling on *The Lady Mary* or *Wye* to Burnham and on 27 July 1885 trains from Templecombe and Shepton Mallet with connections for Wells branch passengers were run to Burnham, connecting with the *Sherbro* which sailed from Cardiff at 7.30am. The fare was 3s return from Glastonbury to Cardiff, but more-affluent passengers paid 4s 6d for the privilege of travelling in the saloon or bridge. The broad gauge rail was lifted from the S&D in 1870.

Excursion trains were also run to Glastonbury and Wells from Burnham and Highbridge such as on Bank Holiday Monday, 7 August 1876, the return fare to Glastonbury or Wells was 3s first class and 1s 6d third class. This incidentally was known as 'Black Monday' on the S&D due to the disastrous collision at Radstock in which 13 people died. The working timetable for May 1892 shows two direct passenger trains to Bridgwater running from Wells at 7.30am and 7.30pm. Burnham never developed as a port, with the S&D abandoning the operation of the passenger service in 1888 on its own account. Messrs P. & A. Campbell operated occasional passenger services between South Wales and Burnham in the 1890s but had ceased in 1900.

With the connection now open allowing GWR trains to steam through its station, albeit without stopping, the Somerset & Dorset continued in its own inimitable fashion with day returns from Priory Road to Burnham costing 1s 3d in 1901 and circular trips from Bath (S&D) via Evercreech to Wells being very popular, with trains returning via Bristol and the GWR. The traffic superintendent of the S&DJR suggested in January 1906 that 'motor cars with an engine strong enough to pull two trailers would be adequate for the Bridgwater and Wells branches'. This would save £450 per annum by not using two engines and four carriages. The Joint Committee, impressed with this idea, gave orders for two motor cars at a cost of £4,000 each. However, the order was cancelled in April as it was considered too costly in relation to the projected savings. The LSWR now stepped in with the loan of one of its 'H12' class steam railcars for trials and August 1906 witnessed the arrival of No 1. Seating eight first class and 32 third class passengers, the railcar was not a success, especially on market days, and was unable to pull a six-wheeled carriage containing additional passengers. The railcar returned to the Bishops Waltham branch of the LSWR shortly afterwards.

The Wells branch services were at their peak in 1914 when 10 trains ran each way between Wells and Glastonbury, with one of the services working through to Highbridge. Excursions to Bournemouth from Wells were also very popular between the wars. Two fast trains ran in each direction in 1890 between Bridgwater and Templecombe

GREAT WESTERN RAILWAY

GRAND CHORAL FESTIVAL
AT WELLS!

Excursion To Wells!

ON TUESDAY, AUGUST 5TH, an EXCURSION TRAIN
will leave

		A.M.	FIRST CLASS	COV. CARS.
Weymouth	at	8.45		
Dorchester	,,	9.0	6s	4s
Yeovil	,,	9.45		
Sparkford	,,	10.5	4s	2s 6d
Castle Cary	,,	10.5		
Bruton	,,	10.35	2s 6d	1s. 6d
Witham	,,	11.0		
Cranmore	,,	11.10	2s	1s
Shepton Mallet	,,	11.25	1s	6d

returning from Wells the same day at 7.0 p m.
No Luggage allowed.
Bristol, 26th July 1862.

SOMERSET CENTRAL & DORSET
CENTRAL RAILWAYS.

Festival in Wells Cathedral

TUESDAY, August 5th, 1862, First and Second Class SINGLE TICKETS TO COVER THE DOUBLE JOURNEY, will be issued on this day from all Stations on these lines, to WELLS, by any train up to 11.33 a. m. from Temple Combe, and 1.15 p.m. from Highbridge, both inclusive.

Above: A Grand Choral Festival at Wells on Tuesday, 5 August 1862 gave the GWR and the Somerset Central and Dorset Central railways the opportunity to run excursion trains to the event.

Above: The S&D locomotive shed at Wells, opened in March 1859, comprised two roads with a gable-style roof over each road. A handsome Johnson 0-4-4T, No 55, stands on shed on 11 April 1914. The locomotive, complete with 'SDJR' picked out in gold on the bufferbeam and tank sides, is in immaculate condition. No 55 was constructed at Vulcan Foundry in 1884 with fellow members Nos 52-54 especially for the S&D and used on main line trains between Bath and Wimborne. Some fast running was expected from the 0-4-4 tanks as the 11.50am Wimborne to Bath was timed to cover the 64-mile journey in two hours with two stops, at Blandford and Shepton Mallet. The Johnson tanks lasted on the main line services until 1891 when they were replaced by the Johnson 4-4-0s and relegated to local duties, particularly on the Wells and Burnham services. The shed officially closed in 1947, remaining open as a stabling point until 1951. *Ken Nunn Collection/LCGB*

Below: Portraying a timeless branch line scene, Johnson 0-4-4T No 54 approaches Wells with the 12.15pm from Glastonbury on 11 April 1914. The train is formed of five six-wheeled carriages. Push-and-pull services began on the branch in 1928 at the same time as on the Bridgwater line. *Ken Nunn Collection/LCGB*

stopping at Edington Junction, Glastonbury (for connections with the Wells branch) and Evercreech, the distance of 35 miles taking 66min to connect with the LSWR expresses to Waterloo. The outward fast trains departed from Bridgwater at 10.20am and 6.10pm with return services departing from Templecombe at 1.52 and 8.15pm. However, this fast service from Bridgwater was withdrawn in 1914. As late as 1923 there was a summer through working in each direction between Burnham and Bournemouth with connections being provided at Glastonbury for Wells branch passengers. S&D trains, while shunting in the yard or standing alongside the platform at Priory Road, effectively blocked through passage to the GWR services, and in order to save line occupation, branch trains between trips to Glastonbury usually waited in a lay-by siding alongside the station, this siding also being used for stabling oil tankers for the Anglo American oil depot.

The Somerset Central locomotive shed opened in March 1859 and was used by the Bristol & Exeter broad gauge engines until the SCR started running its standard gauge services. The B&E gave up all interest in the shed from December 1868 although the SCR still maintained one mixed gauge track in the shed until 1870 with the arrival of the Cheddar Valley line. Prior to the opening of the branch to Wells, there is evidence of a locomotive shed existing at Glastonbury, and as this was the end of the line until the opening of the Wells branch in 1859 there must have been accommodation or facilities for locomotives. Various extracts from the Bristol & Exeter minutes give a fascinating glimpse into the past. 29 August 1855: '. . . to procure an estimate for putting a turntable at Highbridge and Glastonbury. Mr Castle undertook to ascertain whether the Somerset Central Company will pay part of the expense.' 30 January 1856: 'Authorised to order from Dell Brothers two clocks for the Glastonbury and Yeovil engine houses.' 13 February 1856: 'Mr Fox shewed a plan for an engine shed at Glastonbury.' 12 March 1856: 'It was agreed to accept Mr E. Streeter's tender for piling the foundation of the engine house at Glastonbury for the sum of £38 0s 10d.' 28 August 1856: 'An additional engine shed has been erected at Glastonbury station.' 25 January 1860: 'The secretary was directed to write to Mr Read requesting him to remove the engine shed from Glastonbury to Wells and proposing to him to purchase the shed at valuation.'

The two-road SCR shed at Wells, measuring 40ft by 40ft, was constructed in Mendip stone with a gable-style roof over each road. The locomen's cabin and office was also constructed in Mendip stone under a tiled roof. The northerly road was extended through and past the shed after 1902, this forming a siding for the locomotive coal wagons. Coaling was accomplished by reversing a locomotive up to a coal truck, whence the tender or bunker of an engine could be coaled by hand.

The first S&D locomotives were the small 2-4-0 tender engines purchased in 1861 from the London firm of George England & Co. One early locomotive worthy of mention is S&D No 11, a 2-4-0T constructed by England at its Hatcham Ironworks in 1861. This locomotive was exhibited at the Great Exhibition, Hyde Park in 1862 and was at work on the Wells branch in 1863. It was painted in Prussian blue and is reputed to have had influence on the famous blue livery of the Somerset & Dorset Joint Railway in later years, the locomotive being nicknamed 'Bluebottle'. The original SCR livery was dark green, this being changed to Midland light green from 1875, and for some years after 1883, Midland red, but in later days the famous Prussian blue was adopted and retained until the last days of independent working.

Mr John May was the stationmaster and goods manager in 1875. At one time the locomotive shed housed two locomotives — this was reduced to one occupant from the late 1930s. Replacement of the original trackwork in the locomotive shed caused a temporary closure in April 1938 with S&D locomotives using the facilities at the GWR shed. The Wells branch, by 1939, was the only part of the Somerset & Dorset using push-and-pull services, and for this purpose 0-4-4 tanks Nos 1303, 1307 and 1346 were retained by Highbridge. Footplate staff at Wells was now made up of two drivers and two firemen. Highbridge men covered the branch workings in times of sickness or holiday. Engine changeover took place at Glastonbury on Saturdays with the 'fresh' locomotive arriving on the 4.15pm Highbridge to Evercreech Junction; the branch engine would then return for boiler washing etc to Highbridge. A 10,000gal water tank served the depot, supplies being pumped into the tank via a pump driven by a water wheel from a stream. However, water was in short supply at times during the summer months when the stream would dry up. At these times the 'water train' would arrive from Highbridge. Formed of redundant six-wheeled locomotive tenders the water train would bring supplies from Shepton Mallet, or on occasions from Highbridge itself. If supplies were short at Glastonbury and Highbridge, then the water train would collect from Wells for delivery thereto. The shed officially closed in 1947 but was retained as stabling point until closure of the branch in October 1951, and was demolished in December 1955.

From the turn of the century, 0-4-4 tank engines designed at Derby and built by the Avonside Engine Co of Bristol were the main movers of passenger trains on the branch, leaving the 0-6-0 tender engines built by Vulcan Foundry to convey the freight traffic. Coaching stock was mostly formed of six-wheeled vehicles, remaining largely unaltered until 1928 when the S&D introduced push-and-pull working on the branch, with S&D bogie non-corridor thirds being converted for this purpose. The original S&D 0-4-4 tanks were scrapped and replaced by the handsome Johnson 0-4-4 tanks of which Nos 30A, 31A, 32, 54 and 55 were fitted with the LMS vacuum system of motor control for use on the Wells branch (as well as the Bridgwater and Burnham lines). Some of the push-and-pull services ran as mixed trains, thereby replacing one of the two daily return goods working over the branch. Under the Southern Railway Act of 1923, the Somerset & Dorset Joint Railway Co was dissolved, becoming vested in the Southern and the London, Midland & Scottish railway companies jointly from 1 July 1923. The locomotives ceased to be the property of the Joint Committee from 1 January 1930 and were taken over by the LMS which provided the motive power, while the rolling stock was divided between the Southern and the LMS. All the old SDJR coaches were withdrawn in 1938 and replaced by LMS stock. Far from its place of origin, ex-Lancashire & Yorkshire 0-6-0 No 12140 was at work on the branch in April 1934, being another LMS import.

Also in the 1930s, the branch trains were utilised to convey excursion passengers to Glastonbury in order to meet main line services to Burnham. The S&D goods shed at Priory Road contained two 1½-ton cranes, and a 7-ton crane was situated in the yard. Six sidings served the needs of the local traders and there was a cattle dock and coal wharfage. Freight brought along the branch from Glastonbury and the S&D main line included timber for the well-known firm of John Snow & Co, agricultural machinery, cattle, general goods and coal from the major Somerset collieries including Braysdown, Clandown, Writhlington and Norton Hill. Parcels

Above: The Tyers No 1 Tablet instrument seen here in the S&D box at Wells *c*1936 replaced the earlier train staff and ticket working from 1895. The 5½-mile section between Wells and Glastonbury was worked as a single block section.
Scrimgeour Collection-Signalling Record Society

were loaded into a bogie van daily for onward delivery via the main line. Those parcels from another local company — Clares — were also transported by rail, but the main exports from Wells via the railway were the milk and cheese products of Wilts United Dairies.

The S&D signalbox (A) dating from c1876 and comparable to a B&E design stood near the junction of the S&DJR and GWR tracks and controlled movements through Priory Road station and the branch to Glastonbury. The original frame contained 32 levers and was positioned at the front of the box. This was replaced in 1949 by a 28-lever frame located at the rear of the box. The box was installed with a closing switch in 1930 in order for it to be shut when the line to Glastonbury was not in use, this enabling the section between East Somerset and Tucker Street to be worked as a single-block section. From 1 October 1934, GWR trains called at Priory Road, although with Tucker Street station only a few chains away, the reason for their stopping seemed rather vague.

The largest and heaviest locomotive seen at Wells appeared on 25 November 1949 when Bulleid 'West Country' class Pacific No 34092 was named *Wells* (later renamed *City of Wells*) in a ceremony at Priory Road. The locomotive, which had been sent down especially for the occasion from Stewarts Lane shed, arrived at Wells tender first, hauling three coaches, one of which was a dining vehicle. The coaches were stabled in an adjacent siding, while the loco-

motive was placed in the loading dock for the naming ceremony. Civic dignitaries, railway officials and the Bishop of Bath and Wells enjoyed an excellent dinner in the dining car after the ceremony.

There were six trains from Glastonbury and five from Wells prior to closure. Branch passenger services were usually in the hands of the 0-4-4 tanks until closure. During the last few years a total of 10 passengers a day had used the line. Freight, which had once totalled 80-100 wagons per day including coal, had dwindled to 10 or less. The other final regular traffic was petrol from the refinery at Fawley for the Esso Co which was now the occupier of the Anglo American Petroleum Co premises adjacent to the station. With the Western Region gaining control of the former S&D route, the writing was on the wall, and closure by stealth was implemented. The 10.40am ex-Glastonbury was carefully timed to miss a connection at Priory Road with the 10.45am to Yatton and Bristol, but by walking to Tucker Street the same Bristol train could be caught, as it did not leave there until 11.10am.

The last train ran on 29 October 1951, this being the 6.30pm to Glastonbury formed of ex-LMS push-and-pull coach No M24465 propelled by 0-4-4T No 58086, formerly MR No 1423, and the last survivor of a class that had been introduced to the S&D in 1877. Driver Frank Banwell, Fireman Clarence Rawles and Guard Bob Fry were the crew on this sad occasion, a crowd of local people filled the platform for the final train, and there was a sad feeling of nostalgia in the air as the train steamed out. It returned from Glastonbury to a fusillade of detonators, before returning to Highbridge as empty stock.

Ironically, the first station to open in the city, was the first to close. With Priory Road station closed trains running between Yatton and Witham now steamed through without stopping in the same manner as they had in 1878. Wells 'A' signalbox remained in use controlling access to the goods yard, which closed on 2 December 1955, being replaced by a two-lever ground frame and a replacement 27-lever frame installed in East Somerset box to work the revamped layout. After closure of the S&D branch, a short section of track was retained as a headshunt to give access to the goods yard. The block section now became Wells East Somerset-Wells station and worked by EKT (electric key token) — possibly the shortest section of track with tablet working in Great Britain, a distance of approximately 400yd. An Annett's key on the token was used to unlock the ground frame for access to the goods yard which was now served by Cheddar Valley trains. Priory Road station after closure was used as the district zonal offices where freight traffic accountancy work was carried out for many years. Lifting of the trackwork on the Glastonbury-Wells branch began on 13 February 1955, and unusually was not completed until early 1957 as the local permanent way staff did the work at weekends. The roof of Priory Road station was removed in 1955, and No 2253 hauled the crane used for its removal to Wells. The former Wells 'A' signalbox was demolished in 1960. The sidings in the goods yard at Priory Road were taken out of use on 12 October 1964 and subsequently lifted. The goods shed was dismantled in December 1988 with most of the masonry being transported to the present-day East Somerset Railway at Cranmore and used to construct a shop and restaurant at the station. The small wooden building used as an office for the goods shed was saved by the Somerset & Dorset Railway Trust and can be seen at Washford station on the West Somerset Railway which is home to the museum and rolling stock of the S&DRT, and is well worth a visit. The Wells relief road has completely obliterated all traces of the railway at Priory Road except for some pieces of concrete fencing etc. The former corrugated iron Anglo American depot still survives in the yard of Messrs Tincknell alongside the relief road.

During 1942 an incident happened, the outcome of which has become part of the folklore of the Somerset & Dorset. A Government stores train was running from Witham to Highbridge, the load consisting of jerrycans full of petrol in sheeted open wagons. An inspector who was riding in the brake van with the guard was rather wary of pinning down the wagon brakes at Shepton Mallet for the 1 in 47 from Dulcote in fear of sparks from the brake blocks or an overheating wagon wheel causing a fire amongst the petrol cans. Therefore the inspector explained his reasons to the driver, asking him to rely on the brakes of the locomotive and brake van only, to which the driver reluctantly agreed. The unfortunate result was that the train started to run away while coming through the cutting at Dulcote, with the footplatemen blowing the locomotive whistle violently to attract the attention of the signalman in Wells East Somerset box — 'train running away' — to which the signalman reacted swiftly by opening the level crossing gates and asking the S&D signalman for the road. As Priory Road box controlled the junction between the GWR and the S&D the signalman could have directed the train in either direction, but instead offered it to his counterpart in the GWR signalbox at Tucker Street. The runaway ran through the station at a very fast rate, eventually coming to a halt near Wookey. A Board of Inquiry was subsequently held in the waiting room of Priory Road station. The GWR signalmen were commended for reacting to what could have been a very serious incident. The S&D signalman was then asked why he had let the train run towards Tucker Street rather than along the Glastonbury branch, to which the signalman, who in common with many of his comrades on the S&D had a very low opinion regarding the GWR in any shape or form, replied in true Somerset & Dorset fashion, 'Well, 'twas their train, so I let 'em 'ave it.'

I know full well from my own working experiences that life on the railway can be dirty, physically demanding, and at times often dangerous and even death may be the unfortunate result. However, on the opposite turn of the coin, railwaymen (except for a few!) have a very positive sense of humour and I am indebted indeed to Paul Fry for the following amusing collection of anecdotes. Paul, the son of a former S&D railwayman, and a railwayman himself, started his career at Priory Road in 1949 working at various stations on the old S&D until returning to Tucker Street. He lived in the station house at Priory Road for 24 years. An eminent local historian, and Divisional Superintendent of the Wells Division of St John Ambulance for 30 years, he is also the secretary of the Wells Railway Fraternity, a member of the Somerset & Dorset Railway Trust and the Bristol Industrial Archaeological Society. I will now let you peruse his highly amusing recollections.

No 1 Self-importance
'Self-importance was inevitably deflated on the branch, like the day a somewhat self-opinioned GWR porter, proud that he was acting as porter-guard, and who had taken to giving flamboyant waves of his flag as right-away, was guard on a freight train into Wells on the Cheddar Valley branch. Having stopped at a wayside station he noticed the stationmaster in conversation with an inspector and he left his guard's van to make himself prominent, whereupon one of the signal and telegraph linesmen, giving the nod to the engine driver, slipped along the train on the blind side and quietly uncoupled the guard's van from the rest of the train.

The guard, unaware that anything had taken place, blew his whistle and gave an exaggerated right-away signal with his flag, the driver opened the regulator smartly and took the train out of the station, leaving the guard's van behind and the guard sheepishly running down the platform shouting "Stop! Stop!" in full view of the stationmaster and inspector. Poor fellow. The event was relayed by telephone right down the branch so that all got to know.'

No 2 The Tin Mallard
'A young public school-educated junior clerk tried to impress his workmates as to his knowledge of ornithology by pointing out one morning to the station staff that he had seen a very rare wildfowl in a local stream. Upon investigation by some of the staff, nothing could be seen except an old rusty tin can. Later in the day a bird's nest, made by human hands and complete with egg shells, appeared outside of the office where the clerk worked, together with a notice which read:

Eggs & Nest of the Greater Tin Mallard
(Tincanus Rusticus Vealii)

Its reddish brown plumage and habit of remaining stationary for weeks on end easily distinguish the Greater Tin Mallard, also known as the rusty-necked sewer wader, or Priory Road pippet. It frequents shallow streams and can often be seen on rubbish dumps. One great difference from other ducks is its note, instead of the melodious "Quack" (eg Moatii or Bombayii) it gives a dull "clang" hence when a tin mallard lays an egg it is known as "Dropping a clanger". The species Vealii was thought to be extinct until rediscovered in 1958 by a distinguished ornithologist.

No other attempt was ever made to impress his workmates about knowledge of feathered friends.'

No 3 The New Boots
'A porter at Priory Road came to work with a brand new pair of hobnailed boots of which he was very proud. But an amusing thing happened later in the day when a local farmer brought to the station for despatch by passenger train several very young heifers all done up properly in sacks for the journey. They were tethered to suitable rainwater pipes waiting to be loaded into the train. When it was time for the heifers to be loaded, the porter undid one of them and was leading it along the platform, when suddenly it took off at high speed up the station yard with the porter being towed along, unable to get a grip with his hobnailed boots. To the amusement of all watching he was taken up the yard and out into Priory Road before the heifer could be brought to a stop with the help of a passing motorist.'

No 4 A Pigeon Special
'The railways were always able to provide a service to pigeon fanciers by way of enabling them to send their racing pigeons by train for release. Whole trainloads of them were taken over the Mendips to Dorset from the Midlands. The railways also made arrangements for small fanciers to take their birds to a station in special baskets to be forwarded to wherever the fancier desired and upon arrival the birds would be released. The time of the release would be noted on the label of the basket which was sent back carriage-free to its home station. From this information the flight times could be calculated when the homing pigeons returned to their lofts. We had several fanciers in Wells who made use of this service. One particular man lived at Godney, about four miles from the station, and would regularly bring a basket of birds to Priory Road for despatch up North. Having

paid his carriage charges he would depart for home. One bright sunny morning he laboured in with his basket, did the necessary and departed. The basket of birds was left on the platform to go off on the next available train.

'Unfortunately, there was a young new porter on duty, and seeing the basket, he mistakenly thought it had arrived by the last train into Wells, whereupon he took the basket out into the station yard and released the pigeons, properly noting the date and time of release on the label. The first any of the station staff knew of the occurrence was when the poor man came cycling back to Wells from Godney with the birds again. The pigeons had returned home before he had and were in their loft when he arrived. He was not amused, and said so! Sixteen miles' cycling for one basket of birds; he was certainly dedicated to his hobby.'

No 5 The Goat with an Appetite for Glue
'The manufacturing company of Clares used to send a considerable number of cartons by rail from Priory Road. One day we had a consignment of 20 or 30 items to go away. We had a glue pot with a large brush to affix the ledger labels to the cartons which were then loaded into the guard's van to travel to Glastonbury. Also on this day there was a goat travelling on the same train, and the animal was also put into the guard's van. It appears that on the way out to Glastonbury the goat took a fancy to the glue and licked all the labels off, not only the ledger ones but the destination labels as well. As the station staff at Glastonbury could not make out where the parcels had to go, they were returned to Wells by the next train. We had to telephone Clares and tell them that we had some of their parcels, and didn't know where they had to go! They had to relabel all their parcels, thanks to a goat with an appetite for glue.'

No 6 An Angry Clergyman
'Due to its prominence as a cathedral city a large number of clergymen travelled to Wells by train for conferences and meetings etc. Living in the station house at Priory Road I used to spend most of my spare hours as a young man mooching about in the goods yard, or playing up the porters and booking clerks etc. One night during the war I was in the booking office with the late-turn porter. The blackout was on and there were no lights showing outside, and the few that existed on the platform were rather dim. A train had arrived from Shepton Mallet and the driver unfortunately had misjudged the station a little bit, so instead of being under the overall roof, the coaches ended up past it. We went out on to the platform, and as nobody seemed to get off, we went back into the booking office. However, about five minutes later, the door suddenly opened, and standing in the doorway was an apparition — it was a clergyman covered from head to foot in cow manure and bleeding from a cut to his forehead. The first words which he uttered really shocked me — "I have just fallen down a bloody great hole". What he had done when getting out of the train on that part of the platform that was unlit was, instead of turning right and through the station in the normal way, he had in fact walked straight across and had fallen about three feet into the part of the cattle loading dock where all the manure was washed down. He was not amused and put in a claim for his clothes etc. We never heard any more regarding that incident but it always upset me that a vicar should swear. However, after falling about three feet into a pile of cow manure I can quite understand his feelings.'

No 7 The Overloaded Diesel
'I was on duty in the booking office at Tucker Street when someone wanted to book a Sunday school outing to Weston-super-Mare, and after telling him the cost, he then went on his way. Come the day of the outing he arrived with about 60 children, and the thing that I had failed to remember when

Above: A Johnson 0-4-4T complete with its mixed train has reversed out of Priory Road station in 1936 and stands in the loop adjacent to the S&D signalbox in order to clear the line for a GWR Yatton-Witham service, for which the lower quadrant signal arm to the right has already been lowered. Tucker Street station can be seen to the far right, and coaches stand on the site of the former B&E locomotive shed. The S&D signalbox in the centre of the photograph was known at times as Wells A. Built to a Bristol & Exeter design, it originally contained a 32-lever frame which was replaced by a 28-lever frame in 1949. The single-line section between Wells and Glastonbury was originally worked by block telegraph, replaced in 1886 with train staff and ticket working, and replaced again in 1895 with electric train tablet working using Tyers No 1 instruments. Although the Glastonbury branch closed in 1951, the box remained open to control access to the goods yard, eventually closing on 2 December 1955, being replaced by a two-lever ground frame. *H. B. Priestley*

Priory Road station closed in 1951 with the last passenger train to Glastonbury departing at 6.30pm on 29 October. The overall roof was removed in 1955. No 8714 (82B) and 'Toad' brake van trundle through the now-closed and roofless former S&D station in April 1959.

RAS Marketing

Having left Tucker Street station, a '45xx' 2-6-2T complete with a two-coach 'B' set hustles across the S&D/GWR junction at Wells with a Yatton to Witham train in 1936. The Johnson tank standing on the loop adjacent to the S&D signalbox has reversed from Priory Road station and awaits entry to the station before departing for Glastonbury. *H. B. Priestley*

Above: Tucker Street station as viewed from underneath the Burcot road overbridge in 1957. Water columns were situated between the tracks at either end of the station. With the opening of the junction over the S&D metals on 1 January 1878 and the closure of the East Somerset station, the GWR concentrated its passenger services upon Tucker Street as traffic, both goods and passenger, was always heaviest on the Wells to Bristol section. *J. H. Moss*

Below: A view of Tucker Street taken from the footbridge in 1957. Coaches can be seen stabled on the former B&E locomotive siding. The right-hand siding formerly included a turntable. Sheldons grain mill can be seen to the left of the down platform. The Bristol & Exeter advertised market trains in 1877 from Wells to various local destinations including Axbridge, Bristol and Highbridge. *J. H. Moss*

Above: The waiting room situated on the up platform at Tucker Street was constructed in brick and equipped with a large attractive canopy. The 27-lever signalbox opened on 15 September 1901, replacing the original box located between Burcot road bridge and the footbridge on the down platform. *R. Lacey collection*

the booking was made was that the train they were travelling on was a limited-accommodation (GWR) diesel railcar. When the train arrived at Tucker Street, all the children climbed aboard and it was totally overloaded. I remember it going out of the station surrounded by a cloud of blue smoke where the diesel engines were having to work a little harder. I had my leg pulled about this incident for many years after.'

Tucker Street Station

The contractors of the line from Cheddar had taken possession of a number of cottages that lay at the western end of Tucker Street on the road to Burcot in March 1868. The dwellings stood on the route of the railway and their demolition was required. The unfortunate inhabitants were without alternative accommodation, as housing shortages, it was reported, were very acute. The landlords of the remaining houses which 'staggered' up Tucker Street between the Cheddar Valley and Mermaid hostelries squeezed as many of the homeless as they could into already overcrowded conditions, the extra rent being an incentive to find extra room. Dust from centuries-old lath and plaster filled the air as the buildings came crashing down, along with the acrid smoke from the bonfires of discarded timbers. The steel tyres of many carts rumbled and grated to and fro over the rutted, debris-strewn road.

A works locomotive arrived at the Somerset & Dorset station in Priory Road on Thursday, 26 March from Highbridge. For its final journey of approximately three quarters of a mile to join the limit of the contractors' line from Cheddar, it was loaded on to a road carriage. Unfortunately, its weight of 30 tons proved too much for the soft ground upon which the carriage stood, causing the wheels to sink into the earth. With this dilemma, upward of 20 horses were attached to try to pull it free, but to no avail and additional attempts that day were postponed. Further endeavours were

made the following day, but to no avail. However, a team of 23 horses plus the added support of numerous men did the trick, with the carriage and its load making its way across Tucker Street to the site of the new bridge taking shape at Portway Hill, where the engine was safely transferred to the rails. As spring turned to summer, many of the cuttings were nearing completion, and by June of the same year a second contractor's locomotive was at work on the line.

The Bristol & Exeter opened its broad gauge line from Cheddar to Wells on Tuesday, 5 April 1870, making a junction with the S&D, thus completing the trio of stations situated within a third of a mile of each other, the B&E premises being located 15 chains west of the S&D Priory Road station. There was no ceremony at Wells for the opening of the line, which was only advised as late as the preceding Saturday, when Captain Tyler RE inspected the line, in company with Mr Wall the General Traffic Manager and Mr Fox, with the former gentleman expressing his approval of it. It seems as if the B&E was in a hurry to open for the accommodation of those people attending the County Quarter Sessions at Wells. However, a large number of persons were reported as passing over the line, and the last train from Wells consisted of 12 crowded carriages. Although no celebrations were held at Wells, it is reported that in the morning the fife and drum band of the workhouse played a 'merry' selection on the platform at Axbridge in honour of the completion of the railway.

The B&E provided six trains each way on weekdays and its easier and quicker connections to Yatton and onwards to Bristol soon made this section the busiest of all the three lines for freight and passenger traffic. The 1870 timetable shows the first train to Yatton departing from Wells at 7.55am with a booked arrival in Bristol of 9.30am, the first class fare costing 5s 6d. The final train of the day for Bristol departed at 7.50pm. Down trains started from Bristol at 8.30am with the final evening train leaving at 8.40pm. No Sunday services ran between Yatton and Wells until 1886.

Above: The exterior of Wells Tucker Street station, seen here in 1957, was constructed in the usual solid style of the Bristol & Exeter Railway. The station opened on Tuesday, 5 April 1870 with the completion of the broad gauge line from Cheddar. The single-storey station building was constructed in Mendip stone with two matching wings, each having arch gabled roofs with alternating plain and patterned red tiles. Decorative bargeboards also adorned the building, including the entrance porch as viewed here. The station became Tucker Street from 20 July 1920, although the name was used by *Bradshaw* much earlier and in fact featured in the B&E timetable of 1877. This grand building was demolished (the term 'destroyed' would suit better) in 1975. *J. H. Moss*

Below: The main station building at Tucker Street showing the same attention to detail as viewed from the forecourt. Passengers entered the platform from the booking office and waiting room via the central doorway under the small canopy in the centre of the building. The valencing even extended to the footbridge as seen to the left. When the line from Cheddar was being constructed, the contractors took possession of a number of cottages at the western end of Tucker Street on the road to Burcot in March 1868, which had to be demolished. Newspaper reports suggest that the unfortunate inhabitants had to be rehoused in less than satisfactory conditions by their landlords in houses that 'staggered' between the Cheddar Valley and Mermaid hostelries. *J. H. Moss*

WELLS TUCKER STREET STATION
MAIN PASSENGER BUILDING

Viewed from the platform

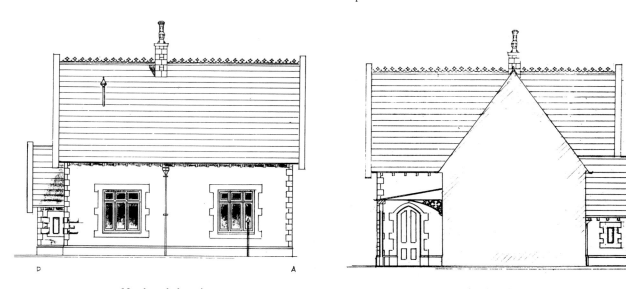

North end elevation

section looking north

Front porch elevation

Drawings by Terry Morgan

Above: Wells Tucker Street signalbox diagram with the line from Wookey approaching from the left. *Signalling Record Society*

The B&E 4-4-0 saddle tanks worked the line in its early years. The main station building was located on the down platform, built in Mendip stone with a large awning and the usual decorative features that were typical of the Bristol & Exeter. It was a single-storied building complete with two matching wings with arch gabled roofs and red tiles in alternating patterns of plain and patterned laid as six courses of saw-tooth and four of plain. Decorative bargeboards also adorned the building. The station building contained the usual offices, waiting room, ladies' waiting room, booking office and stationmaster's office, etc. A footbridge connected the two platforms which were constructed on a curve, and a brick-built waiting shelter complete with a fine awning was constructed to the GWR style at a later date on the up platform. Locomotive watering facilities were situated at the ends of each platform.

An engine shed and a 40ft turntable were established to the east of the station on the up side behind the S&D signalbox and near St Andrews stream, the engine shed closing in 1876. A signalbox containing 12 levers was installed on the down platform between the overbridge and the station buildings which is believed to have been of similar design to the Saxby & Farmer boxes installed at other locations on the Cheddar Valley line such as Cheddar and Axbridge. A road bridge carried Burcott Road over the railway to the west of the station. Goods sidings were located west of this, again on the down side, together with a goods shed constructed in Mendip stone.

It was always the intention of the Bristol & Exeter to project its line through the S&D goods yard and station to link up with the East Somerset station. The Somerset & Dorset, which by this time was a standard gauge railway, had granted the necessary running powers to the B&E using its metals for nine chains, and a rental was agreed. The Board of Trade was having none of it and objected to broad gauge passenger trains running at right angles and crossing 'narrow gauge' sidings on the level. The S&D, seeking payment, took legal action against the Bristol & Exeter for loss of rent at £400 per annum for allowing its trains to cross S&D metals, despite the fact that the Board of Trade had disallowed passenger traffic across the connection! The

B&E countered this by quoting the Acts of 1864 and 1865 giving 'to the Bristol Company a free and unrestricted communication for purposes of all traffic whatever between the Cheddar Valley and the East Somerset Railway.' The clause mentioned unfortunately did not give 'free' passage over that important nine chains of the S&D. A decision was made in favour of the Somerset & Dorset. Another attempt by the B&E quoting the same clause to persuade Parliament to over-rule the judgement of the Board of Trade failed in 1871. In March of the following year Mr MacKay, the secretary of the ESR, was asked by his board to write to the GWR and the B&E urging them to use the junction, as its use for goods traffic did not require the necessary sanction from the Board of Trade. A reply from Grierson, secretary of the GWR, erring on the side of caution, indicated that his company would hesitate to use the junction without the authority of the Board of Trade. A further letter from the ESR secretary mentioned that Mr Malcolm of the Board of Trade had informed Paget (vice chairman of the ESR) that it (the Board of Trade) had no power to prevent it being used for goods traffic, and the ESR directors thought it desirable to work it before any prohibitory legislation was made on the subject.

The ESR had been converted to standard gauge in 1874. The Cheddar Valley line from Yatton, however, was still broad gauge. In order that the Board of Trade might be persuaded to allow through running, an exchange platform was constructed in the East Somerset station yard for interchange of passengers between trains of the differing gauges. The redoubtable Colonel Yolland appeared at Wells in April 1875 to make the necessary inspection for the Railway Department of the Board of Trade. The report is interesting in the fact that the connection and level crossing gates were in situ and just awaiting clearance by the Board of Trade. The report is lengthy, so I have condensed portions for the reader's interest:

'I have inspected the single line connecting the three

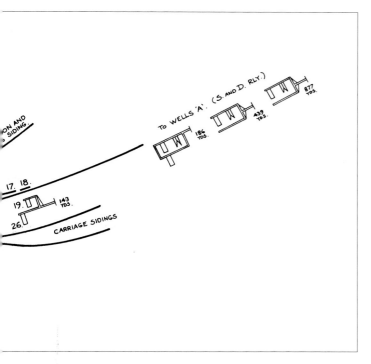

stations together at Wells which belong to the East Somerset branch of the Great Western, the Somerset & Dorset and the Cheddar Valley branch of the Bristol & Exeter Railway companies which line runs across the goods lines of the Somerset & Dorset Railway Company on the level . . . And the line crosses an important Turnpike Road on the level also with the sanction of Parliament at the eastern end of the Somerset & Dorset station by a single line of rails . . . An exchange platform has been constructed in the East Somerset station yard for passengers to change carriages who may be proceeding in the narrow gauge trains of the Great Western Railway eastwards or in the broad gauge carriages of the Bristol &

THE PROPOSED JOINT RAILWAY STATION.

The following letters on this subject were read by the Acting Town Clerk :

"Great Western Railway, London Terminus, Paddington, W.—25th February, 1881.—DEAR SIR,—I beg to acknowlege the receipt of your letter of yesterday enclosing memorials from the Council of the City of Wells and from inhabitants of the city, suggesting the provision of a joint station at Wells for the lines of this company, the Midland Railway Company, and the South-Western Railway Company. An opportunity will be taken of submitting those memorials to the directors of the company.—Yours faithfully, FRED. G. SAUNDERS.—R. L. Foster, Esq., Town Clerk's Office, Wells, Somerset."

"South Western and Midland Railway Companies, Somerset and Dorset Joint Line, Derby, March 24th, 1881.—DEAR SIR,—I brought before the joint committee at its last meeting your letter of February 24th, enclosing memorial respecting the Somerset and Dorset Station being used in common by the two companies at Wells. In reply I was advised to inform you that the Great Western Company already possess power under which they can use the station of the Committee in Priory-road, and that the Committee have no objection to their exercising it.—I am, yours faithfully, R. SPEKE.—R. L. Foster, Esq., Wells."

The Town Clerk added that he had written a second letter to the Great Western Railway Company, but had as yet received no reply. It was suggested that they were awaiting a meeting of the directors before replying to the memorials.

The following letter was, however, read at a subsequent stage of proceedings :—

"Great Western Railway, General Manager's Office, Paddington Station, London, W., April 30th, 1881.—DEAR SIR,—In reply to your letter addressed to Mr. Saunders I beg to inform you that the question of the suggested joint station at Wells is under the consideration of the directors, and I hope to be able very shortly to write to you further upon the subject.—Yours truly, J. GRIERSON.—R. T. Foster, Town Clerk, Wells."

Above: The proposed joint station at Wells was a matter of some discussion in the *Wells Journal* of 5 May 1881.

CHEDDAR VALLEY LINE.
UP TRAINS.

STATIONS.	WEEK DAYS.						
	1 2 3 Class.	1 & 2 Class.	1 & 2 Class.	1 & 2 Class.	1 & 2 Class.	1 & 2 Class.	1 2 Cls.
	a.m.	a.m.	noon	p.m.	p.m.	p.m.	
WELLS.........dep.	7 45	9 40	1153	2 20	5 30	..	..
Wookey .... ,,	7 50	9 45	1159	..	5 35	..	..
Lodge Hill .. ,,	7 59	9 54	12 8	2 29	5 44	..	..
Draycott .... ,,	8 6	10 1	1216	2 36	5 51	..	..
Cheddar .... ,,	8 13	10 8	1224	2 44	5 58	..	..
Axbridge .. ,,	8 20	1015	1230	2 50	6 5	..	..
Winscombe.. ,,	8 27	1022	1237	2 59	6 12	..	..
Sandford & Ban ,,	8 32	1027	1242	3 5	6 17	..	..
Congresbury.. ,,	8 40	1035	..	3 14	6 25	..	..
YATTON ...... arr.	8 45	1040	1251	3 18	6 30	..	..
Yatton ......dep.	9 22	1042	1 5	3 20	6 50	..	
BRISTOL ......arr.	10 0	11 5	1 40	3 43	7 23	..	

CHEDDAR VALLEY LINE.
DOWN TRAINS.

STATIONS.	WEEK DAYS					
	1 2 3 Class.	1 & 2 Class.	1 & 2 Class.	1 & 2 Class.	1 & 2 Class.	1 & 2 Class.
	a.m.	a.m.	p.m.	p.m.	p.m.	p.m.
BRISTOL ......dep.	8 10	1130	1230	4 0	6 0	..
Yatton ......arr.	8 53	1153	1252	4 20	6 34	..
YATTON ......dep.	9 30	1155	1 10	4 23	6 45	..
Congresbury ,,	9 35	12 0	1 15	4 28	6 50	..
Sandford & Ban ,,	9 44	12 7	1 23	4 36	6 58	..
Winscombe.. ,,	9 49	1212	1 28	4 41	7 3	..
Axbridge.... ,,	9 58	1218	1 35	4 48	7 10	..
Cheddar .... ,,	1011	1224	1 42	4 55	7 17	..
Draycott .... ,,	1019	1232	1 49	5 2	7 24	..
Lodge Hill .. ,,	1027	1240	1 56	5 9	7 31	..
Wookey .... ,,	1036	1249	2 5	5 18	7 40	..
WELLS.........arr.	1042	1255	2 10	5 23	7 45	..

WELLS AND WITHAM BRANCH.
NO SUNDAY TRAINS.

UP	1 2		1 2 3	1 2 3	exp		1 2		1 2		
Wells	6 10	..	9 40	10 3	15	..	5 20	..	8 0	..	..
Shepton Mallet ..	6 23	..	9 53	10 25	30	..	5 40	..	8 15	..	..
Cranmore	6 32	..	10 5	10 35	40	..	5 53	..	8 20	..	..
Wanstrow........	..	..	1015	..	..	..	6 10	..	..	..	..
Witham	6 45	..	1025	10 50	55	..	6 25	..	8 45	..	..
DOWN.	1 2 3	1 2		exp	1 2	1 2	1 2				
Witham...........	6 45	12 0	..	2 10	40	6 60	9 0	..	..	..	..
Wanstrow........	8 50	..	..	..	..	..	..	..	..	..	..
Cranmore........	9 5	1215	..	2 30	4 35	6 45	9 15	..	..	..	..
Shepton Mallet ..	9 15	1225	..	2 40	4 45	6 57	9 25	..	..	..	..
Wells	9 30	1240	..	3 5	5 0	7 20	9 40	..	..	..	..

Above: Timetables for the Cheddar Valley and East Somerset lines for July 1875.

Exeter Railway westwards along the Cheddar Valley Railway. Provision is made for the engines of the Great Western Railway Company to run round their trains after arriving at their Wells station from the east, by means of a mixed gauge loop line lying south of the Bristol & Exeter passenger line and which is also used by the engines of the latter company.

'From the position of the points the Great Western engines cannot get from the western to the eastern end of their trains without first closing the level crossing gates partly closing the Turnpike Road and shunting back along the loop line, and it is quite possible that hereafter, complaints may be made on this subject by the Turnpike Authorities . . . The arrangements thus carried out comply with the requirements of the Board of Trade and great pains have been taken to make such arrangements of the sidings points and their connections with the signals by interlocking as to provide against the danger inherent on crossing so many goods lines on the level, but it must be distinctively understood that these arrangements are not suitable for working the passenger trains through Wells, as a through station . . . I must not moreover be understood to assent to the present construction of this station so far as it renders it necessary to shunt engines across the turnpike road . . . A good deal has been done by the Bristol & Exeter Railway Company in carrying out these works to render the

working into and out of the Somerset & Dorset passenger station safe but there are still sidings lying south of their passenger lines which are not provided with blind sidings or throw-off points to prevent vehicles from being brought out of them without the sanction of the signalman on duty.'

The level crossing gates were always a cause of complaint to the ESR, SCR and the City Council, and local newspapers were always a chamber of debate on the subject. The gates and crossing, although not used by through passenger trains due to the ban by the Board of Trade, nevertheless had to conform with signalling regulations such as when a train arrived at the Somerset Central station, the gates had to be closed to road traffic until the train had come safely to a halt, thence the gates were reopened to road traffic. The occupants of horse-drawn carriages etc did not understand why they had to be halted on their journey by a train which did not use the crossing! The same operation would of course happen when a train arrived at the ESR station. The connection did not open until 1 January 1878 when passenger trains could at last steam across Priory Road level crossing en route to Yatton or Witham. The East Somerset and Bristol & Exeter railways had been under the control of the Great Western Railway since 1874 and 1876 respectively, and both routes were now to the standard gauge. Although the GWR could now pass unhindered through the Somerset & Dorset Priory Road station, its trains did not stop there until

Above: Passengers gather on the platform at Tucker Street on 21 August 1957 as 2-6-2T No 5525 arrives bunker-first under Burcot road bridge with the 9.35am from Yatton. Ivatt Mogul No 46517 awaits the ex-Yatton train to clear the section before collecting the single-line token and proceeding with a freight train to Bristol. *H. B. Priestley*

Above: The 2.45pm Yatton-Witham headed by 2-6-2T No 82040 departs from Tucker Street on 16 June 1962. The East Somerset and Cheddar Valley lines were always worked as two separate branches with some services having a lengthy wait at Wells. *Ian Allan Library*

1 October 1934. Appearing in the 1864 SCR Cheddar Valley Line Act was the proposal for a spur line from the S&D near to the engine shed and curving over St Andrews stream into the GWR station at Tucker Street. This would solve some of the problems created by the level crossing, but nothing came of this interesting idea when the Act was transferred to the B&E. The idea for the curve was again brought forward in the 1880s but to no avail.

Two minor accidents occurred during the months of March and May 1882 when engines ran into the gates; damage was slight and no one was injured, a press report describing the March incident at the S&D station thus: '. . . but the incident proved the danger of a level crossing on such a road, where there was considerable traffic — being one of the principal entrances to the city, and also a favourite walk of nurse-maids and children.' The idea of a 'joint' station was also discussed at various times between the City Council and the GWR, the upshot of it being that the railway company would consider the idea, providing the city would contribute materially towards the construction of the station! It is no surprise that the council replied: 'The Council has no power to devote the public funds to and in the erection of a joint station.'

An interesting survey was carried out by the GWR in 1880 for the whole of the year regarding the numbers of passengers travelling eastwards, which totalled 200 passengers, or approximately 11 per train. One of the GWR staff was placed in the signalbox for 12 hours a day from 6am to 6pm to record the number of people, vehicles and animals using the crossing. This interesting report shows that on an average day 463 pedestrians, 175 vehicles and 65 cattle used the crossing, compared with a market day when 823 pedestrians, 489 vehicles and 589 cattle used the crossing. The replacement of the level crossing by a bridge was also the feature of various debates over the years — even Brunel himself, when in the process of planning the route of the

East Somerset line, had suggested the idea of an overbridge carrying the line over the road. However, this had been rejected due to the suggestion of apparent flooding in the area. An overbridge was the subject of debate in 1882 when Colonel Yolland, the Inspector for the Board of Trade, arrived in Wells on 21 June and met officials of the GWR and the S&D, plus the Mayor, the town clerk and various councillors. As well as gathering information regarding various accidents at the crossing he also attended a meeting held in the S&D station and stated he would recommend to the Board of Trade that the GWR should build a bridge, taking the road over the line, and remove the gates. However, it was obvious that both the GWR and the S&D would not spend the necessary money to improve the situation, and the level crossing would survive until the closure of the line.

With the opening of the junction to passenger traffic over the Somerset & Dorset goods yard on 1 January 1878 and the closure of the East Somerset station, the GWR concentrated its passenger services at the Cheddar Valley station. Opened as Wells, the station became Tucker Street from 12 July 1920 (although the name was used by *Bradshaw* much earlier, and features as Tucker Street in the 1877 timetable), being renamed Wells from 6 May 1950 although the goods depot remained as Tucker Street. The original signalbox was replaced on 15 September 1901 by a box with a 27-lever frame located on the east end of the up platform. Known as Wells Tucker Street, the box was renamed Wells Station from 1950 and closed on 9 April 1964.

Traffic, both passenger and goods, was always heaviest on the Wells to Bristol section to the detriment of the line to Witham. Water columns were situated at both ends of the station between the tracks, the former locomotive shed and turntable tracks being used as carriage sidings. Although the engine shed closed in 1876, the 40ft turntable was extant until 1927. Train services arriving from Yatton as down trains became up to Witham and vice versa. A private siding agreement between the GWR and A. Sheldon & Sons was signed in 1936, the siding leading off the Priory Road end of the down platform being in use from 1936 until 1966. A bracket signal giving entry to the siding was placed on the same post as the platform starter. Station staff included a stationmaster, booking clerk, porters, shunter and four signalmen. Staff names included: wartime porter — Bill Speed; signalmen in 1963 — Joe Wheeler and Ernie Griffin; porter/shunter (1963) — Gordon Collins; passenger guards 1963 — Matt Biggs and Walt Burchell. Stationmasters were: Albert Barber April-November 1870, promoted to Yatton where he remained until retirement in 1905; Edward Tookey, November 1870-January 1872; Mr Holcombe, January 1872-June 1873, transferred to Barnstaple; William Bartlett, June 1873-January 1878; William Henry Randall, January 1878 and still there in 1889 residing in the house that would be the home of all future GWR stationmasters (1 Davis Terrace, Tucker Street); H. C. Titball, 1920-37 from Devizes; C. W. Broom, 1937-51 from Marlborough; S. C. Marshall, 1951-6 from Ilfracombe and left to be assistant stationmaster at Swindon, and Richard Hayes, 1957-64, previously at Holsworthy and the last stationmaster at Wells before closure.

For a short period from 1964, Wells came under the Glastonbury stationmaster, H. A. Killeby. The wagon examiner during the 1960s, Mr Bert Isles, had his office in the pump house behind the water tank at Tucker Street. The 1871 Census shows the following Bristol & Exeter staff at Tucker Street: Stationmaster Edward Tookey, aged 26; porters John Cosh (18), George Addison (30) and Charles Sharland (17); telegraph clerk Francis Sharland (17); clerk William Morse (20); locomotive crew, Driver Alfred Ridge (22), stoker John Drissol (22) and engine cleaner William Evans (18); railway labourers William Marsh (22), John Coombes (22) and Charles Jones. It would appear that the railway labourers arrived as part of the 'navvy' force during the construction of the line, and stayed on as permanent way gangs. The Bristol & Exeter advertised Wells in its 1877 timetable '. . . as provided with accommodation for loading and unloading carriages and horses and omnibuses meet all trains.' The B&E advertised market trains in 1877 from Wells to various local destinations including Axbridge on the second Tuesday in each month departing at 7.45am and 9.55am, Highbridge on the first and third Monday in each month at 7.45am, Bristol on Thursdays at 7.45am and 9.55am — Saturdays also brought market trains from Bristol to Wells picking up at Bedminster, Bourton, Nailsea, Yatton, and stations on the Cheddar branch. A market train also departed from Weston-super-Mare at 8.40am for Wells on the same day.

Six daily trains ran in 1910 and this level of service ran more or less into BR days. The GWR timetable for 1947 shows the following passenger services at Tucker Street. The first up train, the 7am from Wells, arrived Bristol at 8.18am. This was followed by the 7.10am from Yatton, arriving 7.45am, terminating and departing for Bristol at 8am (arrive Bristol 9.11am). Then two through trains, the 7.58am Yatton-Witham and 8.25am Witham-Yatton would cross at Tucker Street arriving at 8.41 and 8.58am respectively. Another terminating service, the 10am from Yatton, arrived at 10.41am. A GWR diesel railcar formed the 10.20am Witham-Bristol arriving in Wells at 10.55am (Bristol 12.11pm). A long gap then occurred before the next service to Witham departed at 12.7pm, and an even longer gap before the 1.20pm Witham-Yatton arrived at 1.52pm. The 2.45pm Yatton-Witham arrived at 3.28pm; this was also booked to a diesel railcar. The 3.37pm Witham-Yatton

called at 4.17pm, the 5.20pm Bristol-Wells, booked as a diesel railcar, arrived at 6.28pm before returning to Bristol at 7pm. The 6.50pm from Witham terminated at 7.26pm before departing as the 8.15pm to Yatton, the 6.10pm Yatton-Witham arriving at 6.52pm. The final evening train from Yatton (the 8.8pm) arrived at 8.50pm with the 9.20pm from Witham terminating at 9.57pm. There were two Saturday-only services, the 1.5pm from Yatton which terminated in Wells at 1.51pm before departing for Yatton at 2.40pm. There was one Sunday service in each direction in 1947, the 2.10pm from Bristol which stopped at all stations before arriving in Witham at 3.51pm, where there was a lengthy wait before departing at 5.30pm and arriving in Wells at 6.2pm with another lengthy wait before departing for Bristol at 7.20pm.

Passenger services between Wells and Bristol were always well patronised, especially the early morning trains which were popular with commuters. Although branch trains normally terminated or started at Witham some branch passenger workings were part of the 'full circuit' as it was known by footplate crews, departing from Bristol via Radstock to Frome on the North Somerset branch and then returning from Frome, traversing the main line to Witham and thence via Wells, Cheddar and Yatton to Bristol. From the 1920s until the mid-1950s, when replaced by Ivatt 2-6-2Ts, these services were worked by GWR Prairie tanks from Frome and Bristol sheds. GWR diesel railcars also worked the 'circuit', one such service in 1951 involving an arrival at Frome via the North Somerset line at 8.2am, then forming the 8.10 to Bruton and return (a former steam auto service) at 8.35am, thence departing Frome at 10.10am to Bristol via the Cheddar Valley line (dep Witham at 10.20am) returning to Frome at 4.53pm (2.45pm ex-Yatton) via the Cheddar Valley line, and setting off to Bristol along the North Somerset line at 6.6pm. Most of the goods traffic was directed towards Bristol rather than towards Witham and it was always worked as two separate branch lines — Yatton to Wells and Wells to Witham. A camping coach was kept on the goods shed dead-end road at Tucker Street from 1958 until 1963 with No W9927 noted as being there in September 1962.

Peter Woods, fireman at Wells locomotive shed, recalls his firing days on the branch especially with fast trips with an empty stock train from Frome.

'It all hinged on if we wanted an hour's overtime or not; if not a fast run from Cranmore would be the norm, then after crossing a train at Shepton Mallet we would run like the wind down Dulcote Bank and some unofficial fast runs were recorded, albeit in safety with the vacuum-braked stock. Other trains remembered are the 7.5am from Wells to Yatton, which although steam-hauled was set to diesel car timings, the 18 miles to Yatton being booked in 37min with eight stops. The fireman kept a good lookout when approaching Wookey, and if no passengers were waiting for us, then we would pass through without stopping. The same would apply at Lodge Hill as very few got on there. At Draycott, passengers would always be waiting, so we would lose a few minutes there, and go like the "clappers" in order to reach Yatton on time. At Winscombe many commuters were picked up and the train would be so full that you would be lucky to get a seat. On the odd occasion, that we would be late in arriving at Yatton, it was not considered to be very funny by the commuters collected from Winscombe as they had to meet their connecting train. During the summer service, an extra train was provided at 10.30am from Wells giving a direct connection

Above: Having arrived from Yatton smoke drifts lazily from the chimney of 2-6-2T No 4595 while taking water at Tucker Street before proceeding with a Wells-Witham service. *R. S. Carpenter*

Below: GWR diesel railcar No 28, hauling a single coach, arrives at Tucker Street from Yatton. Dating from December 1940 the unit was fitted with an AEC direct injection diesel engine supplied by the makers, the body and undercarriage being constructed at Swindon. The railcar was at first allocated to Ebbw Junction, then moved to Yeovil and Worcester before being withdrawn from Bristol in September 1960. Weighing 35 tons 13 cwt No 28 had a seating capacity of 48 and could haul a tail load of up to 60 tons. Having arrived from Yatton as a down train, the railcar will now depart as an up train to Witham. *Ian Allan Library*

to Weston-super-Mare. An extra two coaches were added to the normal two coaches, and Burcott Road estate would empty on to that train for the return fare of 3s 6d and passengers would be in Weston by 11.30am — a real case of the railway serving the community. The only opposition to the railway was a single-decker bus. One of the full circuit workings was performed by Bristol crews with a 'D63xx' diesel leaving Bristol travelling to Frome, thence down to Witham and along the branch. We used to cross this train at Cheddar and it was always late, as this class were only small diesels and not very fast. We used to be asked why we were late, and the driver would always reply: "My fireman is no bloody good." Strawberries would be thrown at us between Cheddar and Axbridge, and if they hit the hot pipes in the cab they smelt awful. Not long before closure a lot of the branch was relaid, and we had to work on Sundays especially with the relaying at Dulcote.'

The 7.5am train was known as the 'alarm clock' of the Cheddar Valley, as the sound of the locomotive whistle as it approached various stations along the route would awaken many residents, and when the passenger services came to an end, the silence, without the familiar whistle call of the 7.5am on the first Monday of closure and for many days after, was felt by many people.

Terry Morgan recalls his memories of trains at Wells, plus a family member who arrived at Wells in the days of the broad gauge.

'My earliest recollections of the route between Witham and Yatton would be at the end of World War 2 when I was four years old. At that time my father kept an allotment in Camp Field, which was bounded on its southern edge by the East Somerset branch line to Witham. My father's rented piece of "Digging for Victory" was roughly opposite the cold store. I can remember this depot being shunted at one time by what must have been a Collett "2251" class and this was also a good spot to watch coal wagons being propelled toward the gasworks, usually by a pannier tank. My rail journeys from Wells Tucker Street were predominantly towards Yatton, although I did traverse the East Somerset on a number of occasions. The earliest, again in the '40s, was with my mother when we visited relatives in Bruton, having to change at Witham to be picked up by the next stopping train which was sometimes drawn by a "Hall" for the next station on the Wilts, Somerset & Weymouth section. A combined local secondary schools summer trip to Windsor and Eton in 1953 used the branch, for which a train of 10 coaches arrived at Tucker Street.

'I can still remember our astonishment, counting the carriages as they drew into the station. The train was double-headed as far as Witham and the journey up the

Above: Ivatt 2-6-2T No 41207 has her tanks refilled at Tucker Street while working a Yatton-Witham passenger train.
A. W. V. Mace Collection/Milepost 92½.

Above: Steam escapes from the safety valves of 0-6-0PT No 3696 at Tucker Street on 31 August 1963 while departing with the 3.28pm Witham-Yatton. *Hugh Ballantyne*

bank to Shepton Mallet in bright sunshine was, I recall, a bit of a struggle and very slow. Journeys on the Cheddar Valley line in the immediate aftermath of the war comprised a weekly expedition to Draycott with my mother to visit my grandmother's relatives who farmed close by the station level crossing. The purpose of these outings was to collect dairy products which were still in short supply in the days of postwar rationing. The train was usually a GWR diesel railcar, or the "Flying Bananas" as they were later to be nicknamed. I was always disappointed when it wasn't a steam-hauled service. The stationmaster at Draycott, who wore a pill-box hat, always startled me on our arrival, as he would really bellow out the station name as the train drew to a stop. With the revision of secondary education in the 1950s, many pupils travelled into Wells by rail from the Cheddar Valley villages, the wait for the home train giving the opportunity for a bit of romantic snogging.

'During the latter years of the line's existence, and before the days when we all owned cars, a gang of us, with our hair "Brylcreemed" into something resembling Tony Curtis hairstyles would set off for Weston-super-Mare on a 3s 6d Bank Holiday return, arriving with great bravado at Locking Road excursion platform. With the corridors packed solid on the homeward journey, there would be the chance for a good old scrummage with the opposite sex on the Bristol train as far as Yatton, at which point we would have to say our farewells and transfer into our connection, which would be waiting in the bay alongside the down platform. The final leg of the trip, which I remember being in single compartment carriages, was enlivened with the

trousers of some unfortunate victim being passed from window to window along the train!

'The Bristol & Exeter Railway Company, incidentally, had a significant part to play in the course of my family history, as my great grandfather, Frederick Hodges Morgan, was born close by the B&E main line on Sunday, 19 September 1847. Four months off his 17th birthday, on 6 June 1864, he followed his uncle Jim Hodges into the locomotive department of the B&E under James Pearson at Bristol. Starting in the tradition of all locomotive men as an engine cleaner, he had progressed to a goods fireman by December 1867, and in March 1870 to branch fireman, based at Watchet. Moving through the grades he was promoted to engine turner in February 1872, thence relocating to Bristol, from whence he made his first journey over the Wells branch before being based there, a short time after, as a passed fireman/driver. Fred married my great grandmother, Emma, at Union Street Congregational Chapel on 23 October 1874, his best man being William Marsh, a railway ganger from the village of Street. Fred and Emma departed from Wells on 8 July the following year as he had been promoted to main line goods engineman at five shillings a day, and directed to report to Exeter. Although Fred stayed officially based at Exeter, his company record shows he had many stopovers in Bristol, sometimes working north over the Midland joint line to Gloucester, as well as forays over the Cheddar Valley line.

'He was appointed to first class engineman in June 1890 and directed to "remove" himself to Truro and the last outpost of the broad gauge empire. The remaining years of his railway career were not without incident, as he was the

Above: The view from the up platform at Tucker Street in 1957 looking towards the single line climbing through Portway cutting. The trailing access to the goods yard can be seen curving to the right under the road bridge. *J. H. Moss*

Below: The goods shed at Tucker Street was situated west of the station. Two wagons, one of them a 'Conflat' complete with container, await collection by the next goods working. The signal arm is set lower down the post for ease of sighting under the roadbridge. The goods shed still survives and is in use as commercial premises, although the scene today in the year 2000 is of course vastly different from that portrayed here. *J. H. Moss*

Above: No 41209 awaits departure from Tucker Street with a Yatton-Witham train on 10 November 1962. Unusually, the destination board on the coach is displaying the destination of 'Par', a station in the delightful county of Cornwall, far away from the ultimate destination for this train of Witham. *Ben Ashworth*

driver of the "Cornishman" from Plymouth North Road which was implicated in the Doubledois, Bodmin Road accident of 13 April 1895, his train actually preceding the one that derailed. The make-up of both trains was identical, each double-headed by two of William Dean's "3521" class, which were essentially broad gauge rebuilds of an 0-4-4 wheel arrangement that rode very roughly, and created severe lateral oscillations. Another accident, on the Falmouth branch shortly after, in which both of the crew died, prompted their conversion into 4-4-0 tender engines. Fred retired due to failing eyesight in June 1908 at Bristol having completed 44 years service.'

Closure to passenger traffic between Witham and Yatton occurred on 9 September 1963. Crowds awaited the final train at Wells which, as with all railway closures, was a very sad occasion. Mournful whistles echoed around the darkening sky lit by fireworks and the sound of exploding detonators resounded around the station. With the train pulling away to more evocative whistling, it was all over: the signal arms clattered back to danger, the crowds eventually dispersed and silence fell over Tucker Street station. The signalbox at Tucker Street closed on 9 April 1964 and freight trains ran to Wells until 13 July 1964 when all three goods yards closed. Closure to freight traffic between Yatton and Cheddar occurred on 1 October 1964, and the track was lifted the following year. Tucker Street signalbox and the waiting room on the up platform were demolished in April 1965. With the East Somerset box at Wells closing in 1965 the line to Cheddar from Cranmore was worked as a long siding with the majority of sidings and loops being lifted, the remaining trackwork soon becoming weedgrown and the buildings derelict.

The section from Cheddar to Dulcote Quarry officially closed on 26 April 1969 and the very last passenger train of all — the RCTS 'Cheddar Valley Scenic' — ran from Paddington to Cheddar via Witham on 31 May the same year. The scene at Wells as the four-car DMU arrived was so very different from earlier years. The former East Somerset yard was now shorn of sidings with weeds growing everywhere, level crossing gates broken, no signals or signalboxes and just a single track running through the former Tucker Street station with its loop removed. The signalbox and waiting shelter on the down platform were now demolished, but surprisingly the main station building was still standing although in a very sorry state. When the special train returned to Wells from Cheddar and onwards to Witham this would be the very last train before the demolition trains arrived. The main station building at Tucker Street was demolished in 1975; however the Bristol & Exeter goods shed that once served Tucker Street station still survives and is in use as commercial premises. The former railway workers' houses erected by the B&E are also extant. Nearby in Tucker Street, the 'Cheddar Valley Inn' has a steam locomotive on its sign reflecting early railway days. When one stands today alongside the relief road with its never-ending streams of traffic polluting the atmosphere of the smallest, and in my view, the loveliest cathedral city in England, it is hard to believe that at one time, not one, not two but three railway stations used to stand within a few yards of the spot now covered by tarmacadam. Will the generations to come, as our roads become more and more gridlocked, ever understand the logic of destroying the very best form of transport that our forebears had the foresight to build and entrust to us? The Wells relief road on the site of the former S&D and B&E stations is known today as Strawberry Way.

The up platform starter at Tucker Street is lowered for Ivatt tank No 41209 (82B) with a Yatton–Witham train on 10 November 1962.
A rail tank from United Molasses stands in Sheldons siding, the small arm on the signal bracket giving access to the siding, and a warning board at the entrance to the
siding proclaims 'Only the following engines may use this siding 0-6-0 Standard Goods 0-6-0T 57xx 2-6-2T 45xx and 55xx'. *Ben Ashworth*

Running in under light steam with regulator closed. No 3795 passes the goods shed and yard at Tucker Street with the 11.12am (SO) Yatton-Witham. Wagons await shunting or collection and the cattle pens at the far end of the yard are ready for their bovine occupants. *R. E. Toop*

Above: The timber-built signalbox as seen here when in use as a ground frame, was set forward on the long single platform at Wookey due to the proximity of the adjacent road bridge. The station, which had a staff of six in 1926, opened on 1 August 1871, one year after the extension from Cheddar to Wells opened. Many excursion trains stopped here over the years with passengers disembarking to visit the nearby caves at Wookey Hole. The station platform was demolished in 1965 with the shell of the signalbox existing until 1969. The goods shed survives today in private ownership. *Author's collection*

Below: The down home signal arm at Wookey has been lowered in preparation for a Yatton-Wells train in 1947. The station had a timber-built waiting room/booking office plus a signalbox. The stone-built goods shed stands to the right, with the sidings and goods loop in the distance. The line curving to the right in the mid-distance leads to St Cuthberts Paper Mill. Coal for the mill was supplied by Norton Hill Colliery, Midsomer Norton, and transferred to Wells by the S&D and onwards to Wookey via the GWR. Locomotives were not allowed past the gate into the mill siding. *Ian Allan Library*

Wookey–Cheddar

Wookey

Approaching Wookey from Wells, trains ran past Wookey stone siding which was equipped with two ground frames allowing access from either direction. Stone was brought down from Underwood Quarry by an overhead cable conveying tubs of limestone, and where it crossed the Wells–Wookey road a safety net spanned the road to stop any material dropping on to passing vehicles. The private siding agreement ran from 30 March 1920 until 9 July 1948 with the sidings being removed in 1950. The land for the station site at Haybridge, of approximately two acres on the outskirts of Wells, was purchased from the owners of the nearby paper mill for which a siding was brought into use in 1879. Named Wookey, the station opened on 1 August 1871, one year after the extension from Cheddar to Wells came into use. It was formed of a long single platform upon which a small timber-built station building and a signalbox were situated. The signalbox was set forward due to the proximity of a nearby road bridge, thereby giving a good view of the line in each direction. The box had a Saxby & Farmer frame and operated the electric key token to Wells and Lodge Hill until Wookey was abolished as a block post with running signals removed on 29 August 1954 and reduced to a two-lever ground frame known as Wookey East Ground Frame. This closed on 21 September 1965 when the mill siding was taken out of use.

An intermediate key token instrument was provided to lock freight trains in the loop siding when required, and the existing Wookey ground frame positioned at the west end of the crossover operating the facing points from the Cheddar direction became known as Wookey West Ground Frame. The EKT section then became Wells to Cheddar which was a long section if a train found itself in trouble. As with all branch stations, services between the wars were prey to the expanding local omnibus routes. Passenger tickets issued in 1903 had totalled 8,322 dropping to 5,581 in 1923 and down further to 1,789 in 1933. Freight traffic was good with 3,484 tons being forwarded in 1903 remaining fairly constant until 1933 with 3,488 tons. General goods received in 1903 amounted to 9,153 tons while the tonnage for coal and coke received that year was 18,105 tons, with figures of 16,548, 13,606 and 7,294 tons for 1913, 1923 and 1933 respectively. Coal for St Cuthbert's Paper Mill was supplied by Norton Hill Colliery and transferred to Wells by the S&D and onwards to Wookey by the GWR. Vanloads of paper were transported by rail from the mill, and trains of esparto grass were also brought in by rail from Avonmouth for the paper mill. Locomotives were not allowed past the gate into the mill siding. General goods traffic was withdrawn from the station on 3 June 1963 but traffic into the paper mill existed until 1965.

RAILWAY ACCIDENT AT WOOKEY HOLE.

On Thursday evening an accident of an alarming nature, though fortunately not attended with serious personal injury, occurred at Wookey Hole station on the Wells branch of the Bristol and Exeter Railway. It appears that the 3.20 luggage train from Wells stopped at Wookey station to pick up and set down trucks, and consequently had to run into the siding. After trucks had been detached and others attached to the train it left for Bristol, and the points should then have been turned for the 5.20 train from Bristol; but this by some extraordinary oversight appeared to have been neglected, and when this train came up, instead of keeping to the main line it ran into the luggage siding before the driver was aware of it — there being considerable fog, and the lamps not having been lit. Two trucks were standing on the siding at some distance from each other, and the luggage station, and with these the passenger train came into collision successively, knocking them on either side the metals. The trucks were broken, and the engine considerably damaged and partially disabled. Happily the train was about to stop at Wookey, and consequently had slackened speed; otherwise it must have run into the luggage station, and considerable loss of life as well as damage to rolling stock have been inevitable. The passengers, we understand, were somewhat shaken by the collision, though no bones were broken. Omnibuses were at once telegraphed for to Wells, and these promptly arrived and conveyed the passengers to their destination. A telegram was also sent to Bristol, and Inspector Rudd sent away a special train to Cheddar. In the meantime the driver of the engine had made sufficient repairs to enable him to proceed to Wells and bring the passengers on to Cheddar, where they were transferred to the special, after some delay. The points in question are worked by what is called an auxiliary signal, which is so arranged that when the points are open a red light is shown. The dense fog which prevailed at the time obscured the signal, and the pointsman was on the platform waving his white light for the train to come in, so that the driver did not hesitate to go on.

Above: The railway accident at Wookey Hole on 18 December 1873 as reported in the *Wells Journal*.

An accident occurred in dense fog at the station on Thursday, 18 December 1873 when the 3.20pm 'luggage train' from Wells stopped to pick up and set down trucks, and consequently had to run into the siding. After trucks had been detached and attached, the train departed for Bristol. The points should then have been turned in readiness for the 5.20pm passenger train from Bristol, however, due to an

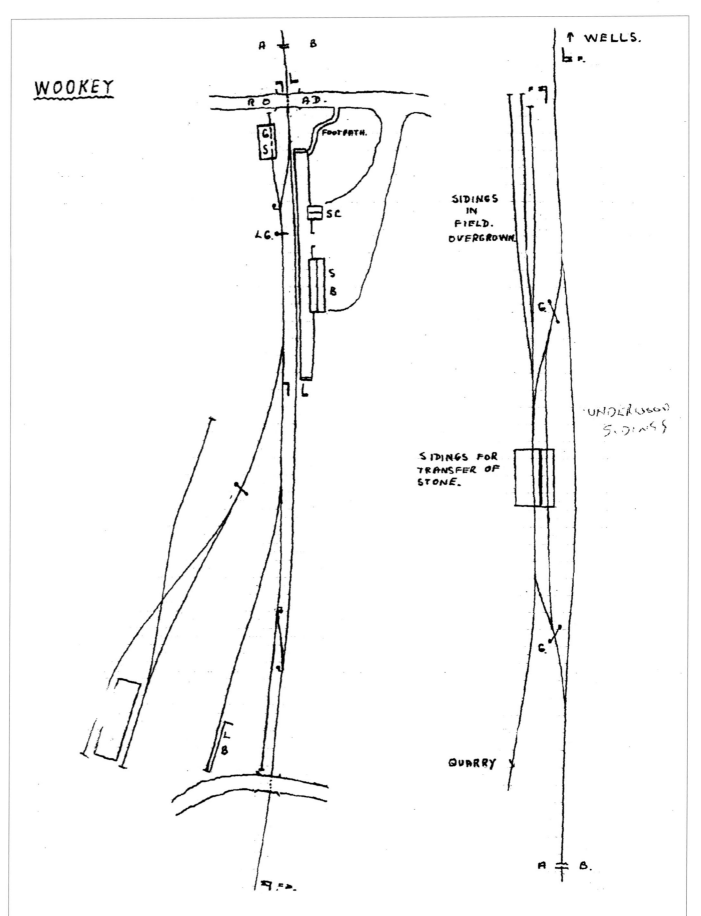

WOOKEY

WELLS.

ROAD.

FOOTPATH.

SIDINGS
IN
FIELD.
OVERGROWN.

SIDINGS FOR
TRANSFER OF
STONE.

UNDERUSED
SIDINGS

QUARRY

Wookey Stone Sidings and Wookey station layout from a sketch plan drawn by Joe Moss when he visited the line in 1948.
J. H. Moss

Above: Stationmaster Danny Williams and Mr Moss (father of Joe Moss, who took the photograph) stand outside Wookey signalbox. The box was equipped with a Saxby & Farmer frame and operated the electric key token to Wells and Lodge Hill until Wookey was abolished as a block post with all running signals removed on 29 August 1954. The box was reduced to a two-lever ground frame known as Wookey East Ground Frame, the EKT section then becoming Wells-Cheddar which was a long section if a train found itself in difficulties. In this view looking towards Wells, we see that the Wookey up home signal stands at danger. *J. H. Moss*

oversight this did not happen, and the Bristol train ran straight into the siding from the main line. Fortunately, it was due to stop at the station and the driver had slackened speed, but could not stop before coming into collision with two trucks standing on the siding, damaging them considerably, with the locomotive also being damaged and partially disabled. There was no loss of life, although the passengers were badly shaken, but with no bones broken. It appears that the signal lamps were unlit; combined with the thick fog and incorrectly set points, something was bound to go wrong.

Omnibuses were at once telegraphed from Wells, and these conveyed the passengers to their destination. A telegram was also sent to Bristol and Inspector Rudd sent away a special train to Cheddar. The driver of the train involved in the crash meanwhile had made sufficient repairs to his engine to enable him to proceed to Wells and bring the passengers on to Cheddar, where they were transferred to the special after some delay. It appears that the 'pointsman' (as described in newspaper reports) was on the platform waving his white light for the train to come in, so that the driver did not hesitate to go on. Until this crash occurred, it seems that no-one was unduly worried about lighting signal lamps at night, and even the rule book omitted the instruction that invisible signals should be regarded as being set at danger. The Bristol & Exeter however was always a safe railway, and even its one serious accident, at Creech near Taunton in 1852, when a locomotive left the track at high speed, did not injure any of its passengers.

The celebrated cave of Wookey Hole with its three magnificent chambers has always been a magnet for tourists.

The Southern Railway in 1939 ran excursions on 6 and 20 August from Portsmouth to Salisbury, Wells, Wookey and Cheddar. The fare from Portsmouth to Wookey was 5s 9d return, departing from Portsmouth Harbour station at 10.28am arriving in Wookey at 2.19pm, the return journey starting from Wookey at 6.56pm on the 6th and 7.12pm on the 20th.

Freight facilities included a goods loop, goods shed and a rail connection to St Cuthbert's Paper Mill from 1879 until 1965. The paper mill is the main industry for Wookey and was established there by virtue of the River Axe, which is sourced in the caves of Wookey Hole. A camping coach was in use at the station from 1935 until 1939 and when Harry Viles was promoted to fireman in 1941 he was transferred to Swindon for a few months, and before returning to Wells one of his first turns was to take the Wookey camping coach from Swindon to Highworth for storage.

Mr C. Cockram was stationmaster in 1875 and the GWR records show a staff of six at the station in 1926. Mr Danny Williams was the stationmaster from 1929 until his retirement in the 1950s, the station coming under the jurisdiction of the Wells stationmaster at the end of passenger services. Bert Marshman was the porter in 1963. During World War 2, Mrs Dalwood was the signalwoman, with D. Greenman (later at Axbridge) and Joe Wheeler (later at Tucker Street) being the signalmen from the early 1950s until closure of the box in 1954. Norman Collins was the shunter in the 1950s and Albert Sheldon the porter at the end of passenger services. The station platform was demolished in 1965, with the shell of the signalbox existing until 1969, while the goods shed survives today in private ownership.

119

Above: A view of Wookey goods shed taken from the adjacent overbridge with St Cuthberts Paper Mill in the background. General goods traffic was withdrawn from the station on 3 June 1963 although traffic into the paper mill continued until 1965. Trainloads of esparto grass were delivered to the mill from Avonmouth, and box vans of paper were transported out by rail. *Author's collection*

Above: Collett '22xx' 0-6-0 No 3215 rumbles into Lodge Hill with a Wells-Bristol freight in 1948. Note the down starting signal at the end of the platform. Lodge Hill was abolished as a block post on 21 September 1952 with all running signals removed. The small building with the corrugated iron roof was the eight-lever platform-mounted signalbox. *J. H. Moss*

Lodge Hill

Lodge Hill was also formed of a single platform. An impressive station building in the grand Bristol & Exeter style complete with decorative bargeboards etc stood on the platform. A goods shed was served by a single siding which ran through the building forming a small bay line behind the platform and a head shunt existed at the Cheddar end of the layout. The station is close to the village of Westbury-sub-Mendip, but the name Westbury was not chosen, due to the proximity of the GWR junction with the same name in Wiltshire; instead it was named Lodge Hill after the 212ft mound of the same name arising from the flat floor of the Cheddar Valley. The platform-level eight-lever signalbox, which had a signalwoman during World War 2, was abolished as a block post with all running signals removed on 21 September 1952 and was replaced by a two-lever ground frame released by an Annett's key on the EKT to gain access to the siding and goods shed.

Passenger tickets issued in 1903 were at their peak with 10,854 being issued; 107 season tickets were issued in 1933 although the number of passenger tickets had dropped to 5,575 in the same year. Livestock was also handled with 58 trucks handled in 1903 dropping to seven in 1933. A camping coach was stabled here from 1936 until 1939 and returned briefly after the war. Mr McGuire was the stationmaster during the 1950s. Mike Horwood recalls his schoolboy days: 'As a schoolboy in the early 1950s I attended Wells Central Secondary School and had a season ticket for the school train. I seem to recall that the train was very well used, with some of the pupils boarding at Yatton. I remember very well seeing soldiers, complete with escorts, on their way to Shepton Mallet Military Prison on most Mondays, to begin their sentence. The name "Lodge Hill" was marked out in a flower border on the other side of the track from the platform. This was allowed to grow over during the war so as not to be spotted from the air. I used to spend quite a few hours with the porters — Bert Atkinson and Jim Iveson — as I was a railway enthusiast, and also recall Mr Mcguire the stationmaster. There was also a holiday coach at the station for several years in the '50s.'

Mike also remembers the big freeze of 1963 when a young man of 22 and living in Cheddar. He decided to visit his parents at Westbury-sub-Mendip but villages were cut off by the heavy snowfalls. The roads being impassable, he decided to walk along the railway line, where he found '22xx' 0-6-0 No 2277 complete with snowplough firmly stuck in the snowdrifts between Cheddar and Draycott. Another engine, No 46406, was sent on a rescue mission, but also became stuck about 100yd behind the snowplough. A 'Hymek' diesel, No D7046, arrived the following day and unfortunately derailed. Another '22xx', No 2217, appeared with an inspector and a PW gang and their equipment, which was contained in a coach, two bogie vans and a box van, to rescue the errant locomotives.

Andy Viles recalls: 'I can remember as a boy, going up on the hill above where we lived at Wookey with my father during the cold spell of 1963 and watching two Class 22xx locomotives working from Yatton to Wells charging snowdrifts on the Lodge Hill side of Wookey and then working into Wells.' The steam locomotives used in the snow clearance of the line came from Bristol Barrow Road and the 'Hymeks' from Bath Road. The locomotive on shed at Wells at the time was BR Standard 2-6-2T No 82007 which was not used in snow clearance work, but it was kept in steam for 24 hours a day during the worst of the cold spell, and when the line was blocked it would be taken and left at the signal near the end of the locomotive sidings by East Somerset box. The crew would return to the drivers' cabin and a roaring fire. Harry Viles recalls that as the line would soon be closing the railwaymen went to a lot of trouble to clear it, especially after one footplate crew spent hours stuck on the footplate at Draycott. After it was all over, the then Minister of Transport, Mr Marples, came down to Bath Road and was introduced to this particular crew, and after being told about how many hours they had spent marooned in the snow, his reply was, 'Well they got paid for it.' This was a sad indictment, reflecting the managerial attitude of the day.

Ivatt Class 2MT 2-6-2 No 41208 was involved in a blowback incident while working the 6.55am Yatton-Wells passenger train bunker-first between Draycott and Lodge Hill on

Below: Lodge Hill signalbox diagram; the station was removed as a block post from 21 September 1952. *Signalling Record Society*

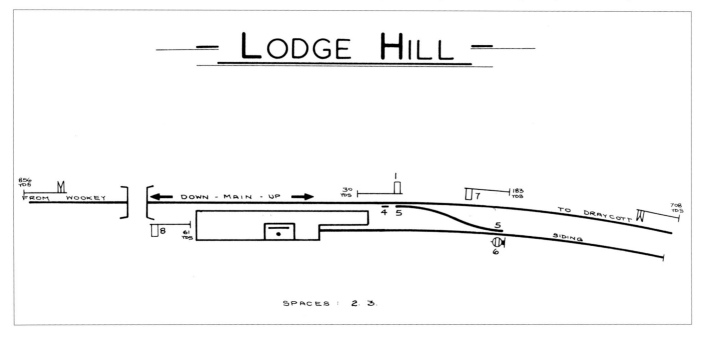

With bunker sprinklers turned on to stop the coal dust from swirling around the cab while working bunker-first, BR Class 3MT 2-6-2T No 82035 calls at Lodge Hill with the 11.12am (SO) Yatton-Witham on 2 July 1960. The stationmaster's house is seen to the right. The platform-level eight-lever signalbox was abolished as a block post with all running signals removed on 21 September 1952 and replaced by a two-lever ground frame released by an Annett's key on the EKT, to gain access to the siding and goods shed. Goods traffic was withdrawn on 10 June 1963. The station site today forms part of a small industrial estate with the goods shed in private ownership. *R. E. Toop*

12 August 1961. The Bristol crew — Driver George Whitman and Fireman Michael James — jumped from the cab to escape the flames, and the train carried on through Lodge Hill to be brought to a stop on the embankment just before Easton Cutting by the guard, Derek Palmer. Driver Harry Viles and a fireman came out from Wells by car and found No 41208 with her safety valves lifting, and when they climbed into the cab they found pieces of waste cloth and a locoman's cap still burning on the footplate. They took the train to Tucker Street, dropped off the coaches and took the engine to the shed. Apparently when it was taken to Bristol, the locomotive was tested at Westerleigh yard but nothing was found wrong, and it was believed that the cause of the blow-back could have been a severe wind coming off the Mendip Hills. Both the Bristol men were taken to hospital, the fireman being badly burned.

The station became partially unstaffed from 2 October 1961 and goods traffic ceased on 10 June 1963, the year of closure to passenger traffic. In the mid to late 1960s, the goods shed featured in the TV drama *Softly Softly*. The main station building was pulled down in 1989 and the stone transported to Cranmore to build the new shop and restaurant. The station site today forms part of a small industrial complex, and the goods shed exists in private ownership with part of the station canopy still standing in a builder's yard at the rear of the goods shed in 1999.

Below: Lodge Hill station as viewed from the adjacent road overbridge on 2 July 1960 with the goods shed and siding situated at the Cheddar end of the station. The goods shed featured in the TV drama series *Softly Softly* in the 1960s. As always, the station buildings reflect the B&E style of construction. *R. E. Toop*

Above: The platform and station buildings at Lodge Hill looking towards Wells in the 1960s. The station became partially unstaffed from 2 October 1961. Passenger tickets in 1903 were at their peak with a total of 10,854 being issued with the total for 1933 dropping to 5,575, reflecting the growing bus services in the area. The station building was pulled down in 1989 and the stonework transported to Cranmore station to construct the new shop and restaurant complex. *Author's collection*

Below: Mike Horwood, who has related his schoolboy days at Lodge Hill station, lived in his father's village shop/post office in Westbury-sub-Mendip, seen here with advertisements for Fry's chocolate and cocoa. The window blind has been pulled down to keep out the strong summer sunshine. *Mike Horwood*

Above: The wooden hut housing the ground frame that operated the points into the siding stands in the foreground in this view of Draycott looking towards Cheddar. The station was one of the areas where strawberries were loaded in great quantities when in season. Paraffin lamps and milk churns can be seen on the platform in the background. *Author's collection*

Draycott

Another single-platform station with an attractive 'bungalow' stone-built station building, the extended gabled roof with its decorative bargeboards reminding one of a Swiss chalet. The impressive stationmaster's house, also built in Mendip stone, was located on the platform at the Cheddar end. The station name was set in stone above the doorway leading on to the platform from the booking office. A small timber-built GWR platform signalbox stood between the station building and the stationmaster's residence. The only level crossing between Wells and Yatton existed here at the Cheddar end of the platform and was operated by a gate wheel in the signalbox. A single siding existed mainly for the strawberry traffic but coal and coke was received for the local traders with 343 tons arriving in 1903, rising to a peak of 724 tons in 1923. A wagon turntable served a siding and a crane at right angles to the main siding; the turntable was removed in 1949.

A serious accident occurred in January 1894 when a goods train arrived and shunted a coal truck into the siding; William Hallett the stationmaster was moving another truck from the right-angled siding on to the wagon turntable when his wagon was struck by the incoming coal truck, causing him to fall underneath it. He was pulled out alive, but unfortunately he died before reaching the hospital at Wells.

As with all of the stations in the Cheddar Valley, passenger tickets were at their maximum in 1903 with 9,720 issued, dropping to 3,340 in 1933. The station was close to the centre of the village and services to Bristol were very popular especially for business people. Draycott was once a block post equipped with running signals but these were removed on Sunday, 10 May 1896 with the box abolished as a block post. A ground frame was installed to operate the points into the siding. However, as Draycott had a level crossing, the distant signals were retained under the Board of Trade regulations with targets and lamps fitted to the gates. When closure to passenger traffic occurred on Monday, 9 September 1963 the level crossing gates were disconnected, to be operated by the train crews, with the distant signals becoming 'fixed'. The signalbox itself closed on 9 March 1965.

Until the closure of the line between Cheddar and Dulcote Quarry, North British Type 2 diesels would arrive from Witham hauling bogie parcels vans for the strawberry traffic which were reversed into the siding for loading purposes. When loaded, the trains would depart for Cheddar where they would be run round before returning back through Draycott, heading for Wells and Witham. The station has been superbly restored and even the name is still extant above the doorway, the building being used today as a holiday home.

125

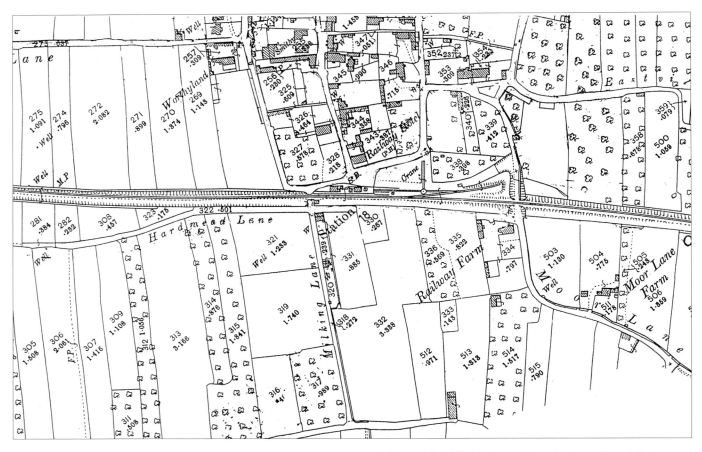

Above: The 1903 survey for Draycott station showing the wagon turntable and right-angled siding in the goods yard. *Crown Copyright Reserved*

Below: Draycott, looking towards Wells, with the small GWR signalbox standing between the stationmaster's house and the station building. The station was a block post at the opening of the line between Cheddar and Wells worked on the train staff and ticket procedure. With the introduction of the electric train staff on the line between Yatton and Witham on Monday, 11 May 1896, and to cut down on the locations where it was considered unnecessary and to save money, such as places where crossing loops did not exist, as with Draycott, the running signals were removed. The signalbox, which contained the wheel for opening and closing the level crossing gates, closed on 9 March 1965. A springer spaniel poses for the camera on the platform, with the small goods yard seen in the background. *Author's collection*

Above: Draycott station building, signalbox complete with a stack of fruit boxes, and small goods shed as viewed from the trackside in 1956. The Bristol & Exeter even placed their decorative bargeboards on a small station such as this giving a Swiss chalet style to the building, and the station name is set in dressed stone above the doorway. The station today, superbly restored, is in use as a holiday home. *J. H. Moss*

Below: Draycott, seen here looking towards Cheddar in 1950, had the only level crossing between Wells and Yatton. The substantial stationmaster's house is glimpsed on the right standing on the single platform. Empty strawberry punnets are dotted about on the platform. *J. H. Moss.*

Above: The small goods yard at Draycott with its solitary siding seen here in 1949, was one of the major rail loading centres for strawberry traffic in the Cheddar Valley along with Cheddar and Axbridge. *J. H. Moss*

Left: A glance back towards Draycott goods yard and siding, complete with loading gauge, from a Yatton-Witham train in May 1948. *J. H. Moss*

Below: Draycott, looking towards Lodge Hill, showing the ground frame that operated the points leading into the siding; the frame was operated by the Annett's key on the end of the single-line tablet. *J. H. Moss*

Above: A Wells-Yatton train hauled by 2-6-2T No 5547 runs into Draycott in 1955. Strawberry boxes are stacked alongside the signalbox and upon the platform barrow at the far end of the platform. *J. H. Moss*

Right: The Draycott platform-mounted signalbox, seen here in 1955, contained the wheel and locking levers for the level crossing gates. Note how substantial the decorative bargeboards are on the station building. *J. H. Moss*

Above: During the big freeze of 1963 the villages of the Cheddar Valley were cut off by heavy snowfalls. Mike Horwood decided to walk along the line from Cheddar on 4 January to visit his mother in Westbury-sub-Mendip. Fortunately he was carrying his camera, and managed to photograph the locomotives stuck in the snowdrifts between Cheddar and Draycott. Collett '22xx' 0-6-0 No 2277 complete with snowplough is seen stuck in snowdrifts with 2-6-0 No 46506 also marooned approximately 100yd behind. *Mike Horwood*

Below: A closer view of No 2277 stuck in the snow between Cheddar and Draycott during the heavy snowfalls of 1963. *Mike Horwood*

Above: Cold and lifeless, Ivatt Mogul 2-6-0 No 46506 awaits rescue in the Cheddar Valley during the depths of winter in January 1963. *Mike Horwood*

Below: Beyer Peacock Type 3 'Hymek' No D7046 arrived from Cheddar to rescue the errant steam locomotives; unfortunately the diesel became derailed, and the PW staff are seen here clearing snow from the bogies before the arrival of the breakdown train. The signal in the background is the Draycott down distant. Even in a small cutting such as this, the depth of the snowdrift is seen to good effect. *Mike Horwood*

Above: The rescue train headed by No 2217 has arrived at the Draycott down distant signal to extract No D7046 from its predicament. The headlamp code is for a breakdown train going to clear the line, and not an express, which of course was the same code. *Mike Horwood*

Below: Bristol Inspector, Jack Whitney, stands to the right on the framing of No 2217 while the PW staff gather to plan the rescue. Pieces of timber and re-railing ramps for the operation can be seen under the smokebox. *Mike Horwood*

Above: Steam issues from the 0-6-0 as Inspector Jack Whitney, standing on the locomotive framing, gives the signal to the driver to reverse and pull the diesel free. Note the heavy duty cables attached to the coupling hook of the locomotive. *Mike Horwood*

Below: Having been re-railed and extricated from the snowdrift the 'Hymek' is seen here at Cheddar with the front end and bogies showing the effect of driving snow. *Mike Horwood*

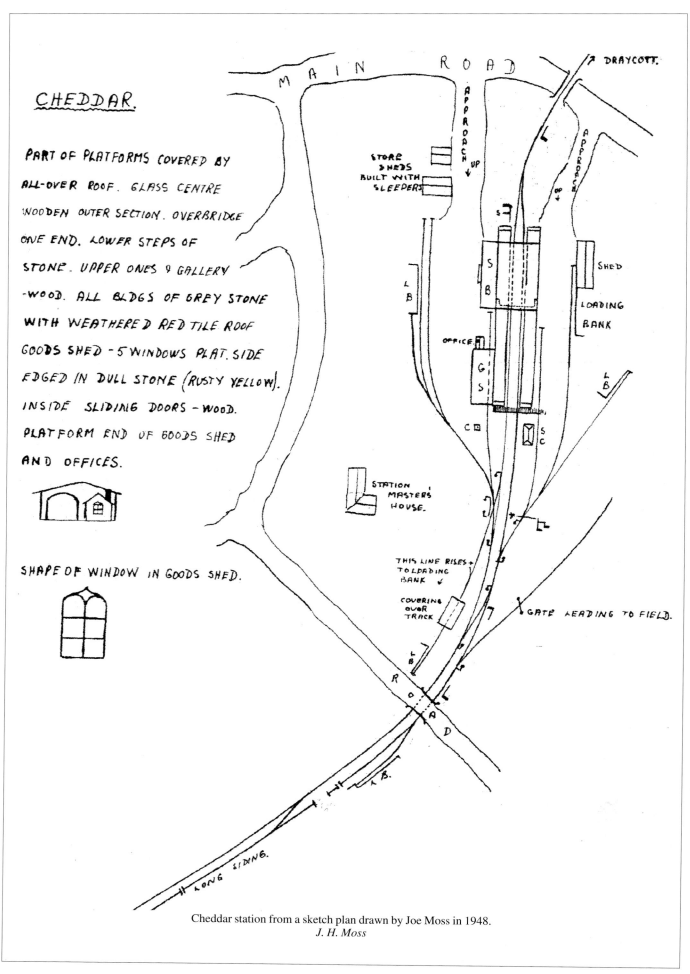

CHEDDAR.

PART OF PLATFORMS COVERED BY ALL-OVER ROOF. GLASS CENTRE WOODEN OUTER SECTION. OVERBRIDGE ONE END. LOWER STEPS OF STONE. UPPER ONES & GALLERY -WOOD. ALL BLDGS OF GREY STONE WITH WEATHERED RED TILE ROOF GOODS SHED - 5 WINDOWS PLAT. SIDE EDGED IN DULL STONE (RUSTY YELLOW). INSIDE SLIDING DOORS - WOOD. PLATFORM END OF GOODS SHED AND OFFICES.

SHAPE OF WINDOW IN GOODS SHED.

MAIN ROAD

DRAYCOTT.

STORE SHEDS BUILT WITH SLEEPERS

APPROACH UP

APPROACH UP +

SHED

LOADING BANK

L B

S B

OFFICE

G S

L B

C

S C

STATION MASTER'S HOUSE.

THIS LINE RISES + TO LOADING BANK

COVERING OVER TRACK

GATE LEADING TO FIELD.

L B

R O A D

L B.

LONG SIDING.

Cheddar station from a sketch plan drawn by Joe Moss in 1948.
J. H. Moss

134

Cheddar

Cheddar opened as a temporary terminus when the broad gauge line from Yatton opened on 3 August 1869, lasting as such until the line was open through to Wells the following year on 5 April. The directors' special train, which had left Yatton at 11am on the opening day, arrived at Cheddar complete with dignitaries from Axbridge whereupon the directors were invited into the station for an elegant refection of cake and champagne which had been prepared for their refreshment. The Vicar of Cheddar, the Rev A' Court Beadon in his welcoming speech said he was deputed to welcome them to Cheddar and, in his opinion, the main cause of the prosperity of the railway was that the directors were a God-fearing body ('hear, hear!'). They had not run on the Lord's Day those monster excursion trains by which the Sabbath had been desecrated and the people demoralised! He wished them all success for their line (loud applause). The Earl of Devon replied on behalf of the directors of the Bristol & Exeter Railway. Several bottles of champagne were then opened and the usual toasts were drunk.

The station building was incomplete when the line opened from Yatton, passengers being accommodated in the goods shed until the station was finished in May 1870, and newspaper reports on Saturday, 7 May the same year stated: 'The new station will be opened in the early part of next week.' Another report dated 26 May described the station as: 'Monstrous gay, decked with flowers and devices.' Mr George of the Swan Hotel in Wells had the foresight to advertise a horse-drawn omnibus departing from his premises at 6.45am to Cheddar station in order to meet the train from Bristol which arrived at 9.30am. He also met the train arriving at 8.50pm, but with the opening of the extension to Wells the omnibus was discontinued.

Without a doubt Cheddar was the grandest station on the line, although a station such as this should have graced the fair city of Wells. A grand overall roof in the

---

THE NEW RAILWAY STATION AT CHEDDAR.—This handsome station, just erected at Cheddar, will be opened in the early part of next week. The Bristol and Exeter Company are making every arrangement for a large traffic during the season, and if the tradesmen aid the company with a liberal and popular scale of tariff, Cheddar will doubtless receive an immense number of visitors during the summer.

Above: The completion of Cheddar station as reported in the *Wells Journal* of Saturday, 7 May 1870.

Above: Driver Fred Western from Wells locomotive shed stands between the tracks alongside his locomotive, No 5512, at Cheddar while working a Witham-Bristol train in May 1948. *J. H. Moss*

Above: Steam blows everywhere from 2-6-2T No 5512 with a Witham-Bristol train at Cheddar in May 1948. *J. H. Moss*

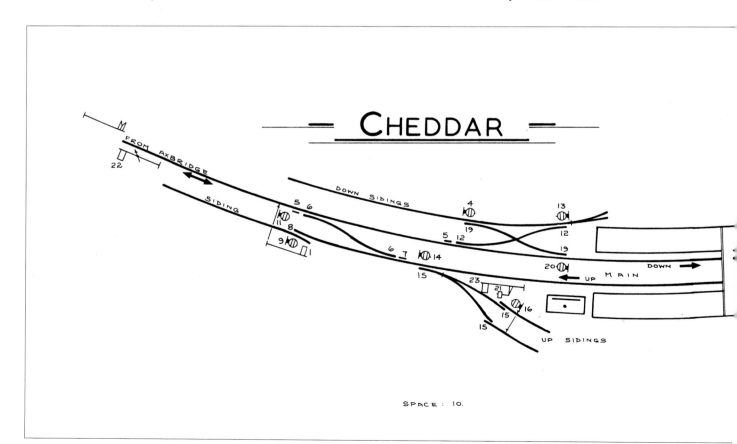

Above: Cheddar signalbox seen here in 1948, was erected by the signal engineering company of Saxby & Farmer, constructed in brick under a plain tiled roof in the distinctive Saxby & Farmer style with oval toplight windows set above the main window frames. The original 17-lever frame was replaced by a 24-lever version in February 1908. The signalbox, dating from 1876, closed on 3 May 1965. *J. H. Moss*

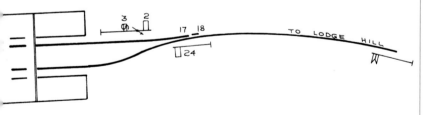

Left: Cheddar signalbox diagram showing the box positioned off the Yatton end of the up platform.
Crown Copyright Reserved

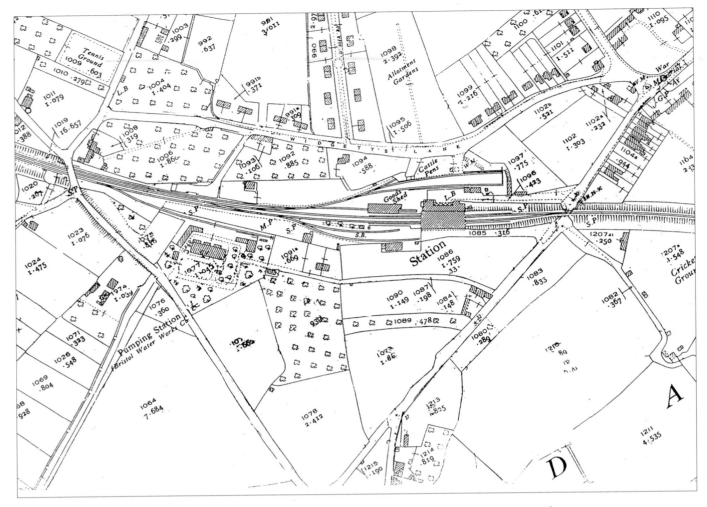

Above: The survey for Cheddar showing the large layout for a small country station. *Crown Copyright Reserved*

Brunellian style supported by walls of Mendip stone spanned the tracks. An internal overbridge at the Axbridge end of the station connected the platforms, the lower steps being constructed in stone, and the upper steps and gallery built in timber. The main station building, located on the down side of the layout, was also constructed in Mendip stone with the usual decorative bargeboards and the roof decked out in red tiles, and as was the B&E style, set out in alternating bands of plain and patterned tiles. A handsome canopy greeted passengers as they stepped down from their horse-drawn carriages. The station offices, first and second class waiting rooms, ladies' waiting room, booking hall, toilets, stationmaster's office and porters' room were all set on the down side of the station together with a prestigious refreshment room which was run by the manageress, Miss Ellen Sainsbury in the 1870s. Except for platform seating no facilities existed on the up side of the station although a small awning was set over the entrance.

The first stationmaster was Mr David Jefferies who lived in Cheddar with his wife and two children. The goods shed was also constructed in Mendip stone. Sidings were situated on the down side at the Yatton end and included the cattle pens and a 6-ton crane. Further sidings were located on the up side of the station, also at the Yatton end. The refreshment room was also the venue in the early years for the annual dinner of Bristol & Exeter staff, although such jollifications were usually confined to stationmasters and managerial staff. Such a gathering occurred for the Passengers Department of the B&E in January 1872 when the room was artistically decorated for the occasion by Mr Sandy of

Wiveliscombe, and a 'capital collection' of foliage, plants and ferns was lent by Dr Lawrence of Cheddar and Mr Hardwich of The Cottage, Westbury. A fine dinner was provided by the caterer, Miss Sainsbury, with about 160 employees from Clevedon, Bristol, Axbridge, Yatton, Sandford, Cheddar, Draycott, Wookey, Lodge Hill and Wells sitting down under the presidency of Mr T. W. Walton, the Superintendent of the line. The usual loyal and patriotic toasts were proposed including 'Success to the Bristol & Exeter Railway' and 'Health to the General Manager, Mr J. C. Wall'. Mr Wall did not attend the gathering but did send a letter wishing the dinner a success, amongst the points raised in the letter being: 'Please assure the men that I am anxious to separate the drones from the bees — getting rid of the former, and taking care of the latter.'

The B&E station staff at Cheddar in 1871 comprised the following: David Jefferies (stationmaster), George Symonds (inspector), William Banbury, Isaac Brimble and Edward Smith (porters). Stationmasters over the years included William Hallet (1881), James Wilkins (1883-99), George Tett (1902), John Richard Tucker (1906-14), Henry Swainson (1919), H. J. Wilson (1923) and R. P. Wilson (1927).

A signalbox erected by the signal engineering company of Saxby & Farmer stood off the end of the up platform. It was constructed in brick under a plain tiled gable roof with the distinctive Saxby & Farmer style of oval toplight windows set above the main window frames. The box was in use from c1876 until it was closed on 3 May 1965. A 24-lever frame, including one spare, replaced the original 17-lever frame in February 1908. It is interesting to note that the GWR

Left: The interior of Cheddar goods shed in 1955 showing the hand-operated crane, a lone wagon awaiting the next shunt by a pick-up goods and merchandise that has been unloaded and awaiting delivery to the local community by the railway delivery lorry. Note the position of the loading gauge which is affixed above the shed entrance. *J. H. Moss*

Below: The substantial goods shed at Cheddar constructed in the well-known style of the Bristol & Exeter Railway. The equally well-constructed stationmaster's house seen in the background was situated in Widgetts Lane. *J. H. Moss*

Above: Cheddar station, looking towards Wells in 1950, showing the width between the tracks — a legacy of the broad gauge. Part of the goods shed can be seen on the left with the imposing B&E station buildings beyond. The all-over roof supported on walls of Mendip stone is seen to good effect, although it has lost some panes of glass over the years. Part of the small awning situated over the entrance to the up platform can be seen to the right. *J. H. Moss*

Below: The east end of the station, looking towards Axbridge on 28 May 1960 with the signalbox at the far end of the up platform. The ravages of time have not been kind to the woodwork on the overall roof, with a prop having to support the building at the far end. *R. E. Toop*

Above: The two sidings running behind the signalbox at Cheddar, seen here on 3 September 1963, dated from 1898 with one known as the 'Jubilee'. *Scrimgeour Collection-Signalling Record Society*

replaced the Saxby & Farmer signalboxes at Axbridge and Wells but not the one at Cheddar. Severe weather has always caused havoc to the railway over the years, and the inclement conditions of March 1891 badly affected the Cheddar Valley line on Tuesday the 10th with the 7.20am Wells-Bristol hauled by two locomotives only reaching Draycott before encountering trouble. After the two locomotives were dug out from the snowdrifts the train returned to Lodge Hill at 6pm and the guard walked to Wells, arriving on Wednesday morning after a 10-hour wait. Two locomotives, complete with a gang of men, were sent from Wells to rescue the stranded train, but only reached the Portway Cutting before being brought to a halt, with no further progress made. A locomotive was derailed at Cheddar, and although a snowplough was also waiting to proceed to Wells from there, the severity of the snowfall made it impossible to do so. The line was eventually cleared on Friday evening with traffic resuming on the Saturday.

Bad weather had also severely affected the area 10 years previously when there was a bad snowstorm in January 1881 that began on the night of the 16th and continued throughout the following day. The 3.35pm Wells to Glastonbury was brought to a stand at Polsham on the S&D line, and a GWR train was blocked in at Wanstrow but with the assistance of a following goods engine reached Wells at 9.11pm instead of 5.35pm. Another train was marooned at Cheddar, the snow in the cutting at Easton being some 25ft deep such was the severity of the weather, and it had to be cut out lump by lump.

Two sidings were added behind the signalbox in 1898, one of which was known as the 'Jubilee' (after Queen Victoria's jubilee, celebrated in the previous year). General goods, coal, coke and timber for the local traders, gasworks

and the quarries, including local consumption, were dealt with in the goods yard. During the 1930s three coal merchants rented wharfage in the station yard, where they could bag up and weigh coal straight from the rail wagons for local delivery at half the charge then applying to deliveries by road traffic. Mr Alfred Perry was one of the several coal merchants who used the station and had his own private rail wagons in both four- and five-plank versions. Limestone from Batts Combe and Crow Catchpole quarries was constantly being transported by rail and a private siding agreement for the use of sidings and loading docks at Cheddar was drawn up between the GWR and Bernard Butcher & F. P. Ford, trading as the Batts Combe Quarry Co on 19 July 1926 (Batts Combe Quarry Ltd from 25 April 1935). Roadstone was transported by lorries between the quarries and the station where the companies had separate loading banks. Lime from the Callow Rock Lime Co was also dealt with, the siding for which was covered in order to keep the limedust dry. It was constructed on a gradient so that rail wagons could be moved forward without using a locomotive. The private siding agreement between the Callow Rock Lime Co and the GWR dated from 27 September 1922, the siding being in use until 1969. Agreements for an additional loading dock and an extension to the siding for Callow Rock Lime were made on 29 December 1924 and 20 November 1926 respectively. The Callow Rock Lime Co used two steam road vehicles, one Foden and one Sentinel, to convey the limedust from the quarry to the station.

A private siding agreement for the Bristol Waterworks Co was authorised on 4 October 1922. L. W. Bryant Quarries had a siding agreement from 18 October 1935, but this was regarded as being at an end on 22 October the following year when the firm went out of business. Two sleeper-built

Cheddar Gorge

Above: The Lion Rock at Cheddar, a focal point for visitors to the Cheddar Gorge by rail or charabanc. *Author's collection*

Below: The limestone cliffs tower in the background in this view of the entrance to Cheddar Gorge with Rose Cottage to the left, long before the mass invasive effects of the motor car. *Author's collection*

Above: Station staff and growers pose for the camera at Cheddar while loading strawberries in the early 1900s. Note the racking for the strawberry punnets inside the GWR vans, the open sides of which kept the fruit ventilated and fresh during the journey. *Author's collection*

store sheds were situated in the station approach, the largest of which was used before World War 1 as a garage for the GWR bus. This journeyed around the local villages delivering luggage and parcels, as well as collecting passengers who had booked in advance.

Strawberries and truckles of Cheddar cheese were loaded into passenger trains, which also had bogie vans tacked on for the summer harvest. Traffic was very heavy during the strawberry season, with the growers queuing in Station Road waiting to unload from a variety of conveyances ranging from prams and handcarts to horse-drawn carts, vans and lorries. The fruit was despatched in eight-wheeled bogie vans, which were branded 'Return to Cheddar'. Separate vans were despatched to Sheffield, Liverpool, Bradford, Newcastle, Manchester and Leeds on the 5pm special fruit train. Strawberries destined for Birmingham and Cardiff went forward with the normal service at 8.30pm. Special arrangements were given in the footnotes of Cheddar signalbox for a van or vans to be propelled to Draycott to collect the loaded vehicles and then be hauled to Cheddar to be formed into the main special train. Due to the gruelling ascent to Shute Shelve Tunnel, loaded freight trains were split to half the capacity of the locomotive, which then proceeded to Sandford & Banwell, thence returning to Cheddar for the second half of its train which was rejoined at Sandford and Banwell for the journey onwards. Freight trains calling at the station on weekdays in the summer working timetable of 1956 were: 3.50am Bristol West Depot-Wells East Somerset (arr Cheddar 5.59, dep 6.15am), 9.30am Bristol West Depot-Wells East Somerset (arr Cheddar 12.27, dep 1.42pm), 9.45am Wells East Somerset-Bristol West Depot (arr Cheddar 11.55, dep 12.50pm), 2.45pm Wells East Somerset-Cheddar (engine and brake van, arr Cheddar 3.9pm, then work 4.45pm Cheddar-Witham),

4.40pm Wells East Somerset-St Philips Marsh (arr Cheddar 5.30, dep 6.15pm).

Cheddar was a very busy station in Victorian days, with trippers arriving by excursion trains from Bristol and other areas. Local carriage operators were kept busy transporting visitors to and from Cheddar Gorge with its limestone cliffs towering to over 450ft and the famous caves which are as popular a tourist haunt today as in times past, with delicious cream teas and tasty Cheddar cheese. The Cheddar Pink, a rare flower that only grows wild in the gorge, can be found here. Excursion traffic from London and Bristol to Cheddar (as well as Wookey, opened in 1871) was at one time prolific, with well-loaded trains arriving under the echoing roof of the station, doors swinging open and hordes of expectant passengers swarming through the exit and walking towards the village centre heading for the caves. The well-off would climb aboard the waiting horse-drawn carriages and travel in style, the B&E timetable for 1877 advertising at Cheddar 'Conveyances meet every train for the cliffs. Fare 4d each passenger.' At the end of the day, the tired but happy trippers would walk back to the station from the Gorge and climb aboard their waiting trains for the journey home. Combined circular road and rail excursions were popular, as in April 1906 when the GWR advertised excursions from Bristol, picking up at Clifton Down, Redland, Montpelier, Ashley Hill, Stapleton Road, Lawrence Hill, Temple Meads and Bedminster. Passengers had the choice of No 1 or No 2 Tour. The first was advertised as 'To Winscombe by rail, thence by charabanc or brake to Cheddar, via Shipham, Charterhouse and Cheddar Gorge, returning by rail from Cheddar.' Tour No 2 was advertised as 'To Cheddar by rail, thence by charabanc or brake to Winscombe via Axbridge, Compton Bishop and Webbington, returning by rail from Winscombe. The service between Winscombe and Cheddar

Above: A view from the station, looking west towards the signalbox and goods yard in 1955. The internal footbridge had its lower steps built in stone, with the upper steps and gallery constructed in timber. *J. H. Moss*

Below: The west end of Cheddar as viewed from the internal footbridge in 1949 with part of the goods shed seen to the right. *J. H. Moss*

will be performed by Mr Alfred G. Weeks's well-horsed charabanc or other similar vehicle.' Return fares for tour No 1 were 5s, 4s and 3s 6d for first, second and third class respectively, and for No 2, 4s 3d, 3s 3d and 2s 9d. The refreshment room closed on 19 September 1925 and, as with licensed rooms on railway stations, it was rented out and not operated by the railway. However, the old refreshment rooms had a new lease of life in 1950 when a group of teenagers set up the Cheddar Youth Club with the membership soon growing to over 50.

The Southern Railway also ran excursions to Cheddar from Portsmouth and Salisbury in 1939, advertising Cheddar as 'Famed for its majestic Gorge and entrancing stalactite Caverns.' The return third class fare from Salisbury was 4s 2d departing at 12.22pm with a booked arrival in Cheddar of 2.36pm, leaving at 6.40pm. Fares from Paddington via Bristol and Yatton in 1953 to Cheddar were 61s 4d and 40s 10d return for first and second class respectively. But the railways, although having it their own way at first with excursion traffic, would eventually face competition from that enemy of the railway — the motor omnibus — and with expanding and better motor charabanc services rather than horse-drawn, by the 1950s much of the traffic had been lost to road transport. The Sunday service during 1953 consisted of a train from Bristol to Witham and return, which involved

a lengthy wait at Wells, so that connections with main line trains at each end of the branch could be made. Sunday trains did not call at Lodge Hill, and on Sundays when the weather was good as many as 50 passengers have been known to travel from Bristol to Cheddar and back. If conditions were wet then passengers entraining would be sparse, although a few passengers would be exchanged at Witham where connections would be made with main line trains. On Sunday, 21 June the same year, as well as the regular Sunday train, No 8795 was reported at Wells with a Southern utility van, returning to Bristol to collect another utility van at Draycott and another at Cheddar. No 46525 was also at work on the same day, hauling an engineering departmental train.

A camping coach stabled on a siding on the down side of the layout was in use from 1935 until 1939, returning in 1952 and lasting until 1963. No W9902W, an ex-GWR clerestory coach was noted at Cheddar in 1956/7/62 and 1963. The camp coach cost £4 per week to rent in 1935, this being an eight-berth version, compared with other coaches on the Cheddar Valley which were six-berth. The GWR, financially astute as always, had the proviso that occupants of the camp coaches (the GWR called the vehicles 'camp coaches', the term 'camping coaches' appearing after World War 2), purchased a minimum of six monthly return tickets

Below: The layout at the west end of Cheddar in 1949 with the station in the far distance. The siding on the left was used to load limedust on to rail wagons by the Callow Rock Lime Co. The building covered the loading area in order to keep the limedust dry. The main running line runs alongside the wall, with the line below the signal being a long siding. The track running to the gate on the right leads to the Bristol Waterworks siding, for which a private siding agreement was authorised on 4 October 1922. *J. H. Moss*

Above: A GWR diesel railcar leaves the up platform at Cheddar in 1949 on a Bristol service. *J. H. Moss*

in connection with the hire. Cooking and lighting was by oil, with the railway company supplying blankets, sheets, towels, tablecloths, crockery and cutlery etc.

A roof prop was necessary in the final years, this being placed between the tracks at the Yatton end of the station. The Clevedon motor trains would make a trip to Cheddar and return to Yatton once a day for many years. Signalmen in the 1940s were Alfie Robertson and Jack Williams, in the 1960s Len Wheeler and Jack Padfield, and the shunter from c1937 until closure was Bert Adams. The footbridge at Cheddar was boarded up in later years as it was too dangerous to use. The private siding agreement for the Bristol Waterworks Co was terminated on 1 July 1961, and that of the Callow Rock Lime Co was terminated by English China Clays Quarries Ltd on 28 March 1969. Class 5700 0-6-0PT No 4607 (82D) failed at Cheddar on 1 November 1958 while working the 10.20am Witham-Bristol passenger train. Fortunately, an Ivatt 2-6-0, No 46525 (82B) was standing in the goods yard and was swiftly coupled on to the train, taking it onwards, while the pannier tank was left behind at Cheddar trying to raise enough steam in order to travel light engine to Bristol, but it had not proceeded beyond Sandford & Banwell by 3pm. Trains leaving Cheddar for Yatton ran alongside Axbridge Reservoir before tackling the 1 in 100 to Axbridge station. The reservoir was constructed by McAlpine & Co for the Bristol and Minehead corporations between 1933 and 1937. Temporary standard gauge sidings for the contractors' locomotives and rolling stock for transportation of machinery and materials to the works were laid alongside the running line in 1933. The private siding agreement dated from 11 December 1933 and terminated in 1937. The contractors' locomotives were all Hudswell Clarke

0-6-0 saddle tanks: No 46 inside-cylinder (of 1924) ex-Southampton Docks extension contract, No 57 (of 1927) also ex-Southampton, No 68 (of 1934) builder's No 1608 new to the Cheddar contract, and No 69 (of 1934) (No 1609) also new to the Cheddar contract.

The last down passenger train, the 8.20pm from Yatton to Wells, arrived on 7 September 1963 packed with more passengers than it ever carried in normal service, and a far cry from that distant day in August 1869 when another train had arrived, conveying the Earl of Devon, the chairman of the Bristol & Exeter Railway and other important personages to open the line from Yatton. The platform was then packed with cheering and happy people, bands playing and flags being waved, yet within 94 years it was all gone. The overall roof, which was the work of Francis Fox of the Bristol & Exeter Railway, was removed in 1964. The line between Yatton and Cheddar closed on 1 October the same year with the termination of the line approximately 400yd on the Yatton side of the station. Stone traffic from two quarries in the Mendips delivered by lorry to the station for loading in rail wagons continued until 28 March 1969, the track layout remaining more or less complete, with the points operated by hand throws.

The line from Cranmore to Cheddar was worked as a siding; trains operated as a 'Q' working (Saturdays excepted) with the train crews operating the level crossings at Kilver Street, Priory Road and Draycott until the line was closed as far as Dulcote Quarry on 26 April the same year, but not before the 'Cheddar Valley Scenic' special arrived on 31 May. This allowed the enthusiasts of the RCTS to wander around the deserted station and remaining rusting trackwork for a short while before boarding the waiting DMU which

Above: Cheddar, looking towards Axbridge in 1949 with the main running line to the right showing quarry wagons stabled as far as the eye can see. The wagons in the left foreground have recently been filled with limestone from the adjacent loading dock. Limestone was transported by lorries between Batts Combe and Crow Catchpole Quarries to the loading banks at the station. *J. H. Moss*

Right: One of McAlpine's Hudswell, Clarke 0-6-0 saddle tanks is pictured on the contractor's sidings at Cheddar on 26 October 1935. The sidings were used for the transportation of machinery and materials in connection with the construction of the nearby reservoir for the Bristol and Minehead corporations.
Kenneth Leech Collection, courtesy Barry Hayward

purred away in a cloud of diesel smoke, leaving the station to lapse into silence, broken only by birdsong and the hum of traffic from the main road nearby. A 15mph speed restriction was applied to the section between Cranmore and Cheddar as the line had not been used since the mineral traffic from Cheddar had ceased a few months earlier. The permanent way gang had to spend the week preceding the arrival of the special train, clearing the line of rubbish etc, as the track was not in the best of condition. The former station is known today as Brunel Stoneworks, and under the auspices of Wells Cathedral Stonemasons now echoes to the sound of stone cutting as the dressed stonework is skilfully carved into exquisite designs, keeping the heritage of Wells Cathedral and other ecclesiastical buildings alive. The craftsmanship of the Bristol & Exeter Railway stonemasons who built the station so long ago is still evident.

Top: A look back towards Cheddar station from a departing Yatton-Wells train in May 1948. *J. H. Moss*

Above: The view towards Wells from the down platform at Cheddar in the summer of 1948 with the single-track line curving away on the embankment in the distance; gas lamps stand on both platforms. The shunt signal (complete with letter S) below the down starting signal arm enabled locomotives of down trains terminating here to run around their stock. *J. H. Moss*

Driver Reg Mapstone from Wells shed, smiles for the camera of Joe Moss after arriving bunker-first with 2-6-2T No 5512 — the locomotive was a long-time stalwart of Bristol Bath Road shed — alongside the down platform at Cheddar with a Yatton-Witham train formed of a two-coach 'B' set in 1948. *J. H. Moss*

Collett 0-6-0 No 2220 from St Philips Marsh shed stands alongside the up platform at Cheddar in 1949 awaiting entry to the single-line section to Axbridge with a Wells–Bristol freight. Agricultural machinery can just be seen on the second wagon. *J. H. Moss*

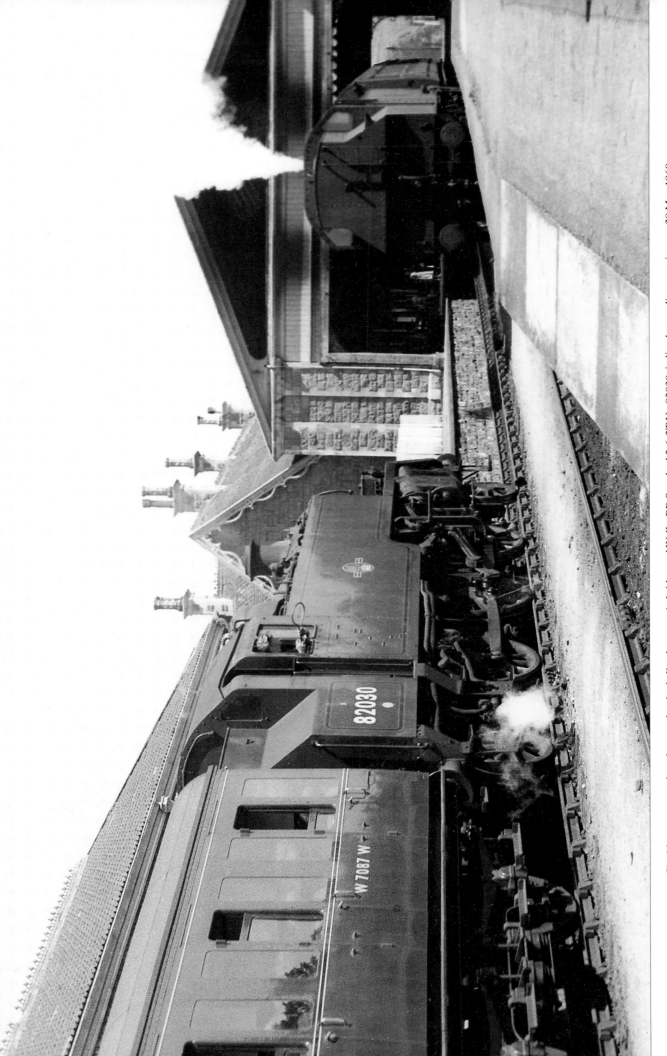

Cheddar was a crossing place on the single line between Axbridge and Wells. BR Standard 2-6-2T No 82030, in lined green livery, arrives on 28 May 1960 with a Yatton-Witham train, the fireman of which has the single-line tablet for the section to Wells in his hands. Steam escapes from the safety valves of Ivatt 2-6-2T No 41240 while standing alongside the up platform with a Wells-Yatton train. *R. E. Toop*

Ivatt 2-6-2T No 41245 runs into Cheddar under the echoing overall roof with the 3.28pm Witham–Yatton on 17 August 1963. Accommodation on the down platform was lavish with the station offices, first and second class waiting rooms, ladies' waiting rooms, booking hall, toilets, stationmaster's office, porters' room and refreshment room being provided. *Hugh Ballantyne*

The Cheddar signalman, complete with the single-line tablet in his hand, chats to the driver of No 41245 at the head of the 3.28pm Witham-Yatton on 17 August 1963. The massive prop and associated timberwork supporting the overall roof can be seen between the tracks. *Hugh Ballantyne*

Class 4575 2-6-2T No 5535, having left Cheddar, now bowls along with a Witham-Yatton train in 1936. The locomotive was at first allocated to Cheltenham in June 1928, thence Bristol Bath Road from where it was withdrawn in June 1957. *Author's collection*

Above: Cheddar station, viewed on 24 December 1967. The overall roof has been removed, and decay and desolation have now set in, although the building still reflects its Bristol & Exeter ancestry. *J. A. Sommerfield*

Below: A three-car DMU organised by the Bath branch of the LCGB stands at the disused Cheddar station on 16 November 1968. The tour had departed from the closed S&D station of Bath Green Park. This was the penultimate railtour to visit the station; the accolade of the final tour to Cheddar was to fall on the RCTS special on Saturday 31 May the following year. *J. A. Sommerfield*

With the fireman holding the single-line token, and the up starter arm lowered, No 41240 pulls away from Axbridge with a train to Yatton on 2 July 1960. Ahead lies the climb at 1 in 74 to the tunnel at Shute Shelve. The station was one of the primary loading centres for the prolific strawberry traffic, and at one time there was a diagram for a complete trainload departing from Axbridge in the late evening, bound for Birmingham (Moor Street). *R. E. Toop*

Axbridge–Yatton

Above: A member of the station staff stands by the timber-built waiting shelter on the down platform as '45xx' 2-6-2T No 5546 (82A) drifts into Axbridge with the 11.35am Yatton-Witham on 19 August 1957. The footbridge connecting the platforms was extended to carry a public footpath to Frys Hill behind the down platform. *H. B. Priestley*

Axbridge

The southern slopes of the brooding Mendip hills, which form the natural backdrop to Axbridge, were once the royal hunting grounds of Prince John, although the oldest building in the town square, known as King John's Hunting Lodge, was not constructed until the year 1500, more than 200 years after the king's death. However, the royal hunting grounds had been well and truly dispensed with when the official train arrived on the opening day. The Brislington Band who had accompanied the directors' train from Bristol and had played some 'agreeable selections' found themselves upon arrival at Axbridge in competition with the Axbridge Workhouse Fife and Drum Band, the wildly cheering throng on the station platform, and the pealing of the bells from St John's Church standing immediately behind the station. The directors of the Bristol & Exeter Railway, including the Earl of Devon, alighted from their saloon carriage, to be met by the Mayor, Mr G. Millard, and the Corporation of Axbridge including Mr Trew (alderman), Mr Richard Lewis (chamberlain), Mr W. Maggs (deputy chamberlain), Mr George Smith (MD), Mr J. P. Mayne, Mr J. Brooks, Mr James Collins and Mr W. Trew. In the waiting room of the station the town clerk read the welcoming address to which the Earl of Devon answered for the

directors, whereupon his speech was cheered. The train then departed for Cheddar carrying the Axbridge dignitaries for the welcoming speech. It seems that the Cheddar dignitaries had been put out by the welcome awarded by Axbridge to the arrival of the train. The train, conveying some of the gentlemen of Cheddar, then returned to Axbridge where a sumptuous repast had been laid out in the town hall to which the Mayor and Corporation had invited the directors of the railway. The Mayor, in toasting the health of the Bristol & Exeter Railway Company, remarked, before the railway was opened, 'Into Axbridge — Out of the world' (laughter), but he hoped now, they would be able to reverse this, and that success would attend the line. Again, the Earl of Devon replied. Dinner and tea were provided for 200 poor people of Axbridge, the inhabitants having liberally subscribed for this object, and Messrs J. Let and W. Trew did their best to carry out the arrangements.

The substantial main station buildings were situated on the up platform and constructed in the solid B&E style as described for other locations on the Cheddar Valley line. A booking hall, waiting room, parcels office, ladies' waiting room and toilets comprised the main accommodation, and people today still remember the blazing fire in the waiting rooms on dark cold winter nights. A stone-built goods shed, sidings and cattle pens were located off the up loop at the

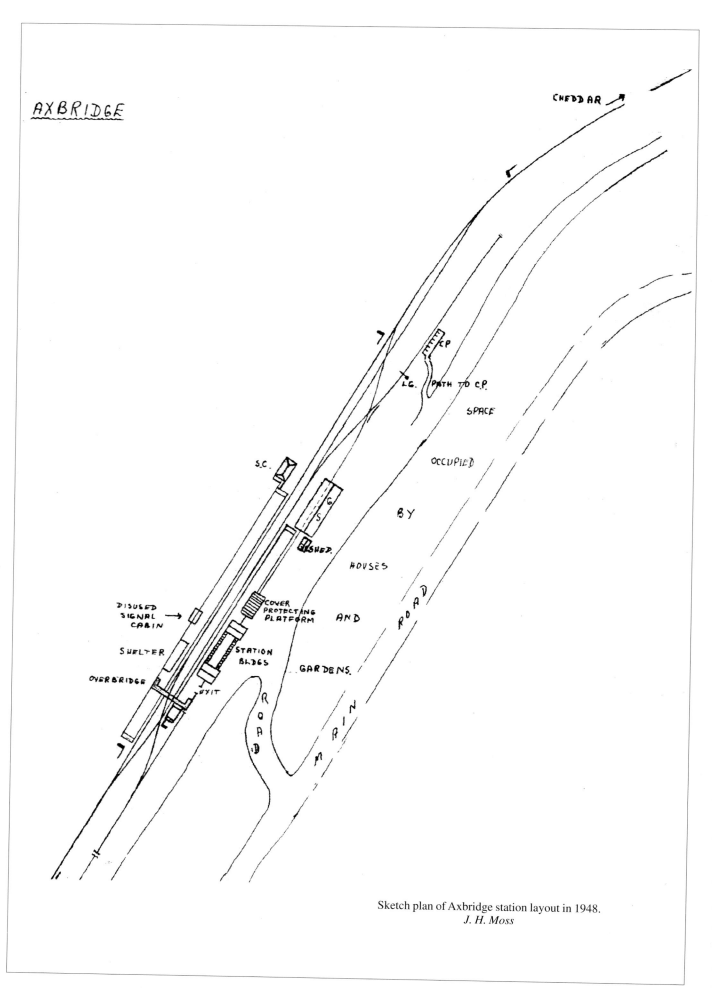

AXBRIDGE

CHEDDAR →

C.P.

L.G.   PATH TO C.P.

SPACE

OCCUPIED

BY

HOUSES

AND

GARDENS.

ROAD

MAIN ROAD

S.C.

G

S

SHED.

COVER
PROTECTING
PLATFORM

DISUSED
SIGNAL
CABIN →

SHELTER

STATION
BLDGS

OVERBRIDGE

EXIT

Sketch plan of Axbridge station layout in 1948.
J. H. Moss

Above: The brooding Mendip Hills dominate the skyline as '22xx' 0-6-0 No 2225 runs past the goods shed into Axbridge with a Wells-Bristol freight in 1952. The signalbox opened on 14 July 1907 replacing an earlier Saxby & Farmer box that stood on the down platform. *J. H. Moss*

Cheddar end of the station, another siding serving a loading dock at the Yatton end also on the up side of the station layout. Passengers awaiting trains on the down platform had a wooden waiting shelter in which to escape the severe weather that can occur at times in the Mendip Hills. Fog, severe frost and heavy snow are no strangers in this region. A Saxby & Farmer signalbox constructed on a Mendip stone base originally stood next to the waiting shelter on the Cheddar platform. The box was in use until 14 July 1907 when the GWR opened a new signalbox located off the end of the down platform at the Cheddar end. A footbridge connecting the two platforms was later extended to carry a public footpath to Frys Hill behind the down platform. The Bristol & Exeter once advertised 'Conveyances may be hired of Mr R. Hutchings, Lamb Hotel'. The stationmaster's house stood alongside the down line at the Cheddar end, reached by a footpath leading from the ramp of the down platform. Access for passengers to the station was gained either via steps from St John's churchyard, or Station Road, both routes leading to the up platform. A canopied shelter for strawberry traffic was erected on the up platform in 1924, the produce being loaded directly from the up platform into vans, usually bogie 'Siphons' or 'Fruit Ds' attached to passenger trains, one of which was the 3.20pm Frome to Bristol (4.20pm ex-Wells). At one time there was a diagram for a complete trainload departing from Axbridge in the late evening bound for Birmingham Moor Street and running via Witham, Westbury, Thingley Junction and Swindon. The coming of the railway was a boon for the growers, who could at last have a speedy delivery for their precious fruit. In the pre-railway era, at least 120 horse-drawn carts would pass through Axbridge nightly in the season, heading for Covent Garden, London.

Passenger trains on the branch in the 1950s consisted mainly of 'B' sets hauled by '57xx' or '45xx' tank engines. However, from the mid-1950s Ivatt 2-6-0s began working most of the freight and some of the passenger trains. Bristol Bath Road shed had inherited from South Wales a number of displaced BR Class 3MT 2-6-2Ts in the late 1950s and it was not long before they were working branch passenger services. One of the last ex-GWR '45xx' 2-6-2 small Prairie tank duties was on 9 July 1960 when No 5508 headed the 9.47am Westbury to Bristol via the Cheddar Valley line. Coal, timber, general goods and agricultural machinery were handled in the goods yard and shed; livestock was also handled, plus milk churn traffic from the nearby farms. At one time, almost every station on the line handled milk churns, and up until prior to 1939 the one Sunday train included eight loaded milk vans destined for London. The tonnage of coal received totalled: 1,788, 1,652 and 1,507 tons in 1903, 1913 and 1923 respectively with parcels forwarded being 48,797, 37,369 and 32,244 for the same years. Passenger tickets from the station were at their peak in 1903 with 22,971 issued, dropping to 12,606 in 1923 and lower still in 1933 to 2,683. A camping coach was in use at the station from 1936 until 1939. The original B&E signalbox

Above: Axbridge signalbox and station on 3 September 1963. Note the soot on the footbridge caused by steam locomotives blasting away on the gradient from the station. *Scrimgeour Collection-Signalling Record Society*

Below: Axbridge station in 1959 viewed from the footbridge, showing the descent at 1 in 100 towards Cheddar with the main station buildings and goods shed on the up platform to the right. Part of the stationmaster's house can be glimpsed behind the signalbox. *J. H. Moss*

that had closed in 1907 was removed during the 1950s. Closure to goods traffic came on 10 June 1963 and although some records show the signalbox closing from the same date, Andy Viles can remember exchanging the single-line staff with the signalman in August that year, while travelling on the footplate with his father, Harry Viles. Trains still crossed here until the end of passenger working, and it is believed the box closed at the end of freight working on the Yatton-Cheddar section on 1 October 1964.

Mr Greenman began his career on the GWR in 1905, being stationmaster of Winscombe in 1914 before moving to Steventon, then being appointed stationmaster at Axbridge in January 1925, serving the railway until he retired in 1949 when replaced by Mr King. When Mr Greenman retired he could not get permission to build a house on land he owned near the station in Chestnut Avenue, so he purchased a railway carriage from Swindon. Its last journey was to Axbridge, where with the help of his two eldest sons he converted it into a house, naming it Cosy Nook. Mr Greenman's wife was a signalwoman at Axbridge for the last 2½ years of the line. Signalmen from the mid-1950s to the 1960s included Reg Kitchen and D. Greenman, son of the former stationmaster, who also worked in the box at Wookey. The station buildings and goods shed are still in existence today, standing alongside the Axbridge bypass which is a much-needed road for the traffic-strangled town although the old buildings will always remind us of our lack of foresight in the haste to close so many branch lines in the 1960s.

Trains bound for Yatton, after swinging out of the up loop and passing the outer home signal at Axbridge on to the single line, passed north through a deep rock cutting on a 34-chain radius and crossed the A38 trunk road via a girder bridge which had a limited clearance to road traffic, and being narrow often caused congestion to summer traffic. Trains now heading north were faced with a climb of 1 in 74 to the 180yd-long Shute Shelve Tunnel. The single-line track was laid dead in the centre of the tunnel, and a joke at the expense of a hapless fireman was often shared by locomotive drivers, especially if the fireman was new to the route and gawping over the side of the footplate. A shout of 'Mind your head!' would startle him into jerking his head back into the loco cab, when in reality there was no danger to anyone's head, as the tunnel had been built for broad gauge track. One of the twin-car diesel railcars caught fire due to overheating at Shute Shelve Tunnel in 1947 with No 37 being severely damaged. The vehicle, dating from 1941, was stored until taken out of stock on 23 September 1949, its place in the twin set being filled by No 22 from 19 April 1948. Another railcar, this time a single-ended version hauling a single coach to Witham, found itself in trouble at the other end of the line on Tuesday, 10 September 1946 when its engine caught fire at Three Arch Bridge between Wells and Shepton Mallet. The fire was quickly extinguished, and there was a 45-minute delay before the Westbury goods loco came down from Shepton Mallet and worked the train onwards. The tunnel today forms part of a public footpath and cycleway and is well worth a visit, especially as this is the major engineering feature of the line which proved a serious difficulty through Shute Shelve Hill. Once through the tunnel, trains ran down the 1 in 100 to run over a road bridge into Winscombe station.

Below: Axbridge, looking west in 1959, with the up platform starting signal to the left. The single line curves to the right in the distance leading through a deep rock cutting on a 34-chain radius before crossing the A38 trunk road via a girder bridge. *J. H. Moss*

Above: The roadside view of the goods shed at Axbridge in 1959; closure to goods traffic occurring on 10 June 1963. As with the station building, the goods shed still survives today. *J. H. Moss*

Below: The main station buildings at Axbridge, seen here in 1959, comprised a booking hall, waiting room, parcels office and ladies' waiting room. The station building survives today, standing alongside the Axbridge bypass that has been constructed on the course of the former trackbed. *J. H. Moss*

Above: When the Axbridge stationmaster retired in 1949 he purchased an ex-GWR clerestory coach which was delivered by rail from Swindon to Axbridge and converted it into the handsome dwelling seen here on land that he owned near the station. *J. H. Moss*

Above: A look back at Axbridge taken from a Yatton-Wells train in May 1948 showing the cattle pens and goods shed. *J. H. Moss*

Above: The Axbridge signalman stands in readiness to collect the single-line token from the fireman of Ivatt 2-6-2T No 41240 arriving with a Yatton-bound train on 2 July 1960. Part of the stone-built goods shed and sidings are seen to the right, with the substantial stationmaster's house standing on the left. *R. E. Toop*

Above: Axbridge is a scene of desolation with tracks removed on 31 May 1966, a far cry from the days when the Bristol & Exeter Railway once advertised in its timetable that 'Conveyances may be hired of Mr Hutchings, Lamb Hotel'. Despite the ruination depicted here, the station building and goods shed with most of the original B&E features still in situ, survive in the year 2000 standing alongside the Axbridge bypass. Cars and lorries pound past the old station buildings instead of 2-6-2 tanks running on local trains between Yatton and Witham. *R. C. Riley*

Opened as Woodborough, the station was renamed Winscombe on 1 December 1869. The standard design GWR building shown here opened on 9 January 1905, replacing the original wooden structure. The small timber-built hut at the left-hand side is the original B&E signalbox which was converted to a ground frame when the running signals were removed in 1896 with the installation of the electric train staff between Yatton and Witham. *Author's collection*

WINSCOMBE STATION.

Above: A closer view of the station building at Winscombe taken in 1910 with passengers awaiting the next train. Even a small station such as this had a separate waiting room for ladies, booking office and waiting room, parcels office and cloakroom. Milk churns, oil lamps and a weighing machine complete the scene. *Author's collection*

Winscombe

Winscombe was opened as Woodborough but was renamed on 1 December 1869. The station building, constructed in timber due to the instability of the new embankment, but of similar design to Draycott station, was erected on the down side of the line. The locality soon developed in the late Victorian era as a wealthy residential area, with many of the residents commuting to jobs and businesses in Bristol. The original station building was found to be inadequate and was removed. A local shopkeeper purchased the old building, which was hauled away on rollers by a traction engine, preceded by a man with a red flag, to be used as part of the village shop. The new single-storey station building on a single platform opened on 9 January 1905. Constructed to a standard GWR design in red brick, it had varying amounts of relief in the form of blues for plinth, corners and window apertures. The large standard canopy was cantilevered from the wall on a steel frame made from factory-assembled components and had a pitched roof clad in corrugated iron on the front slope, and 'Invincible' glazing on the rear. A parcels office, cloakroom,

booking office, waiting room, ladies' waiting room and toilet facilities were provided. Commuter traffic to and from Bristol was always prolific, even to the end of the branch, passengers preferring the railway instead of sitting in traffic queues on the A38.

A single-loop siding existed on the down side of the line at the Yatton end of the station and a 3-ton crane was installed in the yard. With the electric train staff being installed from Yatton throughout to Witham in 1896, and to cut down on the expense of installing the ETS at various locations, the signals were removed from Winscombe and the ground frames controlling the points had to be unlocked with the Annett's key fitted on the end of the train staff. The siding served the local traders with 1,055, 1,340 and 1,338 tons of coal received in 1903, 1913 and 1923 respectively. Passenger tickets issued in 1903 totalled 18,880. Milk in churns was handled at the station, being loaded into trains from the platform by the station staff. A camp coach was stabled here from 1936 until 1939 then returned from 1952 until 1960, with No W9909 noted during the 1950s. Closure of the goods yard came on 10 June 1963, the station being completely demolished circa 1973.

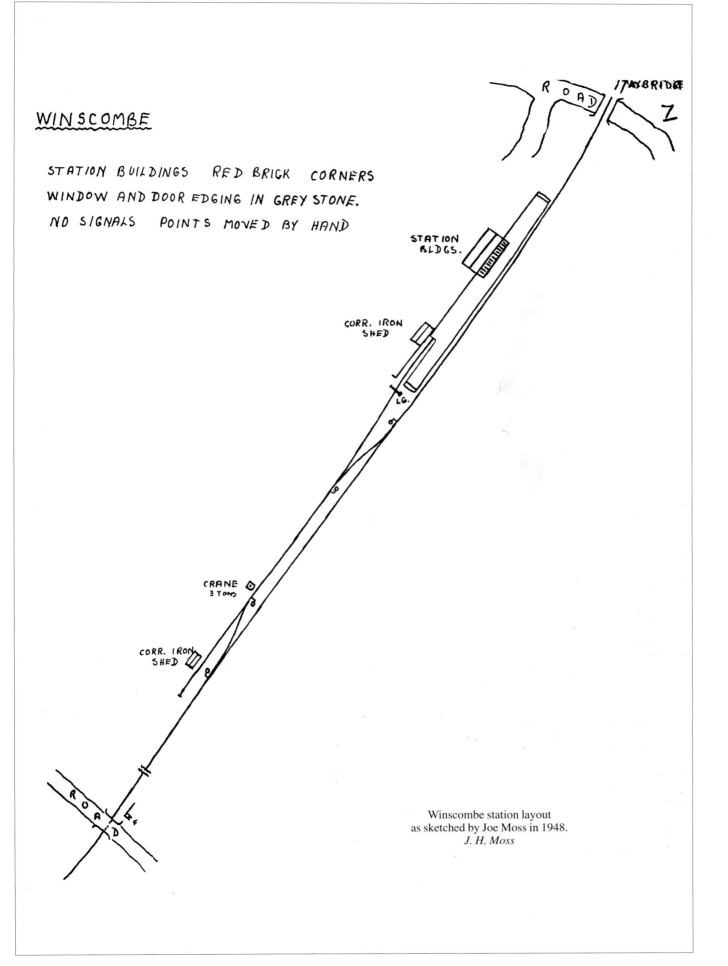

WINSCOMBE

STATION BUILDINGS RED BRICK CORNERS
WINDOW AND DOOR EDGING IN GREY STONE.
NO SIGNALS POINTS MOVED BY HAND

ROAD

ITAYBRIDGE

Z

STATION
BLDGS.

CORR. IRON
SHED

LG.

CRANE
3 TONS

CORR. IRON
SHED

ROAD

Winscombe station layout
as sketched by Joe Moss in 1948.
J. H. Moss

167

Above: Winscombe, as viewed from the station approach in 1955, built in the distinctive style of the GWR. *J. H. Moss*

Below: Winscombe, looking towards Yatton in 1955, showing the single-loop siding on the right, and the 3-ton crane which can be seen at the far end of the siding past the goods wagons. Compared with the 1910 view, the ground frame hut now stands alongside the branch line with another at the far end of the layout in the distance. *J. H. Moss*

Above: Winscombe seems relatively unaltered in this view taken on 13 August 1960 looking towards Axbridge. The building was constructed in the standard design of the GWR in red brick with varying amounts of relief in blue bricks for plinth, corners and window apertures. The large canopy was cantilevered from the wall on a steel frame and made from factory-assembled components with a pitched roof clad in corrugated iron on the front slope, with 'Invincible' glazing on the rear. Commuter traffic to and from Bristol was always prolific from Winscombe. The station was completely demolished c1973. *H. B. Priestley*

Above: The entrance to Winscombe goods yard in 1955 with a clerestory-roofed camping coach standing in the yard. A camping coach was stabled here from 1936 to 1939, then returned from 1952 until 1960. No W9909 was here during the 1950s. *J. H. Moss*

Right: A glance back towards Winscombe from a Wells-Yatton train in May 1948 showing the goods yard and dead-end siding upon which the camping coach was stabled 1936-39 and 1952-60. *J. H. Moss*

Above The station of Sandford & Banwell had originally opened as Sandford until being renamed in December 1869. The station buildings and goods shed were constructed on the down side of the branch line. The goods loop in the foreground opened on 12 December 1905, as did the signalbox in the distance, situated mid-way along the long goods loop. Vast quantities of limestone traffic originating from the nearby Sandford Quarry at Banwell were dealt with here. The signalbox was reduced to a ground frame on 28 October 1963, with the goods loop remaining in use until 1 July 1964. The signalbox/ground frame ultimately closed on 1 October the same year. *Ian Allan Library*

2-6-2T No 5511 (82A) arrives at Sandford and Banwell with a train from Yatton on 21 June 1958. The signalman waits to exchange the single-line tokens with the locomotive fireman. No 5511 had been allocated to Bristol Bath Road in November 1927 until ending her days at Plymouth Laira (83D) in December 1961. The goods loop to the left also allowed freight trains to be 'shut in' when a passenger train was expected. The station buildings have been impeccably restored by Sandford Stone and are now listed as protected buildings, forming part of the impressive showground of the company, which manufactures ornamental garden stoneware that is exported to many countries throughout the world. *Mark Warburton*

SANDFORD & BANWELL

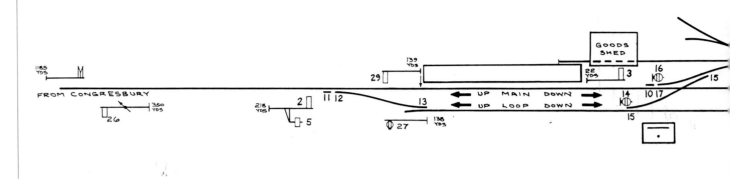

SPACES: 1.8.9.23.24.25.31.

Above: The main station buildings of Sandford & Banwell as viewed from the trackside. The attractive canopy would shelter passengers while awaiting their train to Yatton or Wells. *J. H. Moss*

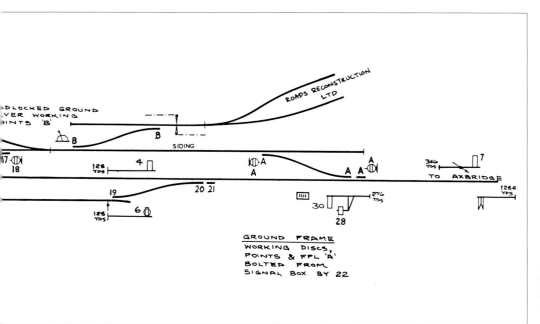

Sandford and Banwell

From Winscombe the line dropped at 1 in 100 giving footplate crews a chance to rally an engine around if they had been having steaming problems on the climb from Axbridge. The line levelled out approximately for one mile before arriving at the single platform of Sandford & Banwell. Opened as Sandford and close to the village of Banwell, the station was renamed Sandford & Banwell in 1869; the name Banwell is pronounced 'Banell' in the local dialect. The platform and station buildings, constructed in the style of the B&E, were situated on the down side of the branch. The goods yard and goods shed were also on the down side of the layout with all the buildings including the stationmaster's house constructed in Mendip stone. A goods loop was completed on 12 December 1905 and a new signalbox replacing the original opened on the same date, situated midway alongside the new loop which was used for goods trains only with reversible working. This allowed traffic to be 'shut in' when a passenger train was expected. A ground frame at the Winscombe end of the loop operated the points and ground signals from the branch to the goods yard headshunt. Considerable limestone traffic was dealt with from the nearby Sandford Quarry at Banwell. Access was gained from the loop via the goods yard as far as the gate to the private line which ran for approximately half a mile to the quarry, crossing the Sandford to Woodborough road on the level. The sidings were in use from 1903 under various quarry owners, the most prolific owning company being Roads Reconstruction. A narrow gauge tramway served the quarry while standard gauge sidings connected with the branch line, the 2ft system closing in 1931 but reopening in 1935 to serve the kilns only, using a Deutz diesel locomotive. Rail traffic was replaced by road vehicles from September 1964.

Standard gauge locomotives operating at the quarry have included:

Bulford, 0-4-0ST Hudswell, Clarke No 1045 of 1914, ex-Sir John Jackson Ltd, Bulford Camp Wiltshire construction contract, c1915. After use at Sandford it went to Selby Oil & Cake Mills Ltd, Yorkshire.
Finetta, 0-4-0ST Avonside No 1565 of 1911, ex-War Department, Codford, Wiltshire October 1919; previously Teign Valley Co. Ltd, Devon. After use at Sandford it went to Conygar Quarries at Clevedon (another Roads Reconstruction concern).
No 1700, Sentinel No 6219 of c1927, an interesting locomotive being a vertical-boilered, geared steam locomotive rebuild of an 0-4-0 Manning Wardle petrol-mechanical locomotive No 1954 of 1918 which arrived by June 1926 from Vobster Quarries near Frome, and was scrapped in August 1960.
No 153, 0-4-0 diesel-mechanical, John Fowler No 19645 of 1932, new to Sandford, then to Roads Reconstruction, Cranmore depot then to New Frome Quarries in 1942; returned to Cranmore depot in 1943.
No 758, 0-4-0ST Vulcan Foundry No 798 of 1876, from A. R. Adams & Son Ltd, Newport, Monmouthshire 1942, then to New Frome Quarry in 1946.
No 1262, four-wheeled geared, vertical-boiler tank locomotive, Sentinel No 9391, new to Sandford in 1949 and then to New Frome Quarry in September 1964.
2ft gauge locomotives have included two 0-4-0 outside-cylinder tank engines from the Avonside Engine Co which are known to have worked here before returning to Cranmore depot; 0-4-2ST Kerr, Stuart No 856 of 1904, ex-Air Ministry, Winchester, Hampshire, by April 1924, then to Sandford from Cranmore depot by January 1927, and returned to Cranmore by March 1931, and 0-6-0 diesel-mechanical Deutz No 88153, returned to Cranmore 1942.

As with other stations on the line, general goods, coal, timber and livestock were handled with 1,665 tons of coal received in 1903 and 14,514 passenger tickets being issued that year, dropping to 3,941 in 1933. The goods yard ceased to handle traffic from 10 June 1963. Approximately three years before closure of the Cheddar Valley line, three loaded wagons of ballast ran away from the quarry, down through the goods shed and smashed the lamp hut on the platform. Under the original deeds of the line with the Bishopric of Bath and Wells, the lamp hut was completely rebuilt to the original 1860s plans, including the intricate bargeboards, roof ends and finials. Staff during the late 1940s and early '50s included Bill Chubb, Jack Frost, and in the late '50s, Jack Leslie. The

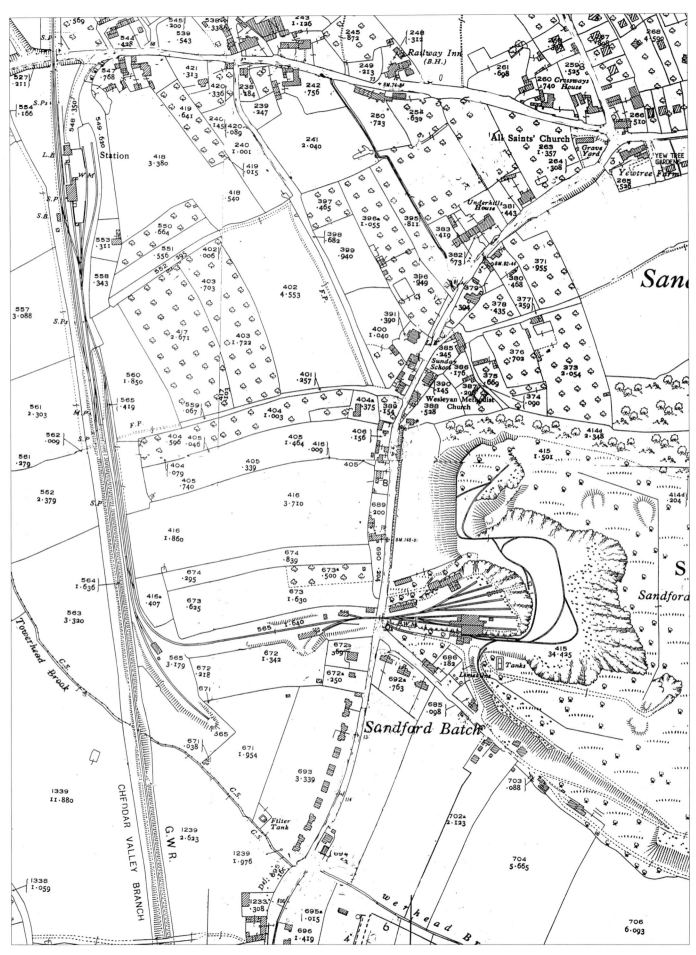

Above: The survey for Sandford & Banwell showing the connection to the quarry. *Crown Copyright Reserved*

Above: Sandford & Banwell station and goods shed, as viewed from the approach road in 1949. A total of 14,514 passenger tickets were issued from here in 1903 with 9,116 parcels being forwarded in the same year. *J. H. Moss*

signalbox was reduced to a ground frame on 28 October 1963, the goods loop remaining in use until 1 July 1964 with the signalbox ultimately closing on 1 October 1964.

Following the lifting of the branch, the station buildings, remarkably, were not demolished, and stand today being impeccably restored by Sandford Stone and are now listed and protected buildings. The architecture of the old Bristol & Exeter buildings is reflected in the quality of the products being manufactured here today. Sandford Stone manufactures ornamental garden stoneware which is exported to many countries including the USA, Japan, Saudi Arabia and Europe. Visitors to the showground can view the products which are reproduced in locally quarried materials, and at the same time wander along the platform to the station building which still has its original interior right down to the

booking office window. The highly decorative B&E barge-boards are still in place as is the varied tile pattern on the roof. The goods shed forms part of the works, and the stationmaster's house, which was located at the rear of the goods yard is still standing and complete. It is well worth having a look around, including having a cup of tea in the cafe and perhaps nostalgically listening for the sound of a whistle as a GWR pannier tank trailing a 'B' set runs in from Congresbury heading for Wells or Cheddar and stops with a squealing of brakes at the platform. Up trains leaving Sandford & Banwell trundled over the stone bridge carrying the line over the A368 Churchill to Weston-super-Mare road before running along fairly level ground to Congresbury. Approaching the station, the main branch line was joined by the Blagdon branch swinging in from the right.

Left: The sound of scraping shovels resounds around Sandford & Banwell station during a quiet moment as the local permanent way gang work on the goods loop near the signalbox in 1949. *J. H. Moss*

Above: The signalbox and goods shed, looking towards Yatton in 1949. The goods yard ceased to handle traffic from 10 June 1963. A Sentinel four-wheel steam locomotive in the livery of Roads Reconstruction, stands on the goods shed road. A standard gauge system operated by the quarry locomotives connected the quarry to the exchange sidings at the station. *J. H. Moss*

Below: Diesel railcar No 32 runs into Sandford & Banwell with a Bristol-bound service in 1949. Part of the meandering quarry line can be seen to the left of the signal behind the railcar. *J. H. Moss*

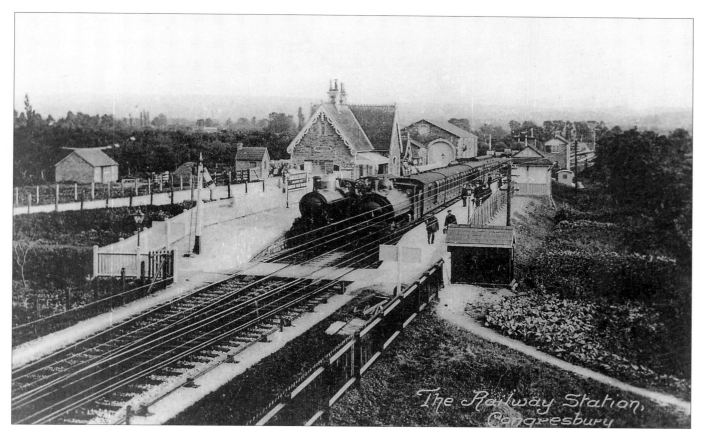

Above: Congresbury, looking north with an 0-6-0 saddle tank heading a Yatton-bound train of six-wheeled carriages and having the road; the starter for the up platform can be seen in the lowered position. This was situated on the down platform for sighting purposes. A freight train also bound for Yatton has been 'shut in', awaiting its turn to proceed. *Author's collection*

Congresbury

The station at Congresbury (the local pronunciation is 'Combesbury') when opened consisted of a single platform and a siding serving a goods shed containing a 2-ton crane. The station was the first block post from Yatton and worked on the train staff and ticket system. With the installation of the ETS system between Witham and Wells in 1896, Congresbury had all the running signals removed and its points locked and unlocked by the Annett's key fitted to the train staff. The small signalbox which stood on the platform to the south of the main building was then closed, remaining in use as a porters' room. The station was lit by oil lamps until closure of the line. With the construction of the Wrington Vale Light Railway, the station area received quite complex alterations which came into use on 14 April 1901 eight months before the branch to Blagdon opened. A separate up platform complete with a cast-iron gents' urinal and timber-built waiting room which had a shallow bay window under a tiled half-gabled roof was installed, plus a crossing loop 640yd in length. A new signalbox standing off the up platform at the Sandford end of the station was also brought into use at the same time. Other new works provided at this time consisted of an additional connection to the goods yard on the down side, with two new up sidings, one of which was a loop. As there was no footbridge, a sleeper crossing was installed between the tracks at the Yatton end of the platforms.

Unusually, in the case of a junction station, no separate bay was provided for the Blagdon services, as it was originally decreed that trains arriving from the branch would run direct to Yatton and connect with the main line services. However, it was decided that for the summer timetable. Blagdon trains would terminate at, and connect with Wells trains at Congresbury. Trains from the up platform proceeding to Yatton were signalled by a starting signal positioned at the Yatton end of the down platform. The layout at the southern end of the station was quite impressive with sidings on either side of the loop, the Blagdon branch curving away to the left and the Wells branch to the right.

Station staff in the 1930s consisted of a stationmaster, two porters and two signalmen, with other porters outstationed at Wrington and Langford attending to the goods traffic and operating level crossing gates. Stationmasters at Congresbury over the years were: 1872-5 William Hunt; 1883-1906 Alfred Hayes; 1910-27 William Braund; 1929-47 William Cockram; 1947-51 Tudor Gibson; 1951-4 J. Hurley and January 1954-September 1963 Arthur Westcott, whose duties also included the Wrington branch, and at a later date, Sandford & Banwell. Arthur Westcott had started on the railway at Wookey in April 1915 as a lad in the office and was a signalman at Axbridge in 1919. Ted Moss and Tom Wheeler were signalmen in the 1930s working shifts 4.40am-12.40pm and 12.40pm until the end of the day. Bob Ford was signalman in the late 1950s. Bill Hodden was the lorry driver in the late '30s. The PW gang in the 1930s included Bob Lawrence, Billy Tinknell, Charlie Buxton, Nobby Clarke, Harry Hayman and Bill Brooks. A fatal accident occurred to members of the PW department in 1875. Three packers and a ganger had been collecting hay from the railway embankments and at 1pm they shunted their platelayers' trolley into Congresbury station to allow the 1.5pm train from Yatton to pass. While this train was waiting at Congresbury, the four men mounted their trolley and

CONGRESBURY

SPACES: 1. 2. 5. 10. 11. 20. 21. 24. 25. 30. 34. 35. 36 37. 41. 43.

Above: When opened in 1869, the station at Congresbury consisted solely of a single platform and station building on the down side of the branch, with a siding serving the goods shed. The station and its layout received complex alterations with the construction of the Wrington Vale Light Railway, all of which came into use on 14 April 1901, eight months before the line to Blagdon opened. A separate up platform complete with a cast-iron gents' urinal and timber-built waiting room was installed, plus a crossing loop 640yd in length. A new signalbox situated at the Sandford end of the up platform was also brought into use at the same time. A footbridge was not provided, passengers having to cross the tracks via the sleeper crossing seen here in the foreground at the Yatton end of the station. Unusually, there was no separate bay provided for the Blagdon trains as it was originally intended that trains arriving from the branch would run direct to Blagdon. However, it was decided that Blagdon trains in the summer timetable would terminate and connect with Cheddar Valley trains at Congresbury. *Ian Allan Library*

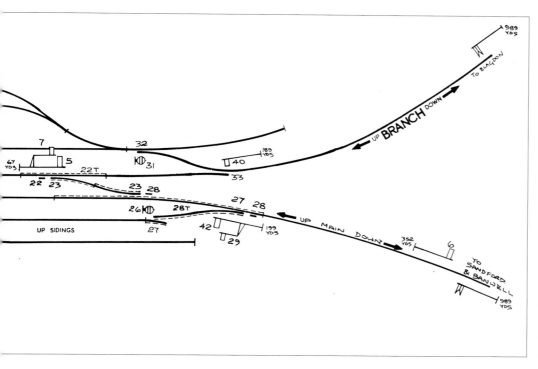

Left: The signalbox diagram for Congresbury after simplification of the junction with the Blagdon branch.
Signalling Record Society

ran it on to the main line, and as the train proceeded towards Wells they got hold of the buffers of the last carriage and fixed the ropes from the trolley to the coupling. As the engine and coaches increased speed, so did the trolley, but before a mile had been traversed, the trolley, for want of sufficient weight to keep it steady, was suddenly jerked with such force as to throw it off the metals and down an embankment. The men were thrown off and rendered for a time insensible. One of the packers, Francis Hemmons, died at the scene. Another packer received a fractured thigh and a severe scalp wound, the ganger suffered fractured ribs, and both men were taken by special train to Weston-super-Mare hospital.

The first train due in the morning was the 3.55am freight train from Bristol West Depot to Wells setting down and picking up wagons for the goods shed, together with traffic for the Wrington line. An engine and brake would arrive from Yatton at 7.36am to work the Wrington Vale goods. The first passenger train arrived at 7.48am (7.15 ex-Wells) for Yatton, followed by the 7.25 from Bristol, booked to arrive at 8.4am. The Wrington goods would return at 8.32 or 9.57 if the train had to go as far as Blagdon, picking up wagons before proceeding to Yatton. At 10.46 the second goods would arrive from Bristol consisting of a station truck from Paddington to Wookey which carried items for Cheddar Valley stations. This train would run direct into the up platform as the following 11.10 Yatton-Wells passenger was booked to pass at Congresbury. Coal, grain, general goods, animal foodstuffs, fertilisers, basic slag, and agricultural machinery were dealt with in the goods yard. Cheddar cheese would arrive in the brake vans of passenger trains for the local shops. A camping coach was stabled in the loading

Above: A view taken from the down platform at Congresbury, showing the diverging routes in the distance, with the Wrington line going straight ahead and the Cheddar Valley route swinging to the right. A clerestory-roofed camping coach can be glimpsed to the left near the goods shed; the coach was later removed to a siding near the signalbox. *Author's collection*

Above: A 2-6-2T bursts under the A370 roadbridge and arrives at Congresbury on 23 June 1953 with the 6.10pm Yatton-Frome. As with most stations along the line, carefully tended allotments were to be found, as seen here behind the up platform to the right. *P. J. Garland collection*

Below: The junction and sidings at Congresbury showing the simplified layout dating from July 1949 when the original scissors crossover, which enabled passenger trains from Blagdon to gain access to the up platform was removed. The camping coach can be seen to the right standing on the No 2 siding showing the steps provided for the occupants. The left-hand arm on the bracket signal is for the Wrington line, with the Cheddar Valley arm to the right. The section between Congresbury and Wrington closed on 10 June 1963 and the track was removed in May the following year. *J. H. Moss*

Above: Smoke and steam issue from a Prairie tank working a Yatton–Wells 'B' set bunker-first at Congresbury in 1952. The starting signal arm is lowered giving passage onwards to the advanced starting signal and the next station stop at Sandford & Banwell. The signalman is seen on the platform chatting to the footplate crew having exchanged the single-line tablets. The corrugated iron lamp hut to the left contained the oil barrel used for the station lamps and signals. *J. H. Moss*

Below: The signalbox at Congresbury, built for the alteration of the layout at the station for the Wrington Vale line, came into use on 14 April 1901, eight months before the line to Blagdon opened. Electric key token working was in use to Yatton West and Sandford & Banwell with a wooden train staff to Blagdon. The EKT working was replaced by 'one train' working from October 1963 with the box closing on 1 October the following year. *J. H. Moss*

181

An up train headed by No 5548 departs from Congresbury on 23 June 1953 with an up service to Bristol. The regular 'B' set has been strengthened with two bogie 'Siphons' and a 'Fruit D' which will be conveying strawberries collected from Cheddar and Axbridge. I worked on this locomotive as a fireman at Yeovil Town when the locomotives were re-allocated from the ex-GWR shed at Yeovil Pen Mill which closed in 1959. I found No 5548 and sister locomotive No 5563 to be good steaming engines when working the Taunton branch and the Evershot bankers. *P. J. Garland collection*

Above: The 'board' has already been lowered for the Cheddar Valley line as the 'Home Counties' excursion special hauled by 2-6-2Ts Nos 4103 and 6148 arrives at Congresbury on Sunday, 6 October 1963. The signalman stands at the trackside preparing to exchange single-line tablets with the footplatemen. Passenger services had been withdrawn the previous month, on the 9th. *R. E. Toop*

bay at the rear of the down platform on the backshunt from the goods shed, but was later moved to a siding to the south of the signalbox. The camping coach was in use at the station from 1935 until 1939, returning in 1952 and lasting until 1962. Coach No W9901 was noted at the station on 8 July 1959 and 15 September 1962.

The Wrington Vale Light Railway, 6 miles 41 chains long, was opened on 4 December 1901 but a special train organised by Mr C. Kislingbury the GWR Divisional Superintendent using the divisional engineer's inspection saloon had conveyed the members of the Press to Blagdon on 25 November. On the opening day, 4 December, a total of 1,500 passengers were carried, but apart from transporting heavy equipment for the reservoir at Blagdon in its early days, the line led a rather quiet existence in the peaceful Somerset countryside for many years. There was no signalling on the branch, except for fixed distant signals as the branch was worked as 'one engine in steam'. A wooden token issued from Congresbury signalbox as the driver's authority, had an Annett's key to unlock the sidings at the stations. From the opening, the line had its own engine and rolling stock, a 2-4-0 side tank No 1384 dating from 1876 and built by Sharp, Stewart for the Watlington & Princes Risborough Railway, which worked the branch for a few weeks before being transferred to the Culm Valley Railway. Known as *Hesperus*, the locomotive ended its days on the Weston, Clevedon & Portishead Railway where it was scrapped in 1937. Rolling stock on the line consisted of old GWR four-wheelers specially fitted with lower than normal step boards for the low platforms. A '517' class 0-4-2T worked the line and on occasions a 'Metro' 2-4-0T was used. The service initially consisted of four trains each way per day, departing Yatton at 8.40am, 11.50am, 3.30pm and 6.50pm, stopping at all stations. Services from Blagdon

were at 8am, 9.35am, 2.35 and 5.20pm. Two of the trains, the 11.50am ex-Yatton and 5.20pm from Blagdon, were run as mixed when required, but if the goods traffic was too heavy then a special freight train would run. Passenger services were reduced to three each way from 1919 but from October 1921 the Clevedon railmotor made an early afternoon return trip from Yatton, thus returning the service to four trains each way. Thirty minutes were allowed for passenger trains to complete the 8-mile journey from Yatton to Blagdon and all trains were subject to a limit of 25mph except when approaching the ungated level crossings when a 10mph limit applied. The only two level crossings equipped with gates were Wrington and Langford.

There were no embankments or cuttings between Congresbury and Wrington, the line due to its light railway construction following the contours of the land, at times giving a switchback ride for the passengers. The only severe gradient, at 1 in 50, lay between Langford and Burrington where chaired bullhead rail was used to stop rail creep, the rest of the branch being laid with lightweight flat-bottom rail spiked to the sleepers. With the closure of the shed at Blagdon in 1924, train timings were altered to favour the locomotive starting from Yatton, but services remained at four trains per day including a Sunday milk train. That old enemy in the shape of the motor omnibus began poaching traffic when buses direct to Bristol started from Blagdon on 22 December 1922, and from Wrington the following year on 19 May. The GWR began an early morning Mondays only service from Yatton at 7.20am (return departure, Wrington at 7.38am) in the autumn of 1926. This was not a success and was withdrawn from 4 July 1927. Service levels remained at four trains each way per day, including the Sunday milk train, until complete withdrawal of passenger trains occurred on 14 September 1931.

Former Worcester (85A) allocated BR Standard 2-6-2T No 82038 (82A) runs past the signalbox at Congresbury arriving with a Wells–Yatton train on 20 August 1960. Part of the platelayers' hut used as a tool store can be glimpsed behind the signalbox. *R. E. Toop*

Class 5700 0-6-0 pannier tank No 7772 awaits passage from Congresbury with the 1.30pm SO Witham-Yatton as Ivatt 2-6-2T No 41207 arrives with the 2.45pm Yatton-Wells-Witham. No 7772 was allocated to Aberdare in March 1931 and spent most of its working life in South Wales including being based at Merthyr shed before ending its days at Stourbridge in November 1961. The overbridge carrying the A370 Weston-super-Mare to Bristol road over the line was completely demolished when major road improvements took place over the course of the railway, of which nothing now exists at this site. *R. E. Toop*

Above: Having arrived with an up pick-up goods and with part of its train standing on the main branch line, St Philips Marsh-allocated 2-6-0 No 46506 pulls forward and prepares to shunt into the down goods yard at Congresbury on 19 August 1957. *H. B. Priestley*

Below: With the vista of the Mendip Hills looming in the distance, we view the remains of the former station at Congresbury. The up loop was taken out of use on 1 July 1964 with the signalbox demolished in April the following year along with the waiting room on the up platform. The Cheddar Valley line closed completely between Yatton and Cheddar on 1 October 1964. The main station buildings were demolished in October 1968 and nothing remains today of Congresbury station except for a few remnants of masonry strewn amongst the undergrowth. *R. C. Riley*

Wrington Vale Railway

WRINGTON STATION

Above: The Wrington Vale Light Railway, 6 miles 41 chains in length, opened on 4 December 1901. In this view of Wrington, looking towards Blagdon, passengers and staff await the next train at the distinctive station building, and the low height of the platforms (2ft 6in) is evident. A substantial coal traffic was dealt with in the goods yard. The building behind the platform proclaims the name Barber Brothers, coal and coke merchants. *Author's collection*

Wrington

After leaving Congresbury the line curved east, continuing in a straight line for two miles and traversing two level crossings before running across the gated crossing at Station Road and into Wrington station. As with all stations on the line, the single platform was only 2ft 6in high, upon which a single-storey building in red brick and half-timber to the standard GWR design was situated. The roof was carried down over the eaves on the platform side to make a simple canopy. A cast-iron gents' urinal and a corrugated iron parcels shed complemented the platform. The station was oil-lit from opening until closure. A total of 11,020 passenger tickets were issued in 1903, with 3,606 parcels being forwarded, rising to a maximum of 10,128 parcels in 1913. Thirteen trucks of livestock were handled in 1903 compared with a total of 56 in 1923. Milk churn traffic was also catered for, as was a considerable trade in coal traffic for Tincknell the local coal agent. A goods loop, siding and loading dock were situated on the down side at the Blagdon end of the station. The only yard crane on the branch was installed here and was rated at 30cwt.

Before the opening of the Wrington Vale line, a two-horse omnibus operated by Mr Henry Player of Wrington ran to Yatton station, departing from the Golden Lion, Wrington at 8am, 12.15 and 5.50pm, returning from Yatton at 9.45am,

1.15 and 6.50pm. The fares each way were 9d inside and 6d outside. It was at the Golden Lion that the men of Somerset 'challenged the rest of the world' to meet them at cudgel playing in 1780. Mr W. G. Gait was the stationmaster in October 1923, and was appointed stationmaster for the whole line when they were withdrawn from all of the stations except Wrington in 1925. The senior porters at each station were then made responsible to the Wrington stationmaster. However, from 1936 only the porter at Wrington remained on the line, his duties including the handling of freight traffic and operating the crossing gates. After opening the gates at Wrington for the daily goods, he then travelled with the train to Langford opening the gates across the A38, travelling to Blagdon and repeating the process on the return journey. Class 5800 0-4-2T No 5809 was seen on the line on 31 August 1950 returning to Congresbury with seven wagons and a brake van. A regular Monday to Friday daily freight train was diagrammed at this time as there was sufficient coal and other traffic to justify the service on most weekdays, which was in the hands of Dean Goods, 2-4-0s and 0-4-2 tanks. The line was closed between Wrington and Blagdon on 1 November that same year. A visitor to Wrington station in 1954 noticed that about a dozen coal wagons were in the yard, with the layout consisting at that time of a run-round loop just beyond the platform with one siding, and that the trackwork had recently been relaid. The station had been demolished.

The RCTS ran a special train to Wrington on 28 April. Starting from Waterloo the train ran via Reading to Bristol whereupon two Ivatt 2-6-2Ts, Nos 41202 and 41203, hauled it to Wrington. The section between Congresbury and Wrington was closed on 10 June 1963 and the track removed in May 1964. With passenger services ceasing between Yatton and Witham in September 1963 the electric token working was replaced by 'one train' operation from October of the same year. The up loop was taken out of use on 1 July 1964 with the signalbox at Congresbury closing on 1 October, the Cheddar Valley line closing completely from Yatton to just west of Cheddar on the same day. The signalbox was demolished in April 1965 along with the up waiting room. The cast-iron gents' toilet which had previously stood on the platform had been removed in the 1950s, and the main station buildings were demolished in October 1968. Today, nothing remains of Congresbury station except for a few remnants of stonework.

Above: The branch train from Blagdon arrives at Wrington in 1903 formed of the usual set of three four-wheeled coaches. Note how the station roof is carried down over the eaves to form a rudimentary canopy. A total of 11,020 passenger tickets were issued in 1903. The stationmasters at all of the stations on the branch except Wrington were withdrawn in 1925, leaving the senior porters at each station responsible to the Wrington stationmaster. The line was abandoned between Wrington and Blagdon on 1 November 1950 with the track between Congresbury and Wrington being removed in May 1964. *R. Lacey collection*

Below: Shunting takes place in the goods yard at Wrington in 1940. The station had the only crane on the branch, which was rated at 30cwt. *Ian Allan Library*

Above: Langford station, looking towards the level crossing gates across the A38 which caused considerable delay when the road became a major trunk route between Bristol and Exeter. From here, the line climbed towards Burrington at 1 in 50 for approximately one mile. The station building was demolished in 1958 but the platform and one level crossing gate could still be seen in 1999. *R. Lacey collection*

Langford

From Wrington the line curved sharply, running southwards as far as Langford station. The station building again, as with Wrington, was constructed in red brick and half-timber, with the roof of the structure carried down over the eaves to give a simple canopy. Standard oil lamps of GWR style, speared finial railings, cast-iron gents' toilet, wooden seats and the usual white-on-black cast-iron nameboards completed the scene. The goods loop and siding was situated on the down side of the line prior to the station as approached from Wrington. Coal for local traders was received, although there was only one wagonload of livestock in 1903 compared with 11 in 1911. The goods yard was a collection point for salvaged metal during World War 2. Trains departing for Burrington crossed the A38 over the gated level crossing causing many hold-ups to vehicular traffic when this road became a major trunk route between Bristol and Exeter. The station building was demolished in 1958 but the keen observer could still see the platform and one level crossing gate in 1999.

Left: A view of Langford station, looking towards Wrington, showing the building constructed in timber and brick. The goods loop and siding situated on the down side of the line can be seen in the distance. *R. Lacey collection*

Above: Burrington station, looking towards Langford in 1949. The goods loop, part of which can be seen on the left, came into use to deal with coal and general goods traffic on 1 December 1903, at the Blagdon end of the platform which was devoid of any buildings until 26 September 1907. The station house seen in the background, also came into use the same year. An annual excursion from Bristol was run for many years, conveying worshippers to the spot in Burrington Combe where the well known hymn 'Rock of Ages' was inspired. The station building was demolished in 1958 but the station house remains. *Ian Allan Library*

Left: The Reverend Augustus Toplady, the vicar of Burrington 1762-4, when taking shelter from a storm in the cleft of a rock in nearby Burrington Combe was inspired to compose the famous and beautiful hymn 'Rock of Ages, cleft for me, Let me hide myself in Thee'. The location was known henceforth as the Rock of Ages. *Author's collection*

Rock of Ages. Burrington Combe

THE REV. TOPLADY.

When taking shelter in a cleft of the Rock during a Storm, composed the famous Hymn, "Rock of Ages, cleft for me, Let me hide myself in Thee."

Burrington

From Langford the line climbed towards Burrington at 1 in 50 for approximately one mile before running under an overbridge and into the station which was situated in a cutting. The gradient would at times make the Clevedon steam railmotor run short of steam. The platform was devoid of any buildings until 26 September 1907. It was when sheltering from a thunderstorm in the cleft of a rock in Burrington Combe that the Rev Augustus Toplady, then vicar of Burrington (1762-4), was inspired to write the well-known hymn 'Rock of Ages, cleft for me'. An annual excursion was run from Bristol for many years to convey worshippers to the spot where the hymn had been composed.

A goods loop opened on 1 December 1903 at the Blagdon end of the station to deal with coal and general goods traffic. Milk traffic in churns was handled at the platform. A station house situated near the road junction by the road bridge was built in 1907. In 1903, 4,800 passenger tickets were issued and 12,093 parcels forwarded from the station. Goods facilities were withdrawn on 1 November 1950. The station building was demolished in 1958 but the station house remains occupied.

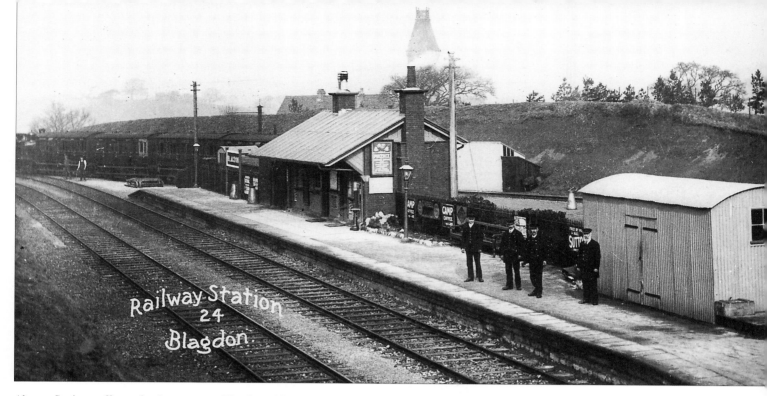

Above: Station staff pose for the camera at Blagdon while the locomotive shunts its coaching stock into the goods yard and it seems that a six-wheeled coach has been added to the normal four-wheeled stock. The similar style of station building to Wrington and Langford is evident. The corrugated iron building on the platform formed the goods shed. A locomotive was allocated here until 21 March 1934 when it and the footplatemen were transferred to Yatton. *R. Lacey collection*

Blagdon

The line turned east towards the terminus at Blagdon and approximately half a mile before the station a short spur diverged off the branch on the down side, descending at 1 in 30 before branching into four terminal tracks at the Bristol Waterworks yard, which had originally been installed for the building of the pumping station for the reservoir. Four compound beam engines built and erected by Glenfield & Kennedy of Kilmarnock operated the pumps. Coal traffic was delivered by rail until 1931 and the four terminal sidings were lifted soon after. Mekin & Dean, the contractors for the building of the reservoir which was under construction from 1899 until 1901, used the following standard-gauge locomotives: 0-6-0ST (inside cylinder) Manning, Wardle No 21 of 1861, ex-Birkenhead contract Cheshire, and after the end of the Blagdon contract it went to the Hundred of Manhood & Selsey Tramway, Sussex as No 2 *Sidlesham* c1907. 0-4-0ST Beyer Peacock No 1736 of 1877 went new to the works and was then sent to Farrington Collieries, Somerset between Farrington Gurney and Paulton, in 1885.

A narrow gauge tramway was used in the maintenance of the reservoir after its completion, with the equipment remaining on site out of use for many years until final disposal in 1971, when the locomotive was acquired for preservation. It is now at the Abbey Light Railway in Leeds. The gauge was 600mm and the locomotive was an 0-4-0 petrol-mechanical, built by Baguley Cars Ltd, Burton-on-Trent (No 736 of 1918).

A small siding near the junction of the spur served Coombe Lodge, the home of the Wills family, and the estate of Lord Winterstoke of the famous Bristol Tobacco Co. He took his title from Winterstoke Hundred in which the village of Blagdon is situated. Unfortunately the noble lord died childless in 1911 and his barony became extinct. Coombe Lodge was rebuilt in imitation Tudor style in 1930-2. The area was known locally as 'Imperial Valley' as the profits made by tobacco generated much of the local wealth. Half a mile further on, climbing at 1 in 75, the line ended at the terminus which lay in a shallow hollow with the station building set on a single platform, as at Wrington and Langford. A run-round loop, mileage sidings and a loading dock comprised the station layout which included a corrugated iron goods shed set on the platform at the terminal end. A locomotive was allocated here until 31 March 1924 when transferred to Yatton with the men.

The drivers at the Blagdon stabling point before closure in 1924 included Driver Oliver Oliver, consequently known as 'Twice Oliver'. The fireman was Mr Boyce and there were two firemen at Blagdon, one being a passed fireman. Although mention has been made in the past of an engine shed which burnt down in 1912, there is no evidence either in photographs or plans of such a building. Driver Arthur Jones, Fireman Frank Slater and Guard Bert Maslen worked the last passenger train in 1931.

Extra traffic was dealt with when a sack factory making sandbags was set up nearby during World War 2. Goods facilities lasted until 1 November 1950 when the line beyond Wrington was abandoned. A camping coach was a feature of the station for many years, and when the line closed to passenger traffic, the campers were advised to travel from Bristol by bus! Linen for the camping coach arrived at Congresbury from the GWR laundry at Swindon by passenger train, to be taken to Blagdon in the guard's van of the daily goods along with water and oil for the lamps.

The station is now in private ownership and has been beautifully restored and integrated into a two-storey extension which has been tastefully designed and constructed, and in no way detracts from the original building.

The Great Western Railway withdrew the passenger service from the branch on 14 September 1931 and from this date a daily goods train ran until 7 June 1963. The line was abandoned between Wrington and Blagdon on 1 November 1950 and lifted between January and April 1952.

A camping coach, seen here in the goods yard, was a feature at Blagdon for many years, and after the withdrawal of passenger traffic the intrepid campers were advised by the GWR to travel from Bristol by bus. An old grounded coach body can be seen behind the platform. The track was lifted between Wrington and Blagdon between January and April 1952. *R. Lacey collection*

WRINGTON VALE LIGHT RAILWAY.

Down Trains.		a.m.		a.m.			p.m.		p.m.		Up Trains.		a.m.		a.m.		p.m.		p.m.	
Yatton	dep.	8 40	...	11 50		...	3 50	...	6 50		Blagdon	dep.	8 0	...	9 35	...	2 35	...	5 20	
Congresbury	,,	8 44	.	12 0		.	3 54	.	6 54		Burrington	,,	8 4	.	9 39	...	2 39	.	5 24	
Wrington	,,	8 52	...	12 11	Mixed	...	4 2	.	7 2		Langford	,,	8 8	.	9 43	...	2 43	...	5 30	Mixed
Langford	,,	8 59	.	12 23		.	4 9	.	7 9		Wrington	,,	8 14	.	9 49	...	2 49	.	5 40	
Burrington	,,	9 5	...	12 34		.	4 15	...	7 15		Congresbury	,,	8 24	...	9 59	...	2 59	.	6 0	
Blagdon	arr.	9 10		12 40			4 20		7 20		Yatton	arr.	8 30	...	10 6	...	3 6	.	6 7	

**On Bank Holidays several Trains shewn in these Tables will not run, and others will run at altered times.—
See Special Announcement.**

Above: Timetable for the Wrington Vale Light Railway for 1902.

Above: Looking towards the terminus at Blagdon which lay in a small hollow, with the run-round loop to the right and the goods yard to the left. A total of 9,419 passenger tickets were issued in 1903. *Ian Allan Library*

Above: A closer view of the station building and platform at Blagdon on 22 May 1929 with '517' class 0-4-2T No 540 awaiting departure with the 7.20pm for Yatton. This locomotive, dating from January 1869, was allocated to Llanfyllin in 1922 before being moved to St Philips Marsh from where she was withdrawn from service in May 1933. Passenger services were withdrawn from the Wrington Vale line on 14 September 1931. *Rail Archive Stephenson*

Above: Weeds cover the run-round loop at Blagdon c1949, the station building looking in remarkably good condition after the withdrawal of passenger services in 1931; the building survives today in private ownership. *J. H. Moss*

Below: The rear of the station building and platform at Blagdon in 1949 showing the lifted goods yard. This view shows the construction of the roof on the platform side of the building which was carried over the eaves to form a rudimentary canopy. *J. H. Moss*

Above: 'Bulldog' class 4-4-0 No 3451 *Pelican* stands at Yatton on 9 September 1929 with a Bristol-Exeter stopping passenger train. The locomotive, dating from January 1910, was one of the final batch named after birds (Nos 3441-55) to emerge in 1909-10. Originally numbered 3741, renumbering to 3451 occurred in 1912. Previously allocated to Weymouth, the locomotive ended its days at Exeter shed from where it was withdrawn in April 1951. *H. B. Priestley*

Yatton and the Clevedon Branch

Trains leaving Congresbury for Yatton passed under a roadbridge carrying the A370 Weston-super-Mare to Bristol road with a short run over level ground for approximately 1½ miles before running into Yatton station. The Yatton up Cheddar fixed distant was situated 1,194yd from Yatton West signalbox. Trains from Yatton passed a loop siding operated by a ground frame released by a key on the EK token, then approached a bracket signal which would guide Cheddar services either across the junction with the main lines into the up platform, or into the Cheddar bay alongside the down platform. A small shunt signal on the same bracket signal would usher a light engine or freight into one of two sidings lying between the Cheddar bay and the loading dock, from where access to the goods shed and turntable road was gained.

The Bristol & Exeter Railway Co was inaugurated under the Act of 19 May 1836 to construct a double line from the GWR 'in a certain field called Temple Mead' to meadows in the Parish of St Thomas in Exeter. The choice of gauge was not finally decided upon until a meeting on 5 March 1839 confirmed that the line was to be constructed to the broad gauge. Due to financial troubles and being unable to fund rolling stock, the B&E decided in March 1840 that the line should be leased to the GWR which would work the services and retain half the gross receipts, although staff and virtually everything else were to be provided by the B&E. The line was complete as far as Bridgwater in May 1841 with public traffic starting on 14 June which was 16 days

before the GWR main line from London to Bristol was fully completed. Taunton welcomed the railway on 1 July the following year, and it opened through to Exeter on 1 May 1844. Isambard Kingdom Brunel was engineer, although his assistant, William Gravatt, did much of the work on the line which was impeccably laid out, and unusually for a main trunk route, constructed without an application for additional capital. The GWR showpiece express covered the 194 miles from Paddington to Exeter in five hours during March 1845. Two months later this timing was reduced to 4½ hours. By 1848, Daniel Gooch's 8ft singles were accomplishing the London to Bristol section in 2½ hours. The 'Flying Dutchman', named after the Derby winner of 1849, was at that time the crack express running between Bristol and Exeter.

The GWR started running its first new express for 17 years in 1879 between Paddington and Plymouth, and as this was the year of the Zulu War, the train soon received the nickname 'Zulu'. The Bristol & Exeter did not start working its own services until 1 May 1849 with 28 locomotives to the design of Gooch, and a steam railcar, after which date the GWR did not work services west of Bristol or east of Exeter. Through trains of Great Western stock were hauled between the two cities by locomotives of the B&E, this state of affairs lasting until the GWR and the B&E amalgamated in January 1876. The B&E engineer, C. H. Gregory was in charge until James Pearson, previously the Atmospheric Superintendent on the South Devon Railway, was appointed Locomotive Superintendent in May 1850. Locomotive workshops were built by the B&E at Bristol, opening in September 1854. The B&E operated 4-2-2 express engines

Above: Main line trains are signalled in both directions as a 2-6-2T stands in the Cheddar Valley bay at Yatton with a train for Witham during the 1930s. The station opened as Clevedon Road with the public opening of the line to Bridgwater on 14 June 1841. The branch to Clevedon opened on 28 July 1847, becoming one of the earliest GWR branch lines and the main line station was renamed Yatton from the same date. The handsome overall roof over the Clevedon bay to the left of the up platform was removed in 1956. A staff of over 40 was employed at the station including four locomotive crews and two shedmen. *Ian Allan Library*

Below: Looking towards Bristol at Yatton as No 1454 (82A) stands in the Clevedon bay complete with auto-train while the up starter and Yatton East up distant signals have been lowered for a Bristol-bound train. *J. H. Moss*

Above: Lower quadrant signals abound at Yatton as Cardiff Canton (86C)-allocated 'Hall' class 4-6-0 No 4913 *Baglan Hall* approaches with an up empty stock train in 1957. The Clevedon auto-train headed by No 1454 is seen to the right. The signal arm with holes at the end of the up platform is a backing signal. Coaching stock can be seen stabled on the Cheddar Valley branch to the far left. *J. H. Moss*

which were smaller versions of the Gooch 'Iron Duke' class with their 7ft 6in driving wheels, with the first 10 constructed by Stothert & Slaughter and the others by Longridge & Co. Also used were 0-6-0 tender goods engines, as well as five 2-2-2 tank engines, which were the first locomotives designed by Pearson. Probably the most well known of his designs were the 4-2-4 back and well tanks. These famous 'nine footers' built for the Exeter expresses were the fastest locomotives of their day.

The station at Yatton opened as Clevedon Road in anticipation of a line opening to the fashionable Victorian resort of Clevedon when public services started to Bridgwater on 14 June 1841. The main station buildings were located on the up platform with a footbridge connecting the two platforms at the Bristol end of the station. The broad gauge, 3 mile 45 chain branch to Clevedon opened on 28 July 1847, the main line station being renamed Yatton from the same date. The branch was worked by the GWR under the original agreement of 1840. This was one of the GWR's earliest branch lines and was converted from broad to standard gauge on Sunday, 28 September 1879. Clevedon trains used a bay complete with an overall roof at the rear of the up platform at Yatton.

Mixed gauge was laid to Bristol and Taunton in 1875, extending to Exeter in March the following year. With the opening of the line to Cheddar, a bay was provided at the rear of the down platform for the services. Work on the 17 mile 55 chain-long route had started in March 1867, and by 1868 it was reported that rapid progress had been made and by June all the cuttings were completed. Two locomotives were in use by the contractor and all the overbridges were constructed for a double line, although only single track was

laid. The contractor's estimate was over £100,000 but this did not include the cost of rails, sleepers and land. Colonel Yolland of the Board of Trade inspected and passed the new line on 30 July 1869 and on the opening day, 3 August, a special train conveying the Earl of Devon, the chairman of the Bristol & Exeter Railway and other directors, departed from Bristol at 11am and arrived at Yatton in fine style before journeying down the branch to Cheddar. The temporary terminus of the line at Cheddar was described as incomplete, and after a short stop for refreshments including champagne and cake, returned to Bristol. B&E 4-4-0 saddle tanks hauling four-wheeled coaches worked the service. The line was extended to Wells, opening on Tuesday, 5 April the following year, having been inspected by Captain Tyler, representing the Board of Trade, on the previous Saturday in company with Mr Wall, General Traffic Manager of the B&E. The station layout had been expanded considerably by 1898 with a goods shed on the down side of the station complete with sidings adjacent to the Cheddar line while alongside the down main, west of the junction with this line, were loading docks and further sidings. The up side of the station had also been developed with sidings laid alongside the up main line on the Bridgwater side of the West signal-box and adjacent to the Clevedon branch.

A combined engine and carriage spent most of its short life on the Clevedon, Tiverton and Weston branch lines. Built by W. B. Adams at the Fairfield Works, Bow, London to the order of the B&E engineer Mr C. H. Gregory in 1848 and known as *Fairfield*, this early form of railcar consisted of a carriage mounted on four 3ft 6in wheels with accommodation for 16 first and 32 second class passengers. It was attached to an articulated platform which supported a vertical tubular

Above: One of the legendary 'Star' ('4000' class) 4-6-0s, No 4056 *Princess Margaret* (82A), arrives at Yatton with a down stopper on 25 May 1953. No 4056 was held in high regard by footplatemen and was known as the best 'Castle' that Bristol Bath Road ever had, reflecting the small margin in performance between the 'Stars' and the 'Castles', although the latter were larger and more modern with a vast improvement in power output. *R. C. Riley*

Below: The coronation of HM Queen Elizabeth II in 1953 was a cause of happiness and celebration throughout the land, and the outstanding display seen in the station gardens at Yatton on 25 May 1953 was no exception. *R. C. Riley*

Above: A train hauled by '4575' class 2-6-2T No 5547 arrives from the Cheddar Valley branch, and crosses over to the up main line near the West signalbox at Yatton on 30 August 1958. An auto-fitted member of the same class, No 5529, can be seen behind the signalbox. *Mark Warburton*

boiler, with cylinders set horizontally driving the single driving wheels of 4ft 6in diameter. The combination was 40ft long, with the coach portion having wooden wheels, and painted sky blue. Trials by the GWR took place on the West London Railway. Daniel Gooch noted: 'It is a very small engine and carriage all in one frame but is of little use.' The railcar began working on the Tiverton branch after 1 May 1849 before working later on the Clevedon branch. Alteration to the vehicle came in 1851 when the engine was separated from the carriage and a pair of 3ft trailing wheels provided. The B&E sold *Fairfield* in 1856 to Hutchinson & Ritson (contractors to the Yeovil branch, and owners of a timber creosoting plant at Bridgwater) after converting it into a four-wheel coupled locomotive, for £600.

Small 2-2-2 tanks constructed by Longridge in 1851 for the B&E, were also used on the Clevedon branch until the gauge conversion. The final conversion of the broad gauge took place on Saturday, 21 and Sunday, 22 May 1892 with 177 miles of broad gauge trackwork altered to the standard gauge between Exeter and Penzance by 4,000 men drafted in from all parts of the system. By this time there was mixed gauge track from Paddington to Exeter and from Truro to Penzance. The last broad gauge train to leave London for Penzance, the 10.15am 'Cornishman' was hauled by *Great Western* on the 20th. The final down train of them all was the 5pm Paddington to Plymouth headed by 4-2-2 *Bulkeley*, this locomotive also hauling the last train into Paddington, the up mail which arrived at 5.30am the next morning. All the broad gauge rolling stock standing between Penzance and Exeter was collected and stabled in various sidings east of Exeter, to be worked over the mixed gauge to the reception sidings specially prepared at Swindon. What a sight for a spectator standing on the platform at Yatton, as train after train of broad gauge stock trundled through for the very last time heading for the scrapyard at Swindon!

Four-wheeled carriages in sets of three or four were the norm, hauled by '517' class 0-4-2Ts (Nos 528 and 1433 are known to have been used) until 1908 when they were replaced by steam railmotors. Two of these were stationed at Yatton and one worked a daily service to Swindon. Other destinations worked by the railcars included Blagdon, Wells and Highbridge. Four cars were based at Yatton for part of 1909-10, then this reverted to two. The summer of 1911 had the Yatton steam railmotor working the Clevedon line on Sundays only, as during weekdays it worked the Swindon trip which was a long haul, out via Badminton and return through Chippenham, as well as a trip to Avonmouth. A Bath-based car at this time worked the weekday Clevedon services. The locomotive allocation for Yatton in 1921 included one steam railmotor, No 95, 'Metro' 2-4-0T No 630 and '517' class 0-4-2T No 1428. Two cars were allocated for part of 1923, one for part of 1925 and one from December 1927 to August 1929. After that date a Bristol-based car worked the branch with No 92 being recorded at work on the line on 2 March 1935, with all steam railmotor services withdrawn from the autumn of the same year and replaced by push-and-pull sets. Class 5800 0-4-2T No 5800 and '4575' class 2-6-2T No 5529 were allocated here in 1934. The allocation for 1947 was 2-6-2T No 4563 and 0-4-2Ts Nos 1415 and 1463. Prairie tank No 5527 was recorded on shed in May 1953. Other members of the '14xx' class 0-4-2Ts at work on the branch in the 1950s included Nos 1402 and 1454 while Nos 1463 and 5813 were recorded on shed in March 1956. Replacing an earlier broad gauge depot, the locomotive shed opened in 1879. Measuring 70ft by 16ft, it was constructed in stone under a slate roof and was situated west of the station on the Clevedon branch. An old grounded broad gauge van body situated behind the shed was the locomen's cabin until a new cabin was constructed. Four locomotive crews and two shedmen formed

Above: Yatton West signalbox pictured here on 2 September 1963 showing the diverging routes to the Cheddar Valley line on the left, and Clevedon to the right. *Scrimgeour Collection-Signalling Record Society*

Below: The interior of Yatton West signalbox on 2 September 1963 showing the spick and span condition and polished floor so typical of the mechanical boxes. Levers have been pulled for an arriving service, and the signalman, with cloth in hand, stands at the end of the 129-lever frame watching for the indicator lamps to light up on the diagram box as the approaching train enters the 'circuit'. He will then reverse the levers into the frame, placing signal arms at danger to protect the train. This was a busy signalbox with the sounds of ringing telephones and block bells resounding around the interior, along with the slamming of signal levers. *Scrimgeour Collection-Signalling Record Society*

Above: The 129-lever signalbox photographed on 2 September 1963, received the suffix 'West' from 6 April 1925. The line to Clevedon can be seen passing under the road bridge to the right. *Scrimgeour Collection-Signalling Record Society*

the shed staff in the 1950s. Closure came on 7 August 1960 with DMUs working the branch from the following day. Yatton, a sub-depot of Bristol Bath Road, had the GWR numerical code of 182, the number 2 reflecting the Bristol Division number, and as sheds in each division were listed alphabetically, Yatton, being the 18th in the list, became 182. Wells for example was 152 and Frome 72.

With Clevedon developing as a dormitory town for Bristol, business traffic was brisk and between 1924 and 1936 a through carriage for season ticket holders left the terminus at 8.47am for Temple Meads with a return working from Bristol at 5.15pm, the coach being slipped at Yatton and hauled to Clevedon by the branch engine. In later years a through train hauled by a '45xx' 2-6-2T would leave Bristol at 1.10pm and return to Temple Meads at 2.17pm. During the 1960s this service consisted of a GWR diesel railcar and a single coach. There were 20 trains per day on the Clevedon branch at the Grouping and 30 under BR. Services to Clevedon were disrupted for five hours on 20 March 1952 due to a wagon derailment at Clevedon, a bus service having to be run between the two stations until the line was cleared.

The brick-built B&E signalbox at Yatton, complete with decorative barge boards and standing alongside the up main line almost opposite the junction with the Cheddar Valley line, was opened pre-1884. It originally measured 50ft x 14ft, the box being extended to 70ft in 1897. A new horizontal-tappet three-bar frame was installed in 1917. From 1 January the same year, the signalbox at Clevedon was closed and relegated to a ground frame, running signals were removed and the electric train staff withdrawn. The branch was then run under the 'one engine in steam' principle and drivers issued with a wooden train staff fitted with a key to unlock the ground frame as their authority to work the line. The ground frame was abolished from 22 April 1964. The main lines west of Yatton were quadrupled from 1921 to provide

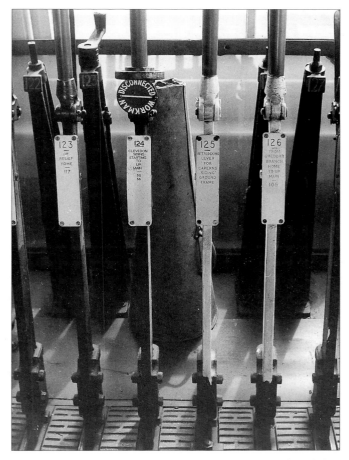

Above: A view of some of the levers in Yatton West box, from left to right: 123 up home relief; 124 Clevedon siding starting to up main; 125 Caperns siding ground frame interlocking lever and 126 Cheddar branch home to up main. *J. A. Sommerfield*

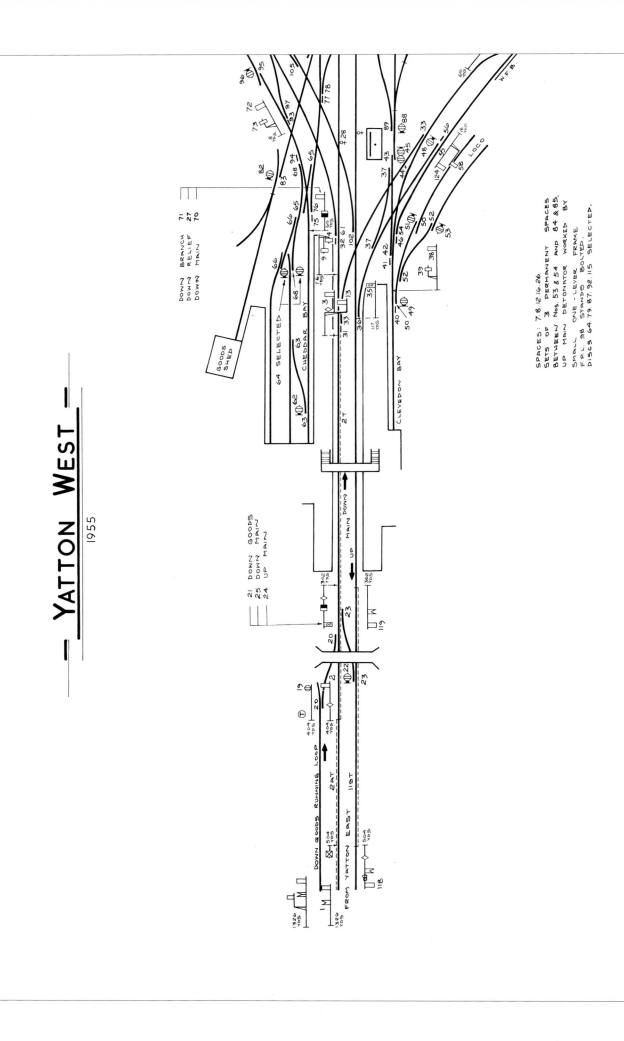

YATTON WEST

1955

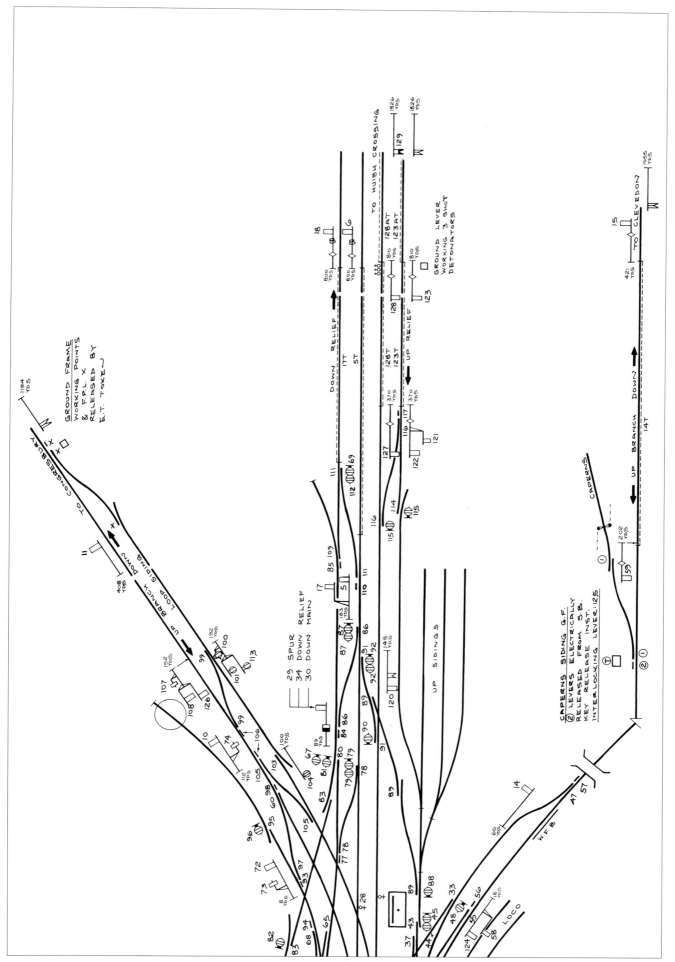

The signalbox diagram for Yatton West showing the massive layout under the control of the signalmen. *Signalling Record Society*

– YATTON EAST –

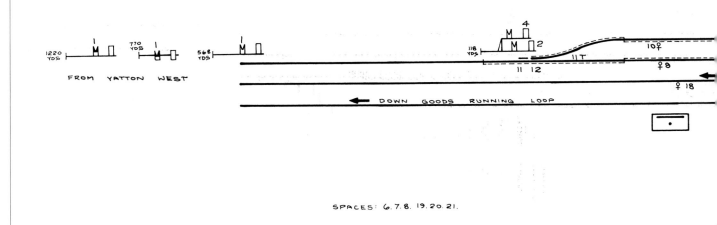

SPACES: 6. 7. 8. 19. 20. 21.

CLEVEDON G.F.

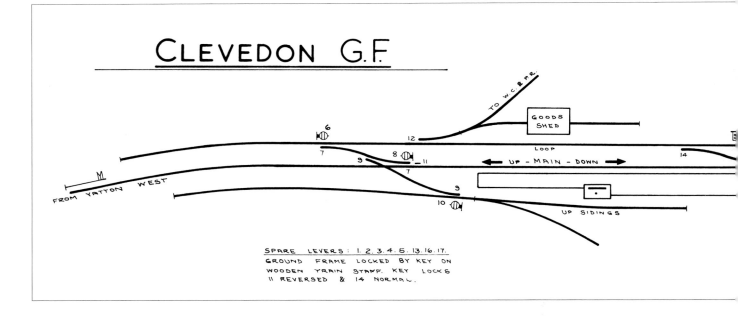

SPARE LEVERS: 1. 2. 3. 4. 5. 13. 16. 17.
GROUND FRAME LOCKED BY KEY ON
WOODEN TRAIN STAFF. KEY LOCKS
11 REVERSED & 14 NORMAL.

up and down relief lines. Quadrupling also occurred east of the station in 1925, giving up and down relief lines. A new signalbox, opened on 6 April 1925 alongside the down goods running loop, was designated Yatton East and the 129-lever Yatton signalbox received the suffix West at the same time. Yatton East was open from 6am to 9.50pm Monday to Saturday and closed on Sundays, although in busy summer periods it would be opened to loop excursion traffic etc. However, the West box was open continuously. The quadrupling of the tracks east and west of the station did not continue through the station due to the high cost of obtaining the land. With the resignalling and construction works associated with the quadrupling, it became possible for the first time to have access to both up and down main lines from either branch line, and in the case of the Clevedon line this occurred halfway along the down platform, 122yd from the West box. A signal at the Bristol end of the down platform had a display box giving access to down goods, down main

and up main. The up starter also shared the same post as the Yatton East up distant arm. A down starting signal positioned off the end of the down platform also had a display box with access to down branch, down relief and down main. Another signal guarding the exit from the Cheddar Valley bay to the down relief line had a display box to spur, down relief and down main. A plethora of signalling controlled the up and down relief lines and sidings. The station had a staff of 40 including the four footplate crews and two shedmen. Signalmen in the West box in 1963 were Malcolm Wathen and Jimmy Waters; passenger guards in the late 1940s and early 1950s were Edgar Skinner and Bert Lynch, and goods guards were Walt Blagdon and A. Maslin. The down platform had a splendid canopy halfway along its length and the platform was unusual in having two GWR water towers at the Exeter end.

Passenger tickets issued from the station totalled 55,898 in 1903 rising to 55,958 and 62,245 for 1923 and 1933

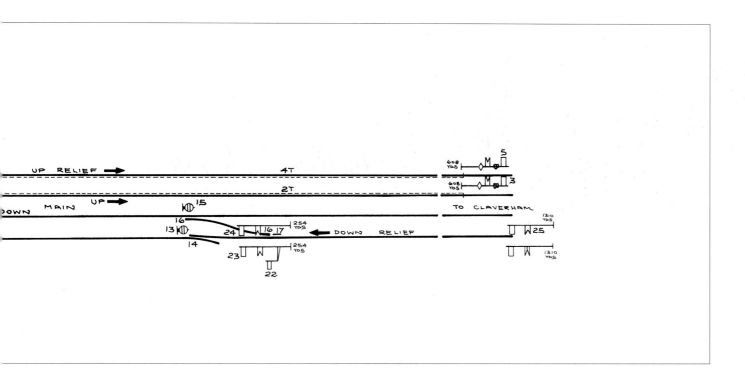

UP RELIEF →

4T

2T

DOWN MAIN UP →

15

16
13

24 16 17 254 YDS ← DOWN RELIEF

14

23 254 YDS

22

608 YDS M 5

608 YDS M 3

TO CLAVERHAM

1310 YDS

25

1310 YDS

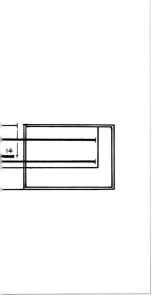

14

Above: Yatton East box diagram showing the signalbox standing alongside the down goods running loop. *Signalling Record Society*

Left: The diagram for Clevedon ground frame. *Signalling Record Society*

respectively. In 1923, 787 season tickets were issued with 29,952 parcels forwarded in the same year. No 1454, operating with a three-car 'sandwich' auto, worked services to Clevedon on August Bank Holiday Monday 1955, and on the same day BR Class 5MT 4-6-0 No 73039 with seven coaches worked tender-first from Yatton to Clevedon at 7.5pm, returning at 7.35pm and running through to Avonmouth.

The Clevedon bay overall roof at Yatton, a relic of the days when steam railmotors worked the services, was removed in 1956 and replaced by an umbrella awning with a curved corrugated iron roof which itself had come from Dauntsey station. On Whit Monday, 21 May 1956 No 1402 and two auto-trailers carried well over 1,000 passengers between Yatton and Clevedon. For a few days at the end of June in the same year, motor-fitted pannier tank No 5406 (82D) replaced the usual '14xx' engine on the Clevedon services. GWR diesel railcars worked the full circuit between Bristol-Yatton-Witham-Frome-Bristol. One of the

services worked in 1952 was the 1.5pm SX and 1.22pm SO ex-Temple Meads which would arrive at Yatton (at times hauling a single coach) and when its passengers had disembarked would reverse into the Clevedon bay to form the 2.18pm return to Clevedon. This returned the branch tank and auto coach to the shed for engine requirements and crew changeover. Upon return to Yatton the diesel, after dropping off its passengers and coach, would reverse into the Cheddar Valley bay before departing at 2.50pm for Witham stopping at all stations en route, arriving at Witham at 4.31 before departing via the main line to Frome. Another wait occurred there before following the 5.55pm semi-fast to Bristol along the North Somerset branch, stopping at every station before arriving in Temple Meads at 7.27pm. The GWR continued its policy of improvement, especially on branch services where the ageing four-coach, four-wheeled close-coupled sets were often the cause of complaint, by constructing between 1924 and 1936 a series of two-coach close-coupled sets formed of brake composites. All the coaches were built to the Collett design of steel-panelled sides and steel roofs. The new coaches were designated 'B' sets and Bristol was the first division for allocation of the new carriages, which were eventually put to use on the Cheddar Valley trains. The top end of each coach was branded 'Bristol Division Train' with the set number underneath. Sets Nos 10 and 15 are known to have been at work on the branch in 1934.

During May 1939 a special circular tour was arranged by the GWR and worked by a streamlined diesel railcar. Unfortunately no details have come to light regarding which of the cars was used on this interesting working. However, the train left Bristol at 9am, arriving in Cheddar at 9.35 where a stop enabling passengers to visit the nearby gorge and caves was made for two hours before departing for Wells at 11.40, where a further sightseeing stopover took place before leaving the city at 2pm for Witham and thence down the main line to Weymouth, arriving at 3.25. It departed from there at 5.40, returning via Westbury and Bath to Bristol with a booked arrival of 7.20pm. Single-ended twin-set railcars with a trailer coach between were used on the circular Bristol-Wells-Witham-Frome-Bristol workings. Bristol had

Above: The terminus at Clevedon, 3 miles 45 chains from Yatton, opened on 28 July 1847. The fine overall roof constructed by the Bristol & Exeter, can be seen in the background. A single platform was provided plus watering facilities for locomotives and a goods shed. A service of 20 trains a day at the Grouping and 30 under BR ran between the two stations. At one time during the postwar period, a through train ran from Bristol on weekdays. The line closed to all traffic on 3 October 1966 and the station site is now occupied by a Safeway supermarket. *Author's collection*

Right: The starting signal arm has been lowered for No 41209 (82B) to exit from the Cheddar Valley bay with a Yatton-Witham train on 10 November 1962. The signal and destination box could direct a train either to the down branch, down relief or down main. *Ben Ashworth*

Right, inset: The 1956 weekday summer freight timetable between Yatton-Wells-Witham and Yatton-Clevedon.

four railcars allocated in June 1947 rising to a total of five in October 1955. DMUs started work on the Clevedon branch on 8 August 1960 with goods traffic ceasing three years later, on 10 June.

The Sunday service on the Cheddar Valley line, of one train each way between Bristol and Wells was prematurely withdrawn on 28 July, leaving the final trains to run on Saturday, 7 September 1963 and not the following day. The last down through train on the Cheddar Valley line, headed by No 2268, departed at 6.15pm. The final service passenger train — the 8.20pm Yatton to Wells crewed by Driver Will Hodges and Fireman Tony Harris from Bristol with Guard Bernard Still from Weston — pulled away from the station amidst the noise of exploding detonators and blasts on the locomotive whistle. Packed with enthusiasts eager to savour the last rites of the Cheddar Valley line, the train passed the

advanced starter on to the single line and, with its red tail lamp flickering away in the gloom, headed towards Congresbury; signal arms clattered back to danger in its wake and the noise from the locomotive exhaust became fainter until it was gone for ever. The Cheddar Valley line from Yatton would never see passenger trains again. Lingering smoke and steam from the last train finally evaporated into the atmosphere as members of the public wended their way home. The last train of all, the empty stock of the 8.20, returned from Wells arriving at Yatton, and with wheel flanges squealing, passed over the junction and on to the main line heading for Bristol.

Retraction in signalling and track layout came about in 1964 with the Clevedon branch facing connection from the down main line and the loop on the aforesaid branch removed. The down bay used by Cheddar branch trains was converted

Above: The Clevedon branch curved sharply to the west past the locomotive shed upon leaving Yatton. The branch is seen in the foreground with the main lines and the rear of Yatton West signalbox in the background in 1952. The coaling stage and line into the shed can be viewed on the far left with a '1400' class 0-4-2T steaming away. *J. H. Moss*

WEEKDAYS   YATTON, WELLS AND WITHAM   B117

SINGLE LINE, worked by Electric Train Token Yatton to Witham, Intermediate Crossing Places : Cranmore, Shepton Mallet, ‡Wells (East Somerset), Wells, Wookey‡, Lodge Hill‡, Cheddar, Axbridge, Sandford‡, and Congresbury.
‡—Wells (East Somerset), Wookey and Sandford are only available for crossing two Freight Trains or a Freight and Passenger Train, but in no case may a Passenger Train be put into the Siding at either place for another train to pass.   Only a short Freight Train can be shunted at Wookey.

Mileage				Ruling Gradients 1 in		K	K	K		K	K	K	K
										3.30 am SX 3.30 am SO Bristol West Depot		9.30 am Bristol West Depot	To Westbury	
M	C						SX	SO		SX		SX	SX
1	46	YATTON .... dep	—			am 4 50	9 10	PM		am 10 33		PM	PM
		Congresbury ... ... dep	434 F			5 0	R			R			
4	40	Sandford and Banwell ... arr	100 R			5 23	9 25			10 48			
5	55	Winscombe ... ... arr	100 R			5 35				11 45 11 53			
8	2	Axbridge ... ... dep	74 F			5 43				12 0 12 11			
9	65	CHEDDAR ... ... arr	100 F			5 51 5 59				12 20 12 27			
11	71	Draycott ... ... dep	286 F			6 15		SUSPENDED		1 42 R		4 45	
14	3	Lodge Hill ... ... arr	174 F									Mondays excepted	
16	38	Wookey ... ... dep	77 R			6 39				1 56 2 4			
17	43	WELLS ... ... arr	119 F			6 49				2 20 2 29			
17	60	Wells (East Somerset) ... dep	86 R			6 55		1 30		2 45 2 50		4 25	5 30
19	45	Dulcot Siding	46 R			6 59							
22	52	Shepton Mallet (High St.) arr	46 R					1 52				4 47	6 42
25	79	Cranmore ... ... arr	70 F					2 23				5 5	6 59
27	63	Stop Board	86 R					2 35				6 10	7 45
29	30	Wanstrow ... ... arr	54 F					2 45				6 19	7 54
29	59	Stop Board	511 F					3 5				6 30	8 7
31	55	WITHAM ... ... arr	47 F					3 17				6 41	8 15

DOWN TRAINS / UP TRAINS

WEEKDAYS   YATTON AND CLEVEDON

SINGLE LINE, worked by a Train Staff and one engine in steam at a time or (b) by Train Staff and two engines in steam coupled together or (c) by a Train Staff and one engine coupled to Rail Motor or a second engine coupled to an Auto Car.   The Train Staff stations are Yatton and Clevedon.

Mileage		DOWN	Ruling Gradient 1 in			UP	Ruling Gradient 1 in	Mixed
M	C							
3	45	YATTON .... dep	—			CLEVEDON .... dep	—	PM
		CLEVEDON .... arr	249 R	am 5 30 5 41		YATTON ... ... arr	249 F	10 30 10 39

Above: A side view of Yatton shed with an 0-4-2T in GWR livery standing to the right. On the left is the grounded broad gauge body, which was used as the locomen's lobby until the construction of the concrete block-built cabin on the right. The chickens and their coop in the vicinity of the shed would not look out of place in a scene from the well-known comedy railway film *Oh! Mr Porter. Ian Allan Library*

to a siding and the turntable road removed on 12 July. Complete closure between Congresbury and Cheddar occurred in the same year with the track being lifted in 1965, leaving a stub of the branch line as a long siding at Yatton. From 6 September 1964 the down goods line from Yatton East was taken out of use and the box closed, with the former West box now becoming Yatton. The goods yard closed on 29 November 1965 but it had only handled coal traffic in its final six months. Passenger traffic was withdrawn from the Clevedon branch when it closed to all traffic on 3 October 1966. From 31 December the same year, the up sidings and Clevedon branch were taken out of use, with the signalbox closing on 31 January 1972 when all semaphore signalling was removed and replaced with colour lights controlled from Bristol.

Yatton today still has its Bristol & Exeter buildings on the up platform, but both the bay platforms have been filled in and cars are now parked where trains once stood before

departing for Clevedon or the Cheddar Valley branches. The footbridge has lost its roof, and the Railway Hotel, which at one time the B&E timetable mentioned that 'Flys and other conveyances may be had on application' still stands opposite the entrance to the up platform. Grass and weeds now mark the spot where the Cheddar Valley line once ran from Yatton. Along the valley itself on the Monday after closure to passenger traffic, there was an uncanny silence from the railway, with not a whistle call, or the sound of escaping steam from an engine drifting into Cheddar, or the clatter as a signal arm was lowered at Axbridge as a straining goods train headed for the tunnel. With the closure to passenger traffic the heart had been ripped out, and although remnants would survive for a limited time, the line, as with many others, yet to close, had now passed into history. Only the memories, now remain.

Left: The grounded broad gauge horsebox body and the side of the locomotive shed at Yatton plus the chickens etc in 1952 strongly reflect the country atmosphere of this small shed which replaced a former broad-gauge version in 1879. Constructed in stone with a slate roof, the shed was situated west of the station on the Clevedon branch.
J. H. Moss

Above: A Bristol to Weston-super-Mare local hauled by '5100' class 2-6-2T No 4142 arrives at Yatton in 1949. The water tank seen to the right supplied the water towers at the station, one of which can be seen to the left on the up platform. The down platform was unique in having two similar towers positioned at its Taunton end. *J. H. Moss*

Below: Steam escapes from the safety valves of No 3702 while taking water at Yatton on 17 August 1963 before working the 2.45pm to Witham. Collett '22xx' 0-6-0 No 2268 stands in the goods dock to the right; a single-car DMU can be seen in the Clevedon bay to the left. Diesel units had begun working on the Clevedon branch from 8 August 1960. *Hugh Ballantyne*

Above: 'Hall' class 4-6-0 No 4947 *Nanhoran Hall*, with plenty of steam to spare, arrives at Yatton with a Bristol to Weston-super-Mare local passenger train while 2-6-2T No 41249 awaits departure on the right with a Cheddar Valley line train. A diesel railcar ticks over in the Clevedon bay to the far left. *R. E. Toop*

Below: A clinker shovel lying precariously on the ground for someone to step on, a gas lamp and the block-built footplatemen's cabin plus the old stone-built shed in the background portray a timeless scene as the footplate crew pose for the camera at Yatton shed on 25 May 1953. No 5527 (82A) along with other members of the class (15 in total) was fitted with auto-apparatus between August and November 1953 and allocated to the Cardiff Valley lines and Bridgend for working on a regular interval passenger timetable which was introduced in September 1953 and called for an increase in auto-fitted locomotives. However, the introduction of diesel services on the Cardiff Valley lines in 1958 resulted in the auto-fitted engines being made redundant, and No 5527, dating from May 1928, was withdrawn from Whitland shed in June 1960. Four locomotive crews and two shedmen formed the Yatton shed staff in the 1950s; closure occurred on 7 August 1960 with DMUs working the Clevedon branch from the following day. *R. C. Riley*

Above: Two London to Weston-super-Mare trains a week, the 9.45am and 10.45am ex-Paddington were steam-hauled on Saturdays during the summer service of 1963. Here, the last 9.45 from Paddington arrives at Yatton on a wet 7 September 1963 hauled by 'Castle' class 4-6-0 No 7036 *Taunton Castle* (81A). The fireman filling the tanks of No 41245 before working the 1.45 Yatton-Wells looks on at the finality of another steam service. *Hugh Ballantyne*

Below: The Clevedon auto, formed of '1400' class 0-4-2T No 1415 and auto-trailer No W233, stands under the Bristol & Exeter overall roof at Yatton during the 1950s. The auto-trailer, in crimson and cream livery, was built by the Western Region in 1951 designed to the style of the earlier GWR trailers, reverting to the saloon type but with modern sliding ventilators to the windows. A GWR railcar can be seen on the right alongside the up platform and may have worked up from the Cheddar Valley line. *Author's collection*

Above: The pannier tanks of No 3758 are filled at Yatton before departure for the cathedral city of Wells on 15 April 1963. When the original Clevedon bay overall roof on the up platform was removed it was replaced by a canopy from Dauntsey station, Wiltshire. *J. H. Moss*

Below: One of the more successful diesel locomotive designs, Brush Type 2 A1A-A1A (Class 31) No 5528, rumbles through Yatton with a short southbound freight train on 17 December 1973. The locomotive, dating from April 1959 and allocated at first to Norwich (32A), was renumbered 31110 in February 1974. Now owned by EWS and named *TRACTION Magazine* and painted in BR green livery it was still in traffic in late 2000. The Clevedon bay is already used for car parking while the Cheddar Valley bay lies derelict. *J. A. Sommerfield*

Above: Snow covers the ground at Yatton on 9 December 1967 as Class 52 No D1017 *Western Warrior* approaches with the 09.00 Plymouth-Liverpool. All traces of the crossover upon which trains from the Cheddar Valley branch gained the up main line have been removed. *J. A. Sommerfield*

Below: WR diesel-hydraulic No D1005 *Western Venturer* arrives at Yatton on Sunday, 26 January 1969 with the 09.00 Plymouth-Liverpool. No D1005 was built at Swindon and introduced to traffic on 18 June 1962 allocated to Laira (83D). Withdrawal came in November 1976 with the locomotive being cut up at BREL Swindon in June 1977. *J. A. Sommerfield*

Above: The prototype Brush Type 4 Co-Co No 1200 *Falcon* enters Yatton with the 13.40 Weston-super-Mare to Paddington on 26 July 1972. MAS signalling has now replaced the former semaphores, as can be seen by the colour light signal at the end of the down platform.
J. A. Sommerfield

Below: Laira-allocated Class 52 No D1002 *Western Explorer* departs from Yatton on Sunday 3 May 1970 with the 09.00 Plymouth-Liverpool. Equipped with twin Maybach MD655 pressure-charged V-type engines and weighing 108 tons with a maximum speed of 90mph, the 'Westerns' entered service on the Western Region in 1962-3. Seven members of the class, Nos D1010/3/5/23/41/8/62 escaped the scrapyard and have been preserved. *J. A. Sommerfield*

MONDAYS to THURSDAYS

DAY EXCURSION BOOKINGS

To LONDON (Paddington)

FROM	DEPART						RETURN FARE	
							FIRST CLASS	SECOND CLASS
	a.m.	a.m.	a.m.	a.m.	p.m.	p.m.	s. d.	s. d.
HIGHBRIDGE for BURNHAM-ON-SEA	—	9 17	10d 4	—	—	—	54/9	36/6
WESTON-S-MARE	6 30	9 35	10 35	11 40	12 35	1 40	52/6	35/0
CLEVEDON	6a 35	9a 48	10a 20	—	12a 25	—	51/0	34/0
YATTON	6 45	9b 34	10 47	—	12 47	—	49/6	33/0
NAILSEA and BACKWELL	6b 17	—	10b 36	—	—	—	48/0	32/0
				p.m.	p.m.	p.m.		
PADDINGTON arr.	9RB35	12RB28	1RC36	2RB46	3RB30	4RB36		

Return from Paddington the same day as follows:—

To Nailsea and Backwell at 4b45, 6b45 or 7b45 p.m.
To Yatton at 4-45, 6-45 or 7-45 p.m.
To Clevedon at 4a45 or 6a45 p.m.
To Weston-Super-Mare at 4-45, 6-45, 7-45, or 11-50 p.m.
To Highbridge for Burnham-on-Sea at 5a55 p.m.

a—Change at Yatton.   b—Change at Bristol T.M.
c—Change at Yatton and Bristol T.M.   d—Change at Weston-Super-Mare.
e—Change at Swindon and Bristol T.M.
RB—Buffet Car Train.   RC—Restaurant Car Train.

EACH SUNDAY

To LONDON (Paddington)

FROM	DEPART	RETURN FARES	
		FIRST CLASS	SECOND CLASS
	a.m.	s. d.	s. d.
WESTON-SUPER-MARE	8 0	52/6	35/0
YATTON	8 17	49/6	33/0
PADDINGTON arr.	11 52		

Return from Paddington by any train the same day affording a service through to destination.

MONDAYS to FRIDAYS (inclusive)

To WEYMOUTH

FROM	DEPART			RETURN FARES SECOND CLASS
	a.m.	a.m.	a.m.	s. d.
WESTON-S-MARE	7 0	8a 30	10 16	20/0
CLEVEDON	7c 0	8b 28	10c 20	18/6
YATTON	7 16	8a 44	10 30	18/0
Arrive:—	10 26	11 51	p.m. 1 57	

RETURN the Same day by any train affording a service through to destination.

a—Change at Bristol.   b—Change at Yatton and Bristol.
c—Change at Yatton.

MONDAYS to FRIDAYS (inclusive)

To WEYMOUTH

FROM	DEPART	RETURN FARE SECOND CLASS	ARRIVAL ON RETURN
	a.m.	s. d.	p.m.
WELLS	9a 0	11/9	6a 54
SHEPTON MALLET (High Street)	9a 13	10/9	6a 43
CRANMORE	9a 21	10/0	6a 35
WANSTROW	9a 28	9/6	6a 28
WEYMOUTH arr.	11 29	a—Change at Witham.	

Return from WEYMOUTH at 4-30 p.m. the same day.

Mid-Week Holiday Return Tickets

Travel Midweek at reduced fares and save approximately 5/- in the £. These tickets are issued during the months of May to October, Second Class only, between any pair of stations in Great Britain for rail journeys of not less than 100 miles in each direction, outwards on TUESDAYS, WEDNESDAYS or THURSDAYS, for return on TUESDAY, WEDNESDAY or THURSDAY within one calendar month except during the week of date shown on ticket.

Each Monday, Tuesday, Wednesday, Thursday and Friday

Minehead, Exeter, Dawlish, Teignmouth, Newton Abbot, Torquay, Paignton and Plymouth

FROM	DEPART		RETURN FARES, SECOND CLASS ONLY, TO							
			Minehead	Exeter	Dawlish	Teignmouth	Newton Abbot	Torquay	Paignton	Plymouth
	a.m.	a.m.	s. d.	s. d.	s. d.	s. d.	s. d.	s. d.	s. d.	s. d.
CLEVEDON	7a 0	8f 0	14/0	16/6	18/6	19/0	20/0	21/0	21/0	29/6
YATTON	7a13	8a11	13/9	15/6	17/6	18/0	19/0	20/0	20/0	28/6
WESTON-S-MARE	7 46	8a28	11/6	14/0	16/0	16/6	17/6	18/6	18/6	27/6
HIGHBRIDGE for BURNHAM-on-SEA	7a50	8a47	9/6	12/0	14/6	15/0	16/0	17/0	17/0	25/0
MINEHEAD arr.		10 49								
EXETER arr.	9 18	10 31								
DAWLISH arr.	10c 8	10 56								
TEIGNMOUTH arr.	10c15	11 4								
NEWTON ABBOT arr.	10 0	11 13								
TORQUAY arr.	10b40	11b37								
PAIGNTON arr.	10b47	11b47								
PLYMOUTH arr.	11 5	p.m. 12 23								

a—Change at Taunton.
b—Change at Newton Abbot.
c—Change at Exeter (St. David's).
d—Change at Weston-S-Mare.
e—Change at Yatton and Weston-S-Mare.
f—Change at Yatton and Taunton.
Return the same day by any train affording a service through to destination.

Day Return tickets are available from Weston-super-Mare and Highbridge Stations to Bridgwater and Taunton, issued on Weekdays and Sundays available in each direction by any train the same day.

Each Sunday, To

Minehead, Exeter, Dawlish, Teignmouth, Newton Abbot, Torquay and Paignton

FROM	DEPART		RETURN FARES, SECOND CLASS ONLY, TO					
	A	B	Minehead	Exeter	Dawlish	Teignmouth	Newton Abbot	Torquay or Paignton
	a.m.	a.m.	s. d.	s. d.	s. d.	s. d.	s. d.	s. d.
YATTON	7 20	10 34	13/0	15/6	17/6	18/6	19/0	20/0
WESTON-S-MARE	7 45	10 50	11/6	14/0	16/0	16/6	17/6	18/6
HIGHBRIDGE for BURNHAM-on-SEA	8 3	11 5	9/6	12/0	14/6	15/0	16/0	17/0

A—Arrive Exeter (St. David's) 9-35, Dawlish 10-11, Teignmouth 10-20, Newton Abbot 10-30, Torquay 11a14, Paignton 11a27, Minehead 9b50 a.m.
B—Arrive Exeter (St. David's) 12-22, Dawlish 12-44, Teignmouth 12-53, Newton Abbot 1-3, Torquay 1-26, Paignton 1-39 p.m. Minehead 12b50 p.m.

a—Change at Newton Abbot.   b—Change at Taunton.

Return the same day by any train affording a service through to destination.

EACH WEEKDAY

TO

CHEDDAR. WOOKEY and WELLS

(Change at Yatton in each direction.)

FROM	DEPART			RETURN FARES SECOND CLASS		
	S	SX	S	Cheddar	Wookey	Wells
	a.m.	a.m.	p.m.	s. d.	s. d.	s. d.
CLEVEDON	—	11 13	1 20	3/0	4/0	4/0
WESTON-super-MARE	10 35	10 35	1 25	3/9	5/0	5/0
		noon	p.m.			
CHEDDAR	11 35	12 0	2 13			
WOOKEY	11 56	12 13	2 29	S—Saturdays only.		
WELLS	11 59	12 17	2 32	SX—Saturdays excepted.		

RETURN SAME DAY BY ANY TRAIN AFFORDING A SERVICE THROUGH TO DESTINATION.

A special ticket can be obtained on application at the time of booking which admits bearer to either Messrs. Cox's or Gough Caves at Cheddar (but not both) or Wookey Hole Cave, at a reduced charge, payable at the Cave Turnstile.

DAILY

(INCLUDING SUNDAYS WHERE THERE IS A TRAIN SERVICE IN OPERATION)

TO

NEWPORT and CARDIFF

FROM	DEPART	RETURN FARE SECOND CLASS, TO	
		NEWPORT	CARDIFF
		s. d.	s. d.
HIGHBRIDGE for BURNHAM-ON-SEA	BY	14/0	16/0
WESTON-SUPER-MARE	ANY	12/0	14/0
CLEVEDON	TRAIN	11/0	13/0
YATTON		10/6	12/6

Passengers may return by any train the same day affording a service through to destination.

Index

Accidents
   Congresbury (1875) 177, 179
   Draycott (1894) 125
   Dulcote (1904) 73
   Lodge Hill (locomotive blow-back 1961) 121, 123
   Wells East Somerset Yard (1916) 86, 87
   Wookey (1873) 117, 119
Axbridge 157, 158, 159, 160, 161, 162, 163, 164, 156-64

Bath Arms, Warminster 9
Bathampton 9
Batts Combe Quarry 141
Blagdon 14, 15, 191-4
Bradford-on-Avon 9
Bramble Ditch Quarry 58
Bristol & Exeter Railway 12, 13, 104, 105, 195
Bristol Waterworks Co 14, 141, 146
Brock, William 13
Burrington 15, 190

Callow Rock Lime Co 141, 146
Central Cornwall Railway 14
Cheddar Station 14, 134-55
Cheddar Valley & Yatton 12, 13
Cheddar Valley Inn 113
Cheddar Valley Scenic Railtour 113, 147
Clevedon 197, 199, 200, 201, 204, 205, 206
Clevedon Road 197
Congresbury 13, 14, 177-93
Coxley 89
Cranmore 40-55, 58, 63
Cranmore Railway Co 53
Croscombe 10
Crow Catchpole Quarries 141

Dinder 10
Dinder House 10
Dorset Central 12, 92
Doulting Siding 58
Downhead Quarry 47, 49
Draycott 13, 111, 125-33, 145
Dulcote Quarry 67
Dulcote Quarry Foster Yeoman 74, 75
Dulcote Quarry Siding 71-5, 79

East Somerset Extension Railway 15
East Somerset Railway 9, 10, 11, 18
English China Clays Quarries 146
English Electric 49
Flying Dutchman 195
Foster Yeoman Ltd 36, 37, 39
Fox, Francis 14
Fox, John, Hingston 14
Frome 9, 15, 19

Gauge Conversion 15
George Hotel, Frome 9
Glastonbury 10, 12, 13, 89, 91, 92
Golden Lion, Wrington 187

Haybridge 117
Highbridge 12, 92

Isambard Kingdom Brunel 9, 10, 195

Kilver Street Crossing 59
King George III 14

La Grange Workshops, Chicago 39

Langford 15, 189
Locomotives
   Alan J. Day 39
   Black Prince 53
   Bulford 173
   Bulkelly 199
   Cossack 29
   Dulcote 36
   Eastnor Castle 27
   Eydon Hall 28
   Fairfield 197
   Falcon 218
   Fawley Court 61, 62
   Finetta 173
   Frank Bibby 84
   Gamecock 42
   Great Western 199
   Hesperus 183
   Homer 63
   Horwich 47
   Keighley 47
   Kenneth J. Painter 39
   Llanstephan Castle 23
   Mendip 36
   Merehead 39
   Nanhoran Hall 212
   Paul A. Hammond 39
   Pelican 195
   Princess Margaret 198
   Seneca 77
   Sidlesham 191
   Starling 84
   Stowe 53
   Tattoo 47
   Taunton Castle 214
   The Green Knight 53
   Thunderer 63
   Village of Chantry 39
   Village of Great Elm 37, 38, 39
   Village of Mells 39
   Village of Whatley 39
   Virgil 76
   Wells 95
   Western Explorer 219
   Western Venturer 217
   Western Warrior 217
   Western Yeoman II 39, 40
   Winslow Hall 23
   Yeoman Challenger 39
   Yeoman Endeavour 39
   Yeoman Enterprise 39
   Yeoman Highlander 39

Lion Rock, Cheddar 142
Lodge Hill 13, 53, 120-4

Marcroft Wagons Ltd 51
Mendip Granite & Asphalt Co Ltd 49
Mendip Granite Works 7
Mendip Mountain Quarries Ltd 49
Mendip Mountain Quarries, New Works at Waterlip 49
Mendip Vale 53
Merehead Quarry 23, 36, 37, 38, 39, 40
Merryfield Lane 53
Moons Hill Quarry 47

Neath Iron Works 14
Newbury Railway 15
North Somerset Electric Supply Co 49
Norton Hill Colliery 117

Pearson, James 195
Phipps & Mackay 9
Polsham 91

Radstock 9
Radstock, Wrington & Congresbury Junction Railway 14
Roads Reconstruction (1934) Ltd 49
Roads Reconstruction Ltd 49, 173
Rock of Ages, Burrington 190

St Cuthberts Paper Mill 112
Sandford & Banwell 13, 143, 170-6
Sandford Quarry 173
Sandford Stone 175
Saunders, Charles 9
Saxby & Farmer 104, 119, 137, 138, 141, 159
Shepherd, David, OBE, FRSA 53
Shepton Mallet Charlton Road 59
Shepton Mallet High Street 63-70, 71
Shute Shelve Tunnel 13, 143, 161
Siberia 51
Signalling, Great Western 16, 17
Signalling, Somerset Central 17, 18
Somerset & Dorset 12, 13
Somerset Basalt Quarry Co 47
Somerset Central Railway 10, 11, 12, 92
Spagnoletti Electric Telegraph 11
Strawberry Way 113

Thingley Junction 9, 15
Torr Works 39

Underwood Quarry 117

Wainwright, John & Co 47
Wanstrow 31, 32, 33, 34, 35
Waterlip Engine shed 47
Waterlip Quarry 7, 42, 47, 49
Wells Cathedral Stonemasons 147
Wells East Somerset Signalbox 16
Wells East Somerset Station 76, 77, 79
Wells East Somerset Yard 75, 79, 81, 83, 85, 87
Wells Locomotive Shed GWR 80-9
Wells Locomotive Shed S&D 91, 93, 94
Wells Priory Road 11, 89-9, 101
Wells Tucker Street 13, 14, 77, 79, 101-16
Weston Clevedon & Portishead Railway 183
Weston Mercury 13
Whatley Quarry 39
Wilts & Somerset Railway 9
Wilts Somerset & Weymouth Act 9
Wilts Somerset & Weymouth Railway 9, 14
Winscombe 13, 143, 161, 165-70
Witham 14, 15, 19, 20, 21, 22, 23, 24, 25, 26, 27, 28, 29, 30, 31
Woodborough 13
Wookey 117-20
Wookey Hole 119
Wrington 14, 15, 183, 187, 188, 189
Wrington Vale Light Railway 14, 15, 17

Yatton 13, 18, 104, 105, 108, 161, 195-222
Yatton locomotive shed 209, 213

Zulu 195

Different shapes from the superb dessert service made in 1830 for King William IV. Underglaze blue ground reserving six panels edged with scrolls in raised gilding and white "jewelling", containing painting of the jewels of the orders of the Garter, the Thistle, St. Patrick, Bath, St. Michael and St. George and Guelphic, in the centre the Royal Coat of Arms. The service is publicly displayed at Windsor Castle and is used once a year on the occasion of the Garter banquet. Photograph reproduced by gracious permission of Her Majesty the Queen.

FLIGHT AND BARR
WORCESTER
PORCELAIN
1783 - 1840

~~~

by Henry Sandon

A study of the history and production of porcelain at Worcester during the periods known as Flight, Flight and Barr, Barr Flight and Barr, *and* Flight Barr and Barr.

© Copyright 1978

The Antique Collectors' Club
World copyright reserved

ISBN 0 902028 75 8

British Library CIP data
Sandon, Henry
    Flight and Barr Worcester porcelain,
1783-1840.
    1. Worcester porcelain
    I. Title II. Antique Collectors' Club
738.2'7   NK4395

    ISBN 0-902028-75-8

Printed in England by Baron Publishing
Church Street, Woodbridge, Suffolk

4

Acknowledgements

I would like to express my gratitude to the many people who have helped in the preparation of this book; especially to Her Majesty the Queen for graciously allowing a photograph of the service made for King William the Fourth to be used and for allowing access to the Royal archives; to various members of the Royal Household in London and Windsor, who have ungrudgingly given of their time and knowledge; the directors of the Worcester Royal Porcelain Company for allowing access to all available records; the Trustees of the Dyson Perrins Museum for permission to photograph and illustrate many of the pieces in their collection; The Corporation of Worcester for allowing access to their records and for allowing the Corporation punch bowls to be photographed and illustrated; Robert Stones, who did a great amount of research into the workmen at the factory; Peter Holloway for unravelling the complexities of the Flight and Barr and Chamberlain merger in 1840; Frank Laney and Malcolm Nixon of the Friends of the Dyson Perrins Museum; Paul Rado, chief chemist and Peter Ewence, chief designer of the Worcester Royal Porcelain Company for much technical help; John Penderil-Church of English China Clays for information about the soapstone quarries and other technical information; Dr Hunt for help on the history of gilding; Cyril Shingler, my predecessor as Curator, for many years of patient build up of knowledge; J.B. Henderson of The Croome Estates for access to the early records of the Coventry family; Leslie Mallabar for permission to consult the notebooks of James Ross; Miss B.C. Monkman of The White House, Washington, D.C.; the ceramic departments of all the auction houses who have assisted with information and photographs of items passing through their hands, especially the London houses of Christie's, Phillips and Sotheby's; the antique dealer specialists who have helped in so many ways that it is invidious to single out one; the collectors of Flight and Barr, both large and small, who have shown me or told me of their collections and prodded me into completing this book, again it is invidious to single out any, but my thanks to you all; and finally to the descendants of the Flights in particular the Eveleghs for so kindly allowing me to study John Flight's diary and publish the important extracts from it, and Bernard Flight for information on the family.

H.S.

Also by Henry Sandon: —
Worcester Porcelain 1751-1793, published by Barrie and Jenkins
Royal Worcester Porcelain from 1862, published by Barrie and Jenkins
British Pottery And Porcelain For Pleasure And Investment, published by John Gifford
Coffee Pots and Teapots, published by John Bartholomew

The
Antique Collectors' Club

Founded in 1966 by a group of keen collectors, the Club pioneered the provision of factual information of use to collectors when buying. Not just information on prices but also details of what to look for and what to avoid.

The *Price Guide to Antique Furniture* by John Andrews first published in 1968 broke new ground. No longer was a book on antique furniture passed out with clutches of museum furniture which no collector could hope to find, or afford it if he did. Instead over 400 photographs were included of the sort of furniture collectors were constantly examining. Comparisons of quality were made, information on improvements was given, and the values of various types discussed. Many other Price Guides have followed, most of them are respected as much for the information they contain as for the help on prices which they give. They do not go out of date as *Price Revision Lists* are available annually for each book.

As the Club grew, the standard and quality of the monthly magazine sent free to members was improved, and a wider range of information provided. It became apparent that information was also lacking on art reference subjects. The first book published on this area of interest was *Dictionary of Victorian Painters* by Christopher Wood. This, and others in this series, have become standard works of reference. They are typified by detailed original research and are sold all over the world.

The third category of books published by the Club covers Clocks and Watches, the first being *Carriage Clocks* by Charles Allix.

Finally, the Club publishes two annual titles: *The Guide to the Antique Shops of Britain,* which as the name implies lists virtually all the antique shops in Britain. It is an indispensable companion to anyone travelling in Britain who wishes to explore the wealth of antiques to be found all over the country. It is published in June each year.

The Antique Dealers' Handbook is also published annually in the Spring, and is unusual in providing a mine of information about the world of antiques: the best books on each subject; specialist dealers on a wide variety of subjects; valuations; supplies of materials for restoration; restorations; transport of antiques, and a great deal else.

Club membership, which is open to all collectors, is £6.95 per annum. Members receive free of charge *Antique Collecting,* the Club's monthly magazine, which contains well-illustrated articles dealing with the practical aspects of collecting not normally dealt with by magazines. Prices, features of value, investment potential, fakes and forgeries are all given prominence in the magazine. In addition members buy and sell among themselves; the Club charges a nominal fee for introductions but takes no commission. Since the Club started many thousands of antiques have been offered for sale privately. No other publication contains anything to match the long list of items for sale privately which appears monthly.

The presentation of useful information and the facility to buy and sell privately would alone have assured the success of the Club, but perhaps the feature most valued by members is the ability to make contact with other collectors living nearby. Not only do members learn about other branches of collecting, they also make interesting friendships. The Club organises weekend seminars and other meetings. As its motto implies, the Club is an amateur organisation designed to help collectors to get the most out of their hobby: it is informal and friendly and gives enormous enjoyment to all concerned.

For Collectors — By Collectors — About Collecting
The Antique Collectors' Club, 5 Church Street, Woodbridge, Suffolk

Bibliography

As this is the first book to deal specifically with Flight and Barr, this bibliography is necessarily on the very short side. The books which have been of the greatest help are *A Century of Potting in the City of Worcester* by R.W. Binns; Chaffers' *Marks and Monograms* (different editions), and Valentine Green's *History of the City of Worcester.*

Other books which have contained a lot of useful information, mainly drawn from the above books, are *Worcester Porcelain* by R.L. Hobson, and *British Pottery and Porcelain 1780-1840* by Geoffrey Godden. Two books dealing with the first years of Flight are *Worcester Porcelain 1751 to 1793* by Henry Sandon and *Caughley and Worcester Porcelain* by Geoffrey Godden. Two books that cover the life and work of William Billingsley are *The Pottery and Porcelain of Swansea and Nantgarw* by E. Morton Nance, and *William Billingsley* by W.D. John.

Collections

The best public collection of porcelain of the Flight and Barr periods is at The Dyson Perrins Museum in Worcester. Other interesting pieces are spread around among many public collections in Great Britain and other countries, but so far relatively little attention has been paid to the superb wares of these periods as most Museum collections tend to concentrate on Worcester wares of the Dr Wall period. Perhaps this book will have the effect of focusing attention on the wares of the years 1783-1840 and produce cases or even galleries devoted to them.

Many fine private collections exist and a number of illustrations in this book are drawn from these. I am sure that much greater attention will be paid to these wares in the near future, in fact a very noticeable increase in prices realised at auction has been recently seen.

Contents

Chapter 1	Flight 1783-1792	11
Chapter 2	Flight and Barr 1792-1804	30
Chapter 3	Barr Flight and Barr 1804-1813	63
Chapter 4	Flight Barr and Barr 1813-1840	100
Chapter 5	The End of the Flight and Barr Era	130
Chapter 6	The Wares of Flight and Barr	160
Appendix I	The Painters, Gilders and Other Workmen and Characters at Flight's Factory	199
Appendix II	Armorial and Crested Services	210
Appendix III	Extracts from the Diary of John Flight 1785-1791	217
Appendix IV	Extracts from the Account Books of James Ross	233
Appendix V	Chemical Analysis of Flight and Barr Porcelain	235
Appendix VI	The Marks of Flight and Barr	237
Index		242

We regret that some colour illustrations are not up to the standard we would like to print. Unfortunately the small colour transparencies from which they were made were the only ones available. As will be seen from the text, they are key pieces in the development of the factory, and as such it was felt that it was desirable to include them.

Chapter 1

Flight 1783–1792

In 1783, the Worcester Porcelain Company was bought for £3,000 by Thomas Flight, who, since 1768, had been the London agent for the Company at the warehouse at 2, Bread Street.

As is noted in the Worcester City records — "Whereas by agreement made 10th April, 1783, and signed by the said Thomas Vernon, William Davis the elder and William Davis the younger, and Thomas Flight, the said Thomas Vernon, William Davis the elder, and William Davis the younger, agree to assign over and convey to the said Thomas Flight the possession of the said manufactory, and all the stock and effects belonging to the manufactory, and also all the house, buildings, and other property which had belonged to them as proprietors of the Porcelain Company, for the sum of £3,000, to be paid in the manner following, that is to say. £500 at signing, £1,000 on or before 24th July next, and the remaining £1,500 on or before 25th March next."

During the years following Dr. John Wall's[1] retirement in 1774 until the purchase of the factory in 1783 by Thomas Flight, the business had been mainly directed by William Davis senior, an apothecary. Great competition with cheap imported Nankin blue and white wares from China, Wedgwood's cream wares and the soft paste porcelain from Thomas Turner's works at Caughley led the Worcester Porcelain Company to cheapen their production, most of this being given over to blue and white printing, at first of patterns similar to the earlier painted ones and later to more complicated "Willow Pattern" type scenes, or else to simple blue borders and gold or black patterns. A certain quantity of higher class productions continued, mainly blue ground and blue scale, the blue acquiring a deeper violet tinge and the translucence turning from a good green to a yellow green and eventually a strawy yellowy orange, caused by allowing the kilns to get dirtier and dirtier during the firing. It is pretty certain that Thomas Flight found the factory in rather a low state, both financially and physically, when he took it over in 1783. £3,000 was a large sum of money to pay and, although he must have been a good business man, it is likely that he did not forsee the troubles that he was laying up for his two sons Joseph and John.

1.   See Appendix I.

Plate 1. Part of a miniature early Flight tea-set painted in late Dr. Wall style in underglaze blue; c.1783-85; no marks. Hunt Collection.

The Thomas Flight (see opposite) who bought the Worcester Porcelain Company was apprenticed to a carpenter in 1741 and presumably practised as one because an apprentice was indentured to him in 1761, but he describes himself as a jeweller in 1759 at the baptism of his son Thomas. In 1769 he was a partner in a banking firm, Pewtress, Flight and Halliday of 34 Lombard Street in the City of London and Master of the Carpenters' Company in 1782, as were later his sons Bannister, Thomas and Joseph and grandson Thomas. He was admitted to Maze Pond Baptist Chapel in 1756, made a Deacon in 1773 and was one of the jurors empanelled to try Lord George Gordon in 1781 after the riots.

He lived in Hackney in the County of Middlesex, then the richest village in England, where also lived his elder brother, Joseph, a turpentine merchant, tallow chandler and linen draper, owning a patent "iron liquor" for printing on linen, and not far away another brother, Hanson, owned one of the complex of five flour mills at Stratford, which supplied not only the whole of London, but Wellington's army in the Peninsular war, with flour.

Thomas's eldest son, Bannister, was a stockbroker and banker; the next son, Thomas, became a stockjobber; Joseph the next son, was a Master of the Carpenters' Company and Hanson a member of the Farriers' Company. More is known about John Flight, especially his connection with the Porcelain Manufactory, because of a wonderfully useful diary that he kept that spans the years 1785 to 1791. This diary, which I have been able to examine for a long time through the kindness of Mr. Evelegh, a descendant of Bannister, is one of the most important documents in English ceramic history and the relative sections that apply to John Flight's work at Worcester are fully given in Appendix III. For this introductory chapter it will suffice merely to give a brief summary of the relevant sections.

The Flights' Family Tree

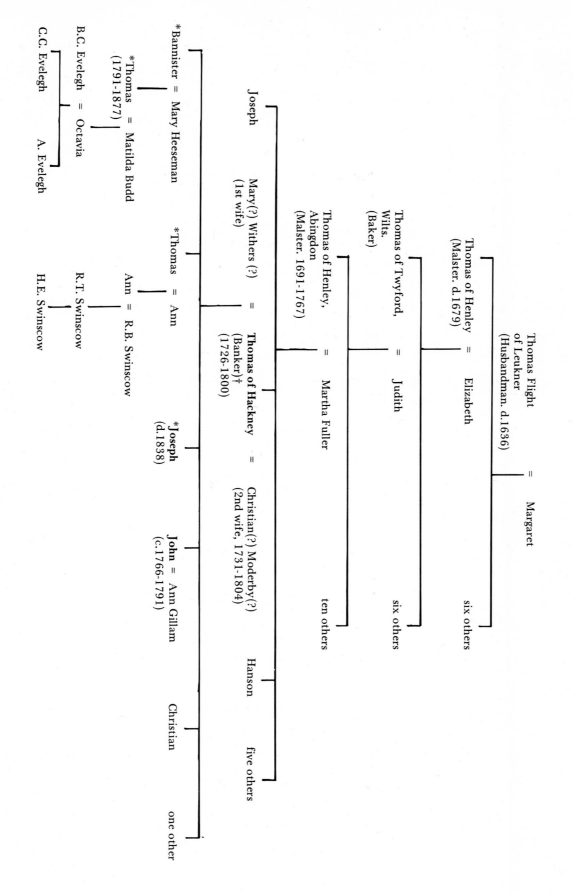

* All served as Master of the Carpenters' Company.
† Pewtress, Flight and Halliday, 34 Lombard St.

13

In the diary John Flight appears as a deeply religious person. In fact the greater part of the first 230 pages is filled almost entirely with religious devotions, thoughts and arguments and only occasional references to his family and no mention at all of his work. When he does mention his family it is in the most affectionate terms but he speaks more of ministers and their sermons. He makes no references to companions of his own age, only of older persons as serious and religious as himself. Now and then he tells us that he has been to a coffee house or chop house, but never to a tavern or a dance.

A casual reader of the diary could easily imagine the young man as being very priggish, or a religious maniac, resenting the fact that life has intruded on the time he can devote to religion and he even discloses that he had lectured his barber "for the good of his soul". On 31st December 1785 he feels remorse at having enjoyed himself over Christmas and in June 1787 he expresses regret that there are no suitably serious minded companions at Worcester. The reader by this time could be excused for thinking that John was a spoilt young man with more money and leisure than was good for him but we must remember that what he wrote was not intended for other eyes and although he was excessively introspective, this was to disappear when he took up his duties at Worcester in 1788.

Plate 2. Early Flight tea cup and saucer of spiral fluted shape, decorated blue and gold; mark "Flight" in script and a very small crescent; 1783-92. Geoffrey Godden.

Plate 3. Typical early Flight spirally fluted tea-bowl and saucer, decorated with blue and gold; mark crescent and Flight in blue; c.1785-92. Hunt Collection.

A year earlier, in June 1787, he had made a long and hazardous journey through Cornwall travelling upward of a thousand miles, "was thrown from my horse four times without sustaining the least injury and preserved thro' many visible dangers". Unfortunately he wrote nothing of the business he was engaged on, only of the preachers he heard, but his journey could well have taken him to the stone mines and clay pits. One thing is clear and that is the difficulty of transportation by road and it is well to remember that in those days a traveller from Worcester to London would make his will before he set out; that one rider was drowned in a pot hole in the main Oxford road and that the main road from Worcester to Droitwich was unpassable for at least three months in the year.

However, it is in July 1788, when he sets out for Worcester to take a fuller part in the manufactory, that the diary takes on a new turn. The religious entries become fewer and are replaced by accounts of the successes and disappointments of the factory, his journeys to the French porcelain manufactories and his short but successful romance. The story of his mastery of the various processes of porcelain making is a fascinating one and one cannot but be astonished at the astuteness, energy, diplomacy and cool business sense that he displays — qualities which were no doubt there all along.

In my book, *The Illustrated Guide to Worcester Porcelain,* I introduced the idea of a middle period of Worcester porcelain between the death of Dr. John Wall in 1776 and the arrival of Martin Barr in 1792, a period that I called the Davis/Flight period, in which there appeared to be a gradual descent into poorer quality of blue printing. By July 1788 this descent had almost reached its bottom and John Flight's move to Worcester was intended to be but a short one to assist his brother Joseph and their father to move their sale shop from the old premises at No. 33, High Street, previously owned by Samuel Bradley, an original partner with Dr. Wall, to new premises at No. 45, nearer the Cross (the centre of town) and the main hostelries at which a lot of business was done by sales of porcelain to travellers. Then his intention was to travel to Swansea to see if it would be beneficial to transfer the manufactory there, where coal was cheaper and there were many experienced ceramic workers to be found.

But for the fortuitous arrival in Worcester of the King, it is possible that within a year or so the factory would have been moved to Swansea and Worcester porcelain become a name of interest only to collectors of wares of the eighteenth century, as Chelsea, Bow or Longton Hall wares are. For make no mistake about it, the Worcester factory was in a very bad way, kiln loads of ware being constantly ruined by sulphur and the chief manufacturing clerk — who we might nowadays call the works foreman — apparently defrauding the firm left, right and centre and refusing to tell the owners their own formula.

The King's visit gave the Flight family great heart, as well as a royal order and its first royal warrant and John's diary record shows what effect it had on him, determining him to keep the factory in Worcester. Many accounts have been written of George III's journey from Cheltenham, where he had been taking the waters, to Worcester, to attend the Music Meeting, or the Three Choirs Festival as it has been known for many years, an annual joining of the choirs of Worcester, Hereford and Gloucester in each city in turn. The most complete account is given by Valentine Green in his "History of Worcester"[1] in which Green, who had worked for Dr. Wall, gives a complete history of the ancient city. A few extracts from this book will give a little of the excitement engendered in Worcester by this visit in 1788:—

> "On the 6th, his Majesty, being a very early riser, had surveyed the Cathedral and its precincts, and walked to almost every part of the town before 7 o'clock . . . On the afternoon of the same day, their Majesties and the Princesses attended by the Countess of Harcourt and

---

1.   The History and Antiquities of the City and Suburbs of Worcester, *Valentine Green. 2 vols. (1st Vol. publ. 1795). The book is of folio size and a great collector's piece mainly because of superb engravings by James Ross.*

16

Plate 4. Flight mask jug of embossed cabbage leaf form, decorated in underglaze blue and gold in the simple style of much early Flight; mark a small blue crescent and the word Flight; c.1785-93. Dyson Perrins Museum.

Plate 5. Three cups decorated with the more common of the ordinary patterns of the Flight period. Left: a coffee cup with the "Queen Charlotte" or Catherine Wheel or Whorl pattern with alternate spiral panels in red, green, gold and underglaze blue; small blue crescent mark. Centre: a chocolate cup and stand with "Royal Lily" pattern of underglaze blue and gilding in form of stylised water lilies; mark "Flight" in script, in blue. Right: coffee cup with "Music" pattern in underglaze blue and gilding; small blue crescent mark. Dyson Perrins Museum.

Oxford, Lord Courtown, Colonels Goldworthy and Digby, walked to Messrs. Flight and Barr's[1] elegant china shop in High Street, where they remained almost an hour, and greatly admired the beautiful porcelain manufactured under the direction of those gentlemen, and gave orders for an extensive assortment of it. . .

"About 10 o'clock on Saturday morning, August 9th their Majesties and the three Princesses, attended by several of the nobility, visited Mr. Flight's china manufactory; as this visit was by appointment, the proprietor had removed some of the branches of the manufactory for the convenience of showing the whole in three rooms; the workmen behaved with the utmost decency, and their Majesties expressed the highest satisfaction. The King gave Messrs Flight the liberty they had requested of styling themselves 'China Manufacturers to their Majesties', and wished success to the manufactory; Their Majesties giving at the same time some additional orders for their china. The King, as usual, showed great knowledge of trade and manufactures by the pertinent questions which he asked; and all the royal visitors were remarkable for their condescension, endeavouring to overcome that awe which so much honour could not but inspire. Their Majesties employed more than two hours in viewing the different departments, and left ten guineas with Mr. Flight for the workmen."

1.   *Green's reference to 'Flight & Barr's elegant china shop' should be taken with a pinch of salt as the firm did not become Flight and Barr until 1792, but as Green was writing in 1795 he naturally referred to the shop as Flight and Barr.*

Examples of services made for members of the British Royal Family. From left to right, top row: for Prince of Wales c.1807, Prince of Wales c.1808, Prince of Wales c.1815. Middle row: Prince of Wales c.1810, George III, George III (Barr's orange ground). Bottom row: Prince of Wales (flowers painted by Astles), Prince of Wales c.1815, Prince of Wales c.1815. Dyson Perrins Museum.

Plate 6. Parts of a Flight dessert service painted with the "Queen Charlotte" or "Catherine Wheel" pattern in iron red and gold on an underglaze blue ground; marks of a crescent and the word Flight; c.1785-90. Sotheby's.

Plate 7. Miniature Flight tête-à-tête service painted and gilt with the "Royal Lily" pattern, some pieces with small blue crescent marks: c.1790; tray 13¾in. Sotheby's.

20

Plates 8 and 9. Rare token or medallion to commemorate the visit of King George III to Flight's factory on August 9th 1788, transfer printed in black, the obverse with the head of the King and the inscription "Georgius III Dei Gratia", the reverse with musical instruments and music of the Music Meeting, a crown and the inscription "Worcester August 6, 1788". 1in. diameter. Dyson Perrins Museum.

It was not only Flight who profited from the royal visit but a number of other Worcester manufactories, especially the carpet industry, at that time well established in Worcester before the major move to Kidderminster. As a local satirical poem put it:—

> "With china vessels, cups and saucers, free,
> Be ready Flight, to catch the Royal Tea;
> On Every dish let fancied Cupids play,
> But yet their fingers on their lips, I pray;
> To show how Silence on the throne should sit,
> And Love himself conceal the schemes of Pitt!
> Watkins, assist, with royal fillets bound,
> To carpet all the country twelve miles around;
> With figures, strange and vast, these strike the man,
> Like Chinese phantoms on a lady's fan!
> Then let the King his Worcester subjects meet,
> And doom all Britain's foes beneath his feet."

Certainly the royal cup of tea, presumably served in the newly bought Royal Lily pattern (newly renamed from Blue Lily), was sweetened by the granting of the Royal Warrant. This reads as follows:—

stamp

seal of
Lord Salisbury

I do hereby appoint Messrs Joseph and John Flight to be Worcester Porcelain China Manufacturers to His Majesty: to have, hold, exercise, and enjoy the said place, together with all rights, profits, priveleges, and advantages thereunto belonging. Given unto my hand seal this 2nd day of March 1789 in the twenty-ninth year of His Majesty's reign.

Salisbury.

21

It is interesting to mention that local Worcester gossipy legend has it that it was while at Worcester that the first signs of the King's madness became apparent and one firm story goes that he was found to be missing from his bedroom in the Bishop's Palace one night and after a hue and cry was found seated in a street doorway in his nightshirt singing "God Save the King". Certain it is that the two magnificent punch bowls made for the Corporation of Worcester in 1792 present a very strange looking portrait of the King although the depiction of Queen Charlotte is not much better and shows her with a ribbon through her hair with the words "God save the King" partly visible. The use of the Aesculapius as part of the decoration may be an illusion to his illness.

However, ill or not, the King gave Flight great encouragement and John's first task was to plan the opening of a London retail shop. John's first appointment as a partner was discussed as was his visit to France but before setting forth he travelled to Newcastle (in the Potteries) in search of a modeller "whom we have since agreed to take on at Michaelmas for 3 years".

Plate 10. Flight tureen and cover, blue ground and gilding; 9in. x 6¼in.; mark a crescent and "Flight"; c.1790. Geoffrey Godden.

Plate 11. Three early Flight pieces with underglaze blue and gilding somewhat in the French style. Left: a sugar and cover vertically ribbed; small open crescent mark in underglaze blue. Dyson Perrins Museum. Centre: a pierced vase or pot-pourri, lower part of body spirally fluted, the cover pierced; similar mark to sugar; 6¼in. Dyson Perrins Museum. Right: a pair of bell pulls; no mark; 2½in. John Sandon Collection.

There is a gap in the diary from September 1788 to June 1789, John, no doubt, being too busy to write but when he resumes, he describes his two visits to France. The first was in October 1788 to Paris where he visited French factories and ordered £300 of porcelain for sale in the Worcester shop. The second, and more important, was in March 1789, again to Paris where through his banker, M. Perregaux, he entered into an exclusive agreement with the Angoulême Manufactory for 5 years, "to supply us only with their china, provided we took to the amount of 50,000 Livres a year of them and that we should not take from any other Manufactory". It may surprise many people to know that Flights, especially in their London shop, were selling Angoulême porcelain, but this was a shrewd business move, helping to augment the rather poor stocks of Worcester, to help break into a class of market in London that loved all things French and also to help the new Worcester modeller see the latest French shapes. Certainly there are a number of shapes produced in the next few years at Worcester that have a distinctly Parisian style about them. It should also be remembered that Flights were also selling many other things such as silver. In fact the account books of James Ross, a Worcester engraver, now in the possession of a descendant, Mr. Leslie Malabar, have four pages full of orders for

Joseph Flight covering the engraving of coats and arms, cyphers, designs etc. on silver articles, such pieces obviously being supplied to customers during the period 1786-1789.

Between the two visits to France, John Flight was in London opening the new shop and warehouse at No. 1, Coventry Street, but on 7th June 1789 he took up residence in Worcester in order to take an active part in the management of the factory and almost at once ran into trouble with Robert Chamberlain,[1] the owner of a rival manufactory, who, apparently behind the brothers' backs, had been negotiating to move into the old shop at No. 33, High Street to sell his wares, which were mainly Caughley wares decorated by Chamberlain, although he was also buying a small quantity of porcelain from Flight.

It was thought at one time that Chamberlain had broken away from the Worcester Company when Thomas Flight bought it in 1783, but Mr. Geoffrey Wills writing in the *Connoisseur* (June 1947) argues convincingly that John's diary entry at this time, "had I known of this the connection most likely would not have taken place between my brother and I and what we could have done had we not met with Mrs Hampton I cannot tell. I see no possible way by which we could have carried on the business", can only mean that Chamberlain had only just severed his connection.

Plate 12. Very unusual vase of hexagonal bottle shape, painted in onglaze colours with gilding and with exotic or fancy birds in each panel divided by rococo gold panels; 16¾in. high; mark open crescent and script "Flight" in gold; c.1790. It is possible that this vase was obtained in the white and decorated at Worcester. Dyson Perrins Museum.

1.   *See also Appendix I.*

24

Plate 13. A range of pieces from the superb dinner service made in 1792 for the Duke of Clarence, each piece painted en grisaille by Pennington with Hope leaning against an anchor within an underglaze blue border with elaborate gilding; mark crown "Flight" and crescent in blue. Christie's.

Certain it is that the first Chamberlain order is for the year 1788 and it is possible that Robert Chamberlain persuaded some of the workers at Warmstry House, the original Worcester Porcelain factory, to join him, for it is clear that he must have had good people working for him, as John states that he and his brother hired three of Chamberlain's men to help build a new kiln. From the outset, the two firms were in opposition and at one stage John even suspects Chamberlain of being behind the trouble they were encountering with the kiln. Chamberlain's attempts to seek a foothold and claim his products as Worcester came at an awkward time for the Flights who were endeavouring to expand and running into baffling problems with the kilns.

Plate 14. Dish from the fine service made for the Duke of Clarence in 1792; mark script word "Flight" below a crown and above a crescent in underglaze blue; 20¾in. x 15¼in. Geoffrey Godden.

The trouble with the kilns seemed endless. Despite alterations "the sulphur continues and spoils the ware" (28th June 1789) and certainly many pieces of blue printed wares of this period, marked with a crescent or a disguised numeral mark, show the effects of sulphuring, mainly a poor glaze appearance and heavy blueing (see also Chapter 6). It was thought that the cause might be rain entering the kiln making it damp and the brothers ordered a smaller kiln from London and considered erecting a kiln "on the Plan of Chamberlain's". Despite their efforts and the assistance of Mr. Kitchen (who John says "seems my sincerest friend") and the able Mrs. Hampton, things show little improvement. Meanwhile, Chamberlain opens his shop and "talks of making a flaming show in about 2 months". John then asks Chamberlain's man for help with the kiln and at his suggestion they burn with saggars, which improves the results "except for the top which was exposed to the Sulpher from the iron". However, liming the kiln helped remedy the trouble and by that time the kiln from London had arrived and was giving good results.

While John was struggling to improve the kiln firings, his brother Joseph succeeded in recruiting a clever painter — John Pennington — from under the nose of Chamberlain. Pennington had come from London, had been apprenticed to Wedgwood and became Worcester's chief artist, specialising in figures and landscapes and painted the Duke of Clarence service of 1792.

Other essential staff were also taken on, including "2 young girls to the burnishing".

About that time (July 1789) John was visited by Mr. T. Whitwell, a Coventry chemist, later to marry Ann Flight, who inspected the kilns and thought he could improve the method of burning. It was not until November, however, that the problem was solved, mainly by John, who found that the fault was in the method of stacking the charcoal and that the vent at the top of the kiln was too small.

But before this discovery, other difficulties were encountered, this time with the glaze and enamel colours, which ran in the firing. With so many troubles coming at once, the brothers' suspicions were roused regarding Shaw, the foreman and manufacturing clerk. It may seem very strange to us living in these days when secret processes and especially the basic formulae, are the automatic property of the owners of the Company, that this was not always so. Shaw was the only one who knew the formula and the brothers began to suspect that he was defrauding them by using inferior materials and that he might even be in the pay of Chamberlain. Industrial sabotage in those days!

John Flight even contemplated visiting Chamberlain to warn him from going too far but was disuaded from this dangerous step by his friends Mr. Gwinnell and Martin Barr, but it is an indication of his alarm that he begins to write some sections of his diary in French, as if to keep these innermost thoughts away from other eyes. This is the first mention of Martin Barr, who was later to join the Company and play a major role in its development after John's death.

With the assistance of Mrs. Hampton, Mr. Kitchen and Thomas Whitwell, however, John Flight experimented with the bodies, glazes and make up of the gold, quickly gaining an incredible insight into a most difficult process and unravelling the secrets of the formula. He also defeated an attempt by Chamberlain to entice away his burnishers.

So things were beginning to look up at last and a visit from his parents and sisters (October 1789) did a lot to cheer John up. During their stay, his father took the coach to Helston in Cornwall to buy a share in a lead mine from Tallach (lead was an important element in glazes and colours) and gave John sound advice on business and the best treatment of Shaw. On another theme, his sisters, who evidently thought it time that he bend his mind to more important matters, endeavoured to interest him in Mr. Trim's two daughters, but without succeeding, possibly because by then he had met Miss Ann Gillam, the daughter to Martin Barr's partner.[1]

For some time John had been planning another visit to France, but was advised against it by Lord Harcourt because of the unrest caused by the French Revolution. Instead he went to the London shop and after examining the stock, sent another large order to the Angoulême factory for an "assortment of ware". The firm must have been selling a great deal of Angoulême porcelain.

1.   *See page 30.*

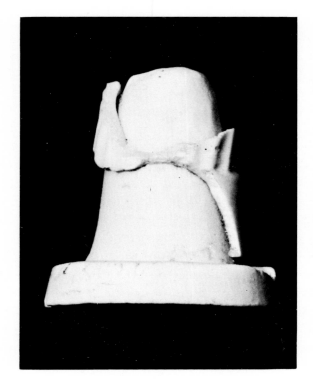

Plate 15. A waster thimble found fused to its firing support during archaeological excavations in 1977, the thimble was spiral fluted with plain lower section and although it was found in the same level as the 1830s trials was probably produced in the early Flight period.

Returning to Worcester, John, with his father's approval, confronted Shaw in Joseph's presence, regarding the various troubles and demanded the secrets of the body recipe. He also told him that his father had ordered him to weigh out the clays and glazes with him. Shaw prevaricated at first but eventually capitulated (to John's surprise) and it was agreed that he should weigh up the ingredients in John's presence. The nagging problem of the recipe was in fact finally laid to rest by Shaw's death in September 1790 when John was able to buy his papers from Shaw's father for ten guineas, having expected to have to pay much more. So the recipe was finally won back, although John had worked so hard to acquire the secrets through his experiments that it was probably really unneccesary to buy them.

The diary records the large order from the Duke of Clarence in 1789 for a service costing £700, the work to be completed in a year. Two quality painters were enlisted and John Flight makes the most interesting note that three specimen patterns were provided, from which the Duke was to choose, on the themes of "Arabesque", "Hope and Patience" and "Peace and Abundance". The Duke chose "Hope and Patience" and the local announcement of the order, coinciding with the "Grand Illuminations" in the City of Worcester to celebrate the Queen's Birthday, brought prestige and publicity to the factory.

There is a gap in the diary from January 1790 to 20th February, 1791, when John was to write his last few entries. These record his proposal and subsequent marriage to Ann Gillam. The wedding was attended by all of his family save Bannister and his wife. He afterwards took Ann to London for three weeks and then made a brief business trip to France for five days, surprisingly making no mention of the Revolution. There was another family reunion in London in December, 1790, when John records that, despite all the worries, it had been a good year for the factory.

The last entry was written on 27th February, 1791, and he described his visit to one of the potters who had been ill for a long time. He found the poor man in a deplorable state, his legs so full of ulcers and sores that he was offensive to come near and had probably been deserted by most. His sick payments had even been stopped by the club to which he belonged as they had been paid for so long, and John promised to look into the matter. As good as his word, he spoke to Mr. Lee, the Attorney, who had influence with the Manager of the Club.

He also records his delight in having received a letter from his brother, Bannister, that after being married for seven years "his wife is in the Family Way".

There is no forewarning of John's untimely end five months later and the cause of his death is not known. The absence of further entries after February 1791 could have been due to a long illness, but equally may have been because he was too busy to write. In his will he appointed Bannister Flight and Martin Barr his executors and bequeathed Ann an income of £2,400 a year.

It is fair to say that John Flight had played a major part in restoring the prestige and profitability of the factory from the very shaky position it had been in when he appeared to take up his part in 1788. In three short years, a position of despair had changed, a royal warrant and several royal orders obtained, a flourishing London shop opened and, more importantly, the factory put in good heart. That most of this was due to the work of John is self-evident from a study of the diary, as his father seems to have kept in the background, leaving John and Joseph to manage the business themselves and only giving advice when it was asked. We cannot tell much about Joseph from the diary but he seems to have been happy to let his younger brother assume control, make all the major decisions and do all the dirty work.

Chapter 2

Flight and Barr 1792—1804

A new partner had to be found to assist Joseph, someone with money and business sense, and it may seem strange that the firm should turn not to Bannister Flight or Thomas Flight junior but to Martin Barr of Worcester. Admittedly, Martin Barr had been appointed one of John Flight's executors and he was a partner of Thomas Gillam, whose daughter John had married, but he apparently had no knowledge of ceramics whatsoever.

The business of Gillam and Barr of High Street, Worcester, is noted as "Drapers, Salesmen, Mercers and Undertakers" in the bill-head that was engraved for them by James Ross. In the Worcester Directory for the year 1794, the firm is listed as "Thomas Gillam, Draper and Salesman, Leech Street" (an alternative Worcester form of Lich Street), this being after Martin Barr had left Gillam. The firm is subsequently referred to in James Ross's work books as "Gillam and Weaver, Salesmen Drapers and Mercers. Funerals Furnished", so Thomas Gillam was some while in replacing his original partner. Another side to Mr. Gillam's many business interests was as agent to the Royal Exchange Assurance and Fire Office, so Martin Barr can be said to have gained a wide knowledge of business in association with him.

On the 2nd January, 1792, Martin Barr was sworn and admitted a Citizen or Freeman of the City of Worcester on a composition or payment of £20 (previously, Joseph Flight on 27th December 1784 and John Flight on 15th November 1788 had been admitted as Freemen on payments of £30).

A most interesting explanation of the way in which Martin acquired the necessary money to pay for the rights to become a citizen and freeman (which gave voting and other rights) and to buy a partnership in the porcelain works is given in a letter from James Knight of Worcester to R.W. Binns, the future Art Director and Managing Director of the Worcester Royal Porcelain Company, dated 7th May, 1877, and referring to the latter's fine book *A Century of Potting in the City of Worcester*.

"Dear Sir,

I am sure I said no more of your work than it deserved. Freely translated, it may be said of you "Iam Marte quam Mercurio".

But I meant to tell you how the first "Martin Barr" got the money, or partly, the money with which he embarked with Flight the second, in the Porcelain Works.

Plate 16. *Flight and Barr tea-service of typical shape, simply decorated in gold with purple flowers; c.1792-96; mark an incised B. Phillips.*

Plate 17. *Early Flight and Barr part tea-service of typical spiral fluted shape, painted simply with a Bourbon Sprig pattern and gilding; c.1795-98; mark an incised B. Phillips.*

Plate 18. Unique pair of Flight and Barr punch bowls made for the Corporation of Worcester, painted in monochrome in the centre with portraits of King George III and Queen Charlotte by John Pennington, surrounded with elaborate gilding of ribbons, oak leaves, aesculapius and horns of plenty; on the outside rim are reserved panels containing the Corporation coat of arms and figures of Justice; mark in script "Worcester China Manufactory established 1751 Flight and Barr 1792" and a crown, together with a very small open blue crescent; made in 1792; diameter 12in., height 5in. In the possession of the Corporation of Worcester.

He was putting up the shutters of his not pretentious — rather humble — shop one evening after dark, when a drunken dragoon officer picked a quarrel with him. From words they came to blows, and the soldier cut Barr severely over the head with his sword. The publication of the business would have led perhaps to his being cashiered — certainly to very unpleasant consequences; so he hastened on becoming sober and conscious of the gravity of the mischief he had done to make pecuniary compensation and stop Barr's mouth. A large sum — for those days — was handed over, and with this money, thus acquired, in satisfaction for his cut head. Barr became a partner in the china works. The late Robert Gillam, so long in practice as a solicitor here, was a son of the Gillam with whom Barr was in partnership in Lich Street. It was commonly said that Barr had made his fortune by his enlivened scence [*sic*].

The Holdships were Quakers. What a capital plate No.3 (Bat printing) "Rustic Subject by Pyne" is.

You say (page 206) that S. Cole was one of Baxter's pupils between 1814 and 1816. Supposing Solomon to have been 12 or 14 at this period, it would make him about 75 years old. Surely he is not so much as that. I have known him tho; for more than 40 years, so it may be. Astles with a cork leg, and Pennington, a prim person (same page) I well remember. Humphrey Chamberlain painted and gave to the *late* C.H. Hebb (surgeon) a beautiful portrait on enamel [here three lines are crossed out]. This I had from Hebb's own lips. Excuse this rigmarole, and believe me.

Very faithfully yours,
James Knight."

Plate 19. Two unusual pieces transfer printed from earlier copper plates of the Dr. Wall period. Left: vase and stopper with the "Draw Well" scene printed in lavender and coloured over in enamels, height 11in; mark a crossed sword with star below in blue, almost certainly Flight and Barr c.1795-1800. Right: a jardinière with transfer prints in black of ruins and King George III; 6¼in.; mark an incised B; c.1792-1800, but might be as late as 1809 to commemorate the King's Jubilee. Dyson Perrins Museum.

Plate 20. An early Flight and Barr spiral fluted tea-bowl of ogee shape, painted with flower sprigs in purple and gold; style of the first half of the 1790s; script writing underneath "J. Cottrill Dec. 22nd 1795", by Joseph Cottrill who, as well as doing the fine hand written marks under the bases of pieces, possibly painted some of the wares of this type; in fact this piece might be one signifying that he had completed his apprenticeship; 2¼in. Geoffrey Godden.

So the firm suffers its first change of name and is called Flight and Barr. The exact year of this change was set by R.W. Binns as 1793 but several pieces of evidence suggest that it should be a year earlier.

For instance, in *Berrow's Worcester Journal*[1] on August 2nd 1792 appears the following advertisement.

"Worcester China Manufactory
Established 1751.
Warehouse No. 45 High Street.

Flight and Barr have the satisfaction in this public manner to say that, patronized by their Majesties and the Royal Family, and liberally encouraged by the Nobility and Gentry, their Manufactory of Porcelain is now so far extended as to constantly employ more than double the usual number of Enamellers and consequently require their whole attention. They are therefore determined to sell off as expeditiously as possible their Stocks of Jewellery, Plate and Sheffield Goods at considerably under prime cost.

Flight and Barr flatter themselves that with the additional Show Room they are now fitting up, their warehouse will display the most elegant assortment of British Porcelain that has ever been exhibited."

1. *I am indebted to the researches of Alderman Brotherton of Worcester in the finding of the advertisement in the files of* Berrow's Worcester Journal, *a newspaper still in publication and probably the newspaper that has been in continuous publication the longest.*

Plate 21. Part of an early Flight and Barr tea-set simply but beautifully decorated with purple and gilt sprigs; mark incised B; c.1792-1800. Hunt Collection.

A later edition of the same newspaper of 1st November, 1792, contained the following snippet of news:—

> "The Corporation of Worcester have been presented by Messrs Flight and Barr, Porcelain Manufacturers to their Majesties, with a pair of bowls of elegant design and workmanship."

This fine pair of punch bowls, are still owned by the Corporation of Worcester and are marked under the base "WORCESTER CHINA MANUFACTORY established 1751" in a circle and in the centre, under a crown "FLIGHT and BARR 1792".

James Ross's account books record the engraving of a card plate and billhead for Flight and Barr on June 18th 1792. (Appendix IV gives a list of all the entries for Flight and Barr in James Ross's account books.)

This I feel is good enough to put the start of the Flight and Barr period as 1792 and not as 1793 as has been held previously.[1]

Valentine Green's book on the history of Worcester contains a splendidly comprehensive account of a tour of Flight and Barr's factory which he made, together with a sideways glance at Chamberlain's establishment, and it is worth quoting this, and the footnote, in full.

1. *I also argue that the change in the name of the Company to Barr, Flight and Barr, usually given as 1807, is more likely to have been 1804. See Chapter 3.*

"The Royal Porcelain manufactory, situated in Palace — row at the bottom of Fish — Street, and extending from thence to the banks of the Severn, is deservedly held in high estimation, as, independent of the pleasure a curious mind must receive from observing the various processes of the business, the consideration of being able with out own materials and industry, to rival, and in fact, supersede that celebrated commodity of India, must afford great satisfaction to every lover of his country.

This manufactory was first established in the year 1751, by the late Dr. Wall, Mr. William Davis and several other gentlemen, under the firm of the Worcester Porcelain Company, and by their appointment, the late Mr. Samuel Bradeley vended the china when finished.

In the year 1783, the whole was purchased by Thomas Flight, Esq. of Hackney, Middlesex: from whom it was conveyed to the present proprietors, Messrs. Joseph Flight and Martin Barr.

The original company confined themselves principally to making blue and white ware: and the very ingenious method of transferring the impressions from copper plates upon the inferior articles, was their invention, and for a long time known only in this manufactory: but the *present* proprietors have engaged in this arduous undertaking with the laudable ambition of not only improving the *strength* and *colour* of the ware, but also of giving the most liberal encouragement to ingenious painters in emblematical compositions, and in landscape.

In the present year (1795) the improvements made in the texture of the ware, and the beautiful paintings now executed, have been so astonishingly great as to rival the royal china manufactories of the French, who, for many years before the present war, exported into this country immense quantities of their finest china ware: but happily in this instance, as well as in many others of great national importance the abilities and perseverance of our countrymen have

Plate 22. Very rare bourdeloue painted in the popular "Kylin" pattern of the Dr. Wall period but made in the Flight and Barr period, c.1795; no mark; 9¼in. by 5½in. Bourdeloues, often called in England "carriage pots", were chamber pots for ladies to use on long journeys. At the Court of Versailles the ladies were said to have had need of them during the sermons of Père Bourdeloue, hence the title. Private Collection.

Above: Barr Flight and Barr honey pot and cover painted panel of shells on an unusual pink/purple and cream marbled ground; script marks; 4½in; c.1805-08. O'Donaghue Collection.

Right: Flight Barr and Barr pot pourri bowl and cover, supported on three gilt winged sphinxes and triangular base, painted with a continuous band of flowers; impressed mark; 7½ins; c.1813-20. O'Donaghue Collection.

Below: Barr Flight and Barr triple spill vase, Barr's orange ground with oval panel of finely painted feathers of a quality which might be by Thomas Baxter; script mark under a crown and incised B; 6⁵/₈in; c.1803-08. O'Donaghue Collection.

Right: Fine Barr Flight and Barr vase with two heavily gilt dolphin and shell handles, salmon and gilt vermiculated ground reserving a large painted panel of Tintern Abbey; script mark; 12¾in; c.1805-10. O'Donaghue Collection.

rendered it totally unnecessary for the curious to apply for gratification in arts and manufactures either to France, or any other nation. And it is highly creditable to the enlightened taste of the British nobility and gentry that they have given the proprietors of this manufactory every possible encouragement to persevere in their exertions to render it an ornament to their country and an increasing advantage to many industrious and ingenious artists. But to his present Majesty the proprietors are under the highest obligations: he is known to the world as the patron and protector of the arts, and of industry: an object so replete with both, and in itself so interesting and important, as the Worcester china manufactory is known to be, could not be lost on the royal observation. In fortunately receiving the distinguished honour of being personally examined by their Majesties and the Princesses, during their visit to this city in 1788, in which its operations were minutely traced through the various stages of preparation, to the complete finishing of the ware, this factory ultimately received that reward to which the active exertions of the proprietors had confirmed its claim, and Worcester has thence the gratification of having the first ROYAL CHINA MANUFACTORY known in these kingdoms established within its walls. It was then also that the king was most graciously pleased to advise the proprietors to open a repository for the sale of their china at the court end of the metropolis. That condescending and encouraging advice was readily followed, and a warehouse at No.1 Coventry Street, Haymarket, was immediately established, under the auspices of their Majesties' patronage: an undertaking honoured by that of the different branches of the royal family, and also of the principal nobility and gentry of the Kingdom.

Plate 23. Flight and Barr dish painted with the "Kylin" pattern in onglaze enamels; 13¾in. by 10in. and 4in. high; mark Flight and Barr Worcester; c.1795. Geoffrey Godden.

Plate 24. Fine Flight and Barr dejeuner set and stand painted with the popular "Kylin" pattern (sometimes wrongly called Bishop Sumner and Bengal Tyger pattern); tea-pot 5in. high, stand 14in. by 9¾in; c.1795-1800. Geoffrey Godden.

The retail warehouse in Worcester was formerly kept opposite the Guildhall, in the High—Street, but the concern having very materially increased after the death of Mr. Bradeley, that place was found too small, and therefore the trade was removed to No.45, in the same street, nearer to the Cross and the principal inns. By applying to Messrs Flight and Barr, the nobility and gentry who visit this city are conducted through their beautiful and extensive shew-rooms *at that house*, and from *thence* have cards of admission to view the manufactory.

The china works are usually shown in the following order. The first operation viewed, is that of reducing the hard bodies made use of in the composition of the china into powder, which is performed by an iron roller, upwards of two tons weight, revolving in a groove not much unlike a cider-mill. The materials are then calcined and afterwards ground at the water-mill; where by a late improvement they are levigated sufficiently fine to filter through sieves, made on purpose for this manufactory, through which no particle larger than the fifty-seventh thousandth part of a square inch can pass. The composition then in its liquid state, is dried upon the slip-kilns till it becomes of the consistency of clay; it is then taken to the throwing-room, where the ware is first formed, and from thence to the stove-room in which it is placed to dry gradually, thereby preparing it for turning and pressing. The articles being applied to the lathe, are reduced to less than half the substance in which they were at first formed; here also are seen the various methods used in pressing the different sorts of ware into their respective moulds. From this department of the works, the first set of kilns, called Buiscuit-kilns, receives the ware, and in which it is burnt near 60 hours. In the second kiln-house, is performed the ingenious operation of making straight such pieces of the china that may have been warped from a too great degree of heat in the buiscuit-kiln. Here also are made the cases, or saggars, in which the ware is burnt. On the opposite side of the building, the dipping or glazing room, in which the china receives its beautiful glaze, is next shewn. From hence it is committed to a third ordeal of fire, in another

39

Two Barr Flight and Barr plates. Left: with the crest of the Duke of Gloucester, painted in the centre with landscape by Rogers on a pale salmon ground, richly gilded. Right: painted with "The High Tor at Matlock, Derbyshire", by Rogers, c.1810. Dyson Perrins Museum.

set of kilns, prepared for that purpose. The painting-room, a spacious apartment, lately enlarged to the length of near 60 feet, next exhibits its never-failing sources of entertainment and delight. After receiving here the embellishments of paintings and gilding, the ware is taken to the fourth set of kilns, called the Enamelling Kilns, wherein the gold and colours are intimately united to the substance to the glazing as to become equally durable with the ware itself. Lastly, from these kilns it is taken to the burnishing-room, where the gold receives that brilliant lustre, which has never yet been seen upon any foreign china.

Plate 25. Two fine Flight and Barr mugs with central oval panels painted with female portraits in sepia monochrome by John Pennington, surrounded by gilt spray and leaf ornament, the right-hand mug with "Conjugal Peace" subject, the title written under the base, together with the mark "Flight and Barr, Worcester" under a crown in script; 5¹/8in. high; c.1795. Dyson Perrins Museum.

In the course of the foregoing operations, many of the finer articles pass through the eight kilns several times, and are burnt, in the whole, near 200 hours. The process of printing the common ware, formerly kept a profound secret, is now openly shewn among the other operations of the manufactory."

An interesting note about the rival Chamberlain factory is also given by Valentine Green:—

"Mr. Chamberlain, senior, was bred in the Worcester manufactory, in which he was the first apprentice under the original proprietory. The ornamental part of the productions of that factory, and the embellishing of the ware, were carried out under the immediate direction of Mr. Chamberlain and his son for many years. This warehouse, opposite the Guildhall, is that, which was formerly occupied by Mr. Bradeley."

A number of interesting factors arise from these statements by Valentine Green, who, of course, knew the factory's production at first hand. The most important of these is the reference to the fact that "In the present year (1795) the improvements made in the texture of the ware . . . have been so astonishing great as to rival the royal china manufactories of the French . . ."

There is no doubt that quite shortly after Martin Barr joined Joseph Flight in 1792 the body and glaze became much harder and brighter, changing from the traditional Dr. Wall type soft paste body seen on the 1792 dated punch bowls, to one beginning to approach a hard paste type, but still not a true hard paste body.

Plate 26. Miniature tea-pot, lacking cover, and coffee-pot and cover; tea-pot decorated with gold sprigs, coffee-pot with brown gold scroll and leaf design; mark on coffee-pot incised B; 4½in. high; belonging to M. and E. Milbourne; tea-pot unmarked; 2¾in. high. Dyson Perrins Museum.

A comparative spectrometric semi-quantitative analysis of the new Flight and Barr porcelain with the earlier Davis/Flight type was done by the British Ceramic Research Association and a summary of their findings is given in Appendix V.

Worcester continued to use soaprock from Cornwall as the major constituent of their body right into the 1820s, with little change in the formula of 1795. Such small changes as there are have the effect of making the body and glaze look

Plate 27. Rare miniature sauce-boat and stand from a toy service painted in brown and gilt with scroll and leaf design; 4½in. long by 3in. high; c.1795-1800. Dyson Perrins Museum.

somewhat harder and more brilliant than the earlier wares, although they still remain a soft paste porcelain. It is very important in considering these later more brilliant appearing wares, to realise that quite a lot of blue scale pieces, decorated with fabulous birds, which were still continuing to be made, are often mistakenly thought to be fakes of a much later period. I will revert to this when considering the wares in Chapter 6.

So Flight and Barr continued to require great quantities of soaprock and also other raw materials from Cornwall and I am grateful for the help of Mr. John Penderill-Church, Company Historian of English China Clays, for various indications of this continuing search. For instance in 1799, one Parry from Worcestershire (we do not know if he was from Flight and Barr's factory) went to Cornwall to bid for a lease of Carloggas, a china clay and stone mine. He was said to come from "the Quaker House in Worcester — people of much money and few words". The reference to the "Quaker House" might have been a backward look at the factory in Dr. Wall's period, when a few of the partners were Quakers; certainly no member of the Flight or Barr families are known to have been Quakers.

In 1791 the main lease of Gew Graze near Mullion Cove, which had been Worcester's main source of soaprock since the Miller & Lund lease had been taken over in 1752, was replaced by a new lease, new seams of soaprock having been found

Plate 28. A selection of shapes from a pretty tea-service of early Flight and Barr, painted in a very simple and restrained way with scrolling leaves in chocolate brown and gilding; tea-pot 6¾in. high; mark incised B or Bx; c.1795-1804. Geoffrey Godden.

there. In 1808 the Company were employing five men at Gew Graze producing between about 15 and 20 tons of soaprock per annum and they were also raising soaprock at Caerthillian Crofts, Predannack Downs, Trethevas and Mullion.

In the diary of R. Warner, 10th October, 1808, is the following entry:—

"When we arrived at Gew Graze today, we saw some activity, with men digging the soaprock and women sorting it nearby. They told us that about 100lb. a week was being dug by each of five men. In a building nearby we saw some three or four women grading the soaprock and packing it into casks for the Worcester factory of Messrs. Flight and Barr."

In 1815 an interesting advertisement by Jethro Hornblower appeared, reading as follows:—

"To Owners of Vessels

WANTED, a VESSEL to remove 80 Tons of SOAP ROCK CLAY, from the Cove at Mullion across the Bay to Penzance. Application to be made to Mr. JETHRO HORNBLOWER, Whitehall, near Redruth, who will contract for the same.

Whitehall, April 19. 1815"

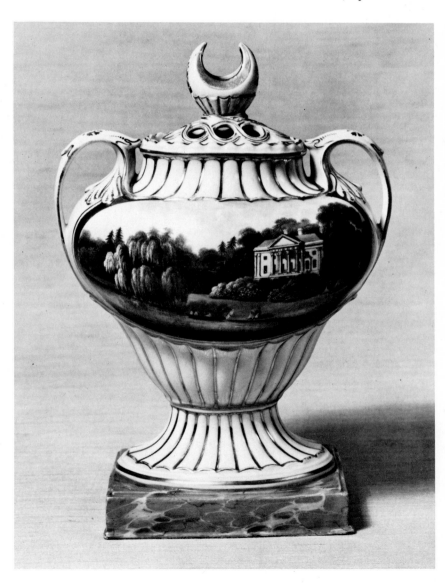

Plate 29. Rare Flight and Barr vase and cover (or possible pot-pourri) with a crescent shaped knop, square base painted to resemble marble, painted with a scene of a house and grounds which is probably that of the Barr's at Henwick, Worcester, the other side with a scene of Worcester from Henwick; 10¾in. high; mark incised B and reversed C incised; c.1795. Dyson Perrins Museum.

This advertisement was for a shallow draught vessel which could get into Mullion Harbour to collect the soaprock and bring it across the bay to Penzance for shipment to Worcester. In 1818, Flight and Barr's quarries were still operating on a small scale at Gew Graze and Dorose but Trethevas and Mullion Cliff were abandoned, and Caerthillian Crofts was being rapidly run down, the latter being closed down in 1820. In 1826 all the quarries were abandoned, no further rock being mined by Worcester. There was no alternative source of soaprock in the United Kingdom, the Shetland steatites being too contaminated with iron to be suitable.

A visit to the factory on 28th May 1796 by Charles Hatchett, a chemist, is recorded in his diary, published in an edition by Arthur Raistrick. This gives an interesting insight into the factory, which, although given by an outsider, is by a highly intelligent person and provides several valuable bits of information.

"Worcester —

Went to see the Porcelain Manufactory belonging to Messrs Flight and Barr.

I have observed that the Steatites of Cornwall is used as an ingredient but could not learn the other component parts of the paste or clay (perhaps it is the decomposed Feldtspar from St Stephen in Cornwall).

When the steatite is reduced to powder in a mill at Worcester, it is sent to some place about 10 miles distant to be mixed and washed: it is then brought back to W — and in a liquid state is passed through fine wire sieves, is dried and tempered with water for use.

When the ware is moulded it is of a brownish white or a very pale brown; it is then gently unperfectly dried. The bottoms and edges are then turned on a laithe and the Ribs if required are formed by pressing it in a Mould, the edges are then scalloped with a knife.

Plate 30. Tureen and stand, double spiral flute, finely painted in monochrome and gilding with grapes and vines; 7¼in. high, stand 8¼in. by 6in.; incised B mark; c.1795-1800. (Note that the double spiral flute is sometimes found on Flight and Barr wares as well as those of several other factories.) Geoffrey Godden.

46

The ware is then perfectly dried and is baked in a kiln, inclosed in pans of coarse clay. It then comes out in the state called Biscuit. If it is to be painted Blue (with cobalt) this is then done and the ware is again baked and then dipped into the glazing liquid which is of a pale red (perhaps contains Millium). The ware is then baked again and the blue colour strikes through the glazing.

If gold or any other colour than blue is to be used these are applied after the ware is glazed. The colours appear to be glazed with oil of Turpentine. The gold appears to be used in the state of Cassius's Precipitate.

Plate 31. An extraordinary Flight and Barr vase and cover in the form of Vaisseau à mat *of Sèvres, blue borders and gilding, painted on the front with a view of Hampton Court, Herefordshire; Script mark; c.1795; 13in. high. This is one of the most unusual of Worcester pieces, probably inspired by their interest in French porcelain. Collection of Mr. Arkwright.*

When the ware is painted with this it is put into a small square brick furnace and is arranged in a square iron pan which has an iron cover with a Pipe. On this cover Kundled charcole is put till the top is full.

The gold when the ware comes out of this furnace is of a dead buff colour and is burnished by women with Burnishers made of Agate or Haematite.

The fuel used in the kilns is a light Pit Coal in large masses with the appearance of charred wood in many places.

Sometimes instead of pencelling the ware they use engraved copper plates which they fill up with the colouring matter, then with rollers take off the impression on a sort of soft tissue paper which they then apply to the ware and rub with cushions of flannel.'

Of particular interest is that the factory was using a site 10 miles away (probably Dick Brook at Shrawley on the River Severn) to mix and wash the raw material; underglaze blue had a special hardening on firing before glazing and they were still producing underglaze blue transfer prints in 1796.

During the years 1796-98 Flight and Barr placed annual orders for 25 to 30 tons of fireclay with the Horsehay Company of Shropshire, one of the Darby/Reynolds group of ironworks, with clay interests too, as noted in a ledger, manuscript 334 of the Shrewsbury Borough Library Collection. The clay was shipped via the Shropshire Canal to Coalport and thence to Worcester (information provided by Roger Edmundson).

In 1800 Thomas Flight, who had bought the factory in 1783 for his sons John and Joseph, died. In his last few years it is doubtful if he had much effect on the working of the factory, but the new century began with Joseph Flight and Martin Barr in sole control; meanwhile Martin Barr's two sons, Martin and George, were being groomed to enter the firm.

Plate 32. Typical marked tea-pot base of the Flight and Barr period, showing the script mark "Flight & Barr Worcester Manufacturers to their Majesties" and an incised B; c.1800. Dyson Perrins Museum.

A superb Flight Barr and Barr vase in the classical style, painted in the centre with a named scene, "Gate of Carisbroke Castle", almost certainly by Thomas Baxter; script and impressed marks; 13¾in; c.1813-15. Dyson Perrins Museum.

Plate 33. Large jug and beaker, possibly for some sort of wine, cider or maybe lemonade (a rare version of this jug is found with cover and strainer at the spout), decorated with grapes and vine leaves, initials of the owner RB in gilding; jug 8½in. high, beaker 4in. high; mark incised B; c.1800. Geoffrey Godden.

Plate 34. Flight and Barr double-handled cider or beer mug, painted border of hops and leaves in pale shaded green, gilt bands and meander band of stylised hops; 7in. high; mark "Flight and Barr Worcester" in script under a crown and "Manus. to their Majs." incised B and reversed crescent and M in puce under base; c.1800. Dyson Perrins Museum.

Plate 35. Flight and Barr cream jug from a very elaborately decorated tea-service in the Japan style with underglaze blue and onglaze colours and gilding; 4in.; mark incised B; c.1800. Geoffrey Godden.

Beautiful small tankard, said to be painted by Thomas Baxter with a black silhouette of himself on the front, the remainder with a continuous panel of flowers with fine gilding; printed and impressed Flight Barr and Barr marks; 3½in; the base is inscribed "Septr. 1814". Dyson Perrins Museum.

Plate 36. A beautiful Flight and Barr dessert service painted with botanical specimens within spirally moulded borders painted in sepia with lily of the valley and gilding, flowers are named on reverse; some pieces with script marks and incised B; c.1800. Christie's.

Plate 37. A rare set of seven custard cups in the form of artichokes on a stand, decorated with gold; c.1800. Christie's.

Plate 38. Flight and Barr ink-stand, complete with inkwell and cover and taper holder, the drip pan supported by a gilt spotted fish; floral decoration on a gilt ground; 4¾in. high; incised B mark; c.1800. Barr Collection.

Plate 39. Different view of above.

54

Plate 40. Pair of Flight and Barr jardinières and separate stands with gilt ring handles, painted with panels of garden flowers on a chocolate ground and gilt with key fret and classical patterns; 6¼in.; incised B marks; c.1800. Christie's.

Plate 41. *Flight and Barr triple spill vase, Barr's orange ground, painted with a panel of feathers; script mark and incised B; c.1800, 6⅞in. O'Donaghue Collection.*

Plate 42. *Trade card of Flight and Barr c.1801, from the British Museum Collection, photographed by R.B. Fleming. This was engraved by James Ross and depicts the Warmstry House factory on the bank of the River Severn with Warmstry slip to the left.*

Plate 43. An interesting jug with a printed scene of Flight and Barr's factory on the front, the front of the factory carrying the inscription "Flight & Barr Royal China Manufactory". Christie's.

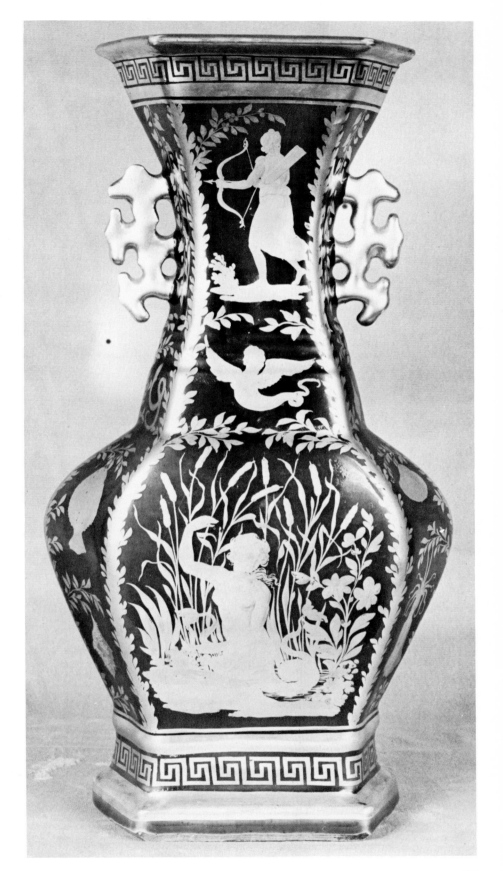

Plate 44. One of a pair of Chinese hard paste porcelain vases, decorated in gilt by Thomas Baxter in London on a cobalt ground, one signed "T Baxter 1801", the other "Thos. Baxter 1803"; this shows the superb gilding of which Baxter was capable in the classical style of the Greek vases of Sir William Hamilton. Barr Collection.

Plate 45. Superb plaque painted by Thomas Baxter, signed and dated February 1802, not factory marked and not necessarily a Flight and Barr production; probably painted at his father's decorating shop whilst Thomas was still a student at the Royal Academy Schools; 8in. by 7in. Dyson Perrins Museum.

Plate 46. Fine pair of Flight and Barr ice pails, covers and liners, bands of gilt fret above and below a band of Barr's orange colour, reserving oval panels finely painted probably by Baxter in London with shells which include those from the harp, cowrie, helmet, volute, screw shell and trochoid families, with two views of the rare cymatium ranzanii, an example of cassis Magdagascarensis, the queen helmet and conus Thalassiarchus; incised B marks; c.1800-05. Sotheby's.

Plate 47. Pair of Flight and Barr jardinières, Barr's orange ground and gilding, reserving panels of finely painted shells, possibly by Baxter in London; incised B mark; c.1800-05; 6¼in. Christie's.

Plate 48. Pair of Flight and Barr apricot ground jardinières, probably decorated by Thomas Baxter in the London studios, with fixed mooring ring handles, superbly gilded with classical figure subjects, one with a staff, the other with a caduceus and cornucopia, on a dot and star gilt ground; incised B marks; c.1800-04; 6¼in. Christie's.

Chapter 3

Barr Flight and Barr 1804-1813

There is some dispute as to the date the company next changed its name from Flight and Barr to Barr Flight and Barr, when Martin Barr junior was made a partner. Although it has been accepted as 1807, on 13th August 1804 Martin Barr had been sworn and admitted as Citizen or Freeman of the City of Worcester (as an apprentice to his father, Martin Barr, China Manufacturer) and there are a number of references to the name of the firm as Barr Flight and Barr from this time.

In James Ross's account book (see Appendix IV) is entered a bill for engraving a bill-head for "Barr Flight and Barr" on 27th December, 1804, and the entries continue under the heading of Barr Flight and Barr for a number of years.

In *Berrow's Worcester Journal* on 13th September, 1804, is the following entry:

"Subscriptions received for the Humane Society — Barr, Flight and Barr £3 3s.3d."

I feel this strong evidence to consider 1804 as the date at which the Company's name changed from Flight and Barr to Barr Flight and Barr.

Following the first Royal Warrant granted in 1789, other warrants followed. In 1807 a warrant was issued by the Prince of Wales:—

By the authority vested in me, I do hereby appoint Messrs. Martin Barr, Joseph Flight and Martin Barr Junr., of Worcester, to be Porcelain Manufacturers extraordinary to His Royal Highness the Prince of Wales, and permit them to have full liberty to erect His Royal Highness's arms or crest in token thereof.

London.

The 12th October 1807.   J. Hulse.
Entered.   Treasurer.
Phil. Fras. Hart.

In the following year a warrant was granted by the Princess of Wales:

By the authority vested in me, I do hereby appoint Messrs. Martin Barr, Joseph Flight, and Martin Barr, Junr., of Worcester, and of Coventry Street, London, to be Porcelain Manufacturers to Her Royal Highness the Princess of Wales, and permit them to have full liberty to erect Her Royal Highness's arms in token thereof.

London.

The 10th August 1808.   A.B. St. Leger.
J.L. Fras. Hulse.   Vice Chairman.

Plate 49. Constituent shapes of a tea-set of Barr Flight and Barr period, slightly different in form from that shown in Plate 28; simple floral meanderings in gold and purple; mark impressed; c.1802-05; tea-pot 10½in. x 6½in; the sugar does not require a cover. Geoffrey Godden.

These Royal Warrants were important in setting the royal seal of approval on Flight and Barr's factory and the growing number of services being made for the Royal Families bear testimony to this. The spill over of this royal approval led to the ordering of great services by great numbers of the nobility, both in England and abroad. (This is dealt with more fully in Appendix II.) It is a truism to say that Flight and Barr never had to advertise. Their advertisements were the fantastic services themselves which envious guests would see when they attended a great banquet in their host's house, sneaking a look under the base of a beautiful plate to see the Flight and Barr mark, either written with a pen by Joseph Cotterill or printed with a wonderful flamboyant and yet at the same time very tasteful trade mark stamp that gave the guest everything he wanted to know about who had made the service and where to order one.

During the Flight period, the Company had experienced the problem of trying to obtain formulae from the recalcitrant Shaw; during the Barr Flight and Barr period they were troubled by two employees, William Billingsley and his brother-in-law, Samuel Walker, imparting their secrets to rival companies.

William Billingsley was one of the most extraordinary characters in English ceramic history. From the time of his becoming a painter of flower subjects at Derby, through his wanderings at such places as Mansfield and Torksey, he established himself as not only a leading painter but also a great expert on ceramic bodies and kilns.

Plate 50. Fine Barr Flight and Barr tea-pot, grey marbled decoration with a panel of shells; incised B inside cover and script mark under base; c.1803-05; 6in. O'Donaghue Collection.

Plate 51. Fine pair of Barr Flight and Barr jardinières and stands, painted and gilt with classical subjects by Thomas Baxter; signed and dated 1804. Christie's.

It was his great experience in the latter that led Barr Flight and Barr to enlist his aid and early in 1808 he arrived in Worcester, accompanied by his daughters Sarah and Lavinia and Samuel Walker who was later to marry Sarah at Claines Parish Church in Worcester on 22nd September 1812. Billingsley had been in some kind of trouble in the North of England and had used an alias, calling himself *Beeley* but whether Barr Flight and Barr knew of this is not certain.

It is certain, however, that both Billingsley and Walker began working for Barr Flight and Barr in 1808, and it is probable that Sarah and Lavinia were also employed, possibly as burnishers. This is hinted at in a fascinating letter from Sarah to her Mother, sent, presumably from the point of escaping detection, addressed to Mr. John Rawson of Blackwell near Alfreton, Derbyshire with whom Mrs. Billingsley was then staying. This letter was first quoted in the *Old Derby China Factory* by John Haslem, who had a copy of the letter in his possession, and later in *William Billingsley* by W.D. John, but it is worth giving it again as it throws such a great deal of light upon life in general at a factory. The Mr. W. referred to is Samuel Walker and it is also clear that the Billingsleys had previously tried for work in Wales, probably at Swansea.

"My Dear Mother,   Oct. 24, 1808.

"I am only this day favour'd with your kind letter, & my dear Grandmother's kind present. I have been very anxious & unhappy till I heard from you, I was fearfull my letter had got lost, or had fallen into somebodys hands it ought not, & might lead to Discovery where we was, and I thought if I wrote again that might share the same fate. However notwithstanding these doubts I had wrote another letter which I intended to have sent in a few Days, but your letter eased my Doubts in that respect, altho' I cannot think what could be the reason of its being above a Month on the road, for yours was Dated Sepr. 20—ever since we have been here we have gone frequently to the Office but they always said there was not a letter. Your prayers my Dear Mother are heard, & we are again in our Native Country, after experiencing very Great hardships, which would fill sheets to recount, but which I shall take pleasure in relating to you when I have the happiness of seeing you, which I long to Do, & I trust it will not be very long first.

"I don't recollect whether I told you after the Storm and we got into harbour that I durst not venture on Ship Board again, but prefer'd walking between 50 or 60 miles. I was so terrified anything was preferable to going on Board again, I thought during the Storm your last words were prophetic when you said you should never see us more; you may Judge of my feelings, I had a thousand anxious fears for you, and I was doubtful whether you would ever hear of our fate on account of the Name we went by—but thank God we are safe from those Dangers. We were all very sick, but I was dreadfully so, I was obliged to be put to Bed, but the Ship was in such Dreadfull Motion that I was knocked from one side of the bed to the other for 7 or 8 hours. There were severall passengers on Board that had been severall voyages, one of them had been in a Storm or two before, but said they never experienced anything so Dreadfull, and I could not think of returning by Sea, so we had to walk all the way back which in the whole amounted to near 400 miles, so you may Judge of our fatigue and we had severall Days very Bad Weather.

"I must now tell you Father has got into a situation, but wages very low for a good hand, indeed he has not any more at present than the Common hands. We were obliged to write out of Wales to get them to advance a little Money to help us back again. I dare not name the place we are at for fear of my letter being opened, but I think you will Judge. My Father's wages being so low & everything so extremely high here that with every frugality we could not subsist on it, & now Lavinia and myself have begun to go to work, I dont know what we are to have a Week but it is I believe very little at first, it is not Burnishing, it is a kind of work you never saw [? Printing]. You may Judge of the low wages here when I tell you that when a young woman first goes to Burnishing she has not more than 3s.6d a week for the first year & never more than 6s. when they have worked 4 or 5 years. Lodgings & House rent is uncommonly Dear, we pay 6s. a week for two rooms, and they are reckoned the cheapest rooms in the Town, we cannot get a bit of Bread Flour under 3s.6d a Stone and everything dear in proportion. We go to work at 7 in the morning and leave at 7 at night, but I am troubling you with what cannot render you any Service. I was very ill for a few days after we got here, but am now very well indeed. Mr. W. has not got a Situation yet, but the person who we work for has promised to think of a place for him as soon as he can. I wish my Dear Mother I had it in my power to send you something, but after relating the particulars I have you will see it is not in my power, but I hope when our wages comes to be settled & Mr. W. gets into work I shall be able to send you something to come to us. So short was we of money that we could not pay the Lodgings, but when your and my Dear Grandmother's kind present came in I paid 12s. of it for the fortnight's Lodgings.

"Will you have the Goodness, my dear Mother, to present my best respects to Mr. & Mrs Adlington and say to them how gratefull I feel to them for their kindness to you, and likewise their kind wishes in regard to my sister & that I hope a time may come when I may have an opportunity of evincing my Gratitude. Do be very particular in observing if the Seal of this letter is safe & write to me very soon, & I will then in my next say where we are and all particulars.

"I am very sorry to hear Grandmother and yourself have been so poorly, but sincerely hope you are both better. Dont forget to give my best respects to S. Rawson and family & also thank

Plate 52. Fine Barr Flight and Barr urn of classical shape, pale blue ground and gilding, painted with shells on a marble topped table, probably by Baxter, the reverse finely decorated with classical forms in brown and gold shown in Plate 53; script and impressed marks; c.1804-10; 13½in. Barr Collection.

Classical Flight Barr and Barr vase and cover with double headed twisted serpent handles and flamiform knop, applied pearls and fine gilding, superb painting of fancy birds in detailed parkland landscape typical of George Davis; mark in script; 9⁵⁄₈in; c.1815. Dyson Perrins Museum.

them in my name, for their kindness, and best love to aunt Boot when you see her. I think My Dear Mother, if you have not been at Derby you had better to a little while, as they expressed such a wish to see you particularly Mrs. Smith and Mrs. Duesbury, each of them wish'd you to spend a few weeks with them. I wish you was with us.

"I am affraid you will hardly be able to make all my letter out, indeed I can hardly see what I have written my eyes ache so with looking at work all Day. Father and Lavinia Joins in Love to you and Grandmother & respects to all. I have many things I could wish to tell you but Durst not for fear of any accident happening to my letter—in yours do tell me all you know about how things are settled have you heard anything of Turner. I had some thoughts of writing to him but hardly knew how to act, as his conduct was so strange.

"Adieu my Dear Mother & believe me your very affectionate Sarah B. Mr. W. desires his best respects to you and Grandmother. Dont forget to say everything for me to Mr. & Mrs Adlington & S. Rawson. Direct your letter the same as the last."

It has never been exactly clear what work Billingsley and Walker did at Worcester. William Billingsley would not seem to have done very much painting, although a very few examples of Barr Flight and Barr pieces exist that are almost certainly painted with his characteristic flowers.

Their main work at first seems to have been in improvements in the kilns with the introduction of a new type of muffle kiln for firing the enamels, but it would appear that in November 1809 an agreement was entered into with Martin Barr for them to work on an improvement of the body to achieve more translucence, possibly by the addition of bone ash to the soaprock body.

Some improvement, real or imagined, must have taken place because Mr. R.W. Binns, later to become Art Director of the Worcester Royal Porcelain Company, quotes a letter sent from Martin Barr to the editor of the London Miscellany in 1810:—

"It affords me considerable gratification to inform you that perseverence has accomplished very great improvements in the texture, whiteness and beauty of our porcelain."[1]

It seems certain that experiments must have gone ahead and that in November 1812 a bond was drawn up between Barr Flight and Barr on the one hand and Billingsley and Walker on the other. The original bond has not been preserved but by a fortunate chance a draft of it was sent to Samuel Walker at Swansea when the Company was considering prosecution and was copied into a book of ceramic recipes by Lewis Dilwyn, proprietor of the Cambrian Pottery and China Works. This was first published in *Analysed Specimens of English Porcelain* by Eccles and

1. *This may, of course, be simply a publicity stunt because to my eye there is no basic difference between the improved harder body of Flight and Barr in 1795 and the wares of the Barr Flight and Barr and Flight Barr and Barr periods, until the very last years of Flight Barr and Barr in the 1830s when some bone china was made. To my knowledge, no finished examples of highly translucent artificial porcelains of the frit type have been found from the Flight and Barr factory, although on the factory site during excavations were found some biscuit and glaze wasters which looked not unlike the finest wares of Nantgarw. It is possible that some finished examples were produced and I should be most interested to learn of any possible pieces.*

Plate 53. The reverse of the vase shown in Plate 52.

Plate 54. Pair of Barr Flight and Barr coffee cans and saucers painted with roses, poppies, bluebells and other flowers on a black ground surrounded by grey marbled ground and gilding; script marks; c.1803-06. Beauchamp Galleries.

Rackham and later, in a reconstructed form, in E. Morton Nance's *The Pottery & Porcelain of Swansea & Nantgarw*:—

Know all Men by these presents that we   are held and firmly bound to   in the Sum of one thousand pounds of good and lawful money of Great Britain to be paid to the said   or their Attorney, Executors, administrators or assigns for the true payment whereof we bind ourselves jointly and severally and our respective heirs executors and administrators for and in the whole firmly by these presents sealed with out seals dated this 17 day of November in the 53 years of the reign of G. 3 and of our Lord 1812, whereas in consideration of the sum of 200£ of Lawful British Money now paid the receipt whereof is hereby acknowledged and also divers sums of money paid in the course of the last three years by way of wages while Experiments were making they the above bounden   have imparted and disclosed to the said   the knowledge of a certain secret relating to a new method of composing Porcelain the principles of which are specified and set forth on the back hereof and have agreed not to reveal the same to any person or persons whomsoever or to make use thereof to their own advantage in any manner Now the considerations of this obligation is such that the above bounden

shall and do from time to time and at all times for ever hereafter forbear from communicating and imparting the secret above mentioned to all and every person or persons whomsoever and shall and do from time to time and at all times refrain from making use or availing themselves of their knowledge of such secret in order to procure any further emolument or advantage whatsoever unless they or either of them or their or either of their Heirs shall at any time hereafter engage in the Trade or Business of a china Manufacturer in which case they reserve to themselves the Liberty of making use of the said secret in carrying on such Business then this obligation shall be void but otherwise to be and remain in full force and effect
Sealed and Delivered being first
duly stamped in the presence of

Flight and Barr quote the following passage from the Bond in their letter to Walker which does not appear in the above:—

"but not to the profit of any partners or yourselves if engaged with other Partners."

Although Billingsley and Walker must have been under some sort of legally binding contract, this did not stop them once more in November 1813 uprooting themselves and slipping off to Nantgarw to make the new body. They have always struck me as a pair of crafty rogues, although I may be doing them an injustice and I know that many people regard them highly.

Plate 55. Parts of a very large Barr Flight and Barr dinner service painted with Royal Lily pattern in blue and gold, rims with brown edge; incised B marks and script marks and gilders numerals; c.1804-06. It is interesting to reflect that this service when sold at auction some 160 years after it was originally made, still comprised two soup tureens, covers and stands, four vegetable tureens, covers and stands, six sauce tureens, covers and stands, salad bowl and stand, 20 oval meat dishes in sizes, 22 soup plates, 73 dinner plates and 31 side plates, a total of 180 pieces and a testimony to its durable qualities. Sotheby's.

The Company directors did not regard their action in a good light and a letter from Flight Barr and Barr (the name had changed yet again in 1813 with the death of Martin Barr senior) addressed to Samuel Walker, again preserved in Lewis Dillwyn's notebooks, is quoted in *Analysed Specimens of English Porcelain*:—

"Mr. S W   Worcester. Nov. 12. 1814.
    Sir

We were a good deal surprized after the kind and liberal treatment yourself and Mr. Billingsley experienced from us, that you both so suddenly left our works—how far this conduct was consistent we leave you to consider—in addition however to this breach of confidence, we are now told that you are about forming some sort of connection with a Person of the name of Young, and also with Messrs. Dilwyn and Bevington Potters of Swansea, and that you are to make for them a composition the principles of which are similar to the one for which we paid you a high premium, besides being at great expences in your wages etc. during the time of your acquiring this knowledge by experiments made at our works.

You well know that you engaged that the secret should be entirely confined to ourselves, or ultimately to you and Mr. Billingsley if ever you should venture to make the Article yourselves, but not to the profit of any Partners, or yourselves if engaged with other Partners—for if this were the case the advantage to be derived from the secret, for which we gave so large a price would be destroyed

Plate 56. Pair of Barr Flight and Barr mugs painted in "India" style with tropical or exotic birds in onglaze enamel colours of blue, red, pink, green, purple and gold; 7in. high, 5½in. diameter; mark an incised B and script "Flight and Barr" under a crown and "Barr Flight and Barr, Manufacturers to their Majesties and Royal Family"; c.1804-06. From collection of Mr. Jessop.

You and Mr. Billingsley are jointly and severally bound to us in a penalty of one thousand pounds to forbear from communicating the secret to any person or persons whomsoever, and if we find upon further enquiry that you really mean to adopt a line of conduct so dishonourable as that before alluded to—we now inform you of our firm resolution of instantly giving our attorney Instructions to commence an Action against you for the amount of the Penalty of one Thousand Pounds named in the Bond given to us the 17 day of November 1812.

We are Sir

Yrs etc,

Flight, Barr & Barr.

PS. We shall wait the return of the Post for your answer before we address a Letter on this subject to Messrs. Dilwyn and Bevington."

Plate 57. Pair of Barr Flight and Barr "Music" candlesticks, salmon ground, vermiculi and key fret gilding, painted landscapes; incised B and script mark of Flight and Barr London and Barr Flight and Barr Worcester; c.1804-10; 5¾in. O'Donaghue Collection.

Plate 58. *Fine Barr Flight and Barr breakfast service painted in the Kakiemon style with two quail strutting among flowering shrubs and prunus within a border of iron-red scrolls; the surviving parts of the service comprise two two-handled porringers, covers and stands, cylindrical butter tub and stand, hot water jug, sugar bowl, milk jugs, seven saucer dishes, sixteen plates, four bowls in two sizes, eleven breakfast cups and twelve saucers, twelve tea-cups, ten large coffee stands, twelve small coffee cans, fourteen saucers; impressed and incised B marks; c.1805. Sotheby's.*

Plate 59. *Superb Barr Flight and Barr desk-set, each piece painted with shells or feathers on a grey marbled ground, comprising kidney shaped inkstand with bird's-head handle set with three pots and covers and pierced with holes for pens; 6¾in. wide, taperstick 2½in; a pen tray of canoe shape, and a pair of large spills of trumpet shape with gilt ring handles, 5in; c.1805-08. Sotheby's.*

Plate 60. Part of a superb Barr Flight and Barr service made for John Prendergast, 1st Viscount Gort; the two urns are decorated with sporting subjects and florals and shells, the 24 plates with named scenes and theatrical scenes; elaborate script mark including Prince of Wales plumes; c.1805-10. James Robinson Inc.

Plate 61. Part of a fine Barr Flight and Barr harlequin dessert service, painted with a range of naturalistic and figure subjects, classical style gilding; c.1810. James Robinson Inc.

No reply would have appeared to have been received from Billingsley and Walker and Flight Barr and Barr must have written to Dilwyn himself complaining about the affair, although reading between the lines it almost seems as if the Company were glad to be rid of them. Lewis Dillwyn, in a letter to Joseph Marryat in 1849 referred to this:—

"While engaged in some experiments for strengthening this body, so that the articles might retain their shape in the kilns, and for removing the liability to craze and shiver, I was astonished by receiving a notice from Flight & Barr, of Worcester, that the persons who called themselves Walker and Beely had clandestinely left their service, and warning me not to employ them. Flight & Barr in the most gentlemanlike way, at the same time convinced me that this granulated body could never be made of any use, and as it was not worth their while to prosecute them, the runaways went back for a few months to Nantgarrow, and I do not know what afterwards became of them. Beeley, under the name of Billingsly, though he had another alias, was well known in all the British China manufactories to be a first-rate modeller of flowers, and Walker whose other name I forget, had married his daughter, and was employed with his father-in-law in Flight & Barr's mixing room . . ."

Plate 62. Pair of Barr Flight and Barr spill vases painted with studies of old people probably by Thomas Baxter from earlier drawings or paintings; mark in script; c.1805-10; 4¼in. Erle Randall.

Plate 63. Barr Flight and Barr vase with two heavily gilt dolphin and shell handles, salmon and gold vermiculi ground, painted with a panel of Tintern Abbey, Monmouthshire; script mark including reference to the Prince of Wales and Royal Family; c.1805-10; 12¾in. O'Donaghue Collection.

It is likely that if Flight Barr and Barr had put this experimental body into production they would have suffered the same problems that befell Nantgarw with the collapse of most of the wares during firing and probably the best thing that happened to Worcester was the flight of Billingsley and Walker. Samuel Walker left for pastures new in the New World and many years later, in 1874, the Worcester Royal Porcelain Company received a letter from him in which he was offering to sell new experiments in porcelain. This letter, quoted in full in my book, *Royal Worcester Porcelain from 1862*, ends with a postscript.

"I was employed by Mess[s] Flight and Barr 50 years ago makeing [*sic*] experiments. I made them a fine China — Mr. Barr gave a £100 for it."

A cheeky rogue indeed!

Martin Barr senior had died on November 10th 1813, aged 56. The local newspaper marked the event in the following words:— "Died the 10th Inst. Mr. Barr, one of the proprietors of the Royal Porcelain Works in this City; after an illness of a few weeks, during which he was eminently supported by the hopes and consolation of a Christian. His removal from a sphere of active usefulness in public and private life will, we feel assured, be long and sincerely lamented." As well as his work at the factory he seems to have been deeply involved with the life of the City. In *Berrow's Worcester Journal* are frequent references to this work, for instance on 10th August, 1804, where he is mentioned as auditor of the Royal Infirmary; 11th July, 1805, as

Plate 64. Rare Barr Flight and Barr garniture comprising a covered vase with rams head terminals to the handles and a pair of jardinière shaped vases with false ring handles, finely painted with panels containing a King Charles Spaniel, a Hound and a Greyhound, possibly by John Pennington, reserved on a Barr's orange ground, richly vermiculated in gilding between bold key fret and entwined Greek key borders; 8¼ins. and 5in; script and impressed marks; c.1805-10. Sotheby's.

Plate 65. Dessert dish of ribbed lobed shape finely bat printed in black with shells and gilding; mark BFB under a crown impressed; c.1805-13. Dyson Perrins Museum.

a director of the Worcester House of Industry (later to become the Workhouse and nowadays Shrub Hill Hospital) and 5th December, 1805, auditor and committee member of Worcester Library.

A copy of Martin Barr senior's will is preserved in the archives of the Corporation of the City of Worcester (as also are those of his sons, and Joseph Flight) and it may be of particular interest to quote this in full:—

"This is the last Will and Testament of me Martin Barr of the City of Worcester Porcelain Manufacturers. I bequeath to my dear wife Hannah Barr all my household furniture, plate and linen, wines and books and also two Policies of Assurances in the London Annuity Office and to whom I also give and bequeath the sum of one hundred and forty pounds per annum for her life by four equal quarter payments to be made by my sons Martin Barr and George Barr in consideration of my share of the Good will of the Porcelain concern carried on in Worcester and London which I give and bequeath to them as Tenants in common and I do hereby charge the same with the said annuity accordingly Provided and in case it shall be more satisfactory to my wife to have the said annuity purchased and well secured I request it may be so by my said sons as aforesaid or she may make such purchase from my other Estate general but in the latter case I direct my said sons to yield and pay an equivilent to the purchase money or an annumity of the same amount into my said other Estate general as for the benefit of all my children for my said wife's life in lieu of the said annuity they are hereinbefore requested to pay any said wife themselves it is my will that what remains due for the purchase money and interest thereon of the moiety of the Porcelain works and the four houses adjoining now enhabited by James Pennington,[1] James Price, Emma Hunt and Joseph Johnson situate in the Parish of Saint Alban in the City of Worcester which were conveyed to me by Mr Joseph Flight should be settled for with him his heirs or assigns out of my other effects in the Partnership concern and further it is my will that the moiety of the said Porcelain works and of the four houses adjoining be valued by persons of skill and integrity to my sons Martin Barr and George Barr their heirs and assigns one person to be named by Mrs Barr and my other Children who shall be of age so to value the premises and after the payment of all my just debts I desire that the value of the said Premises and all the residue and remainder of my real and personal Estate and Effects may be equally divided amongst the said Martin Barr and George Barr and all other my Children and their heirs executors and administrators and assigns respectively equally share and share alike and that the same be paid with Interest by my sons Martin Barr and George Barr as soon as each shall arrive at the age of twenty one years or within three years after my decease or as much earlier as may be convenient and I appoint my dear wife Hannah Barr Executrix and my sons Martin Barr and George Barr Executors of this my last Will and Testament In witness whereof I have hereunto set my hand and seal this second day of November one thousand eight hundred and thirteen — MARTIN BARR — Signed sealed and delivered by the said Testator Martin Barr as and for his last Will and Testament in the presence of us who in his presence and in the presence of each other have hereunto subscribed our names as witnesses — W. Willes — I. Dickens — Ann Williams.

Proved at London 16th May 1814 before the Judge by the Oaths of Hannah Barr Widow the Relict and Martin Barr and George Barr the Sons the Executors to whom admon was granted having been first sworn (by Commission) duly so administered."

Plate 66. Beaker for lemonade or similar, bat printed with rustic figure subjects after Pyne between gilt lines; mark BFB under a crown impressed; c.1808. Dyson Perrins Museum.

1.   Of particular interest in this will is the note that James Pennington and Emma Hunt, who we meet with in John Flight's diaries, were living in houses owned by the factory, probably an indication of the importance of these two employees.

Plate 67. Barr Flight and Barr plate painted in rich Japan or Imari style in red, gold and underglaze blue and pink flowers; impressed and script marks; c.1805-13. Collection of Mrs. E. Collard.

Plate 68. Barr Flight and Barr honey pot with fixed stand and high domed cover, the jar finely painted with "Forge Bridge, Westmorland", the cover with "View from Port Elliot, Cornwall" in panels on a salmon ground, richly gilt with bands of entwined chevron pattern on a vermicular ground; 5½in; impressed and script marks; c.1808. O'Donaghue Collection.

Plate 71. Barr Flight and Barr inkwell, liner and inner cover and foliate cover, kidney shape, with mask loop handle and two flared containers, painted with a scene of Binstead Cottage, Isle of Wight, within gilt foliate scrollwork reserved on a pink ground; 5¾in. wide; script marks; c.1808. Sotheby's.

Plate 69. Barr Flight and Barr honey pot and cover decorated with a panel of finely painted feathers, reserved on a most unusual marble ground; 5in. high; script mark; c.1808-10. Barr Collection.

Plate 70. The feather painted side of the honey pot shown in Plate 69.

Plate 72. Magnificent Barr Flight and Barr vase and cover with shell and dolphin handles made to commemorate the capture of the French frigate La Guerrier *by* HMS Blanch *commanded by Commander (later Sir Thomas) Lavie in 1808. The painting, almost certainly by John Pennington, is symbolic of the victory, the fine gilding comprises naval emblems, the reverse a description of the battle. The vase was a gift to President Kennedy in 1961 and it is still in the White House. White House Collection.*

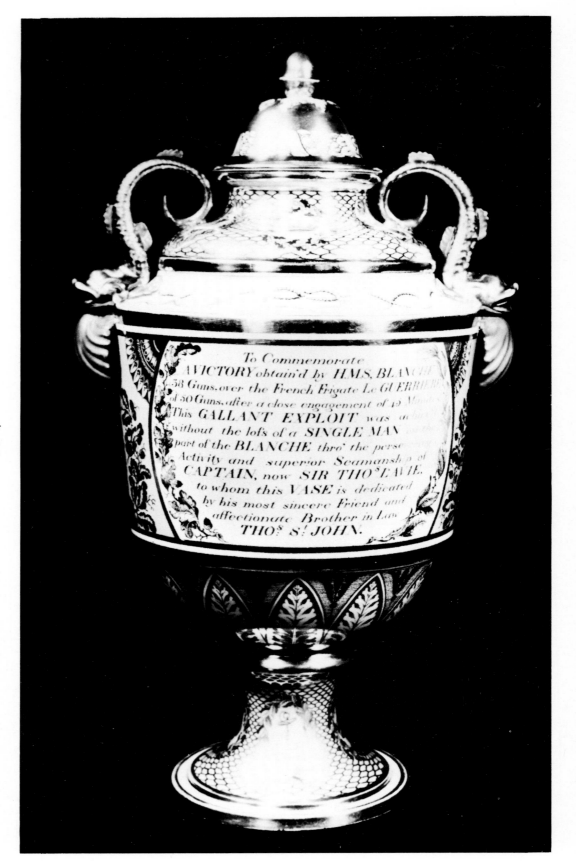

Plate 73. The reverse of the Lavie vase shown in Plate 72, the inscription in gold.

To Commemorate
A VICTORY obtain'd by H.M.S. BLANCHE
58 Guns, over the French Frigate Le GUERRIERE
of 50 Guns, after a close engagement of 19 Minutes
This GALLANT EXPLOIT was achiev'd
without the lofs of a SINGLE MAN on the
part of the BLANCHE thro' the persevering
Activity and superior Seamanship of
CAPTAIN, now SIR THO.ˢ LAVIE,
to whom this VASE is dedicated
by his most sincere Friend and
affectionate Brother in Law
THOˢ Sᵗ JOHN.

Left: Plate 74. A pair of Barr Flight and Barr vases and covers with double eagle and serpent handles in burnished gilding, painted with a named water bird in rectangular panels on a deep claret ground between pearl borders, gilt flamiform knobs, the birds named as Dunlin and Green Sandpiper; 6in; impressed and printed marks; c.1808-13. Sotheby's.

Plate 75. Barr Flight and Barr vase, lacking cover, of depressed urn shape, resting on three gilt Empire style legs with foliate terminals and lion's paw feet, supported on a trefoil base with cracked ice gilding, painted with a scene from The Tempest, Act III, Scene 1, Miranda and Ferdinand, possibly by Pennington, on a rich coral ground heightened with vermiculi gilding; 7½in; script and impressed marks and quotation from the play; c.1810. Sotheby's.

One of a pair of Flight Barr and Barr ice pails, covers and liners painted panels of shells, almost certainly by Thomas Baxter, with deep blue ground and fine gilding; impressed mark; 11¾in; c.1813-20. Dyson Perrins Museum.

Plate 76. Fine Barr Flight and Barr vase and cover with flamiform knob, buff ground with gilding, painted with a view of Amberley Castle, Sussex; impressed and script mark; c.1810; 8¾in. Private Collection, courtesy of Geoffrey Godden.

Plate 77. Pair of Barr Flight and Barr vases of campana shape, two entwined handles, painted in bright colours with sprays and sprigs of garden flowers, reserved on a pale periwinkle-blue ground, above a beaded border, the base with foliate scroll-work gilding; script marks; c.1810. Martin Hutton.

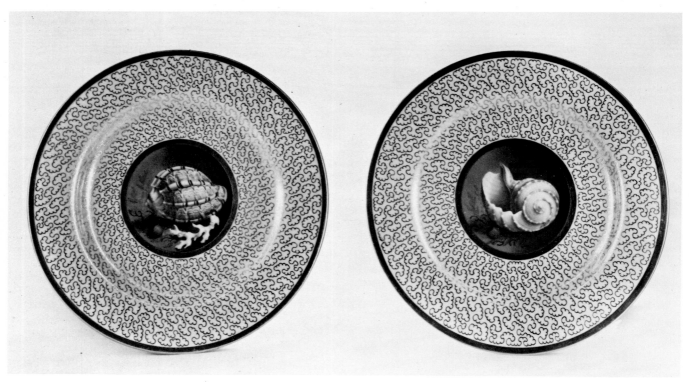

Plate 78. Two plates from a fine Barr Flight and Barr dessert service, finely painted in the centre with shells, corals and aquatic plants, the borders with a full version of vermiculi in gold, the interlinking maze or jigsaw-like pattern that was a long tiring job to do, possibly by young gilders; 8¼in.; marks impressed and printed; c.1810. Sotheby's.

90

Left: Plate 79. Unusual inkwell in the form of an antique oil lamp with swan-neck handle on a rectangular plinth, borders and motifs of grotesque figures and palmettes in the classical style painted in brown and gold; 6¼in. high; no mark; c.1810. Dyson Perrins Museum.

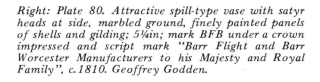

Right: Plate 80. Attractive spill-type vase with satyr heads at side, marbled ground, finely painted panels of shells and gilding; 5¼in; mark BFB under a crown impressed and script mark "Barr Flight and Barr Worcester Manufacturers to his Majesty and Royal Family", c.1810. Geoffrey Godden.

Plate 81. One of a pair of Barr Flight and Barr fruit coolers, superbly painted and gilded by Thomas Baxter; impressed mark; c.1810; 11in. Beaverbrook Art Gallery, Fredericton, Canada, gift of Mrs. Howard W. Pillow.

Plate 82. Left: jug with a central scene bat printed in black with a scene of Worcester from the North West, taken from the garden of the Barr's house in Hallow Road, other bat printed subjects and gilding; height 5⁷/8in. Right: jug elaborately painted with a Japan pattern; 6½in.; impressed BFB and crown mark and full printed circular mark with royal coat of arms and Prince of Wales feathers; c.1810. Dyson Perrins Museum.

Plate 83. Barr Flight and Barr plate, finely painted in the centre with a dead robin and goldfinch lying on a marble table, the rim with a border of palmettes and foliate scrolling in gilding; painted in the style and quality of Thomas Baxter, and could have been decorated at his London studio if made before, or after he joined Worcester in 1814 on earlier stock; 8¾in.; marks printed and impressed; c.1810-13. Sotheby's.

Plate 84. Barr Flight and Barr urn with turquoise ground and a panel painted with "Forge Bridge, Westmoreland", named under base, mounted on top of a square plinth which has oval reserved panels on three sides with gilt decoration, the fourth side painted with a scene of a peasant in a landscape, handles in form of gilt birds with balls in their beaks; 7¾in. high; script marks; c.1810-13. Barr Collection.

Plate 85. Pair of Barr Flight and Barr vases of classical shape, the handles formed as gilt entwined snakes, the sides painted with scenes from the poems of Cowper in gilt framed panels on buff yellow ground, with gilt foliate borders and with gilt rims and pearls; script marks with Coventry Street address and the relevant lines of poetry; 5¼in; c.1810-13. Sotheby's.

Plate 86. Constituent parts of a superb Barr Flight and Barr dessert service made for the Earl of Coventry in 1811, borders azure blue with arms in bronze and different groups of flowers on every piece. The order of the service is given in the book and the total cost was £182.11 shillings. Earl of Coventry and Trustees of the Croome Estates.

Plate 87. Barr Flight and Barr spill vase, mask handles, rectangular panel painted with "Mother's Hope" ("Mother's Hope" is usually a pair with "Father's Darling"), identified under base, and the other side with superb gilt urn in classical style, probably by Thomas Baxter, gilt Greek key fret at top; 5in. high; script and impressed marks; c.1810-13. Barr Collection.

Plate 88. The other side of the spill vase shown in Plate 87, showing superb gilding technique.

Plate 89. Barr Flight and Barr campana shape vase, double entwined gilt serpent handles, applied pearls, painted in bronze with two figures from the Lord Hamilton Vase, probably by Thomas Baxter, above an apricot ground foot, gilt with vermiculi and key pattern; 5½in. high; script and impressed marks; c.1810-13; Barr Collection.

Plate 90. Three plates painted in Oriental styles. Above: plate of octagonal shape, painted in enamel colours with a rare Chinese pattern, probably a replacement; Barr Flight and Barr; c.1810-15. From the collection of Mrs. D. Laney. Bottom left: plate with a popular "Japan" fence pattern with underglaze blue and onglaze enamels; Flight Barr and Barr; c.1810-15. Dyson Perrins Museum. Bottom right: an "India" fence pattern painted in onglaze colours, mainly pink and red; Barr Flight and Barr; c.1810-15. Dyson Perrins Museum.

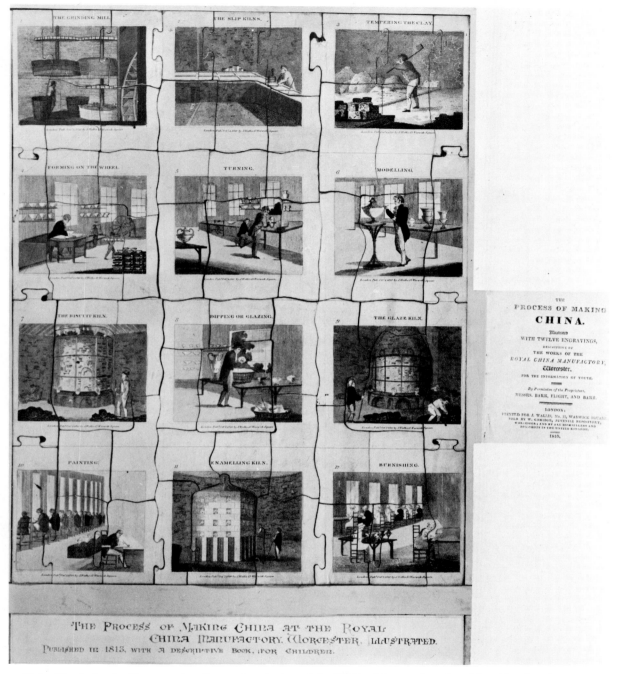

Plate 91. A fascinating wooden jigsaw puzzle issued in 1813 with an educational booklet for the young describing a visit to the Royal China Manufactory Worcester. The twelve sections show the grinding mill, slip kiln, tempering the clay, throwing on the wheel, turning, modelling, the biscuit kiln, dipping or glazing, the glaze kiln, painting, enamelling kiln and burnishing; 16½in. by 12¾in. Dyson Perrins Museum.

Chapter 4

Flight Barr and Barr 1813–1840

The death of Martin Barr led to the final change of name of the Company as Joseph Flight became the principal partner with Martin Barr junior and George Barr, his younger brother, as junior partners. George had been sworn and admitted as a freeman of Worcester in 1808. As might be expected, the name of Flight moved up a peg and the firm was officially known as Flight Barr and Barr, although the London showroom continued to be called Barr Flight and Barr for a period.

A wonderful account of the factory when under the partnership of Flight Barr and Barr has been preserved to us in the words of Solomon Cole, one of the great painters of Flight and Barr, referred to in the previously quoted letter from James Knight to R.W. Binns (see Chapter 2). Cole's account is of the greatest importance in understanding the work and wares of Flight and Barr and although it has been previously quoted in the revised edition of *Chaffers' Marks and Monograms* it is worth giving it again in full:—

"The painting-room was a hundred feet long. There were several peculiarities connected with the manufactory of Messrs. Flight, Barr & Barr, one of which was that of paying the painters by time and not by the piece. This plan was wholly confined to them, and they adopted it to secure the greatest possible degree of excellence in all that they produced. Their business too was strictly of a private character; their orders came from the nobility and most of the distinguished families of the United Kingdom; they kept no traveller nor did they transact business with retail houses.

The slightest patterns produced by them were always painted not printed, as is often the case, consequently their ordinary services were expensive. The quality of their gold has never been surpassed. Mr. Barr always prepared the gold himself and obtained the best possible quality, which was used as well for the slightest patterns as for the most elaborate.

The colours, too, were always ground as fine as possible, and fully prepared for the painter's use. The Bleu du roi was painted upon the biscuit, and consequently under the glaze; hence arose the extreme purity and brilliancy of the gold inlaid upon it.

Before grounds were dusted upon the border of the plate or upon vases, they were laid of one uniform even tint with a large flat brush. This was very skilfully done by James Tomlins, who excelled all others in this peculiar branch. It was the custom of Messrs Flight, Barr and Barr to select those best qualified to paint the different parts in any rich piece, and who excelled in some particular branch. One was chosen to paint the embossed parts to receive the gold, another would be engaged in laying on the gold in armorial bearings, a third would shade the gold, another would be selected to paint the supporters, varying according to the design. If the subject was the royal arms, one would paint the lion in flat gold, another would shade the

100

gold and give expression to the lion after the piece has been burnt. Another would paint the unicorn. The best flower painter would be selected to paint the rose, thistle, and shamrock, and another would write the motto. By these means the greatest perfection was obtained.

Frequently, on Messrs. Martin and George Barr going round the painting-room, which was their custom twice a day, they would say to the painters engaged upon the richest services, 'We want you to consider this as jewellery — we wish you to take all possible pains.' This was particularly the case when the dessert service was being executed for his Majesty William IV., a plate of which service, that was retained by the manufacturers as an example of their productions, has since realised by auction no less a sum than £34. Another mark of distinction was that of never employing females to paint. None were ever employed except as burnishers: and this branch of the manufacture is particularly suitable to them. The burnishing room was over the painting room, and occupied one half the length, 50 feet: the other half was devoted to the finished productions and private use of the firm.

The burnishers were presided over for many years by Mrs Hunt, who devoted most of her time in skilfully papering up the finished pieces ready for the packer. The only other female employed was Mrs Lowe, who had a room to herself, and was engaged principally in printing the names of the firm in a circular form on the back of each rich and important piece, and occasionally printing shells and figures, as already described, in one colour, sometimes in a grey tint, and at others in a warm self colour. On each plate of the very rich services, the names of

Plate 92. *Superb dish from the Stowe service, showing not only the quality of the armorial painting but also the classical style border on salmon pink borders, still so popular in 1813. The Stowe service was one of the finest dessert services made by Flight Barr and Barr. Sotheby's.*

101

Plate 93. Tureen, cover and stand from a superb dessert service made for Richard, second Marquess of Buckingham, known as the Stowe service, dispersed at a sale August 1848, by Christie's, lot 956. The original service comprised two tureens, covers and stands, eight sauce tureens, covers and stands, six oblong dishes, covers and liners, 27 dishes and 119 plates; it realised 28½ guineas. It was probably supplied in 1813 on the death of the first Marquess and the magnificent painted arms comprise quarterly of seven those of Grenville, Temple, Brooke, Lords Cobham, Nugent and Chandos on the male side and on the female Brydges, Bruce, Seymour, Duke of Somerset, Grey, Earl of Dorset, Brandon, Duke of Suffolk and the arms of England quartering France, for Plantagenet. Printed and impressed marks. Sotheby's.

102

Plate 94. Small Flight Barr and Barr mug, black painted silhouette said to be a self-portrait by Thomas Baxter, white and gilt meander bands round the circumference from either side of the portrait reserve at top and bottom, between them a running panel of finely painted flowers, probably painted by Baxter on a dark background; 3½in. high; elaborate printed circular mark under the Royal Arms and the date "Sept 1814" in script under base near footrim. Dyson Perrins Museum.

Plate 95. Flight Barr and Barr plate, blue ground and gilding of palmettes and foliate, surrounding a panel of finely painted shells and seaweed; impressed and printed mark; c.1813-15; 9¼in. Beauchamp Galleries.

the firm, &c., were written with a pen in gold by Joseph Cotterell. He also wrote with a pen in colour the subjects of the figure pieces and names of the views. John Bly, who came from Lowestoft, excelled in shading the gold in arms, and was unequalled in giving a natural expression to the lion in the royal arms or wherever it occurred, and took that part in the grand service made for his Majesty William IV. above alluded to. His son John continued with the firm until the breaking up of that establishment. He painted landscapes, and was occasionally otherwise engaged. Ishmael Sherwin was chiefly engaged in designing patterns and in decorating the rich pieces with gems, &c., and attended principally to the embossed gold. He was a fine ornamental gilder. Thomas Baxter, who was first employed in Worcester in 1815, may be said to stand unrivalled in this country as a classical figure painter on porcelain. He had one advantage over others, that of being a student of the Royal Academy for some years, and was esteemed one of the best draughtsmen of his time.

Mr. Baxter's father had workshops at No. 1 Goldsmith Street, Gough Square, London, for painting and gilding china, obtained principally from France and Staffordshire. Mr. Baxter, jun., his son, established a school of art during his stay at Worcester, from 1814 to 1816; among other of his pupils were Doe, Astles, Webster, Pitman, Lowe, and Cole. His fine productions on porcelain elevated the taste and his tuition cultivated the talent of several others of that period; two of whom succeeded him as figure-painters after his death, which occurred in 1821—viz., Thomas Lowe and Solomon Cole.

It may be said of this manufactory that it was a school of art; not only were those engaged in the higher branches emulated[1] by Baxter's works, but those who ornamented his productions

1.   This is the wording given by Cole in Chaffers.

103

by gilding and adding gems round the subjects were stimulated to the greatest possible painstaking care to render their part of the performance worthy of him who, by his excellent productions, was setting them so good an example; even the potters could not fail to receive benefit from those for whom they were producing such excellent forms, the like of which up to that period had never been produced in this country. Examples of them are rarely to be found except in the collections of the nobility.

It is not always the most elegant forms that are best adapted for porcelain. Messrs Flight Barr & Barr, knowing that the Etruscan shapes presented a greater amount of plain surface than any other, had the good taste to adopt them, being desirous of introducing as much art as possible into their manufacture. These classical forms admitted of figures being painted upon them without the disadvantage of the limbs being distorted by the curvature of the lines, or the building in landscapes losing their perpendicular. The most elegant form in porcelain that can possibly be produced is of little value compared with what it becomes when colour and artistic decoration are added to it; and upon the quality of these is the value of the vase estimated.

While these Etruscan shapes are classical and severe in form, they may be also said to be complex, always having handles, and great skill being required in their production; while ornaments without handles, however elegant in form, cannot please in the same degree, because they can be produced by a more simple means, viz., by the thrower on the wheel in clay or the turner in wood.

At the same time that Thomas Baxter was engaged in painting classical figure subjects on vases, some of which were 22 inches in height, John Pennington was devoting his talent to rustic figures, while Samuel Astles and Henry Stinton were painting groups of flowers on similarly shaped vases. There were also flower-painters subordinate to them. Then there were also Messrs. Thomas Rogers, John Barker, and John Smith at the same time painting landscapes.

Plate 96. A fine covered vase, blue ground with gilt scrolls and handles, painted with fine shells on one side and flowers on the other in the style of Thomas Baxter; printed mark; c.1813-15; 12in. Dyson Perrins Museum.

Central rose painting from an early Flight Barr and Barr dinner plate painted by William Billingsley, showing his technique of applying colour en mass and wiping it away with a dry brush to produce highlights; printed mark incorporating Barr Flight and Barr and Flight Barr and Barr marks, c.1813-15. Alan Willis Collection.

One of a pair of plaques, depicting Worcester from the South, the porcelain factory can be seen between the Cathedral and the tall spire of St. Andrew's Church (the other plaque depicts Malvern); like most Flight Barr and Barr plaques the edges are rather nibbled, looking as though they had been nipped with pincers; 5in. by 3¼in. Shirley Hartshorne.

Fine Flight Barr and Barr inkstand with two pots and covers and centre handle with mask, pen tray either side, on four scroll feet, sky blue ground and painting of flowers, birds and butterflies; mark "Flight Barr and Barr Worcester and No 1 Coventry Street"; 10¾in. long; c.1825-30. O'Donaghue Collection.

Group of five candlesticks. Top left to right: 6-sided, blue ground, panels of flowers; Barr Flight and Barr script and impressed mark; diameter 3¼in.; pale green ground painted feathers and flowers, 5½in.; pale green ground flowers and gilt weed c.1835, 1¾in. diameter. Bottom left to right: Marble ground double snake handle, painted flowers, Barr Flight and Barr, 5¼in. diameter; marbled ground painted panel of shells, 4¾in. diameter. John Broad Collection.

Barker excelled in painting shells, and was engaged in that part of the celebrated service made for Watson Taylor, Esq.; William Doe painted natural birds, feathers, insects, &c.; Charles Stinton painted fancy birds, &c.; Thomas C. Crowther painted flowers, and was particularly gifted in painting the cowslips with great delicacy. At the same period the celebrated bird-painter, George Davis, usually called Dr. Davis, added his brilliant colouring in the rich plumage of his birds to the decoration of these Etruscan forms, a beautiful example of which, painted on one side with exotic birds by Davis, and on the other a group of flowers by Stinton, with a garnet ground, is in the possession of Mr. R.C. Tennant of Kensington.

In the collection of Sir Arthur Guinness (Lord Ardilaun) are three of the Etruscan-shaped vases of the larger size painted by Baxter, and by the same hand, upon smaller vases, are seven other figure subjects set round with pearls and gems.

A fourth vase of an extremely elegant shape, also in the same collection, is painted with flowers by Astles. These choice specimens, with many others, were produced between the years 1815 and 1821, in which latter year Baxter died.

Soon after Baxter arrived at Worcester, and was engaged by Messrs. Flight, Barr and Co., he painted a cabinet plate, the subject of which was Mrs. Siddons in the character of the "Tragic Muse," which the then Marquis of Stafford purchased for fifty guineas. A second plate was afterwards painted by Baxter, precisely the same in all respects, which was in the collection of Mr. H. Rokeby Price. Mr. H.T. Hope the great virtuoso, invited Baxter to view his collection of pictures, china, &c., and during the inspection he handed a plate to Baxter remarking how much it was to be regretted that we had no artist who could paint on china in so good a style, at the same time saying, 'I bought this in Paris' and that 'the like had never been seen in this country'; when Baxter said, 'I have seen this plate before.' 'No', said Mr. Hope, 'that is impossible.' Mr Baxter replied, 'I have not only seen this plate before, but I painted it.'

This was no doubt a French plate painted by Baxter for his father before he left home for Worcester. The painters never marked the pieces at Barrs', not even the superior and highly decorative specimens. The name of the artist was always sent to London with the vase that was painted by him."

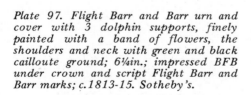

Plate 97. Flight Barr and Barr urn and cover with 3 dolphin supports, finely painted with a band of flowers, the shoulders and neck with green and black cailloute ground; 6¼in.; impressed BFB under crown and script Flight Barr and Barr marks; c.1813-15. Sotheby's.

Plate 98. Urn with double entwined serpent handles, painted with a named scene of Windsor Castle outlined in raised gold; impressed BFB under a crown and script Flight Barr and Barr marks; c. 1813-15. Phillips.

A fine Flight Barr and Barr vase and cover, pierced with alternate diamond and circular holes at the shoulders, turquoise ground and fine modelling and gilding, painted with a continuous freize of shells, possibly by Barker, 18½in.; c.1815-20. Sotheby's.

Plate 99. Flight Barr and Barr tea-pot, cover and stand of attractive boat-like shape, elaborately gilded with seaweed pattern and gadrooned edge; 5¼in. high; mark FBB under crown impressed on stand; c.1813-20. Geoffrey Godden.

An interesting account of a visit to the factory is given by Michael Faraday.[1] In his diary for August 1819 he writes of travelling to Worcester from Wolverhampton. The main artist that Faraday met was Thomas Baxter (whom he refers to as Bagster).

August 1st 1819

We entered Worcester early in the Evening. It was crowded with people dressed in their best who all appeared to be at the summit of gaiety and happiness and they gave a wonderfully animated and fine appearance to the excellent street through which we passed into the city. I left the coach at the Lion Inn opposite the town hall, took tea then rambled out about the town till near nine when I returned and went to bed.

1. *Dsfydd Tomos*, Michael Faraday in Wales, *published by Gwasg Gee.*

Plate 100. Flight Barr and Barr dessert service painted with a bold Japan pattern in underglaze blue and onglaze colours; c.1813-20. Christie's.

Plate 101. Pair of Flight Barr and Barr vases with double gilt scrolling serpent handles and band of applied pearls, painted with named panels of "The Mother's Hope" and "The Father's Darling", reserved on a pale blue ground; 4¼in.; script marks; c.1813-20. Sotheby's and Winifred Williams.

Monday, August 2nd

This day I did Wonders. Immediately after breakfast I went to Flight and Barrs House and presuming on the slight knowledge I had of Mr. Martyn Barr, asked permission to see the porcelain works. Mr. Barr himself was not there being at Malvern but his brother very politely instantly gave me admittance to the works. I went to them and found the old porter whose place it is to show them to strangers, and he immediately took me around regretting however I had come so early as the men generally had not yet come to work. He explained all he could to me and the workmen here and there left off what they were about to show me the series of operations. I was not very solicitous to see and examine at this time for I saw all was not yet in activity and I intended to have better opportunities in the course of the day.

Just in the entrance of the works was a box with an inscription over it forbidding any gifts to the workmen in the place but stating that whatever was put into the box was divided equally among them at the end of the year, so I of course at leaving the place paid my respects to the box. From thence I went to seek out Mr. Bagster an artist employed at Chamberlains to whom I had words of introduction from several friends. I had found out at Barr's manufactory that he lived in Edgar Street and after about half a dozen enquiries at different houses, just as I was going regularly from house to house I found out his habitation. The maid would fetch him from the works and I was forced to submit, though quite a stranger to him, but when he came he brought a large stock of goodwill and good nature and so we were soon familiar acquaintances.

I went with him to Chamberlains, the Manufactory of Porcelain, where I believe he superintended the painting department and as Mr. Bagster professed to be but a bad showman for all the operations, he placed me in the hands of another person who went over the works with me and showed me all very minutely. I will not here detail what I saw in the order in which I saw it but endeavour briefly to describe the porcelain manufacture by and bye. Being later in the day Business had not yet got into its due order and velocity, and the place looked much fitter and more lively than Flight Barrs had done.

Plate 102. One of a pair of Flight Barr and Barr vases painted with panels of Faith and Hope, blue grounds, applied pearls and gilding, printed mark; c.1813-20; 6½in. Dyson Perrins Museum.

Plate 103. Pair of Flight Barr and Barr spill vases with blue grounds and pearls reserving panels painted with "The Hermit" and "Spring" and a vase and cover supported on three dolphins painted with rural subjects; 4¾in. and 7½in.; c.1813-20. Beauchamp Galleries.

When I had seen all there Mr. Bagster would take me home to lunch and on the way showed me the outside of the Cathedral and other old buildings. At home he showed me various paintings and drawings of his own admirably done and a specimen on porcelain entirely the work of his own hands. After lunch he again walked with me and set me on the river side where we parted having promised to meet together in the Cathedral in the afternoon, he to draw and I to see. I, however, broke my promise and I then walked on to the Bridge and other parts of the town and on my way to the Inn called in at Mr. Barr's to thank him for the attention I had received at the Manufactory.

Mr. Martyn Barr, I found had just come home and immediately gone to the manufactory so I and his brother walked after him. On arriving there however we found that Mr. Barr had returned to the house but the Porter soon brought him back again whilst I looked over some parts of the manufactory. On Mr. Barr's arrival I again saw the manufactory more minutely than before and found it far more lively and busy. After an hour or two spent here looking at the processes and some experiments, we left the place and I was persuaded to break my promise with Mr. Bagster, that I might dine with Mr. Barr and afterwards go with him and take tea at Malvern, a fashionable watering place well worth seeing. We had a very pleasant drive to Malvern which is about [10] miles from Worcester and which when we came there appeared to be astonishingly full of people. The Malvern Hills are a range of granite shciss and scenite rocks which rise suddenly from the very flat country about Worcester to considerable elevation and presenting a marked contrast to the neighbourhood around. They offer some very pretty scenery and the views over the flat country are extensive. In consequence of their contrast to the surrounding parts they have become an attraction to numbers who leave the busy town

Plate 104. Flight Barr and Barr garniture, the central vase with gilt animal mask handles, painted with sea urchin, conch and cowrie shells on marble ledges within gilt cartouches on salmon pink ground enriched with gilt vermiculi (possibly painted by Barker); 4¾in. and 9¾in.; impressed and printed marks; c.1813-20. Christie's.

Plate 105. Flight Barr and Barr cabinet cup and saucer, apricot-beige ground painted in bronze with winged birds, classical urns and flower heads in the style of Thomas Baxter, applied white pearls; cup 4¾in. high, saucer 6¼in. diameter; script mark; c.1813-20. Barr Collection.

Plate 106. Flight Barr and Barr garniture of five vases, richly gilt on a pale blue ground and applied pearls, painted with rustic figures in landscapes; height of centre vase, 10in.; left hand vase painted with "The Gamekeeper"; c.1813-20. Beauchamp Galleries.

during the summer. A small village at the foot of the nearest hill has received the name of the hills and of late has rapidly increased in size by the addition of many excellent houses for summer residence. At this moment families were arriving without any place being vacant for them.

After taking tea at Mr. Barr's house with the lady, his mother, we strolled up the hill to get, if possible, a view of sunset but were a little too late. We however, found plenty to fill a long walk with enjoyment. We met many fashionable stragglers about, among whom were Lord Grey and his family and from above they looked extremely well spread about the hillside, the town lying beneath and a cultivated country in the distance.

Returning to the house we had an easy lunch of bread and butter and grapes and then entering the chaise, drove back to Worcester again where Mr. Barr completed his numerous and kind attentions to me by a supper. Not until that was concluded would his good nature permit me to depart so that I did not get to bed till 12 o'clock, though I had to be up at 5 next morning for the London Coach."

Michael Faraday's diary does not seem to present too rosy a picture of the factory in 1819. Visiting the factory after his breakfast it might by thought that he would find work going on at a brisker rate than met his eye. Even when he went on to Chamberlain's factory later in the morning he did not find things much better there. We should be careful in trying to equate this picture of very little going on with the present day appearance of a large ceramic factory with a thousand or more employees producing vast numbers of pieces a day to satisfy huge order books. In 1819 Flight and Barr's factory would probably have had no more employees than the 160 or so that Mrs Lybbe Powys found when she visited it during the Dr. Wall period in 1771. Possibly the working force was smaller in 1819. It is not possible to know for certain as the wages books have not survived but if a comparison is made with Chamberlain's factory, many of whose work books are still in existance, neither factory had as many employees, nor was producing as great a quantity of ware as in the Dr. Wall period.

Certainly life must have been difficult for ceramic firms in 1819. Flight Barr and Barr had seen a number of fine companies go to the wall but probably felt that justice had been done by the collapse of Swansea and Nantgarw in Wales, after their experience with Mr. Billingsley.

Joseph Flight died in 1838 and in his will, signed and sealed on 11th February, 1830, and giving the Coventry Street, London showroom as his address, he left the High Street shop and his proportion of the factory to Martin and George Barr equally. The legacies named in the will are very interesting in showing how rich a man he had become. In a nutshell these were the legacies and obligations:—

"To my brother Bannister Flight	£50
His son Thomas Flight	£50
My brother Thomas Flight	£50
His daughter Ann Flight	£50
My sister Christian Flight	£50

Jeremiah Ford (if he should continue in the service of the Partnership) £100. My friend Samuel Barr (in consideration of my esteem for him and valuable services) £500 plus a life policy for £500 or if the policy should not be paid an amount of £500 in lieu. My partners Martin Barr and George Barr, my property No.45 High Street, Worcester plus my moiety in the china manufactory and the four messuages, plus the tenements and the stable on the north side of Warmstry Slip, plus stock in trade, household goods, furniture, plate, linen, china and library of books and all other residue in equal proportions."

Martin and George Barr were directed to provide a suit of mourning for Jeremiah Ford and mourning rings for all the other persons named in the will.

So was set the scene for the final curtain which was to come down upon this great factory.

Plate 107. Flight Barr and Barr vase, blue ground and gilding, finely painted with scenes from Midsummer Night's Dream *and* Love's Labours Lost, *probably by Lowe; 17½in.; impressed and script marks; c.1813-20. Barr Collection.*

Superb plaque painted and signed by Astles, showing the fine quality of this magnificent flower painter; c.1820-25. Private collection, courtesy of John Twitchett.

Plate 108. Plate from a superb Flight Barr and Barr service made for the Nabob of Oude, underglaze blue ground with gilding in Pompeian style, a delicate gilt border in centre enclosing painted heraldic emblem of two standing tigers and initials NGH; elaborate mark incorporating royal coat of arms and Prince of Wales feathers; c.1814-16. Dyson Perrins Museum.

Plate 109. Superb portrait medallion commemorating Lord Nelson with frame combined, the glazed border with raised jewelling of red, yellow, green and purple surrounded by white pearls on an underglaze blue ground, the interior with a very finely modelled biscuit portrait set in a gilt surround. The flat base underneath is incised with the script initials TB above a trident mark with leafage at the bottom enclosing the date 1805, the year of Nelson's death; 3in. diameter. The medallion almost certainly made in 1814 or 1815 by Thomas Baxter at Worcester (see Appendix I). Rous Lench Court Collection.

A fine Flight Barr and Barr punch bowl, maroon ground and fine gilding, painted with a beautiful view of Malvern Abbey and the hills beyond, with a scene of Worcester on the other side, the arms of Shuttleworth painted in between; script mark; 14in. diameter; c.1820-30. Dyson Perrins Museum.

Plate 110. Superb Flight Barr and Barr urn shaped vase on square pedestal base, twisted vine stem handles, embossed tongue moulding around rim, row of applied pearls at waist, pale beige ground with reserves painted probably by Thomas Baxter, the vase with a scene from Shakespeare's King John, *Act IV, Scene 1, noted under base "For heavens sake Herbert, let me not be bound", the pedestal with a vignette of a tomb; 9½in.; script mark; c.1815. Dyson Perrins Museum.*

Plate 111, Rare Flight Barr and Barr vase, of shouldered double-ogee shape with two high scrolled handles, pale cream ground reserving panel painted with a scene from Comus, possibly by Thomas Baxter, within gilt borders tooled with a linked diamond and oval motif and with gilt classical motifs; 13½in.; script mark and lines from Comus; c.1815. Sotheby's.

Plate 112. Unusual Flight and Barr covered cup, the cylindrical body painted on one side with a view of Downcondra Bridge near Dublin, in an octagonal panel reserved on a pale pink ground, below linked flower head gilded borders, the double-ogee cover with diamond knob; 5in.; impressed BFB and crown and script mark and the view named; c.1815. Sotheby's.

Plate 113. Unusual Flight Barr and Barr dish, possibly a butter dish or compotière, the base forming an integral part with the stand; c.1815. Collection of Mr. J. Amos.

Plate 114. *A magnificent sauce tureen, cover and stand from a dessert service, finely painted with shells, with applied pearls and gilded with classical palmettes; c.1815. Christie's.*

Plate 115. *A very fine Worcester vase with dolphin and shell handles, with flower subjects and elaborate gilding; c.1815. Delomonse.*

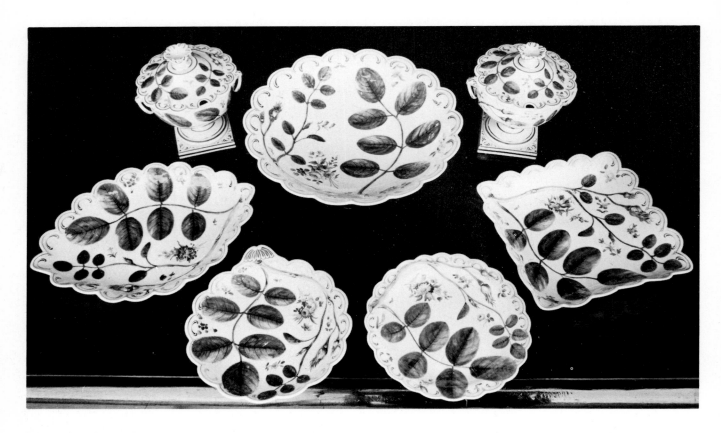

Plate 116. *Constituent parts of a Flight Barr and Barr dessert service moulded and painted onglaze with the Blind Earl pattern, the service made for the Coventry family in about 1815. Earl of Coventry and Trustees of the Croome Estates.*

Plate 117. *A pair of ice pails, covers and liners of Warwick vase type with ram's-head mask handles and a shaped centre dish from a fine Flight Barr and Barr harlequin dessert service painted with named views, fancy birds and bouquets of flowers in circular panels surrounded by insects and gilding reserved on a rare yellow ground; c.1815. Sotheby's.*

126

Plate 118. The Cottrill jug, painted with a hunting scene set in the Worcestershire countryside reserved on a Barr's orange ground with gilding in the classical style; this jug, together with a Barr Flight and Barr stirrup cup in the form of a fox head, was presented to Robert Cottrill by Lord Deerhurst, eldest son of the Earl of Coventry. Cottrill lived at Sandal Lodge, Droitwich, Worcestershire, hunted with the Worcestershire Hunt and entertained Viscount Deerhurst and his servants for weeks at a time. Such presentation pieces were made especially on demand by the factory. Private collection.

Plate 119. Side view of the Cottrill jug.

Plate 120. Coffee-cup, tea-cup and saucer from a Flight Barr and Barr tea-service, green and gold; c.1815-20. Geoffrey Godden.

Chapter 5

The End of the Flight and Barr Era

With the death of Joseph Flight came the end of an era for the company and the two remaining partners, Martin and George Barr, waited only for the proving of Joseph's will in February 1840, before arranging an amalgamation of the company with their old rivals, Chamberlains. The reasons for this are not clear but R.W. Binns suggests in his *Century of Potting in the City of Worcester* that, after making the magnificent service for King William IV in 1831, when Flight & Barr can be said to have been at their greatest, there was a gradual reduction in profitability and quality until 1840. As Mr. Binns put it, "The nobility still patronised their London houses, but the orders were not sufficiently numerous to keep the works fully employed."

R.W. Binns also gave his view of the merger between the two firms:

"1840 was a remarkable year in the history of the Royal Porcelain Works, as it saw the two, hitherto rival establishments, joined as one. We fear the union was a marriage 'de convenance' not of love, the proprietors had hitherto been conducting their business on different principles, and had been activated by widely different motives, both equally delusive and without prospect of success.

By the intervention of friends it was proposed to form a joint stock company, to consist of members of the two firms (joining their plant of moulds, copper-plates and stock) and adding to their number several of the most influential gentlemen in the city to subscribe the necessary capital, which including the valuation of plant, stock etc. amounted to about £40,000. The two London Houses, Coventry Street, and Bond Street, were included in this scheme, with the intention of removing the Coventry Street stock to Bond Street, which was finally accomplished in 1845."

Despite this statement by R.W. Binns, the union of the two manufactories of the Barrs and the Chamberlains appear to have been intended as a take-over rather than an amalgamation, and was a partnership not a joint stock Company. A reading of the contemporary records, kindly allowed by the Worcester Royal Porcelain Company, makes it clear that the two Barrs (Martin and George) were minded to sell-out, completely, to the Chamberlain partnership, merely retaining a minority share-holding and taking no active part in the day-to-day management of the new concern.

The financial problems which beset the two manufactories seem to have stemmed from a failure to adjust their range of wares and patterns to changes in fashion rather

Plate 121. Plate from a superb Flight Barr and Barr service painted with named birds within green ground borders; c.1815-20. Private collection.

than from direct competition the one with the other. But, whatever the causes of their separate problems may have been, by early in 1840 the two groups of partners were ready to set their hands to a scheme of arrangement and did so, formally, at the house of their solicitor, John Brook Hyde.

On the 13th April 1840, Martin and George Barr and Walter Chamberlain, John Lilly and Fleming St.John signed the proposed arrangement which provided for the union of the two manufactories under the title of the "Worcester Royal Porcelain Company". The substance of the arrangement was to be as follows:—

(a) the shareholders in the new concern were to be:—

Martin Barr	with 3 shares of £1,000 each.
George Barr	with 2 shares of £1,000 each.
Walter Chamberlain	with 7 shares of £1,000 each.
John Lilly	with 8 shares of £1,000 each.
Fleming St. John	with 5 shares of £1,000 each.
John Brooke Hyde	with 1 share of £1,000.
George Allies	with 1 share of £1,000.

a further 23 shares of £1,000 each, were to remain unissued for the time being, although the arrangement required £30,000 to be paid-up upon the signing of the formal agreement, a further £10,000 to be paid up on 29th September 1840, and, the balance of £10,000 to remain on three months call.

(b) the new concern was to purchase:—
  (i) Messrs. Barrs works including four dwelling houses, two coach houses, a lease-hold stable, the stock in trade, plant and appurtenances at Worcester, Bransford Mill, and London also, the remaining lease of No. 1 Coventry Street, the goodwill, and the receipts for manufactures. The purchase price to be £13,000 being £4,500 for the works and £8,500 for the stock in trade. The Barrs to be paid £5,000 in shares, issued as fully paid up; £3,000 in cash, on the new concern entering Barr's works, £2,000 in cash on the formal conveyance of the works to the new concern, and £3,000 in three promissory notes of £8,000 each due in six, twelve and eighteen months, successively.
  (ii) Messrs. Chamberlains' stock in trade, the plant, steam-engine and appurtenances at the manufactory and at 59 High Street, Worcester, and the receipts for manufactures. The purchase price to be £14,000, to be paid in shares — to the value of their stock — issued as fully paid-up, forthwith; and the balance, in cash, at the final call.
  (iii) the stock in trade at 155 New Bond Street, at valuation, now stated to lie between £6,000—£7,000, paid as £5,000 in shares issued as fully paid up and the balance, in cash, in two halves at intervals of six and twelve months.

(c) James Yates, the London Sales Manager, was to assign the lease of 155 New Bond Street to the new concern, who were to rent it at £350 a year.

(d) The new concern was to rent Chamberlains' works for 14 years at £250 a year and was to take a lease of 45 High Street, Worcester at an agreed valuation.

The scheme of arrangement then goes on to specify the officers: Walter Chamberlain to be Manager at a salary of £400 a year; John Lilly to be Sales Manager at a salary of £400 a year with residence at 45 High Street, Worcester, rent and rates free; James Yates to be London Sales Manager at a salary of £400 plus £100 expenses a year, with residence at 155 New Bond Street, London, rent and rates free; Flemming St.John to be Treasurer and Secretary at a salary of £200 a year and be allowed an office at 45 High Street, Worcester; John Brook Hyde was to be the solicitor and was instructed to draw up the formal partnership deed; Berwick & Co. were to be the Bankers.

It was intended that the new concern should not commence trading until the capital subscribed had reached £35,000 and the scheme of arrangement raised but £27,000 (£32,000 after James Yates had taken up his holding) of which only £7,000 was in cash. The new concern expected to raise £4,000 from the sale of some of Chamberlains' stock, but these sales could not be arranged before the new concern started trading so that the rapid attraction of fresh capital, in cash, became a matter of urgency.

On the 7th May 1840, the partners, alarmed at the delay in raising the required capital, instructed Flemming St.John to try to borrow £5,000 from the bankers and he wrote to them as follows:—

High Street 6 May 1840

Dear Sirs,

I am directed by the shareholders in the intended Company for uniting the two manufactories of Messers Barr and Chamberlain to apply to you as the proposed Bankers of the Company to know whether, in the event of their commencing business on their present subscribed capital of £32,000 they may rely on a temporary advance from you to the extent of from £3,000 to £5,000 should the same be found necessary. It was the original intention of the partners not to commence business until a capital to the extent of £35,000 was subscribed for but from the advanced state of the London season it is thought that any further delay may be prejudicial to the Company and in the event of a favourable reply from you it has been resolved to commence operations immediately.

I beg to submit a list of the present subscribers with the amount of capital subscribed by each and remain

Dear Sirs
faithfully yours
Fleming St. John.

Mr Martin Barr	£3,000
Mr George Barr	£2,000
Mr Walter Chamberlain	£7,000
Mr John Lilly	£8,000
Mr Fleming St. John	£5,000
Mr J.B. Hyde	£1,000
Mr George Allies	£1,000
Mr James Yates	£5,000
	£32,000

Two days later the Bank agreed to make the loan and things then began to move. Mr. Jabez Allies and Mr. Henry Douglas Carden each subscribed £2,000 and were allotted two shares each, accordingly. Messrs Lilly, St. John, and George Barr were asked to proceed to London, without delay, to value the stock at 155 New Bond Street, although only Lilly and St.John appear to have gone. On the advice of James Yates the partners resolved to trade as a firm under the title of Chamberlain & Co', and to call their works "The Worcester Royal Porcelain Works".

On the 14th May 1840, Fleming St.John, writing from London, suggested to the partners that, in the interests of expediency, the stock at 155 New Bond Street

Plate 122. Fine Flight Barr and Barr pot-pourri urn, cover and liner, of classical shape with double ram's mask handles, underglaze blue ground reserving a broad band containing a continuous landscape with exotic or fancy birds; 16in. high; sepia and impressed marks; c.1815-20. Although the painting of such subjects is usually ascribed to George Davis, they might well be by Charles Stinton. Sotheby's, now in the Barr Collection.

Plate 123. Pair of Flight Barr and Barr ice pails, covers and liners from a dessert service with ram's head handles and pine cone knobs, apple green ground with white reserves painted with sprays of roses, pinks, poppies, tulips, crocus, sweet William and other garden flowers and gilding; mark impressed FBB under crown; c.1815-20. Sotheby's.

should be taken, subject only to cursory inspection, at Yates' valuation, which he gave as:—

Stock including Glass	£6,000
Lease	1,000
Fixtures	500
Yates' expenses	350
	£7,850

The partners baulked at this suggestion and instructed Lilly and St.John to make a physical inspection of the stock and to value it by reference to Yates' purchase ledgers; Yates countered immediately, by refusing to allow any stock-taking to be done unless and until a written agreement between himself and the Company had been executed. The agreement was signed on the 25th May, 1840, and the partnership began trading as Chamberlain & Co. from that day — in passing, it should be noted that the partners' method of valuation resulted in Yates receiving more than would otherwise have been the case. The essence of the agreement was that Yates should be alloted 5 shares issued as paid-up, and be paid £500 in cash,

Left: Plate 124. Flight Barr and Barr vase of a rare shape which sometimes has a cover, finely gilded and painted with a naturalistic group of shells probably by Barker; script mark; c.1815-20; 9½in. Phillips.

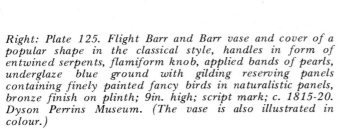

Right: Plate 125. Flight Barr and Barr vase and cover of a popular shape in the classical style, handles in form of entwined serpents, flamiform knob, applied bands of pearls, underglaze blue ground with gilding reserving panels containing finely painted fancy birds in naturalistic panels, bronze finish on plinth; 9in. high; script mark; c. 1815-20. Dyson Perrins Museum. (The vase is also illustrated in colour.)

Left: a plate with fine raised gilding, painted in the centre with a view of Hallow Park, Worcester (the home of the Barrs) from the River Severn. Right: a vase with a scene of Boyne Castle painted by Rogers; script Flight Barr and Barr mark; 6in; c.1825-30. Dyson Perrins Museum.

Plate 126. Fine pair of Flight Barr and Barr vases, claret ground and gilding reserving scenes from Don Quixote *and* The Lady of the Lake, *canto 20 (Then safe though flattered and amazed She paused and on the stranger gazed), probably by Lowe; script marks; c.1815-20; 18in. O'Donaghue Collection.*

together with two promissory notes for £1,548 each payable at intervals of six and twelve months respectively: barely a month later, he resigned. Walter Chamberlain and John Lilly each took up two of his shares and the fifth share was transferred to a trustee for the common benefit of the partnership.

In the meantime the partnership was doing its best to get the business moving; Lane, the traveller, began his northern tour; the Barrs and John Lilly sent out circulars, informing their customers of the new partnership; plans were put in hand for the alteration of No. 45 High Street, Worcester, and for the construction of new kilns on Warmstry House, apparently for the manufacture of encaustic tiles.

By August 1840, however, Walter Chamberlain had persuaded his colleagues that it would be advantageous to concentrate all the work on the Diglis Street site and to close the Barr factory; accordingly, they offered the factory for sale or lease and also determined to sell the lease of No. 1 Coventry Street. Later in the year, they reversed their decision on No. 1 Coventry Street and determined to keep it open, appointing John Turner, then employed by Mortlocks, as manager.

Turner was to receive a salary of £120 a year, plus £65 a year for so long as his son continued to work with him; he was also to have a commission of 2½% on all the sales made at Coventry Street, and, of course, free residence at Coventry Street. In November, he sought and obtained the partners' consent to alterations costing £163.

In January 1841, the partners took steps to dispose of Barr's stock and finally appointed a new salesman to manage 155 New Bond Street, London.

In February 1841, George Allies, who normally acted as chairman whenever the partners met, took-up the fifth share which had been put in trust when Yates resigned. Jabez Allies was appointed Auditor at a fee of seventy guineas a year and the Barrs were voted £50 to discharge certain debts incurred by them during the formation of the partnership.

On the 31st March 1841, the partners declared a dividend of 3½% payable on the 1st May 1841 and increased the salary of Fleming St.John by £100 to £300 a year, retrospective to 25th December 1840. They also decided to dismiss John Parker for failing to introduce new business at 155 New Bond Street.

A month later, the partners decided to increase the capital to £40,000 by raising an additional £4,000 amongst themselves, the four shares being taken by George Allies, J.B. Hyde, H.D. Carden, and J. Allies. They also took the opportunity to record their appreciation of the services of George Barr and granted him a salary of £200 a year.

By January 1842, the partners were again short of cash and endeavoured to raise £3,000 on the security of Barr's manufactory — without success; they decided to try and raise the money from their own resources by issuing non-negotiable bills, payable in twelve months and carrying interest at 7½%. In April Jabez Allies indicated his wish to withdraw from the partnership and offered to accept promissory notes, carrying 5% interest, payable at annual intervals over four or five years. At the same time the partners agreed to take down some of the kilns at Barr's works and to redouble their efforts to dispose of the site, and the remains of the surplus stock.

In September 1842, they entered into a mortgage, with the executors of the Chamberlain estate, for the purchase of the Diglis works, for £4,000, payable in

Plate 127. Vase with pink ground, with three dolphin supports, painted panel of a kingfisher possibly by Doe; script mark; c.1815-20; 7¼in. O'Donaghue Collection.

seven years, carrying interest at 4%. At the same time the salaries of the managers were reduced to £200 a year — until such time as a dividend of 5% was declared on the shares — and a profit sharing scheme was introduced for their benefit. Jabez Allies appointment as Auditor was abolished but John Lilly had his salary increased by £100 a year. In December, 1842, as a further economy measure the partners decided to close 155 New Bond Street, London.

In March 1843, the partners declared a dividend of 2½%, not to be paid until further notice and decided to sell the bricks and materials resulting from the partial dismantling of Barr's works. But on the 1st May 1843, the partners considered it expedient to erect new buildings on the Diglis site and appointed a sub-committee to deal with this project.

Despite the several changes of mind, reflected in the decisions of the partnership, there is nothing in the record to suggest that they were at loggerheads one with the other until September 1843, when Messrs Carden & Hyde challenged the half yearly accounts, by questioning the validity of the "Trade account Manufactory" — the inventory of stock — which had been declared at £20,522. 14s. 8½d. The account was again challenged in October and Walter Chamberlain and John Lilly were given until the 22nd November 1842 to produce a full and detailed inventory of the stock. On the 22nd November 1843, the partners met to consider the revised inventory and again — Chamberlain and Lilly dissenting — rejected the account. A committee of three — W. Chamberlain, G. Barr and Fleming St.John were then appointed to consider the matter and to report to the partnership, before 1st March, 1844. At this meeting H.D. Carden, offered to sell his shares and retire from the firm.

Plate 128. A finely painted Flight Barr and Barr plaque of a long haired bard, the reverse inscribed "The Bard, Loose his beard, and hoary hair stream'd like a meteor to the troubled air : Gray"; crowned script mark; c.1815-20; possibly painted by Joseph Flight. Sotheby's.

Plate 129. Plate from a Flight Barr and Barr armorial dessert service, the crests surrounded by a bold Japan style pattern; c.1815-20. Delomosne.

Plate 130. Flight Barr and Barr vase, the urn shaped body supported by three dolphins on a trefoil base moulded with scallop shell motifs, painted on one side with a still-life of shells and seaweed on a table, possibly by Barker, row of pearls, and gilding; 7½in; full printed mark; c.1815-20. Sotheby's.

Plate 131. Pair of Flight Barr and Barr vases with gilt entwined snake handles, claret ground reserving panels painted with scenes of Worcester Cathedral (left) and Malvern Priory, two favourite subjects; 8in. high; c.1815-25. Christie's.

142

The Committee reported with commendable speed and brevity. On the 10th January 1844 their report was considered by the partnership; it read:—

"Upon consideration of the whole matter and referring to the state of the assets and liabilities the committee are of the opinion that the business cannot be advantageously carried on under the present arrangements.

They take into consideration:—

The proposed retirement from the partnership of Mr. Jabez Allies.

The Notice from Mr. Carden to sell his shares and a similar Notice just received from Mr. Hyde.

That it will be necessary that a dissolution of partnership as regards these partners shall be published in the Gazette.

And they suggest this as a favourable opportunity for a general arrangement whereby the affairs of the present Partnership may be wound up, providing such arrangement can be made to meet the views of all parties.

With this object they suggest the appointment of two of the firm with a confidential party as referee as the most likely means of carrying out this suggestion.

Dated 9th January 1844
Signed Walter Chamberlain
George Barr
Fleming St.John."

Plate 132. Plate from a service made for the East India Company, pink ground and arms in the centre, small sprays of roses; c.1816. Dyson Perrins Museum.

Plate 133. Plaque, or more likely a cut down plate centre, painted by Joseph Flight with a subject of Hippolytus, dated underneath November 14th 1818 and signed Joseph Flight, although the signature has been partially removed probably by someone wishing to pass off the painting as by Baxter; 6⅜in. diameter. Dyson Perrins Museum.

Plate 134. Complete Flight Barr and Barr egg cup set and stand, simply decorated with gilding, each cup has a ridge around the outside of the body to fit in the stand; impressed mark under the flat base; c.1820. Collection of Mr. A.J. King.

The partners adopted the report unanimously and appointed Walter Chamberlain and Fleming St.John, with J.W. Isaac as referee, to work out a suitable scheme. On the 19th January 1844 they submitted the following suggestions:—

"Messrs W. Chamberlain and J. Lilly to take the Manufactory Diglis Street ... with the stock, plant, fixtures and Goodwill also all moulds at the Old Factory (Except the Tile Business and the Stock ... belonging ...) Also to take the stock ... in 45 High Street ... For and in lieu of the 19 shares which they hold in the concern."

And that the other proprietors take:—

"Both the London Houses with the Stocks, Goodwill, Fixtures and Book Debts.
The old Manufactory ... and things therein.
With the Tile Business and Plant Stock Fixtures and Goodwill thereof.
The High Street and Manufactory Debts and all other property belonging to this Concern ...
For and in lieu of their 20 shares in the Concern
    Dated the 19th January 1844

Signed Fleming St.John
Walter Chamberlain"

The partners agreed to consider these suggestions and instructed Fleming St.John and George Barr to proceed to London and take stock at 155 New Bond Street and 1 Coventry Street and to investigate ways of selling such stocks. They also recorded the result of Fleming St. John's investigation of the disputed "Trade account Manufactory".

"it appears ... since the Stock has been taken at the Manufactory that the principle upon which the Profit and Loss Acount has been made out is erroneous and that instead of any profit having been made a Loss has occurred since 1 January 1842 to the 30th June 1843 to the extent of £767:5:4 and instead of the Stock and other Property ... under the head of 'Trade Account manufactory' being of the value of £20,522:14:8¼ as stated in the Balance Sheet the same is not valued in the Stock Book at more than £13,000:8:7. It is therefore expedient that ... (the accounts be adjusted accordingly)."

But worse was to come.

On the 9th February 1844 Fleming St.John and George Barr reported on their visit to London.

"so as to ascertain the exact amount of Worcester Porcelain Bought China and Earthenware and Glass . . .

The valuation of the Stock was made at fair selling consists of . . .

Worcester Porcelain	£4,163: 7: 7½
Bought China and earthenware	2,838:15: 9¼
Glass	2,218:19: 4½
Packing Cases	16: 4: 0
Encaustic Tiles	14:12: 2
	£9,251:18:11¼

and at Bond Street

Worcester Porcelain	£5,436:19: 5
Bought china and earthenware	2,012: 8: 2½
Glass (Chiefly patterns)	421:18: 3
Packing Cases	11:14: 9
Encaustic Tiles	3: 1: 4
	£7,886: 1:11½

which amounts being severally reduced . . . by a deduction of £30 per Cent makes . . . Coventry Street . . . £6,476.7.11 being £412.6.7. more than appears by the Trade Account to the 31st December 1843. And at Bond Street . . . £5,520.12.11 being £744.12.5 less than appears by the trade at the above date."

They then go on to say:—

"We think it right to remark that on investigating the amount of Glass we found the Original Stock was purchased of Mr Yates at £1,249.16.6 being . . . at the highest retail selling prices subject to a discount of £5 per cent only. And at those prices was afterwards invoiced to Coventry Street. We find the Article of Glass upon an average allows a profit of £75 per cent being put upon the cost price, consequently the stock purchased of Mr Yates was £70 per cent dearer than any subsequent additions . . . a large portion of the Original Stock was Old Fashioned and in order to make it saleable had been very much reduced (at subsequent stock-takings) from the Prices at which it was invoiced to Coventry Street . . . a considerable portion of the Original Stock of China and Earthenware has been removed from Bond Street to Coventry Street and was invoiced to the latter House at the very high prices at which the same were taken of Mr Yates and being mostly of Old Date had been also necessarily reduced in price at subsequent Stock Takings (in some Cases one-half) to make it saleable and still hangs on even at these greatly reduced prices . . . a considerable portion of the China and Earthenware at Coventry Street consists of Broken sets which must be made up in order to become saleable. We should also remark that in the last half of the Year 1843 Stock to the value of £400 and upwards was removed from Bond Street to . . . High Street . . . chiefly of ornamental porcelain.

After the valuation of the Stocks . . . we had conversation with Mr Turner as to the best mode of disposing of the Stocks at Both Houses.

We found him quite unprepared for this . . . he had not the means to purchase . . . and could not name any Party likely to embark in so large a speculation . . . as regards One House Mr Turner was of opinion the Stock might be realised within a moderate period without a greater sacrifice than of 30% from the Prices marked at the present Stock Taking but that any attempt to sell both at once would be attended with a very great loss indeed."

The partners adopted, with minor modifications, the solution recommended by Fleming St.John and Walter Chamberlain ". . . it appears desirable that the proposed arrangement should take effect as from the 25th day of March next the Dissolution appears in the Gazette on that day or as soon after as circumstances will permit."

Thus ended the short lived and unfortunate amalgamation of 1840 leaving Martin and George Barr and their sister Maria living at Henwick Hall, Worcester in a *ménage à trois*.

On 28th January 1848, Martin Barr died at Henwick Hall, leaving George as his sole legatee. A few months later, on 21st July, 1848, George died, leaving Maria as his sole legatee. On 23rd August 1848 Maria, described as a widow, died. So passed away, in the space of just a little over half a year, the last owners of the once great Flight and Barr factory.

Plate 135. *Flight Barr and Barr plate, painted in two shades of green and gilded in a very close approximation to the style of Kakiemon with a quail subject, possibly a replacement; mark impressed FBB under crown; c.1820; 9^7/16in. From the collection of Mr. and Mrs. James Amos.*

Plate 136. Flight Barr and Barr sauce tureen, cover and stand, chrome green ground outlined with gilding, painted with a single rose subject; 7½in.; c.1820. Dyson Perrins Museum.

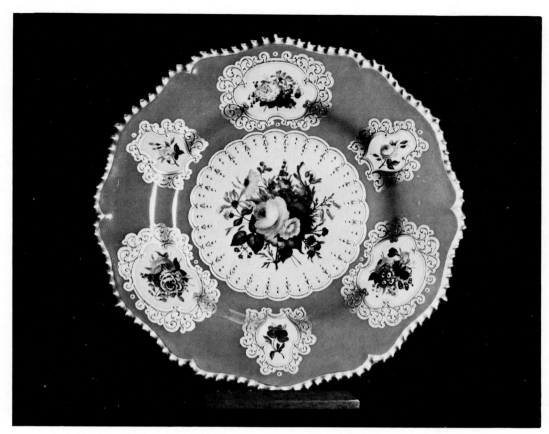

Plate 137. *Superb Flight Barr and Barr dessert plate, green ground, panels of superbly painted flowers probably by Astles, finely gilded; c.1820. Martin Hutton.*

Plate 138. *Three dishes from a Flight Barr and Barr dessert service, apple-green ground reserving central panels of finely painted shells probably by Smith; marks impressed and printed; c.1820. Sotheby's and Beauchamp Galleries.*

Plate 139. Sauce tureen and cover, oval dish and square dish from a Flight Barr and Barr dessert service, each piece finely painted with a named English landscape, including Bothall Castle, Northumberland, Walsingham from the Priory, Norfolk, and view near Dolgelly, Merionethshire, with green ground and gilt gadrooned borders; c.1820; impressed and printed marks. Sotheby's.

Plate 140. Three pieces from a Flight Barr and Barr dessert service painted with panels of fancy birds probably by Charles Stinton, the gilt gadrooned edges with gilt seaweed inside; c.1820. Sotheby's.

150

Plate 141. *Three pieces from a Flight Barr and Barr dessert service with underglaze blue borders, groups of butterflies and insects and named central panels of landscapes; marks impressed and printed; c.1820. Sotheby's and Studio Antiques.*

Plate 142. *A pair of wine coolers and a lozenge shape dish from a Flight Barr and Barr dessert service decorated with a broad apricot ground, picked out with a stylised strawberry meander in gilding, gilt gadrooned borders; impressed mark FBB under crown and printed mark; c.1820. Sotheby's.*

Left: Plate 143. Flight Barr and Barr inkstand of rectangular shape on four scroll feet, finely painted with feathers probably by Doe; script mark; c.1820; 5¼in. Beauchamp Galleries.

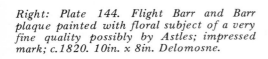

Right: Plate 144. Flight Barr and Barr plaque painted with floral subject of a very fine quality possibly by Astles; impressed mark; c.1820. 10in. x 8in. Delomosne.

Plate 145. Fine Flight Barr and Barr plaque of the Eton boys bathing in the river Thames in front of Windsor Castle, the edges of the plaque showing typical irregular edges; impressed FBB and crown with a small incised cross below and an incised 12 below the cross; c.1820; 6in. x 4½in. Collection of Mr. J. Amos.

Plate 146. *Pair of Flight Barr and Barr pink ground vases and covers, the scroll handles with Mercury head terminals, painted with named views of Windsor Castle and Edinburgh on marbled square bases; c.1820; 9¾in. Christie's.*

Plate 147. *Fine pair of Flight Barr and Barr vases of Empire style, cobalt blue ground with narrow pale yellow ground panels painted with garden flowers and insects, probably by Henry Stinton; height 10½in; mark FBB and crown impressed and script mark; c.1820. Delomosne.*

Plate 148. Pair of Flight Barr and Barr vases painted with fine botanical studies possibly by Astles; 8¾in; mark FBB under crown impressed; c.1820. Delomosne.

Plate 149. Pair of Flight Barr and Barr small vases, applied pearls, painted with flowers on a white ground; 3¾in; impressed and printed marks; c.1820. Delomosne.

155

Two Flight Barr and Barr plates painted by Henry Stinton c.1825-30; green ground, panels of flowers and flies, ivory ground in centre, 9½in; and blue ground, panels of flowers and insects, 9½in. Dyson Perrins Museum.

Above: Plate 150. Pair of Flight Barr and Barr vases on three gilt lion's paw feet above a triangular base, finely painted with sporting subjects of a hound and a doe at lodge, the reverses with gilt urns, applied pearls; 3½in. high; impressed and script marks; c.1820. Barr Collection.

Right: Plate 151. Flight Barr and Barr vase with underglaze blue ground painted with a fine panel of flowers; printed mark; c.1820; 7in. Dyson Perrins Museum.

Plate 152. *Fine Flight Barr and Barr harlequin dessert service, claret grounds and raised gilt scroll cartouches, finely painted with named landscapes, fancy birds in landscapes and bouquets of flowers or fruits on ledges, surrounded by insects and butterflies; c.1820-25. Christie's.*

Plate 153. *Composite parts of a Flight Barr and Barr dessert service painted in camaieu rose with flower sprays and gilt rims, the original comprising two ice pails, covers and liners, sauce tureens, covers and stands with bird's head and ring handles, four oval, four square and four circular dishes and 24 plates; impressed crowned marks; c.1820-25. Christie's.*

Plate 154. Flight Bàrr and Barr tureen and cover of Blind Earl raised rose leaf and rose bud pattern, ring handles and floral knop; 6¼in. high; impressed mark; c.1820-25. Barr Collection.

Chapter 6

The Wares of Flight and Barr

The Flight period, 1783-1792

When Thomas Flight bought the Worcester Porcelain Company for £3,000 in 1783, he probably intended to provide a ready made, going concern of a business for his sons Joseph and John. But he little knew what problems he was presenting them with.

The production of the factory had dropped to a low ebb; the majority of the wares being produced in the years from 1783 to 1792[1] were of the blue printed type — tea and dessert wares, transfer printed in a deep tone of violet blue in the late Chinoiserie style, which were competing with the wares of Caughley, Liverpool and Lowestoft for the trade of the wealthy English. The Worcester wares were still being made from the same old soapstone formula of the great days of the Dr. Wall period but, as John Flight noted in his diary, there were great problems.

The quality of production had declined by 1783 and was to decline even further. The kiln firings were unreliable, resulting in sulphuring which can be described in modern terms as a heavy bluing of the glaze, especially in the form of round patches of blue suffusing the glaze and this is frequently seen on wares of this period. The Royal Worcester kiln men, who worked in the old bottle kilns, described sulphuring as the appearance of a quantity of blackened specs on the surface of the glaze (this was sometimes rather crudely referred to by the potters as "mouse droppings" — or, rather, they used a rather cruder four letter word for "droppings"). The blue could burn off leaving blotches and large pockmarks and the translucency become a strawy-orange as compared with the lovely green of the Dr. Wall period, caused by the dirty conditions of the kiln. Shapes tended to be poor, even existing shapes tended to decline in quality.

The marks of these years from 1783 to 1792 were basically three. A traditional Worcester crescent mark continued in use for some of the blue printed wares and especially for the remaining blue painted wares, such as "Music" pattern (looking like the lines of a music stave with notes on them) or the more popular "Lily" pattern (growing water lilies out of a central circle in the Chinese style) called "Royal Lily"

---

1.   *I discuss this in my book* Worcester Porcelain 1751-1793.

Plate 155. Flight Barr and Barr ice pail, cover and liner from a large botanical dessert service, painted with named flowers including Ollyhock [sic], Iris and Lilac within a broad band of pale blue, gadrooned edges, the whole service comprising two ice pails, two sauce tureens and covers, two centre pedestal dishes, four square, four shell and four oval dishes and 23 out of 24 plates; impressed and printed marks; c.1820-25. Sotheby's.

with royal permission after a service had been bought by King George in 1788. This crescent tends to get gradually smaller as the 1780s move into the '90s and after 1789, when the Royal Warrant was granted, the crescent may have a crown put on top and the word Flight added underneath. Other blue painted patterns of a simple form of spriggs with added gold on the favourite spiral fluted wares can also have a small crescent but similar spiral fluted wares which only have onglaze colours, such as purple spriggs or gold only, quite often have no mark. Very occasionally an impressed word Flight in small block capital letters was used but this is very rarely found. Gilders' numbers in gold to identify the gilder, are occasionally found, usually on the inside of the foot ring.

The new mark known as a disguised numeral mark used on many of the blue printed patterns such as "Bat", "Fisherman and Cormorant" and "Argument", was certainly used during this Flight period of 1783 to 1792 but may not have been used before 1783 when Thomas Flight took over from William Davis. This mark, a number 1 to 9 with usually three squiggles through it to make it look a little oriental, had only been identified as Worcester since the late 1960s, after having been

161

associated with Caughley for many years and anyone interested in this should read my own book *Worcester Porcelain 1751-1793* and Geoffrey Godden's book *Caughley and Worcester Porcelains*. It is not clear why this strange and relatively short lived mark should have been used but I can only assume that it was to disguise the origins of the wares as being Worcester so that the remaining wealthy clients buying finer things would not know that the factory was producing poorer wares.

The other mark was the continuation of the square mark, still being used for the lesser quantity of blue ground and blue scale wares with onglaze decoration of fabulous birds and flowers. It may surprise collectors to know that such production went on even into the Flight and Barr period and such period wares can be identified by the much deeper violet toned blue, by the use of a green in the landscapes which is much yellower than before, and after 1790 at any rate, the use of a harder, brighter, mercuric oxide gilding. The newer, harder and brighter looking glaze, referred to by Valentine Green in his book in 1796 can often be very confusing to people who are only prepared to accept as Worcester the fabulous birds on the old Dr. Wall type body and glaze, and a quantity of Worcester blue and blue scale ground wares are often wrongly called late French or Samson type fakes.

While these Flight wares generally are not as good as those of an earlier period they can still have great charm, even though one particular painter, probably George Davis, had a habit of repeating his birds on different pieces, a thing that would be unthinkable in the Dr. Wall period. One bird that he seems to have liked especially, has poor stumpy wings that look like arms. During this Flight period of 1783 to

Plate 156. *Two attractive Flight Barr and Barr ewers, the one on the left with blue ground and oval medallions painted with a view of Bickleigh Vale, near Plymouth, and on the reverse Kirkham Priory Gateway, with gilt eagle spout, serpent handle and cailloute gilding on the base; the right hand one with a pale green ground painted with a view of Worcester looking upstream from Diglis; height 3½in.; c.1820-25. Sotheby's.*

1792, that is before the arrival of Martin Barr, full ranges of tea and dessert wares were being produced, but relatively little ornamental pieces or dinner wares. An occasional vase shape can be found, mainly in the French style, and the mask jug and other useful objects such as spittoons, continued to be made of the earlier Dr. Wall period shapes. Handles are usually a double curve like the form of the human ear and knobs tend to have a flat button like top and tea-pots change from a round into a barrel form.

The Flight and Barr Period, 1792-1804

In 1792, with the arrival of Martin Barr, confidence seems to have returned to the factory and the wares are generally marked with an incised B, scratched into the body under the base. This B is always of a peculiar form, usually with a small top loop and a larger bottom one, looking a little like a person with a small head and a huge protruding stomach seen from the side, but sometimes this form is reversed with a large upper loop and small lower one. Sometimes there is an additional mark to the right or just below the B of an incised X or a single line stroke, these latter marks probably being workmen's marks or a foreman's checking mark. What the meaning of the main B mark is I do not know. Perhaps as many people have suggested, it simply stands for Barr, who was, after all, putting a lot of money into the venture and this might have been a sop to him. To strengthen this thought very

Above: Plate 157. Garniture of Flight Barr and Barr spill vases, finely painted panels of flowers with gilding of tulip-like classical shapes, pearl-like shapes and vermiculi; centre vase 5½in.; c.1820-25. Christie's.

Plate 158. Flight Barr and Barr vase and cover, supported by three richly gilt mermen on a triangular base, cover with pineapple finial, painted with a view of Warwick Castle; 9¼in; script mark; c.1820-25. Sotheby's.

occasionally the incised mark "F & B" is found with the "B" the same as that found on its own. But if so, it is a strangely anonymous sop. This B mark can be found on the wares of older type glaze, of pre-1796 and those of the harder, brighter, whiter glaze of post-1796, so presumably it does not indicate the change of body. The incised B mark certainly runs on into the early nineteenth century and may have been used as late as 1805 or so.

Unlike Chamberlain and Grainger, Flight and Barr, as we call the period from 1792 to 1804, were not putting the name of the factory inside the cover of pots nor did they use the word "Warranted", which in the case of the rival firms was meant to indicate that the pot was warranted not to crack when you poured boiling water into it. Not that Flight and Barr's teapots were any worse than their rivals but perhaps they did not like to put things like that on their wares. There is a strange sense of anonymity about the wares of the Flight and Barr period, a feeling of caution and a lack of the fantastic spirit of *joie de vivre* that was going to come in the Barr Flight and Barr period. Perhaps it was a hangover from the previous problems of the Flight period, perhaps the caution and reticence of Thomas Flight and his sons with their Baptist upbringing.

Plate 159. *Fine pair of Flight Barr and Barr yellow ground vases of urn shape, flared necks and Empire style gilt handles with panels within fine gold scrolls showing two popular Flight subjects of Malvern Priory with the Malvern Hills behind and Worcester Cathedral with St. Andrew's Church and Flight's factory beyond, taken from the banks of the River Severn downstream of the city in the area called Diglis; impressed and script marks; c.1820-25; 9in. Sotheby's.*

A typical shape of the period is the jardinière, or plant pot holder which has false mooring-ring handles near the neck and a separate base on which the jardinière top sits, although the shape could be made in one piece as a vase or spill. These could be decorated in all sorts of ways, monochrome or *en grisaille* painting by John Pennington, flowers or even with black transfer prints from some of the old Dr. Wall period copper plates. The copper of King George the Third was pressed into service, possibly to commemorate the King's recovery from illness (he had two bouts of madness starting in 1801 and 1804 and the final bout starting in 1810) or in connection with one of his jubilees.

Flight and Barr were also producing some Dr. Wall period patterns to replace broken services and a number of splendid earlier patterns continued in popularity, such as "Blind Earl", "Queen Charlotte" and "Kylin". The latter pattern was also used by Chamberlain who usually put the pattern number "75" under the base of his pieces, whereas the Flight and Barr factory never used pattern numbers. In fact, the growing number of patterns must have made the control and re-ordering of a Flight and Barr pattern a rather difficult and hazardous job and perhaps the ordering was done on the basis of "a service the same pattern as Lord So and so's". The only numbers found on a Flight and Barr piece are gilders numbers in gold.

Flight and Barr's showrooms in the Worcester High Street and at number 1 Coventry Street were beginning to attract better class orders by 1800 or so. As the Rev. Richard Warner wrote when he visited Worcester in 1801,[1] "Amongst the shops which ornament the High Street that of Messrs Flight and Barr particularly engaged our attention, by the rich exhibition it affords of articles from their elegant manufactory . . . We were presented with some coffee cups, made by the order of the Grand Seignor and intended to furnish a golden stand enriched with diamonds." He mentions that the 46 cups in the set, painted with scenes of Nelson's success at the Nile, cost 10 guineas each, which was a considerable amount of money in those days.

So at the turn of the century Flight and Barr were poised to step into the high class trade, which had previously patronised the French firms, most of which trade was stopped in the war. The growing habit of taking dessert at a separate table, usually in a separate room to that in which the family eat dinner, required ever new and more elaborate dessert services. It became a matter of keeping up with the Joneses or rather going one better than the Lords in the next Manor and the richer and finer your dessert table looked the bigger you had scored. Earlier German style, sugar confection, centre pieces had given way to elaborate silver or porcelain ones with figurines decorating the table. It is almost inherent in human nature to want to pick up a piece of porcelain that you admire in someone else's house and see what mark it has underneath and from about 1800 Flight and Barr began to use more elaborate marks that increasingly began to be the best advertisement that could be

1.   *Rev. Richard Warner,* A tour Through the Northern Counties of England and the Borders of Scotland, *1802.*

Plate 160. *Flight Barr and Barr vase of Empire style, maroon ground and raised gilding reserving panel with a named scene of The Franciscan Abbey, Kilkenny; 10¾in; mark FBB under crown impressed and printed mark including London address; c.1820-25. Geoffrey Godden.*

Plate 161. *Fine Flight Barr and Barr vase and cover with claret ground, painted with a view of the City of Worcester from the South West looking from Diglis towards the Cathedral and the porcelain manufactory beyond; 9¾in; script marks; c.1820-25. Sotheby's.*

found. If you admired the porcelain and saw a beautiful mark hand written underneath you naturally went off next day and put in an order for an even finer one from the same firm. So you find elaborate marks reading "Flight and Barr Worcester Manufacturers to their Majesties", under a beautifully drawn crown superceeding the simple scratched B mark, and even after 1804 when the Worcester factory changed its title to Barr Flight and Barr, the London showrooms were still calling themselves Flight and Barr and the very elaborate marks reading "Flight and Barr Coventry Street London/Barr Flight and Barr Worcester Manufacturers to their Majesties and Royal Family" will date from between 1804 and about 1810.

From the simply but superbly decorated punch bowls made for the Corporation of Worcester in 1792, painted by John Pennington, to the elaborate and almost gaudy wares of 1804 there is a gradually increasing sense of development of a new Englishness of quality, a breaking away from the French style. In the 1790s even the simpler wares look French as, for instance, the bell pulls with bands of blue stripes and gilding and the spiral and straight, fluted, tea wares. Even the cider mugs have a French look festooned with hops or flowers. *Vaisseau à mats* in the form of French jardinières were produced rarely (there may even be examples of Worcester decorated French ones in existence). Chocolate and caudle cups continued to be made, as did a few mask jugs and pierced, dessert baskets, although these latter had probably died out by 1800.

Plate 162. Pair of plates from a Flight Barr and Barr ornithological service, painted with a Creeper and White Grouse in landscape vignettes, surrounded by gilt scrolls and foliage, turquoise ground; impressed and printed marks; c.1820-30. Christie's.

Plate 163. Three pieces from a Flight Barr and Barr harlequin dessert service — sauce tureen and cover, plate and lozenge shaped dish, pale blue borders and scattered insects, central panels of shells, flowers, fancy birds and named landscapes; impressed mark FBB under a crown and circular printed mark; c.1820-30. Sotheby's.

Some early plaques were probably produced, mainly painted by outside decorators such as Thomas Baxter, such as a slab painted with a subject after Corbould of three soldiers, a cross and a rock, signed and dated February 1802, and some of these must undoubtedly be of Flight and Barr production, exhibiting the rather peculiar feature of the slab having nibbled edges, almost as if the slab has been cut down from the centre of a large plate or dish, the edges giving the appearance of having been nipped with pincers. Baxter also made some superbly modelled plaques around this time, some of which may be Flight and Barr.

Borders of patterns by 1800 could be of quite rich Japans or Indias and these richer styles of patterns lead the way into the splendours of the Barr Flight and Barr period, truly one of the great periods of English porcelain. "Japan" patterns were basically those in the style of Japanese Imari porcelains, including wares of underglaze blue. The "India" patterns were like the Chinese wares imported by the East India Company, covering an enormous number of onglaze enamelled designs in the oriental style, but without underglaze blue.

Even in the Flight and Barr period some fine pieces could be made, as witness the order for the Earl of Coventry from Joseph Flight and Martin Barr in September 1799 of two Ink Stands with rich flower borders at a cost of eight guineas, and this order was followed up by nine breakfast cups and saucers of Royal Lily pattern, costing £3.7.6d.

Barr Flight and Barr, 1804-1813

The start of the new period of Barr Flight and Barr, which I have put back from the previously accepted date of 1807 to 1804 as discussed in Chapter 3, seems to have co-incided with the introduction of the use of bat prints at Worcester.

The process of bat printing has been very clearly explained by R.W. Binns in his monumental work *A Century of Potting* and I cannot do better than repeat the words of this great character in Worcester's later history.

"As the plates for ordinary transfer printing were either engraved or etched, so as to hold a sufficient body of colour for the transfer operation, the plates for the new style had to be stippled with a fine point, but the principal difference was in the art of transferring, for which no press was required. The copper-plate having been carefully cleaned, a thin coating of linseed oil was laid upon it, it was then bossed by the operator with the palm of his hand until the oil was removed from the surface, except in the engraved spots. Instead of paper, bats of glue were used, which were prepared in the following manner: ordinary glue having been melted so as to run perfectly smooth is poured on to dishes having a very even surface, to the thickness of a quarter of an inch; this paste (which must be kept at a regular consistency), when sufficiently set, is cut into squares the size of the engraving to be transferred. Having the copper-plate charged with oil, one of these glue bats is laid on, with its smooth side to the copper-plate; it must be gently pressed so as to receive the oil out of the engraving, then taken off the copper-plate and laid on the china; this is a very delicate operation, as the workman has not the advantage of a paper transfer through which he can see before pressing it on the ware. In bat printing the operation of transfer must be made correctly at once, requiring a good eye and constant practice. Having thus placed the bat on the china, it is very gently pressed, so as to deliver the oil marks which had been received from the copper-plate. These marks, if placed in the kiln without any other preparation, would burn quite away; the print is therefore gently dusted with the colour required, the superfluous matter being carefully cleaned off with cotton wool.

Plate 164. Flight Barr and Barr small tray or sweet meat dish, gilt gadrooned edge and leaf terrinal handles, painted with fancy birds in a detailed landscape; 5¼in. x 4in: impressed mark; c.1820-30. Barr Collection.

Plate 165. Fine garniture of Flight Barr and Barr vases, dark blue ground, jewelled borders and elaborate gilding reserving panels painted, from the left, with Worcester, Malvern and Warwick; c.1820-30; centre vase 11in. Delomosne.

Ordinary printing in black had been out of favour for some time, and many circumstances had led to this result. So long as the designs and engravings were fine impressions and the work of a clever artist they would command a sale; but the engraver Hancock, who produced this fine work, had long since left the manufactory, and it did not answer to be continually printing from the old plates, which had been worn out or retouched. Black printing on china, therefore as a decoration, when the bat was introduced, was a thing of the past."

A fairly large amount of bat printing was done by Barr Flight and Barr, perhaps not as much as was done by some of the Staffordshire factories, and the process did not seem to retain its popularity at Worcester for very long. by the start of the Flight Barr and Barr period it was certainly on the wane. Perhaps it went against the grain for the factory with a growing reputation to produce something tinted with a thought of mass-production.

Quite a range of different subjects were produced, such as the classical styles of Adam Buck with Roman figures in chariots, rustic groups by Pyne and groups of cupids after Ackerman. One of the finest groups was designed in honour of Nelson and depicted Neptune and Britannia seated in a car, drawn by sea horses, Neptune holding a shield on which a portrait of Nelson is engraved and a cupid representing Fame standing on the front of the car. Shells were also produced in bat prints and sometimes these could be coloured in by hand, with washes of browny reds, and these are the only printing and tinting-in subjects that the factory did, everything

171

else being entirely free hand. Fine scenes of Worcester were executed, several depicting the factory and Cathedral from the other side of the river, almost certainly done from James Ross's coppers. James Ross was a very talented freelance engraver by this time but produced a lot of work for the factory, as did Valentine Green.

The use of shells in bat prints led to the subject being done as superb hand paintings. By the 1810s hand painted shells of exquisite quality were being depicted on a great range of shapes, from ink sets to large vases and also on tea and coffee wares and although the style went on into the Flight Barr and Barr period it had certainly started by 1810 no doubt inspired by the growing custom of having cabinets of shells, which were greatly admired for their form and rarity. The shells are always depicted in full naturalistic detail but were not named underneath the piece and it would be a most interesting project for someone to produce a paper on the Flight and Barr shells, identifying them all. Regretably many sale catalogues tend to ascribe all Worcester shells to Thomas Baxter but it should be strongly stated that there were a number of shell painters at Worcester and I have tried to suggest some of these in the illustrations in this book. Almost certainly any piece fully marked with just the Barr Flight and Barr mark, or the incised B, would not have been painted by Baxter unless he acquired the piece in the white for decorating in London.

Plate 166. Flight Barr and Barr apple green ground dessert plate with finely painted flowers and insects by Henry Stinton within gilt scrolls; c.1825; 9in. Dyson Perrins Museum.

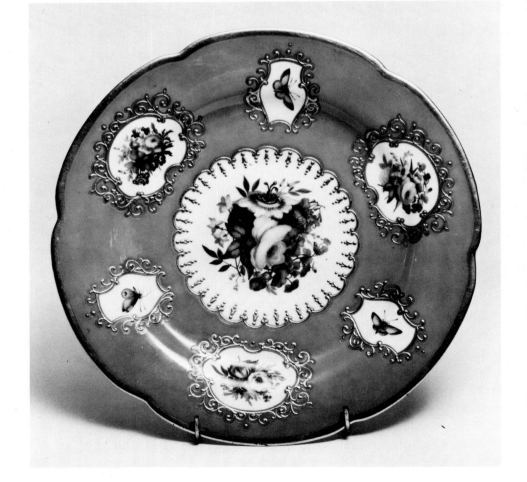

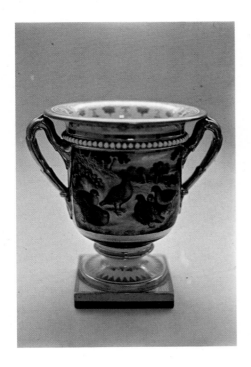

Top left: Flight Barr and Barr vase and cover, on dolphin supports, finely painted with a panel of kingfishers reserved on a pink ground; script mark; 7½in.; c.1830. Top right: Fine Flight Barr and Barr centre vase of a hunting garniture, rope and fox head handles, claret ground, hunting scene described on base "swishing at a rasper" and "going in and out clever"; script mark; 20in.; c.1830-40. Bottom left: Flight Barr and Barr vase, maroon ground and gilding, nicely painted with a panel of six partridges; script mark; 6in.; c.1825. Bottom right: Flight Barr and Barr vase of campana shape and pink ground applied with modelled hops with naturalistic colouring; script mark; 7¹/8in.; c.1830-35. O'Donaghue Collection.

The paintings of naturalistic subjects — landscapes, shells, flowers, birds and feathers — were slowly creeping in at Barr Flight and Barr as an alternative to the popularity of the Japan and India style of patterns, with their bold splashes of blue, red, green and gold. The favourite rich subject seems to have been flowers, either in the form of bunches which on plates can appear the natural way up however you turn them, or set in baskets on a table in the style of the Dutch masters. The flowers could be set inside a border framework of "marbling" or "vermiculi", an extraordinary linking up jigsaw-like pattern in gold that must have been very fiddling to do.

The china receipts of the Earls of Coventry present a dazzling amount of fine pieces bought from the factory. To take just the years 1811-1813 as examples, the delivered orders are set out below a bill head account which reads:—

"Royal China Works, Worcester Established 1751.
Rt. Hon^{bl.} the Earl of Coventry.
To Barr, Flight and Barr.
Manufacturers to their Majesties and the Royal Family."

There is also a fine engraving of the Royal Coat of Arms, surrounded by the words "London Warehouse Flight and Barr, No. 1 Coventry Street", and in date order the orders are itemised and priced, as follows:—

Worcester 1811

Aug. 10	12 Cups and saucers India pattern	£3:12:0
	12 coffee cups and saucers do.	3:12:0
	1 Brunswick Cup and stand Green gold and views.	3: 3:0
Oct. 2	1 Taper Candlestick — Rich Blue & Gold and landscape figure	1: 1:0
Oct. 31	1 Brunswick Cup & Stand with rich painting of flowers	2:12:6
Dec 31	1 Desert Service — Border of azure blue ground with Arms in bronze and different groups of Flowers on every piece.	)
	27 Desert Plates	)
	4 Shell form Dishes	)
	4 Oval do.	) 136:13:0
	4 Square do.	)
	1 Centre do.	)
	1 Stand to do. with columns	)
	2 Cream Bowls	)
	2 Ice Pails	31:10:0
	48 Arms & Crests on the above service	14: 8:0
		£196:11:6

1812

Oct 15	1 Ice Pail pan-French Garland pattern	£— 5:0
Oct 31	1 Imperial form Ink Stand, Blue and Gold vermicilli, green marble & views	6: 6:0
Nov 9	1 Pair Large Match Cases, White & Gold spray work & Landscapes	5: 5:0
	Packing case	—: 1:0

Dec 2	12 Cups and Saucers Rich India with leafage etc.		5: 8:0
	12 Coffee Cans	do	3: 0:0
	2 B & B Plates	do	—:19:0
	1 Slop Bason	do	—: 9:0
Dec 15	1 Pair Brunswick Cups, New French grey & Gold		
	borders & landscapes		5: 5:0
	1 Cup and Saucer New Dresden borders		—: 9:0
Dec 23	India Rock pattern (as under)		
	12 Cups and Saucers		
	8 Coffee Cans		
	2 B & B Plates		
	1 Slop Bason		£12:12:0
	1 Sugar Basket		
	1 Cream Ewer		
	1 Tea Pot & Stand		
	Packing Case		—: 3:0

Sent to Benj^m, Morland Esq., Abingdon, Berkshire.

1813

Apr 9	1 Pair Music Candlesticks — French grey & Gold roses —	
	sent to Lady Augusta Cotton — London	1:11:6
Apr 15	4 Square Dessert Dishes — Vine border	3:12:0
	1 Cream Bowl & Stand do	1: 4:0
	Sent to London.	
Jun 11	1 Centre Dessert Dish on foot (modelled on purpose)	
	Vine Borders. (sent to London)	2: 2:0
Jun 25	12 Dresden form Cups & Saucers	8:12:0
	8 Coffee Cans	3: 4:0
	3 B & B Plates	2: 5:0
	1 Water Bason	14:0
	Sent to Lady Augusta Cotton, London.	
		£63: 6:6

All these orders were paid in full, even the 1813 ones, by September 30th 1813. It was by no means a common thing to pay bills as promptly as this at that time and the Earl of Coventry must have greatly endeared himself to Flight and Barr, for you will appreciate that the amounts were not negligible ones. The splendid dessert service with azure blue ground flower paintings and arms and crests painted in bronze, is illustrated in this book and is typical of the really rich dessert services that were going into the homes of the nobility. At that time the pair of ice pails, which should have an inner liner to be complete, were the main centre display items of the service, and, as you will note from the Coventry orders, it was quite possible to order a separate liner if you had an accident, and indeed you could obtain virtually any replacement piece you required, even if the original came from another factory or country.

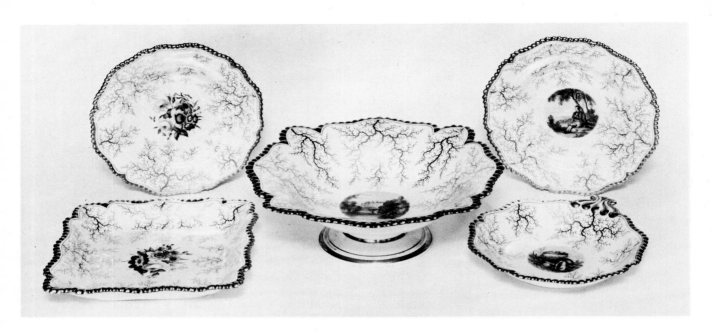

Plate 167. Parts of a Flight Barr and Barr harlequin dessert service with a gadrooned edge, gilt weed border surrounding central panels of landscapes, shells and flowers; c.1825. Phillips of Knowle.

Plate 168. Flight Barr and Barr card tray or basket on four gilt lion's paw feet, apple green ground surrounding a painting of a scene from Paul and Virginia, described under the base "The noise of the water frightened Virginia and she durst not wade through the stream". 10in; script mark; c.1825-30. Dyson Perrins Museum.

Plate 169. Flight Barr and Barr vase of inverted bell shape, lime green ground reserving panel finely painted with a view of Stirling Castle; 11½in; impressed mark; c.1825. Martin Hutton, now in the O'Donaghue Collection.

177

Plate 170. Flight Barr and Barr dessert plate of the Blind Earl pattern of raised rose leaves and rose buds, painted in naturalistic colours; printed mark; c.1825-30; 7½in. Dyson Perrins Museum.

Some of the items mentioned in the Coventry orders need explanations. Brunswick cups were most likely cabinet cups with two handles, a cover and a stand, a match case was what we would now call a spill vase, made in large and small sizes; Barr Flight and Barr sugar baskets were oval shapes with two handles and did not have covers; music candlesticks were of the pillar type with square bases meant to stand on the early pianofortes.

It is interesting that the factory was prepared to make a special piece on request, as witness the dessert dish "modelled on purpose". The shapes during the Barr Flight and Barr period were still influenced by the French styles although they were beginning to move towards the classical forms that were going to be popular in the next period. R.W. Binns, in *A Century of Potting,* said that all their shapes were thrown on the wheel and turned on the lathe, not produced from moulds, and generally the only form of embellishment was of knobs and handles, well designed and beautifully modelled. Where the vases were made in several parts, that is those having large or elaborate plinths or bases, these were usually bolted together with a round headed nut and bolt, the nut under the hollow base and the round head inside the bottom of the vase. This was quite a normal method of manufacture for these difficult shapes and it should not be thought that the vase has been broken and repaired subsequent to the making merely because of the presence of such a fixing.

In the Barr Flight and Barr period the factory mark could range from the simple form of the impressed block capital letters BFB under a crown, to the most elaborate hand script written or printed marks yet put on English porcelain. The written marks are always done in lines under a prettily drawn crown and usually read "Barr Flight and Barr/Worcester/Flight & Barr/Coventry Street/London/ Manufacturers to their/Majesties &/Royal Family", the addition of the three plumes of the Prince of Wales's feathers indicating a date of 1811 or after. The printed marks are even more elaborate; set in an oval form will be some such words as "Barr Flight and Barr, Royal Porcelain Works Worcester, London House, Flight and Barr Coventry Street" and around the outside of the oval appear such words as "Manufacturers to their Majesties, Prince of Wales and Royal Family, Established 1751" with the Royal crown on top of all and with the addition of the Prince of Wales's feathers especially from 1813. Really the mark under the base can often be as beautiful as the decoration on the front of a piece.

Plate 171. Pair of trumpet shaped spill vases painted with named subjects, "The task, forth goes the woodman" from Cowper and "The cottage girl" from Gainsborough, R.A. Cup and saucer with green ground painted with "The peasant girl", Flight Barr and Barr; c.1825-30. A.J. King Collection.

The Flight Barr and Barr Period, 1813-1840

Following the death of Martin Barr senior in 1813, the firm changed its name for the last time to Flight Barr and Barr. As in the previous period the marks can vary from the simple impressed letters FBB under a crown, to script written marks incorporating full details such as "Flight Barr and Barr, Royal Porcelain Works Worcester, London House Coventry Street", or very elaborate printed marks underneath the Royal coat of arms and the addition of the Prince of Wales's plumes between 1813 and 1820 in the Regency period.

The productions reach incredible heights of quality in this period, every piece hand decorated throughout. Services could range from simple, tastefully decorated floral subjects, set in classical borders of palmettes, Greek key fret, or vermiculi, to superb and rich studies of shells, feathers, flowers, birds or landscapes. Some dessert services were produced of a harlequin type with, say a quarter of the service each of shells, flowers, feathers and landscapes. Full landscape services would have a different landscape on each piece, the landscapes drawn from books of engravings depicting landscapes in Great Britain or houses of nobility, the names of the scenes often being written underneath the piece.

Splendid ornamental wares were produced, from small pairs or garnitures of vases, inkwells and desk sets, candle and taper sticks, up to large pairs of vases of classical campana shape. Vases would be for table centre decoration with the painted panels on each side, or for mantelpiece use with the main decorative panel on one side only and simple gilding on the reverse. The basic shapes of vases were complemented by beautiful handles sometimes in the form of twisted serpents or eagle heads, sometimes like Roman or Greek handles or most rarely in the forms of horses' heads, a shape which was probably modelled by Thomas Baxter who joined the factory in 1814, from a horse that was owned by the Barrs. Other decoration was in the form of beautiful pearls, formed of separate balls of rolled clay stuck on to the belly or neck of a vase with slip and then coloured over with white enamel. These pearls have a magical appearance with a three dimensional feeling, so different to the flat effect of pearls produced by moulding. Hand made pearls, hand made vases, hand painting — everything produced by hand superbly well and the result also comes up to expectations. Most great factories' wares are usually of fine quality but could be pedestrian or ordinary, but in the case of Flight Barr and Barr I defy anyone to produce a poor piece.

The gilding should not be forgotten, as this is invariably of superb quality. The gold itself is always mercuric oxide, and had been since about 1790, harder and

Plate 172. Pair of vases pale yellow ground and pearls, painted with flowers; impressed and script marks as shown; c.1825-30; 3¾in. Geoffrey Godden Chinaman.

Plate 173. Flight Barr and Barr urn, handles in the form of the horns of a ram, claret ground reserving a panel finely painted with a goldfinch on a branch, applied pearls; 3¼in; script mark; c.1825-30.

Plate 174. Night light holder and shade in the form of a gothic style cottage, the top lifting off the base, painted in naturalistic colours with flowering plants on the wall; 6¾in. long x 7½in. high; mark "Royal Porcelain Works Flight Barr and Barr Worcester and Coventry Street London" under a crown; c.1825-30. Dyson Perrins Museum.

Plate 175. Three small Flight Barr and Barr pin-trays. Top: painted with a winged cherub's head on an azure blue ground; 4½in. x 3in. Left: painted with a named scene of Kirkham Priory Gateway, Yorkshire, surrounded by gilt weed; 5³/8in. x 4in. Right: onglaze azure blue ground with panel painted with titled scene from Milton "Lycidas — but not the praise Phoebus reply'd and touch'd my trembling ears", copied from an engraved illustration by Richard Westall, R.A., in a book of Milton's poems published in 1827; 5³/8in. x 4in; c.1828-35. Dyson Perrins Museum.

brighter than the earlier type of honey gold. It might be particularly helpful to give a brief account by Dr. L.B. Hunt of Johnson Matthey and Co. Ltd. of the development of gilding of porcelain over the years.

In the earliest days of Meissen and, even before that, in China, gold leaf was applied with some sort of sticky "goo" of white of egg, linseed oil, white lead and so on. The first real process at Meissen used a precipitated gold powder — made by adding a solution of ferrous sulphate to a solution of gold in aqua regia — and a lead silicate flux. At Vincennes and Sèvres, and at Worcester during the Dr. Wall period, the very old method was used of grinding up gold leaf very slowly in honey. The honey was, of course, then washed away in hot water, the gold powder dried, and applied to the ware with a "mordant" of oil of garlic, gum water and vinegar, etc. Around 1780 Sèvres introduced a new method. Gold dissolved in aqua regia was precipitated by adding a solution of mercurous nitrate. This gave not only a much finer powder than was obtained with the ferrous sulphate, but a powder containing some residual mercury compounds which was of help in producing a thin bright film of gold. This produces a much harder and brighter gold when fired and burnished, superior in many ways to the softer, pitted or blistered effect of honey. It is still not clear whether any factory in the eighteenth century actually used the alleged true amalgam made by dissolving gold, either leaf or powder, in liquid mercury.

Plate 176. *Constituent shapes of a typical Flight Barr and Barr dessert service of about 1830, painted with the crest of Pullar — a falcon standing on an ermine — lined puce cap within a wide salmon-pink border enriched with gilt vermiculi; impressed marks. Private collection.*

The painters at the factory — they all seem to have been men, unlike Chamberlain's and Grainger's factories where a number of girls and women were employed to do simple colouring in of outline printed subjects or "slight flowers" — were of outstanding quality. Inspired and trained by Thomas Baxter they could rise to heights of skill undreamt of before and on some of the subjects which were done by a number of painters it is really very difficult to ascribe the name of the painter with any degree of certainty. Thomas Baxter's letter to Haydon, quoted in Appendix I, seems to suggest that Baxter was only given little things to paint, "the littler the prettier", and while I imagine this to be just a general moan and that he undoubtedly worked on some of the major vases, his hand is certainly to be seen on a number of small pieces, such as "Eagle handled cups", as the shape is referred to in an 1814 order for the Earl of Coventry, painted with a landscape and pearled. Certainly these are pretty pieces indeed. But sorting out a Baxter figure landscape from one by Solomon Cole or Lowe, or Baxter's shells from those of Barker is very difficult, and the firm ascriptions in this book are, I hope, accurate, being based upon the very rare signed plaques or positive ascriptions by R.W. Binns. There is a great danger in making ascriptions on the basis of subject or even on a presumed characteristic of technique for, as in the case of a group of painters who received coaching from as fine a teacher as Baxter, the pupils would undoubtedly absorb so much of the master's style and so many of his "tricks" that their work could resemble the master's almost completely.

One painter whose style is very easy to be confident about is that of Pennington. Whether the painting is a monochrome in his early style, for instance in the 1792 Duke of Clarence "Hope" service, or in the later polychrome style, as in the fine vase in the White House in Washington made to commemorate the capture of the French frigate, *La Guerrière*, by *H.M.S. Blanche*, commanded by Captain Lavie in 1808, his work is unmistakable. The amount of painting by Pennington seems to drop away in the Flight Barr and Barr period — perhaps his style was thought to be rather old fashioned with the advent of the new London styles of Baxter — but some vases are found, notably, a fine group at Stourhead, in Wiltshire, originally the home of the Hoare family, which are undoubtedly by Pennington.

Although many fine armorial services had been made in the Barr Flight and Barr period, it was the Flight Barr and Barr period that really brought such services into their own. Not only were great services produced for English royal families and other nobility but they were also being made for countries beyond the seas of Great Britain. From the earlier period of Barr Flight and Barr came such fine services as those for the Duke of Gloucester and the Prince of Wales, who visited the factory in 1807.

In 1814 a superb service was made for Alexander, the Emperor of Russia, the ground colour of rich cobalt blue with raised gilding, and the Imperial arms emblazoned in the centre in proper colours. Another service was also produced for the Emperor at about this time; in fact there must have been a considerable contact with that country. The Nabob of Oude had two services, both of them had his crest of two tigers holding pennants; in the centre of one of the services is a fine landscape of female dancing figures of great quality that R.W. Binns ascribed to Baxter. A very similar style of painting is seen on the service made for Lord Valentia which has a border of anthemions in raised gold and scenes of Greek ruins in the centre, after drawings by W. Page. A beautiful service, made for Lord Amhurst when going out as Govenor-General of India in 1823, has a lovely ground colour which R.W. Binns describes as Saxon green and gilt gadrooned edge — gadroons having come strongly in at Worcester in the 1810s, although they had been used in the Dr. Wall period.

In the 1820s many interesting new ground colours, such as the Saxon green mentioned above, were added to the range of Worcester grounds which up to then had been mainly either cobalt blue or Barr's orange, the latter a very special kind of deep salmon, peculiar to Flight and Barr. A helpful bit of information comes from a receipted bill of an order for the Marchioness of Hastings in 1829. The order of 12 tea cups and saucers, all of completely different ground colours and decorations, must have been quite chaotic if put out on a table together — perhaps they were not intended for use but just as examples. Anyway, full payment of £6.8.0d. was received at London only two weeks after delivery thus earning the discount, so they were obviously not intended as patterns from which a service pattern would be chosen.

The order is as follows:—

1 Tea Cup and Saucer	Rich Gold Sprayage and Gadroon edge.	£—:12:0
1 do	Gold Vermicelli	—:11:0

1	do	Saxon Green & Gold, Vase borders	13:0
1	do	Pink & do	13:0
1	do	Color'd Forgetmenot border	6:0
1	do	Rich Japan Flowers	10:0
1	do	Fawn & Gold Laurel	8:0
1	do	Mazzarine Blue & Gold Scrolls etc.	11:0
1	do	Groupes (of) Flowers on Straw color'd ground etc.	14:0
1	do	White & Gold & Flowers	14:0
1	do	Garnet ground & Gold Vine Leaf etc	12:0
1	do	White & Gold & Bronze border	8:0
		Packing Box.	2:6
			£6:14:6
	Discount for ready Money		6:6
			£6: 8:0

The differences in costing for the different grounds and decorations are very illuminating and reflect the greater difficulty of some effects. I have tried to indicate what the above colours are in this book — Saxon green, pink, fawn and Mazzarine blue (underglaze cobalt) being fairly common grounds and garnet being uncommon. All ground colours by this time were being done by the proper ground-lay process of dusting colour on to an oiled surface and therefore it was a much more even and smooth colour than the eighteenth century grounds which were painted on by brush. The difference is espcially noticeable in the case of green which was now not only ground-laid but also of a different type — chrome green instead of copper green.

By far the finest ground colour was blue, of superb depth and control and it should be clearly recognised that underglaze blue of this quality is one of the hardest things to achieve on ceramics. Probably the finest service produced not only at Flight and Barr but in the whole history of English ceramics, is that made in 1831 for William IV. R.W. Binns said of the ordering of this service that there had been great competition for the order and the Barrs had need of friends at Court to fight off the opposition. Perhaps it was that the King remembered the fine services that Flight and Barr had made for him earlier when he was Duke of Clarence.

The service is sumptuous without being gaudy; it has all the taste of Sèvres without the vulgarity of the English Regency and is of a purely heraldic character. In Mr. Binns's impassioned words,

"The colour of the ground is a dark blue, forming a broad band in which are placed six panels, three large and three small; the centre large panel at the top of the plate contains a painting of the jewel of the Order of the Garter, St George and the Dragon, beautifully executed on a delicate lemon coloured ground; in the corresponding angles are the jewels of the Thistle and St Patrick; between these, and filling the smaller panels, are the jewels of the Bath, St Michael and the Guelphic Order. The centre of the plate is decorated with the Royal Arms of England, excellently painted. The gilding of this plate is very elegant; in lieu of the usual tasteless panels, a light tracery of raised gold is added, together with a very richly

Plate 178. Flight Barr and Barr miniature pot pourri and pierced cover with flower knob, painted with feathers; 3¼in. high; script mark; c.1830. Barr Collection.

arranged ornament of white enamel representing pearls; the edge was a solid gilt gadroon. Altogether this is the handsomest work of Messrs Flight and Barr's which we have seen."

Everything made at Flight and Barr up to about 1830 was of a soft paste porcelain, basically the old Dr. Wall period formula with some modifications and a finer glaze, but the drying up of the soaprock source forced the firm into the production of bone china, a much whiter body, of course, and highly translucent. Shapes became tinged with a slight hint of Victorianism, although like Chamberlain, Flight Barr and Barr could never quite throw off a style based upon the Regency and classical forms. Perhaps the shapes become a little more fluid and less formal, although a lot of shapes continue over from the Regency into the 1830s, such as card trays on four feet with an overhead handle, and handles of a Regency/classical twisted form continue and the basic shapes of dessert, dinner and tea ware do not undergo much change. In fact the firm continued to be very conservative in all they did. The decoration continued to be of fine quality with all the favourite Worcester subjects surviving. Gilded gadrooned edges are more usual than a plain edge and a bold type of jewelling, simulating amethysts, rubies and pearls, is very occasionally to be seen, framing a beautifully painted panel.

Some shapes that seem to be acknowledging a new style to come in are small cups with delicate handles in the form of a folded butterfly's wings, cottages which are combined pastille burner and night light with the candle light shining out through

Plate 177. Flight Barr and Barr vase and cover, one of a pair, painted with a panel of Clio with a pearled border on a green ground supported on the heads of three gilt mermen; printed mark; c.1830; 8in. Dyson Perrins Museum.

Plate 179. Cabinet cup and stand, hexagonal shape with gilt gadrooned edge and three claw and ball feet, painted with insects and flower sprays; Flight Barr and Barr script mark; c.1830-35. Frank Laney Collection.

the thin windows and the aromatic smoke ascending up the chimney, such cottages being in the Gothic style and of superb quality, a long way removed from the crude cottages which were so popular in early Victorian days.

Some miniatures were produced in the last years of Flight Barr and Barr — gorgeous little candle and taper sticks, vases, watering cans, baskets, painted with floral studies, often on a pale lavender ground, such little pieces being so small and delicately beautiful as to deserve a golden dolls' house as a proper setting. Larger items, such as pin trays and baskets were also popular and invariably beautifully painted.

By far the rarest item made in the 1830s is a standing female figurine, of which I have only come across one example, left in unglazed biscuit bone china and marked with FBB under a crown impressed mark. This is quite well modelled and it may appear very strange that the Flight and Barr factory should only have produced one figure subject, when their local Worcester rivals — Chamberlain and Grainger — were producing fairly large numbers of animal and human figurines in the 1820s and 30s. Assuming that no other figurines were made — none have come to light so far — it should be clearly kept in mind that Flight and Barr were the great specialists in table ware of the finest quality and I suppose they felt no need to make figures. Even the production of plaques seems to have been given only lip service, relatively few being found and most of these, as previously mentioned, giving the appearance of being pieces of porcelain cut down from something larger. The very occasional finding of Barr Flight and Barr plaques made for use in furniture is an exceptional event.

The actual year in which Flight Barr and Barr changed from their soapstone porcelain body to bone china is not known. It is certain that by 1830 they were having great difficulties in obtaining new supplies of soapstone and it is probable that in the early 1830s the changeover was made. Relatively little bone china of Flight Barr and Barr is found and it would seem that in the last few years of the 1830s the factory was not producing as large a quantity of ware as in the earlier years.

One of the last services made by Flight Barr and Barr was made as a present from William IV to the Imaum of Muscat. The Imaum in 1836 had sent as a present to the King a small teak battle ship of the line, containing presents of an Eastern character. In return the King gave, as a present, his royal yacht, the *Prince Regent,* which was freshly fitted out with gilding and painting and filled with presents, including musical instruments and the Flight Barr and Barr dinner service — as R.W. Binns put it "Yachts, cots and what-nots, all gegilt and gefamed". The Imaum is said to have been highly indignant at what he regarded as a very tawdry present of a small sailing yacht, having expected a steam vessel. However, the dinner service was really of great elegance, with gilt gadrooned edge, green ground border reserving the Imaum's crest at the top and in the centre of the pieces a remarkably accurate painting of the *Prince Regent* entering Muscat Cove, showing the scene of the approach to the harbour with the forts on the twin rocks guarding the entry.

So the Muscat service of 1837 is the last certainly dated production of this great factory, which had struggled upwards from the difficult years of Flight in 1783, to the hard development years of Flight and Barr in 1792, the achievements of the Barr Flight and Barr period from 1804 to the crowning glories of the Flight Barr and Barr period from 1813 until its somewhat sad and ignominious amalgamation with Chamberlain in 1840.

Plate 180. Pretty Flight Barr and Barr miniature basket with gilded handles, painted with four small bouquets of Spring flowers; 2¾in. high, 3¼in. long, 1in. wide; script mark; c.1830-35. Barr Collection.

Plate 181. Colour trials fired on the rims of Flight Barr and Barr plates, many of them dated between 1834 and 1839, found on the factory site during a short archaeological excavation in 1977. These trials, which were for testing the behaviour of new batches of colour, are similar to present day trials and were found in a level of dumpings from Flight's factory by Chamberlain and Company in the 1840s. The names of the colours are either written on or incised into the colours and comprise such names as Bailey's Best Purple, Key's Hard Rose, Old Blue Green and Chrome Green.

Plate 182. Pair of medallions with pearl surrounds, left painted in black with the bust of Abbas Mirza, Prince Royal of Persia and right in colours with the bust of Futteh Ali Shah, King of Persia taken from prints published by Thomas Dudley, King Street, London; the coffee-cup with green ground and gilding reserving panel painted with portrait; named under the base "Futteh Ali Shah, King of Persia" and script mark Flight Barr and Barr; medallions 2½in; c.1830-35. Dyson Perrins Museum.

Plate from the superb service made for William IV in 1830, which gives some idea of the fabulous quality of which Flight Barr and Barr is notable; printed mark; 9⁷/8in. Dyson Perrins Museum.

Plate 183. Pair of Flight Barr and Barr spill vases, painted with portraits of Fath Ali Shah (Futteh Ali Shah) King of Persia 1797-1834 and his favourite son Crown Prince Abbas Mirza, "the noblest of the Kajah race", died 1833, taken from a coloured engraving "published as the act directs" by Thos. Dudley, King Street, Soho, London; c.1834-40. Sotheby's.

Plate 184. Plate from the service made in 1836 for the Imaum of Muscat, central scene of The Prince Regent entering Muscat Cove, surrounded by a very pale lime green ground with crest of crowned crescent and gilt gadrooned edge. Dyson Perrins Museum.

Plate 185. Superb pair of late Flight Barr and Barr vases with rich claret ground, hunting scenes on each side inscribed under the base "Topping a flight of rails coming well into the next field", "Going along at a slapping pace", "Charging an ox fence" and "Fording a brook"; these subjects were also done at Chamberlain's factory, c.1830-40; 16½in. Delomosne.

Plate 186. Centre vase from the garniture of hunting vases; 20in. Delomosne and O'Donaghue Collection.

Plate 187. Flight Barr and Barr green ground plate from an armorial service with the arms of Barette of India in full heraldic colours. Even in black and white the fantastic quality of painting, ground laying and gilding is evident; c.1830-60. Dyson Perrins Museum.

Plate 188. Very rare Flight Barr and Barr figure subject of a standing female in unglazed bone china; 9½in. high; mark FBB under a crown impressed; c.1835. Dyson Perrins Museum.

Plate 189. Part of a Flight Barr and Barr apple or chrome green ground crested dessert service with gilt gadrooned rims; impressed marks and some with script Chamberlain marks, the latter pieces either replacements or the service completed after the amalgamation of 1840; c.1838-42. Christie's.

Plate 190. Two Flight Barr and Barr egg or coffee cups with butterfly handles, in a bone china body, apple green ground on the right hand one, dentil gilding inside cups, one painted with woodman sitting on a hewn branch, the other a lakeside scene with exotic temple; c.1835-40. Dyson Perrins Museum.

198

Appendix I

The Painters, Gilders and other Workmen and Characters at Flight's Factory

Our knowledge of the employees of the factory has had to be built up from a large number of scattered sources, as none of Flight and Barr's wages books have survived. Such sources as those in the City of Worcester records have been researched by Robert Stones and these have helped a great deal, although with the rival factories of Chamberlain and Grainger on the doorsteps of Flight, it is sometimes very difficult to be certain at which factory the person worked. Much research into the parish records has been done by Mrs. Mansell and these have been a great help. The details left to us by Solomon Cole, taken from Chaffers' *Marks and Monograms* and quoted in Chapter 4, are of the utmost importance and added to these are Mr. R.W. Binns's own remarks given in his *Century of Potting* and although he only came to Worcester in 1852 he obviously made many enquiries from the older workmen.

So the following list is given with a considerable amount of reservation and it should be clearly understood that a small amount of space devoted to a workman is not necessarily an indication of his importance but more likely because of lack of knowledge of him. The references to "blue painter" apply to the painting of the underglaze parts of a decoration in cobalt oxide, the remainder of the decoration being done onglaze in metallic oxides which are then fired into the glaze.

ALLIES, George, involved in the merger of Chamberlain and Flight. The Allies family were leather merchants.

ALLIES, Jabez (1787-1856), brother of George, involved in merger — a solicitor and keen antiquarian and archaeologist.

ASTLES, Samuel, a fine flower painter, pupil of Thomas Baxter, at his school of art, at factory from about 1812 until 1840, exhibited a china painting of flowers after Van Huysum at Royal Academy in 1827, specialised in groups of flowers, especially on vases, was said to have had a cork leg (letter to R.W. Binns from James Knight, who knew Astles).

BARKER, John, a fine painter of naturalistic shells, at factory from at least 1819 until 1840.

BARR, George (c.1788-1848), partner in the business, admitted Freeman of Worcester in 1808, became a partner on the death of his father, Martin, in 1813 and managed the London showroom for some years.

BARR, Martin, senior (1757-1813), a businessman, joined factory as partner in 1792 and elected Freeman same year, subscribed to Greene's *History and Antiquities of Worcester* 1796.

BARR, Martin, junior (c.1784-1848), son of above, admitted Freeman 1804, became partner 1807 and superintended the factory with his father.

BAXTER, Thomas (1782-1821), probably the finest ceramic painter of his time, born in Worcester, worked at his father's decorating studios at 1, Goldsmith Street, Gough Square, London, mainly decorating pieces bought in the white from Coalport but also on some other English and Chinese porcelains. He attended art classes at the Royal Academy school under Henry Fuseli, a distinguished professor of painting, and was greatly inspired by classical Greek and Roman vase painting, publishing in 1810 a book, *An Illustration of the Egyptian, Grecian and Roman Costumes*, dedicated to Fuseli and containing 40 plates of costumes, many taken from vases formerly in the possession of Sir William Hamilton. Some of these designs were subsequently used on Flight and Barr vases and plates. Baxter held that it was to the Greeks that we owe nearly all that is "elegant and dignified" in art. Certainly the faces that he depicted in his ceramic paintings have a great resemblance to those depicted on Grecian vases. Many authors have written that during 1801 and 1802 Baxter painted a series of vases with poses of Lady Hamilton and that these were acquired by Lord Nelson, Baxter subsequently spending some time sketching and painting for Nelson at Merton in Surrey in 1802 and 1803. However this seems to be based wholly on tradition and is not necessarily correct. Three interesting portrait medallions by Baxter exist; a pair in the Los Angeles County Museum depict Thomas Baxter and his father and are dated 1814 and 1815; the third is in the Rous Lench Court collection in Worcestershire and depicts Nelson and bears the date 18-05, but this may be a reference to the year of the death of Nelson and not the date of making. Each is in biscuit porcelain and within glazed frames of typical Worcester coloured jewels of the mid-1810s on a deep blue ground, the quality equal to if not better than Wedgwood counterparts. On the base they have incised initials T B above a peculiar trident with scroll containing the date and were probably made at Worcester in 1814 or later when Baxter moved to the city to work for Flight Barr and Barr and founded a school of art in Edgar Street, teaching many of the Worcester artists, including Astles, Cole, Doe, Pitman and Webster. Painted at Flight's factory from 1814-16, specialising in figure subjects, especially copying the works of Sir Joshua Reynolds, and West, continuing the subjects he had painted in London, where he had been employed by a connoisseur to copy some of the finer pieces in his collection. An amusing story is accounted about this — this gentleman frequently denigrated English artists and after a visit to Paris he showed Baxter a fine piece of porcelain and enquired if such quality could be produced in England; to his surprise, Baxter told him that he had himself painted it while at Goldsmith Street. In 1816 Baxter moved to Swansea, where he worked for Dillwyn. In 1819 he returned to Worcester, painting for Flight and then for Chamberlain. He does not seem to have enjoyed his work at Flight very greatly, if a letter from him to the artist B.R.

Haydon is to be believed; this is written from his house in Edgar Street, Worcester, and is dated 21st July 1819, shortly after his return from Swansea and it reads:—

"Dear Sir,

Five years banishment from all that is great has rather increased if possible my love of the arts. My health of body is very much better for my removal. I cannot say much for my mind as I am employed here on little things and the "littler the prettier", the *dear* little things and the *dearer* they are the better — but I beg pardon for trifling with you. I have really felt great pleasure in looking after *you* in the "Annals of the Fine Arts" but in the last number I was very much surprised to *find myself* directly mentioned in an article respecting Flight and Barr's china works. I was astonished that an editor who professes to be a friend to artists, should insert a mere manufacturer's puff. The two plates which are noticed are my painting, and their figure painting is now done by a pupil of mine named Lowe. It is not very likely that I shall ever paint anything more for them, as the people I am now engaged with [that is Chamberlain] are more liberal-minded and would be much more likely to bring forward what is good if there was a choice of encouragement. They will send an account of themselves to the editor of the "Annals", indeed I think if the editor wishes it most manufacturers of any kind of articles would take the trouble to write for him, if you think so, have the goodness to let him have it — but I trouble you with this business because I think as we were once friends and fellow students you will feel pleasure in serving me, who the editor is and whether he feels my pleasure in the arts I know not, but he professes to serve artists and perhaps your influence might go far towards making him notice so obscure a person as Your Very humble but sincere friend Thomas Baxter".

While with Flight, Baxter is said to have modelled a horse-head handled vase from a mare belonging to Mr. Barr and he was capable of tackling a large number of painting subjects — figures, landscapes, shells, feathers and flowers — but it is naturally very dangerous to accept as Baxter all the pieces ascribed to him without certain proof, as he was a very fine teacher and the work of many of his pupils could approach that of their master and they would have learned many of his particular techniques. He exhibited at the Royal Academy 16 times between 1802 and 1821, listed as an enamel specialist.

BELL, Edward, Worcester artist, exhibited at Royal Academy, British Institute and Suffolk Street between 1811 and 1847.

BILLINGSLEY, Lavinia, daughter of William, probably employed by Flight while her father was at Worcester, died at Nantgarw in 1817.

BILLINGSLEY, Sarah, junior, eldest daughter of William and married Samuel Walker, colleague of Billingsley, at Claines Church, Worcester, 22nd September 1812, employed by Flight and died 1st January 1817.

BILLINGSLEY, Sarah, wife of William, probably not employed by Flight, died at Derby, June 1824, aged 64; apparently never went to Worcester.

BILLINGSLEY, William (1758-1828), one of the most interesting characters in English ceramic history, came to Flight's factory in 1808, together with Samuel Walker, to develop a new porcelain body and improve the kilns, but probably also did a small amount of flower painting. In 1813 went to Nantgarw and for further details see Chapter 3.

BLY, John, senior (1779-1833), came to Worcester from Lowestoft about 1803, went first to Chamberlain in 1799, said to have worked on the William IV services, specialising in doing the shaded gold on crests, and also painted the Lord Amherst service of 1823, died aged 54 in Carden Street, Worcester.

BLY, John, junior, son of above, painted landscapes and general subjects from before 1819 until the end of Flight Barr & Barr, married Sarah and had a child, Jabez Bly, born 7th April 1833, who was a freelance painter.

BRADLEY, James, appears in a list of general decorators or potters at Flights, most likely a potter from before 1819 until 1840.

BRADLEY, James, described as a porcelain painter in the Long Book of Freemen, might have been son of the above, painted animals, portraits and flowers at Kerr and Binns, Worcester.

BRADLEY, Samuel, an original partner of the Dr. Wall period in 1751, was a goldsmith in Worcester, admitted a Freeman, 1741, address 33 High Street, Worcester, where he had his shop. In his History of 1796 Greene writes, "The retail warehouse in Worcester was formerly kept opposite the Guildhall, in the High Street, but the concern being materially increased after the death of Mr. Bradeley . . . moved to No 45 . . . nearer the Cross and the principal inns."

BREWER, Robert (1775-1857), painter, born Madeley in Shropshire, was probably apprenticed at Caughley then went to Flight and Barr before joining Derby in 1797, staying at least until 1816, when he worked as a painter in the City of Derby.

BROADFOOT, William, apprenticed to Dr. Wall's factory 17th December 1765, may have been manager of Flight's retail shop in High Street, and was later a retailer, described in the Worcestershire Directory of 1820 as "Broadfoot and Ballinger, glass and china ware house, 1, The Cross".

CALE, Frederick, Freeman, admitted June 1782 as an apprentice at Flight's, either a potter or a painter but there may be some confusion with a father and son of same name.

CARADINE, Thomas, appears in list of general decorators before 1819 and continued until 1840, appears in the 1851 census.

CARDEN, Henry Douglas, involved in the merger of Chamberlain and Flight, a local businessman.

CHAMBERLAIN, Robert, painter for Dr. Wall; left to start his own factory at Diglis in Worcester in about 1786 or 87. His descendants ran the factory with the assistance of some other partners, through the period of amalgamation with Flight Barr and Barr in 1840 and on until the close of the Chamberlain and Co. period and the start of Kerr and Binns in 1852.

CHAMBERLAIN, Walter, partner in Chamberlains' business, involved in the merger with Flight.

CLEMENTS, Worcester artist, exhibited at Royal Academy between 1818 and 1831, specialised in portraits.

COLE, Solomon, a pupil of Thomas Baxter, and left a great deal of information in the form of reminiscences published in early editions of Chaffers' *Marks and Monograms* which either come from talks with Cole and Chaffers or from R.W. Binns. He succeeded Baxter as the main figure painter with Thomas Lowe in 1821 and continued until 1840 and exhibited 16 portraits at the Royal Academy. A Solomon Cole, probably his son, was admitted a Freeman as the apprentice of Joseph Flight, Martin Barr and George Barr, China Manufacturers on 7th March 1831.

COTTRILL, Joseph, admitted Freeman on 1st October 1804, he is said by Solomon Cole to have done the fine hand writing by pen of factory marks and names of scenes, quotations from plays and poems and other details that appear under the bases of the rich services and vases. He may also have done some painting, especially purple and gilded sprigs.

CROTHER, G.C., mentioned by Chaffers in a list of decorators at Worcester in 1819 and continuing until break up of the factory.

CROWTHER, Thomas, admitted Freeman on 27th October 1806, a painter of flowers, especially cowslips and worked until 1840.

DACK, Peter (possibly Dark), admitted a Freeman, 8th June 1835, described as a china painter.

DAVIS, George, said to have worked at Flights until 1816 and later at Chamberlains, specialising in "fabulous" or "fancy" birds in the old Worcester style. He was known by his workmates as "Doctor" Davis, possibly a mark of respect.

DAVIS, John, admitted Freeman, 26th January 1819, as an apprenticed painter on porcelain.

DAY, C., Worcester artist specialising in architecture, exhibited at Royal Academy between 1835-8.

DOBBS, Thomas, admitted Freeman, 26th February 1819, as a painter on porcelain, continuing until 1840.

DOE, E(noch), listed as living in Worcester, exhibited flower studies at Royal Academy and Suffolk Street between 1823 and 1848.

DOE, William, admitted Freeman, 15th May 1815, a painter of natural birds' feathers, insects and also painted figures and landscapes. A very talented all round artist, pupil of Thomas Baxter, exhibited landscapes at Worcester Society of Arts exhibition in 1818, later did a lot of free-lance china painting, especially of tea-sets, in partnership with Rogers of Chamberlain's factory in a business called "Doe and Rogers".

DOUGHTY, Joseph, admitted Freeman, 1st October 1804, as apprentice to Martin Barr.

DOVEY, Jos., is noted in Chaffers in a list of general decorators in 1819 who continued until the end of their establishment. Three Doveys — Howard, Thomas and William worked at Graingers.

DOVEY, Richard, admitted Freeman, 7th January 1818, as an apprentice of Flight Barr and Barr.

DITTON (DUTTON?), Thomas, noted in Chaffers as a general decorator in 1819 who continued until 1840.

DITTON (DUTTON?), Thomas junior, noted in Chaffers as a general decorator in 1819 continuing until 1840.

DYER, Richard, possibly at Worcester in the 1780s.

FERN, Andrew, admitted Freeman, 23rd December 1811, as apprentice of Martin Barr.

FLIGHT, John (c.1766-1791), son of Thomas Flight and partner in the factory, see Chapter 1 for further details, admitted Freeman, 15th December 1789.

FLIGHT, Joseph (d.1838) son of Thomas Flight and partner in the factory, admitted Freeman, 27th December 1784, subscribed to Valentine Green's *History and Antiquities,* 1796, exhibited 8 miniatures at the Royal Academy 1801-06, address given in Bloomsbury, subjects Mr. C. Townley, Mr. Evans, Mrs. Simmons, Mr. Claremont, Mr. Palmer of Drury Lane Theatre, Portrait of a Gent. and Portrait of an antiquary. An engraved portrait of Alexander Bengo, published in 1814, is after J. Flight. Also painted on porcelain.

FLIGHT, Thomas, London agent of the original factory, bought factory in 1783 for his two sons for £3,000, subscriber to Green's *History and Antiquities*, 1796.

FOSS, Richard, admitted Freeman, 1835, in the 1840 Directory was living at Tallow Hill, described as a potter, in the 1851 census is described as a china presser.

GREEN, Valentine, Flight Worcester engraver and pupil of Robert Hancock, wrote several important books in the eighteenth century. It is likely that he started working for the Company in the Dr. Wall's period.

HAINES, Henry, admitted Freeman, 1st October 1804, to Martin Barr.

HAMPTON, Mrs., is noted in John Flight's diary in June 1789, "I at last agreed with Mrs Hampton to come down and teach us the gilding". On June 21st 1789 he notes, "What we could have done had we not met with Mrs Hampton I cannot tell. I see no possible way in which we could have carried on".

HAYTON, C, probably merely an outside decorator, painting signed floral studies, but mentioned by Chaffers as working for Flight.

HIGGS, Samuel, admitted Freeman, 1835, as a china painter but not noted as being apprenticed to a particular factory. In the local register of births 1832-39 he is described as a "painter" and a "china manufacturer".

HOLLOWAY, Thomas, referred to in Chaffers in the list of general decorators in 1819 who continued until 1840, admitted Freeman, 27th January 1822, apprenticed to Martin Barr.

HOLLOWAY, William, referred to in Chaffers in the list of general decorators in 1819 until 1840, apprenticed 1818, ended apprenticeship 1826, admitted Freeman, 13th March 1826.

HUGHES, William (b.1768), son of James Hughes, Lowestoft modeller, worked as a Lowestoft modeller and moved to Worcester c.1799, possibly to Flight and Barr.

HUNT, Mrs., mentioned by Chaffers as presiding over the burnishers, who also "papered up" the finished pieces ready for the packers.

HYDE, John Brooke, involved in the merger with Flight and Chamberlain.

JONES, John, appears in list of decorators in 1819 who continued until the breaking up of their establishment (a John Jones was apprenticed to Champion at Bristol on

September 19th 1776); in a Board of Health list for Worcester a John Jones of Park Place 1825-28 described as "China Printer".

JONES, Joseph, mentioned in list of general decorators in Chaffers; a Joseph Binns Jones was living in Park Place 1825-28 described as a painter.

JONES, Thomas, admitted Freeman, 15th June 1835, described as a china painter, but where employed is not known.

JOHNSON, John, admitted Freeman, 16th March 1807, to Martin Barr, was living in Copenhagen Street near Flight's factory in 1817 when a daughter, Emma, was born to him.

KITCHEN, Edward, of great assistance to John Flight in the running of the factory.

KNIGHT, Jonathon, admitted Freeman, 1st October 1804, to Martin Barr.

LEAD, John, appears in Chaffers' list of decorators in 1819.

LILLY, John, partner in Chamberlain's factory, involved in the merger with Flight Barr and Barr.

LLOYD, Thomas, admitted Freeman, 27th June 1790, as an apprentice of William Davis, China Manufacturer.

LOWE, James, appears in Chaffers' list of decorators, in the 1851 census he is noted as living in Palace Row, next to Flight's factory, aged 76, from Burslem, Staffordshire, retired burnisher.

LOWE, Mrs., mentioned by Chaffers as having her own room to print the trade mark on the back of pieces and also to print shells in a grey tint or warm self colour.

LOWE, Thomas, mentioned in Chaffers as a pupil of Thomas Baxter and succeeded the latter as the figure painter of the factory, with Cole, going on to "higher branches of their art afterwards"; in a sale at Sotheby's on 10th October 1971, lot 131, was sold "a fine portrait plaque of upright rectangular shape, painted by T. Lowe, signed, with a three-quarter length portrait of a young woman", and dated 1834; admitted Freeman, 14th June 1826; in 1845 exhibited a portrait at Royal Academy, his address given as 40, Ely Place, London.

MANASON, Henry, appears in Chaffers' list of decorators at factory in 1819.

MANASON, Henry, may be son of the above, admitted Freeman, 8th June 1835, as apprentice of Joseph Flight.

MANASON, William, appears in Chaffers' list of decorators at factory in 1819; in the St. Paul's birth records a William Mannison, described as a china painter, was living in Park Place.

MASON, Chaffers refers to an account by a "Mr. Mason who worked at the Chelsea manufactory and whose son (also a china painter) worked many years at the Worcester manufactory, when conducted by Flight Barr and Barr".

MEADOWES, James, admitted Freeman, 10th October 1812, as apprentice of Joseph Flight.

NIBLETT, Jos., appears in Chaffers' list as a decorator in 1819.

PAGE (?), mentioned by Downman and Gunn as possibly a Flight painter.

PAINE, Thomas, admitted Freeman, 16th March 1807, to Martin Barr.

PARKER, John, a retired bankrupt, involved in the merger between Flight and Chamberlain.

PEAT, Charles, admitted Freeman, 27th October, 1806, to Martin Barr; a child, Solomon, was born in 1813 to a Charles Peat, described as a "Chinaman-china slip", probably indicating he prepared the clay.

PENNINGS, Nicolas, appears in Chaffers' list as a decorator in 1819.

PENNINGTON, James, born 1760 in Liverpool, son of John and Jane Pennington and cousin to the next 3 Penningtons, was living in Worcester 1803-11 and probably later but it is not known if he worked at Flight's factory.

PENNINGTON, James, probably came to Flight's factory from Liverpool, lived in China Slip and was described as a Chinaman; lived in Warmstry Slip 1805-16, had 4 sons and a daughter, one son (Thomas) became a potter at Grainger's factory.

PENNINGTON, John (c.1765-1842), brother of above, one of the finest painters for Flight, specialising in monochrome painting of figure subjects, but also produced superb figure subjects in colours. Came to Flight 1789, probably from Liverpool originally and painted the figure subject of Hope on the service for the Duke of Clarence (a John Pennington was admitted Freeman on 12th December 1808, but this may not be the painter of the Duke of Clarence service); Chaffers describes him as painting "Rustic Figures"; probably born in Liverpool, worked in Wedgwood's London decorating shop in 1784 with his brother Robert, is probably the painter mentioned in John Flight's diary 12th July 1789, and likely to have been the son of James Pennington of Liverpool.

PENNINGTON, Robert, brother to John and James, probably born Liverpool 1763, was living in Worcester 1794, may have been a painter.

PEUGH, Thomas, appears in a list of general decorators in 1819, may be the same as a Thomas Pugh who painted landscapes at Coalport from about 1830s.

PIERCY, George, admitted Freeman, 2nd September 1811, but not known to whose factory, described as a "Chinaman" — probably a potter.

PITMAN, C., Worcester artist, exhibited at Suffolk Street in 1828 a painting of horses.

PITMAN, John, one of Baxter's pupils at his School of Art; in the 1841 Directory is described as an animal painter living in the Tything and exhibited paintings of animals at the Worcestershire Society of Arts Exhibition in 1818 and paintings of game at Royal Academy, Suffolk Street and British Institution between 1820 and 1827.

RICHARDS, Charles, appears in Chaffers' list of general decorators in 1819, in the 1840 Directory he was living in Spring Place and described as a painter, in the 1851 census was living in Tallow Hill and described as a painter.

RICHARDS, Thomas, appears in Chaffers' list as a flower painter in 1819, continuing until 1840, had a number of children, including a Thomas, born in July 19th 1822, living at Spring Place.

RICHARDS, Thomas, admitted Freeman, 9th June 1835, described as a china painter, probably son of above.

RICHARDS, William, appears in Chaffers' list of decorators in 1819 who continued until 1840, and is described as doing blue paintings.

ROGERS, Darby, appears in Chaffers' list of decorators in 1819 who continued until 1840.

ROGERS, Thomas, admitted Freeman, 2nd October 1797, as apprentice of Joseph and John Flight; appears in Chaffers' list of decorators in 1819 and is described as a landscape painter.

ROSS, James, Worcester engraver.

SHAW (d.1791), the manufactory clerk, or foreman, during the 1780s.

SHERWIN, Ishmael, mentioned by Chaffers as a painter at factory in 1819 who was engaged in designing patterns and decorating rich pieces with gems etc. and embossed gold, also a fine ornamental gilder. Probably did all the jewelling at the factory, such as on the service for William IV. In Pigot's Directory of 1841 he appears under glass, china and earthenware dealers in Worcester.

SILK, is mentioned by R.W. Binns as a painter of landscapes at Flight's factory.

SMITH, John, mentioned in Chaffers as a landscape painter at factory in 1819, continuing until 1840; in Pigot's Directory of 1841 he appears under "artists", exhibited paintings at the Society of Artists Exhibition in 1818, including a landscape.

SMITH, Samuel, a fine fruit painter, mentioned in Chaffers' list of decorators at factory in 1819 who continued until 1840, admitted Freeman, 16th March 1807.

SMITH, Thomas, admitted Freeman, 30th September 1811, as apprentice of Martin Barr.

SPARE, William, a father and son of same name, the son admitted Freeman, 24th February 1800, as "first born son of William Spare, China Manufacturer".

STINTON, Charles, painter of fancy birds and flowers, noted in Chaffers as a painter at factory in 1819 who continued until the breaking up of their establishment, one of the great Stinton family who continued painting for Worcester until the 1960s.

STINTON, Henry, painter of flower groups on vases, noted in Chaffers as being at the factory in 1819 and continuing until the end of the establishment, admitted Freeman, 13th March 1826, exhibited at Royal Academy, 1830-31, three paintings of flowers, listed as living in London.

ST. JOHN, Fleming, partner in the Chamberlain factory and involved in the merger with Flight and Barr.

TAYLOR, Jos., appears in Chaffers' list of general decorators at factory in 1819 continuing until the end of the establishment.

TAYLOR, William, appears in Chaffers' list of painters in 1819 who continued until the end of the establishment, as doing blue paintings (a William Taylor was a Chelsea/Derby blue painter and oriental subjects and patterns); in a Board of Health list for Worcester a William Taylor of London Road is noted as a China Painter.

Continued as a Kerr and Binns artist, painting flowers.

TOMKINS, John, appears in Chaffers' list of decorators at factory in 1819 who continued until the breaking up of the establishment.

TOMLINS, mentioned by Chaffers as excelling in ground laying at Flights, using a large flat brush.

TOULOUSE, John, senior (d.1809), may have been modeller at Flight's factory; the Toulouse family produced modellers for Chamberlain as well and the mark "IT" or "To" found on some late Dr. Wall/early Flight elaborate pieces may be the repairer's mark of Toulouse and not that of Tebo as was thought.

TURNER, Francis, admitted Freeman, 2nd September 1811, noted as "first born son of Francis Turner, China Potter". R.W. Binns refers to the indentures of Francis Turner, potter, son of John Turner potter, 1st May 1772.

TURNER, George, eldest son of Francis Turner, admitted Freeman, 2nd September 1811, "George Turner as first born son of Francis Turner China Potter".

TURNER, James, admitted Freeman, 17th December 1792, as the "apprentice of Joseph Flight China Manufacturer"; Hurlbutt (*Derby Porcelain, its workmen etc.,* 1925) on page 81 mentions a James Turner as a Derby painter and he may have moved to Worcester from Derby; a James Turner was at Grainger's in 1847.

TURNER, John, father of Thomas Turner who was admitted Freeman, 31st October 1806, as "first born son of John Turner China Manufacturer", and he was probably a potter.

TURNER, Moses, admitted Freeman, 27th October 1806, to Joseph Flight.

TURNER, Thomas, admitted Freeman, 31st October 1806, as first born son of John Turner China Manufacturer.

VARDEN, R., Worcester artist, exhibited a landscape at the Royal Academy in 1843.

WALKER, Samuel, at Worcester 1808-13, came with William Billingsley, entered into agreement with Martin Barr November 1809, married Sarah Billingsley at Claines Church, Worcester, 12th September 1812, went to Swansea, later went to America. Also see Chapter 3.

WALL, John, M.D., born 1708, founded the Worcester Porcelain Company in 1751, left Worcester for Bath in 1774, died in Bath in 1776. The period of production at Worcester from 1751 to 1776 is called "the Dr. Wall period".

WEBSTER, Moses (1792-1870), apprenticed at Derby then joined London decorating house of Robins and Randall in about 1817, moved to Worcester in 1821 where he is said to have received instruction from Thomas Baxter at his School of Art, returned to Derby in 1825 for a short while and left the factory to become a drawing master in Derby town. A very fine flower painter and is also mentioned by R.W. Binns as doing landscapes. Haslem of Derby said of him that while at Worcester the following impromptu verses were made by one of the painters on hearing another observe that Moses Webster was fond of introducing roses into his flower groups:—

"If Moses composes
His posies of roses
Of sweeter he can't them compose;
No flower else that grows
Can compare with the rose,
If you doubt it consult your own nose."

WOODS, William, a figure painter, mentioned in Chaffers' list of painters in 1819 who continued until the breaking up of the factory; three sons are noted as having been born to him — William Henry, George and Frederick.

YATES, James, London sales manager of Chamberlain, more strictly an independent trader, since he had purchased the lease of 155, New Bond Street, together with all the stock.

Appendix II

Armorial and Crested Services

The making of services with full armorials or crests was one of the staple productions of Flight and Barr during the years from 1800 to 1840. Such services could range from a simple badge or crest and motto, put in the centre of an existing standard border pattern, right up to a full armorial centre with possibly a special border designed for it.

Flight and Barr and Chamberlain probably produced the greater proportion of the armorial services made in England. Most of the Chamberlain order books survive and they show a bewildering number of armorial orders, sometimes over a hundred services in a year. Unfortunately none of the Flight and Barr order books are in existence, although if they were they would undoubtedly show that Flights were producing an equal or greater quantity, as the Royal Factory had its foot very firmly in the door of the rich noble families. In fact they proudly claimed that they never had to advertise and the name of the firm written or printed under the base of the plates and dishes for all the guests to see as they admired their host's sumptuous new Worcester service was advertisement enough.

Our knowledge about this side of Flight and Barr's production has had to be built up from a number of sources, for example, from the services that survive virtually complete, from the receipted accounts that remain with the families and from the identification of the names of the original family from the armorial on a piece. Identifying a family, and especially being certain of the actual person for whom it was made, is fraught with many problems. So many people have used similar mottoes and crests, some nouveau riche, without a grant of arms but keen to put on a good show, would not be above having any crest or motto put on a service. Identification of such pieces is not an easy task even for the specialist but I have been fortunate in having the assistance of Bill Price, one of the world's leading experts in this field, who has pinned down a large number of armorials to the actual family, and his work, and that of his mother, is the basis of this Appendix.

It is hoped that Bill Price will produce a specialist book dealing with the armorial services made by the three Worcester factories — Flight, Chamberlain and Grainger.

The following list of Flight and Barr, Barr Flight and Barr, and Flight Barr and

Barr armorials may help the growing number of collectors of such items to identify them. I do not claim it is anywhere near being a complete list of the armorials produced, in fact it may only contain something like ten or twenty per cent of them, and it would be most helpful to hear from collectors or families with positively proved armorials that do not appear in the list. Nor is it certain that the actual family or person has been correctly identified in all cases, owing to the enormous difficulties involved. In fact the following list is meant to be a first ice-breaker into this fascinating side of ceramics.

The list does not include the major English Royal services, which are all illustrated in this book. The family and the original owner is given first, if known, next the details of crest or armorial (often in a very abbreviated form in the case of the tremendously complicated ones), and then the motto, if there is one. An index at the end refers to the number in the list and gives lists of families, mottoes and a main distinguishing object in the crest or arms to help in the identification. The dates given are often approximations but from them you will be able to ascertain the period — whether Flight and Barr, Barr Flight and Barr or Flight Barr and Barr.

	Family	Crest of Arms	Motto
1.	William Frederick, 2nd Duke of Gloucester and Edinburgh	Royal ducal crown; lion passant, guardant, ducally crowned (1808-09).	
2.	Sir Robert Peel impaling Yates	Baronet's helmet; 3 sheaves of arrows, a bee volant, red hand of Ulster (1813-15).	Industria
3.	Shuttleworth (prob. Robert of Gawthorp, Lancs.), m Janet Marjoriebanks	An arm in armour grasping a shuttle; 3 weavers' shuttles and a crescent.	Aequanimiter
4.	George, 1st Earl of Onslow	Eagle, sable preying on a partridge; supporters 2 falcons; 6 Cornish choughs.	Festina Lente
5.	Sir Cecil Bishopp, 12th Lord Zouche, m dau of 2nd Marquess Townshend	(6 quarters) 3 swans' heads, 3 leopards' heads, a label of 3 points (1810).	Pro Deo et Ecclesia
6.	(Probably) Henry Walker	A mound, a wreathed serpent, a dove passant (1808).	
7.	Worcester College Oxford	An armed arm holding a sword out of a mural crown (1807-13).	Deo Regi Vicine
8.	New East India Company	Arms of France and England, the shield ornamented and regally crowned (1820).	
9.	Marjoriebanks of Lees, Co. Berwick	A lion's gamb holding a tilting spear (1810-15).	
10.	Sir Roger Gresley, 8th Baronet, m Sophia dau of 7th Earl of Coventry	(12 quarters) a lion rampant, 3 spades, a fireball, 4 leopards' faces (1825-30).	Meliore fide quam fortuna

Family	Crest of Arms	Motto
11. Duke of Clarence	(4 quarters) arms of England, France, Ireland, Brunswick, Luneburg and Saxony (1789).	
12. Sir John Jervis White-Jervis	Crest a martlet (4 quarters), 3 lions rampant, 3 martlets, red hand of Ulster (1800).	Venale nec auro
13. William Archer and Joseph Archer of Longford, Tasmania	Crest a bear's gamb holding an arrow (1813-40), not granted by College of Arms.	Le Fin couronne l'oeuvre
14. Dixon of Raneshaw, Co. Durham	Crest a cubit arm vested erminois, holding a roundel (1825-30).	
15. Richard, 1st Duke of Buckingham	Crest Marquess coronet, bust of old man in profile (1808-13).	Templa quam delicta
16. Richard, 1st Duke of Buckingham	Crest Marquess coronet, 7 quarters, 2 in pretence and 8 grand quarters, supporters of lion and horse (c.1810).	Templa quam delicta
17. Wykeham of Swalcliffe and Baroness Wenman	(15 quarters) including 3 archers and 3 lions' heads.	
18. William Pitt, Viscount Holmesdale and Earl Amhurst	Baron's coronet (4 quarters), 3 tilting spears, supporters 2 Canadian war Indians (1823-25).	Constantia et virtute
19. Sir Thomas Walmesley	(4 quarters) a gryphon, impaling 3 leopards' faces (c.1830).	Semper fidelis
20. Sir Henry Bold de Houghton	Crest a bull and red hand of Ulster (1810).	
21. Wyndham	Crest a goat's head out of a ducal coronet and a lion's head out of a mural coronet, arms 3 field gates, 3 goats' heads (1808-10).	Legale judicium parium
22. Baretti of India impaling Potts	Crest a demi Bengal tiger, arms a maiden's head, supporters pelicans in their piety (1813-40).	Non sine Deo
23. Taylour	Crest a talbot's head erased grey (1825).	Semper fidelis
24. Ferrier of Hemsby	Crest a horse's head erased proper (1810).	
25.	Crest out of a ducal coronet a hind's head collared (1801-10).	
26. Patrick Barclay Maitland	Crest a lion sejant, arms a lion rampant (c.1810).	Consilio et animis
27.	Crest a Saracen's head in profile wreathed at the temple.	

Family	Crest of Arms	Motto
28. Rundall or Rundle	Crest a squirrel chained, holding a sprig (c.1805).	Unita fortior
29.	Crest, on a wreath, a spur erect between sprays of leaves and acorns (c.1810).	
30. Nabob (Nawab) of Oude	Crest a steeple, arms the letters NGH between 2 fishes supported by 2 tigers rampant holding pennants (c.1815).	
31. Alexander II of Russia	Arms of Imperial Russia, an eagle displayed, double headed, supported by crown of Russia (1814).	
32. George Annesley, 2nd Earl of Mountmorris	Crest Earl's coronet, in profile a Moor's head couped (c.1825).	Virtutis amore
33. James, 8th Earl of Lauderdale	Crest out of ducal coronet a lion sejant, ducally crowned, holding a sword and fleur-de-lis (c.1830).	Consilio et animis
34.	Crest, buca trippant acorn in mouth.	
35.	Out of a ducal coronet a lion sejant in sepia.	
36. Ogle of Ogle Castle Northumberland	Crest an antelope's head, arms 3 crescents (1813-1840).	A Deo Lumen
37. Burgh (Baron Downes)	Crest a cat-a-mountain with collar and chain (1813-1840).	A cruce salus
38.	Crest a lion (1813-40).	Dum spiro spero
39. Warren impaling Mangles	Crest a Wyvern, wings expanded chequy or and azure on a chapeau gules turned up ermine.	
40. Hughes Minet	1804-13.	Quantum est in rebus inane
41.	Crests a stag trippant and a demi eagle (1803-13).	Spes nostra Deus
42.	Crest a crown above double monogram DE and badge of the Baronets of Nova Scotia (1793-1803).	
43.	1807-1840.	Esse quam videri
44. Thomas Everett of Ludgershall	Arms of Everett impaling Ellis (1807-1840).	
45.	1804-13.	Deum cole regem serva

Family	Crest of Arms	Motto
46. Davidson	1813-40.	
47.	Knight on horseback (1813-40).	Deo Juvante
48.	Demi fish (1813-40).	In cruce salus
49.	Hand holding dagger (1813-40).	Vigeur de dessus
50. ? Sitwell	Crest a demi lion rampant holding escutcheon (1813-40).	
51. Futte Ali Shah and Abbas Mirza		
52. ? Richard Suinthill Jay of Cork	Crest, crown and Tudor rose, ship in sail between 2 light-houses (1813-40).	Statio bene fidat carinis
53. Wilkinson	Crest, on a mound, a talbot sejant amid rushes (1813-40).	
54. Amphlett	Crest a dromedary proper (1813-40).	
55. Holgate of Walden	Crest, out of a mural coronet argent, a bull's head sable (1813-40).	Flecti non frangi
56. Brackenbury of Skendleby	Crest, a lion couchant guardant sable, at foot of oak tree proper.	Sans reculer Jamais
57. Coney	Crest, rabbit holding a pansy.	
58.	Out of ducal coronet a unicorn's head argent.	
59.	Crest helmeted head under a thistle (1813-40).	Pro rege et lege
60.	1804-13.	Perfeci perseverantia
61. Blomberg	Crest, out of a crown a lion with 2 tails (1804-13).	
62. Paul of Rodburgh	Crest, a leopard (ounce's) head	
63. Elton of London and Reading	Crest of an arm holding a mullet, out of a mural coronet.	
64. ? Whitgrave	Crest of demi antelope, shield with 4 chevrons.	
65. Prendergast (1st Viscount Gort, 1816)	Crest of antelope's head (1804-1813).	Vincit Veritas
66. Warren-Poynton	Crest, a forked-tongued dragon, displayed, arms a checker board.	
67. Gordon-	Scottish deerhound.	God with us

INDEX OF NAMES
(numbered as above)

Amhurst	18	Lauderdale, Earl of	33
Amphlett	54	Maitland	26
Annesley	32	Marjoriebanks	9
Archer	13	Minet	40
Baretti	22	Ogle	36
Bishopp	5	Onslow, Earl of	4
Blomberg	61	Oude, Nabob of	30
Brackenbury	56	Paul	62
Buckingham, Duke of	15, 16	Peel	2
Burgh	37	Persia, Shah of	51
Clarence, Duke of	11	Pitt	18
Coney	57	Prendergast	65
Davidson	46	Rundall or Rundle	28
Dixon	14	Russia, Emperor of	31
Downes, Baron	37	Shuttleworth	3
East India Company	8	Sitwell	50
Elton	63	Taylour	23
Everett	44	Walker	6
Ferrier	24	Walmesley	19
Gloucester, Duke of	1	Warren	39
Gordon	67	Warren-Poynton	66
Gort, Viscount	65	White-Jervis	12
Gresley	10	Whitgrave	64
Holgate	55	Wilkinson	53
Holmesdale, Viscount	18	Worcester College Oxford	7
Houghton de	20	Wykeham	17
Jay	52	Wyndham	21
		Zouche, Lord	5

MOTTOES

A cruce salus	37	In cruce salus	48
A Deo lumen	36	Industria	2
Aequanimiter	3	Le fin couronne l'oeuvre	13
Consilio et animis	26, 33	Legale judicium parium	21
Constantia et virtute	18	Meliore fide quam fortuna	10
Deo juvante	47	Non sine Deo	22
Deo regi vicine	7	Perfeci perseverantia	60
Deum cole regem serva	45	Pro Deo et ecclesia	5
Dum spiro spero	38	Pro rege et lege	59
Esse quam videri	43	Quantum est in rebus inane	40
Festina lente	4	Sans reculer jamais	56
Flecti non frangi	55	Semper fidelis	19, 23
God with us	67	Spes nostra Deus	41

MOTTOES

Statio bene fidet carinis	52	Vigeur de dessus	49
Templa quam delicta	15, 16	Vincit Veritas	65
Unita fortior	28	Virtutis amore	32
Venale nec auro	12		

MAIN DISTINGUISHING FEATURE OF THE CREST OR ARMS

ANIMALS

Antelope's head	36, 64	Eagle and Partridge	4
Bear's gamb and arrow	13	Falcon	4
Buca	34	Gryphon	19
Bull	20	Martlet	12
Bull's head	55	Swans' heads	5
Cat-a-mountain	37	Wyvern	39
Deerhound	67		
Dragon with forked tongue	66	**HUMAN FIGURES OR PARTS**	
Dromedary	54	Arm, armoured	3, 7
Goat's head	21	Arm, cubit	14
Hind's head	25	Arm, holding a mullet	63
Leopards' heads	5, 62	Helmeted head and thistle	59
Leopards' faces	10, 19	Knight on horseback	47
Lion	38	Moor's head	32
Lion crowned	1	Old man in profile	15
Lion, demi	50	Red hand of Ulster	2, 12, 20
Lion's gamb and spear	9	Saracen's head	27
Lion's Head	21		
Lion and horse supporters	16	**OTHERS**	
Lion and oak tree	56	Arrows	2
Lion rampant	10, 12, 26, 50	Bee	2
Lion sejant	26, 33	Checker board	66
Lion with two tails	61	Chevrons	64
Rabbit and pansy	57	D E (letters)	42
Squirrel	28	Fireball	10
Stag trippant	41	Fish, demi	48
Tigers rampant	30	Gates	21
Unicorn's head	58	Mound	6
		NGH (letters)	30
BIRDS		Serpent	6
Choughs	4	Ship and lighthouses	52
Dove	6	Shuttle	3
Eagle, demi	41	Spades	10
Eagle displayed, double headed	31	Spur	29
		Tudor rose	52

Appendix III

Extracts from the Diary of John Flight
(1785-1791)

A considerable amount of punctuation has been done editorially, as John Flight only infrequently uses punctuation marks; the original spelling has been left unaltered. A number of badly written passages have proved difficult to interpret and I have done my best to get these correct, with the assistance of Miss M. Henderson, a Worcester archivist and Mr. Peter Ewance, chief designer of The Worcester Royal Porcelain Company Limited. The passages in the diary written in French are given as they appear and below each is an English translation by Barry Still.

Saturday 3rd December 1785

Having had that almost inestimable privilidge of being brought up by Religious Parents and Friends I have from the first dawning of Reason been subject to serious impressions which in one way or other I have had continually. Sometimes they have lasted longer and some shorter yet the Lord has been rather remarkably gracious to me in that I have been kept from any allowed outward sins of any kind. Some sins to which I have been particularly prone and which but for a superior power exerted in my behalf I must have gone into these in a very wonderful manner I have been kept from as much as 4 or 5 years ago . . .

18th March, 1786

On Thursday I returned from a journey to Worcester where I have been to assist my Brother in taking Stock and staid there about a month, and I truly find it heavy work to come to self examination. My carelessness has been so very great that I have every reason to fear the Concerns of My Soul are much worse that they were —

Saturday, August the 25th, 1787 8 p.m.

. . . I have been a very long journey and from every danger I am preserved and returned in very comfortable circumstances. Left London Friday the 6th July and went in the coach to Bristol from whence I proceeded on horseback all thro' Cornwall and returned by Worcester and Kimbolton in all upwards of a Thousand Miles; was thrown from my Horse four times without sustaining the least injury and preserved thro' many visible dangers — but alas I have experienced the common effect of travelling instead of having my soul drawn out after God my mind was continually dissatisfied . . .

12th April 1788

I have thought and spoke to my Father about removing our manufactory somewhere into Wales where Coals are cheap, but the practicability of this seems uncertain and the success of it still more so.

Saturday the 10th May 1788, 8 p.m.

... My father etc. went to Worcester yesterday. He is gone with a determination to consult Shaw upon the scheme of building a China Factory somewhere in Wales. I cannot but think such a thing might answer if it could be executed upon a good plan so that in every concern, but especially these great ones, I cou'd beseach the Lord and leave the event with him, when the uncertainty of everything here is a little reflighted upon how very important does this life seem except as a state of preparation, and then it is indeed important ...

Saturday, 28th June 1788, 10 p.m.

... As to my Situation in life I seem extremely unsettled what to wish for. Sometimes I think the best way is to wait some months and improve myself in French etc. as much as I can and see what may turn up. As other times I long to try the scheme of a China Factory about Swansea, which as often I think would not answer. Again I determine to ask Mr. Neal wether he has any inclination to take a partner instead of Mr. Maidment from whom he has separated (what a mercy in all our concerns to be guided by infinite wisdom preserved from vanity and prepared for the heavenly inheritance). May this be my care.

[Folios 226-229 are torn out]

Lords Day the 14 September 1788, 9 p.m.

A variety of interesting occurances have happened since I last thus employed myself. Wednesday July the 31st I sett off for Worcester with the design to assist my Bro[t]. in mooving,[1] make some little stay at Worcr. and then go to Swansea to make enquiry wether there was any probability it would answer to remove our Manufactory there. I had a pleasant journey and found my friends safe and well. The Saturday after, the King, Queen, Duke of York, 3 Princesses and attendants came thro' in their way to Hartlebury on a visit to the Bishop. I just got a glance of them as they passed but little thought of the distinguish'd honor that awaited me. The Royal Family had been a little while at Cheltenham where the King went for the benefit of the waters and as the musick meeting was at Worcester, the time of it was so fix'd that they might be there. The King being of a Curious Mechanical Turn and fond of seeing manufactories of all sorts we hoped he might visit Ours but it was a matter of so much uncertainty that I did not like to mention my hopes for fear of a disappointment. The musick meetg. was the 6 7 8' of Aug. The 5th, the Royal Family (The King, Queen and three Princesses) arrived at Worcester and took up their residence at the Bishops. Palace the same day my Bro[t]. had moved and opened his new shop. The next, in the affn. the Sovereign and his family honou'd us with a visit, totally unexpectedly and came in without any form as a common person wou'd attended by Ladies Harcourt, Pembroke and Courtown, Lords Harcourt and

---

1.   *Probably from 33 to 45 High Street, Worcester.*

Courtown and Oxford, Cols. Goldworthy and Gwynn. They behaved exceedingly familiar and affable, ordered a good deal of china. I took the liberty to ask the Queen to honor us with a visit at the Manufactory, which she condescended after mentioning it to the King to accept and fixed Saturday morning. After staying an hour they left us, well satisfied. On Friday I went to the Palace with some patterns for the Queen and Princess Royal and had the honor of taking further orders from each and the King told me to bring the Bill which he would pay as I did not know how much of him before he left Worcester. On Saturday morng. they visited the manufactory according to appointment and expressed great satisfaction. I had requested the Earl of Oxford to ask permission for us to style ourselves Manufacturers to their Majesty's which was graciously granted. This visit we expect as does everybody else will be of great advantage to our Manufactory and my brother and self began to think of improving the opportunity. The best way appeared to be attending to advice the King had honored us with, that is to have a Retail Shop in London, and after Seriously talking it over we determined with our Fathers approbation to drop the Swansea Scheme and as soon as we cou'd meet with a house, open a Retail Warehouse in Westminster. This renders it necessary to endeavour the improvement of the Manufactory and with Fathers consent went to Newcastle to seek after a modeller. I found one whom we have since agreed to take at Michaes. for 3 years. I now returned to Town and arrived here Friday the 5th of September and immy [immediately] consulted Father upon our Scheems which he seems to approve. I have been looking out for a House and found one, the Rent of which is the only objection. I have wrote particulars to my Father and Bro^t. and expect their determination tomorrow. This, if it takes effect, will make great alteration with me. We talk of entering into partnership and I living at Worcester for the sake of learning the Manufactory, which is of great consequence. One thing preparitory for me we talk of a journey to France. Lord Harcourt promised me a letter to the Duke of Dorset to protect me in visiting the China Manufactories. We think this may be of advantage. He particularly recommended it to improve our Shapes and after we are settled I shall have no more opportunity. Father thinks of my going direct to Paris and then round by Holland home. Add to all this I have changed the place of my abode; have left Mr. Heath and got a room in Mrs. Jeffs house over our Warehouse. Except when I go out I breakfast tea and sleep myself, and dine at a Chop house, its more convenient for me not being confined to time but from what I know of it even yet shoud soon be tired of such a life especially now, my Parents being at Lewes where they went Thursday and purpose staying about a fortnight. All these changes may rationally be supposed to have affected the concerns of my soul but I dont find much difference and yet my expectations do seem more raised with regard to the world. Yet in a serious moment a little thought upon the variety of these concerns brings them for the time to their level. In some sweet moments I can rejoice in the prospect of eternity but alas a very superficial view of myself leaves room to say, God be merciful to me a Sinner. This is all my cry —

Tuesday the 23rd September 1788, 10 p.m.
This day I may properly be said to have begun life, I mean so far as the world is considered. With my Fathers consent, or rather under his directions, I have this day agreed for the 2 houses in Coventry Street and paid the premium in B.$^{ros's}$ name

and my own. This is a great concern in itself and is particularly so to me as being my setting off. I desire now solemnly to commit myself to the Lord and whilst I would resolve in the divine strength to do my best to act soberly, honestly and uprightly I would pray not to fix my affections too strongly on this world but be prepared for those disappointments I shall most certainly meet with. I received on Friday a letter from Lord Harcourt w^h one enclosed for the Duke of Dorsett in which Lord H. says he has strongly recommended me to his Graces protection. I therefore expect soon after my Fathers return from Lewes which will be this week to sett off for Paris and Holland. I can hardly think of going so far in a Foreign country by myself without being very low but I hope it will be of service to us. Lord H. in his letter says there are a great many French shapes in China[1] that would take well here. I have been a little poorly for some days past but thro' mercy begin to get better, or rather am recovered.

Lords Day June 1st 1789, evening

Great indeed have been the changes I have experienced since I last thus employed myself. — I hope that at last am settled, at least in a degree. On Sat^y Oct 4 I left London for Lewes on my way to France, I spent till Tuesday with my B^r and that Ev. embarked for Dieppe where I arrived the next afternoon and reached Paris the Satur.^{y} after. While at Paris I employed myself in look^g about me and over all the French Manuf^{ys} and purchased ab^t 300£ of China. After stay^g there rather more than a fortnight i ret'd to London by way of Boulogn and Dover in Novr. I went to Worcester and took Stock with my Bro^r and finally settled our articles of partnership, after which I returned to London. I now left Mrs. Jeffs, whose house began to be very unpleasant and lived entirely at Hackney. After my return to London my time was much devoted in looking after the work people at Coventry Street till the middle of February when we opened the Shop there. I had previously hired Mr. Gibbons, who formerly lived with Wedgwood, as our clerk and a Porter also, a female my Mother hired for me. This was quite a new nuisance for me. About the middle of March I found or thought it prudent to take an^r journey to France as we wanted French China. I left London on Thursday the 19th of March in the Paris Dilegence and arrived at that place on Monday the 23d. While here thro' the medium of Mr. Perregaux my Banker, I entered into an agreement w^h the Angouleme Manufactory for 6 years[2] to supply us only with their China, provided we took to the amt. of 50,000 Livrès a year of them and that we should not take from any other manufactory. After look^g out a large assortment I returned to London by way of Dieppe and Brighton. Was happy to find on my return that my Father & Brother quite approved what I had done but I was sorry to learn Chamberlain & his Son had taken our old House & intended setting up a Retail Shop.[3] This rendered it necessary for me to come immediately to Worcester to consult with my Brother what was best to be done. Coud not at all agree with Chamberlain so I returned after mak^g great enquiry. I at last agreed with Mrs. Hampton to come down with us & teach us the Gilding & assist us for 3 years. In May my dear Sister Ann was marr^d to

---

1.   *i.e. china or porcelain shapes.*
2.   *The "for 6 years" is entered as an afterthought.*
3.   *33 High Street.*

Mr. Whitwell & the 4th of June in the ev^g I left London to come & reside here in Worcester on Sund^y the 7. Mrs. Hampton arrived the day before. I had been employ'd in building a Kiln. We hired 3 of Chamb$^{n.s}$ men who are now with us — We have fired twice, once of Tuesd^y & ag^n last night but neither have succeeded very well. My Brother left his old Habitation on Mond^y mor^g last — God grant these changes may be for our mutual comfort & that a Blessing may attend us — Thus, besides all other changes in these 9 m^o [months] I have travelled 1800 miles & as the French China seems to answer very well its very likely may go there again soon.

Lords Day June 21st 1789, 6 p.m.
What a surprising change it is that has taken place with me within Twelve months. Wither all that has been done is consistent with sound prudence I will not affirm, but nothing has taken place without the advice of my Father, which in the case of misfortune would be a great comfort to the mind — my dear Brother & I seem very comfortable together & I hope we shall continue so, at least I think we sett out with as good a prospect of it as any persons coud. Wither it is right to say providence guided any of us in our conduct I cannot tell but, under the circumstances this has happened, I think the hand of providence is clear. While my Brother & I were determining upon opening a shop in London, Chamberlain was treating about taking over our old House. Had I known this the commission [connection?] most likely woud not have taken place between my Brother and I; & what we coud have done had we not met with Mrs. Hampton I cannot tell. I see no possible way by which we coud have carried on the business — Thus should we admit & adore the secret influence of God; We act, but how can we tell werein he may be counteracting by defeating our wishes; how often does he confer a greater good — Oh then my soul learn a patient acquiescence in his will. Learn hence to commit thy ways unto the Lord & cast all thy cares upon thy God — Such an unsettled Life as I have led lately had not only been unfriendly to Religion in general but particularly so to the regularity I formerly observed while at Mr. Heaths — It may be usefull to devote sometime every week as formerly to remark past occurences both with respect to Body & Mind and now Sunday Evening seems peculiarly proper for this purpose from after Service in the afternoon. I have nothing that ought to engage my attention except that which will be the best improvement of my time — regularity is very suitable to the genius of Christianity & very useful is it. And by thus statedly employing sometime the mind may be habituated to more close thinking — In my setting out in life I woud consider the Duties to which I am called & make it my daily study & prayer well to fill them up — Indeed at present with respect to our business I need seek wisdom & dependance. We have been obliged to make some further alterations in the kiln last week and now are ready to burn again. It is much indeed that depends on our success & therefore I cannot but be anxious, but after doing all that prudence points out it becomes me to be resigned. — With respect to commissions, as yet I have only kept up our old ones, the Gillams, Fields & Gwinnells, to those three places I have been. Shoud be happy coud I find a friend here but its very doubtful to me whether Worcester will afford one after my own heart. As to my mode of living I would be prudent. While profit is uncertain it becomes us to be carefull. It will be very easy for me hereafter to live, as is called, better but perhaps very difficult to draw in. I purpose attending Mrs. Painting in the

morn^g & Mr. [?] in the afternoon, the both of them seem unlikely to continue, the former being very infirm, the other not liked by the people.

Lords Day the 28th June, 1789, 7.p.m.

The last week has indeed been a very trying one to me and what is worse the coming one will I fear be more so. We burnt the kiln every day in the week & still the Sulphur continues & spoils the ware. On Monday, I thought it was better. Tuesday it appeared to continue to mend and was still better on Wednesday but on Thursday was worse again. We hoped then it was owing to the Rain, which had made the place damp, but it appeared otherwise by being no better Friday or Yesterday. What we shall do I cannot tell. We think of trying to erect one upon the plan of Chamberlains. Wether we can or not I cannot tell. Have rec'd the Smaller Kiln from London which they are now erecting. We must try that in hopes of doing better. What to do I cannot tell and Mr. Kitchen seems my sincerest friend, tho' am sure Mrs. Hampton will do, & does, all in her power. We can by no means ascertain the cause from which this arises. I have need for patience, fortitude and resignation. — Having been informed a man at Derby woud be likely to be very usefull to us I consented to let Doe write to try to get him here. On Friday I rec$^{d.}$ a letter from Duesbury, who has found that somebody here had applied to him & wish$^{'d}$ me to prevent it as the man was valuable to him. I wrote him in reply that tho' the man would be of service to us, nothing more shoud be done to get him away. Yesterday Doe rec$^{d.}$ a reply to his letter that the man was willing to come if I woud assure him a place for 7 years. — After what I had wrote Duesbury, was almost determined not to do anything more in it but it was necessary for Doe to reply to this letter & I consented he shoud tell him that tho' I did not by any means wish to draw him from Duesbury, if he came he shoud be assured of the Place for 3 yrs. I hardly like what have done in this matter but could not tell what else to do. — Having been so much, both as to my time & thoughts, taken up with this business, God & Divinity alas have employed but little of my thought the last week, how foolishly do I apply to these things as the true happiness consisted in them. On Thursd^y night I sup$^{'d}$ at Mr. Gwinnells. Mr. H. Field & his wife were there. Last night I sup$^{'d}$ w$^{h.}$ Mr. Field. — Yesterday Chamberlain opened his shop. I was rather surprised as I thought they were hardly ready yet but they talk of making a flaming shew in about 2 m$^{s.}$ Altogether these things agitate my mind a great deal — I find more envy & selfishness in my temper than is good for my own comfort. How it will end, God only knows but it certainly is a great trial. I shoud learn here from the uncertainty of all sublimary enjoyments indeed upon what a slender thread they all hang. This I had other proof of last night, being kept awake by a very violent tooth ache. When in violent pain what are riches and honors worth. Lord teach me to seek happiness in Thee . . . my interest in Christs Salvation lay nearest my heart.

Lords Day the 12th July 1789 6 p.m.

With respect to my temporal concerns have reason to be so exceeding thankful for the change that has taken place within the last fortnight. When things are come to the worst, they sometimes mend; this was the case with us. — On Mond^y when I consulted Kitchen what further coud be done, we sent for the man who built Chamberlains Kiln, who gave us every necessary dimention & said he coud easily build one for us. However in the interim he proposed burning with Saggars, which we accordingly did, & brought all the ware out good except the top which was exposed to the sulphur from the iron; next time we lined all the inside and found the sulphur cease. 4 or 5 we fired in that way, & pretty well, but the fire kiln which I had got from London now began to get ready for burning & we determined to try in a new way. I had the plates made thinner & all punch'd & instead of iron stands, we had a sm. bar of Iron on each side the kiln, with holes to admit pins to support the plates. This answered our end very well and by lining the plates it does very well & will burn more ware for half the expense of the larger kiln with saggars. Surely it becomes me now to offer my thanksgivings to the Almighty. Our repeated losses & continued disappointment began to make me very unhappy. Oh let me learn from this & observation on all experience to commit my ways to him who knows what is best for me, for devine providence may use the most severe & painful dispensations for the kindest purposes. Oh how foolish is it to rest our happiness on the world; it is unworthy of it. — Trials & afflictions are often very beneficial & are however what I must constantly expect. Let me then learn not to be expecting too much. My Brother has exten^d into an agreement with Pennington, a very clever painter in London. We heard he was eng^d to Chamberlain & this made us first wish to have him. C. had applied to him but he prefered our offer. I expect him on Tuesday — have taken on 2 young girls to the Burn^s [Burnishers] one comes on pretty well, the other very slow. Am to have another tomorrow. — On Satur^y the 6 of July Mr. T. Whitwell[1] of Coventry called on me & he spent last Lords Day here. He looked over our Kilns & thinks he can put us into a much better method of burning & from his representation I rather apprehend it will be much cheaper. I agreed to go to Coventry after his return of which he promised to advise me. He is a chemist & seems a very sensible intelligent man. Was very much pleased with him. My friend has been greatly taken up by cares & anxiety, which almost make me dull; no sooner is one thro' one affliction than another arises, & so it will be. There is a sad proportion of envy & jealousy in me & therefore it is not to be wondered at that the present opportunity of serving C., which I fear will injure us but I ought to be thankfull that we have a tollerable prospect in London & our business in other lines here increases very much. — I had another letter from Duesbury about the man, saying he heard further offers had been made to him. I ord^{d.} another letter to be wrote, to prevent him as far as possible from coming, & wrote again to the same purpose to Mr. D. Altogether I think can hardly justify what I have done in this matter tho' its what he has done to us. — I really wish nothing had been ever said about it. It would be profitable for me to think more on Death & Eternity. Alas how little woud all these things appear & hope of happiness when we leave this world, surely can anything be compared to it. Here is support more than equal to every affliction, & surrounded by Dangers & Death, as we are, surely it is very foolish to be so thoughtless. To be verging towards a precipice into which one must fall, & it very uncertain how soon, what a Fool not to attend to embrace everything that can afford every relief when the period comes. I have sup^d out twice this week, once at Mr. Gillams & once with Mr. Field.

1.   *Thomas Whitwell married Ann Flight, John's sister.*

Lords Day 19th July 1789 6 p.m.

The trifling concerns of time, and the necessary duties of life, have a very sad effect upon me. I have always complained a very dissipated mind, but alas how much more cause have I now than ever to be ashamed of myself on this account for want of practice. A fixed attention becomes almost an impossibility to me & except my worlds interest, trifles only employ my mind. Nothing very particular has happened since last Sunday. The last week we burnt the small Kiln 3 times; the first was but indifferent — it was over fired; the second very good; — the third was last night, therefore I cannot yet tell. How happy woud it be if I paid as much attention to the concerns of the soul as the Body; by misfortunes I gain experience & am exceeding cautious to avoid the same again, but alas the objects of Faith are drowned & lost by those of sence. — On Monday, the man we have agreed with came. He is since got to work & from what little have seen of him, I expect he will [be] an acquisition. To decrease them by indifference, I begin to be anxious about the Manufactory. Shaw seems to be taking all possible pains to keep every thing from me, nor do I take less to get at knowledge. I know not what to think of him. Kitchen is very suspicious of him and says he intends no good to the Manufactory. He thinks if I go to put myself more forward he will not stay — the greatest inconvenience from this, K thinks, will be Shaws telling some other Manuf^y our Process, but I shoud believe that little if I thought coud carry on the business well without him. The method prudence seems to point out to me is care and attention to get all the knowledge I can, especially from Kitchen, who professes to be very ready to give information. Perhaps were Shaw gone, the case would be different. Everything seems to enforce upon me attention to this. — Our Gilding goes on comfortably. The Father of one Pugh has applied me offering to come to work here. On enquiry I find he has the character of a very good hand. I have therefore agreed to take him and hope t'will not be long before he comes. — As to Burnishers, two out of the three girls do very well, but one, I fear, must part with. Partly think I shall take another next week. — I had an application from Dyer respecting a very clever man who he says is willing to come and wish'd me to go to meet this person and consult upon terms. I thought it prudent to write him and request him to state particulars, as it did not suit me to go. — This Dyer, Kitchen told me this week, was a particular friend of his but affronted with him for refusing to teach him to make a Glaze to finish some China biscuit ware. He shew'd me the letter D. wrote him; this makes Kitchen appear in a very honorable light and Dyer rather diff^t., by no means consistent with the pretended concern he has for the success of this Manuf^y. Have had a good deal of trouble the last week about the blue printing, the colors peels off in the burning in and spoils a vast deal of ware. Every possible attention is payed to it to find out the Cause and remedy it, but hitherto without success. Our business, thro' mercy, is tollerable. We have reason to be thankfull. On Wednesday even^g. I sup'd at Mr. Fields and Thursday at the Gillams which is all I have been out this week. — Father writes me word, Chamberlain will lay open to an action if he calls theirs the Original Worcester China Warehouse, or themselves Succ^{rs}· to Mr. Bradley, and has wrote me to give them notice to be cautious what they do. Tomorrow I must attend to this business. I have been reading a very Solemn Sermon of Souinos upon the danger of delaying the work of conversion. With what conviction does he paint the folly of suffering the concerns of the Soul to be second to any other — does not my conscience condemn me. Alas, Alas. Oh for space to realise more the great truths of Heaven and Eternity. What shall a man give in exchange for his Soul

Lords Day 26th July, 1789 6 p.m.

The changes I have pas'd thro' lately have been great indeed, but yet one thing seems gradually to lead on to another so that tho' the alteration upon the whole is amazing it dont appear so great to me. Since I was in the situation I had been for many years and little did I think so soon in so settled a situation as I am now —

Oh Mon Dieu je te leve mes yeux donnez-moi cettee grace que ce que je fait ce que je seroit, j'aurai la Gloire éternel pour mon heritage — la Semaine passé m'a été toujours interessant — Lundi le matin je parlais a M. Gwinnell de m'accompagner a M.C. et fils pour leur avertir de ne pas faire aucune chose qui leur subjugeai aux peines de la loi toucha(n)t leur porcelaine. Mais ce n'étoit pas une chose qu'il avait envie de faire, et il me dit que si je peut trouver un autre person il lui sera plus agreable. M. Barr a qui je parlois apres me donnoit une preuve de son amitié disant qu'il etoit pres de faire ce qui me semblera, bon mais il m'a donné conseil d'attendre un peu de jours parce qu'il croit que leur charte se publiera ce semaine. J'ai écrit sur ce sujet plusieurs fois a Mon Pere et enfin il a resolu de ne rein faire parce qu'ils se sont exprimé bien different de ce que attendoit — et j'en suis bien suis — Mais

Oh my God I lift my eyes to thee; give me the grace that what I do, what I may be, I will have eternal glory for my inheritance — Last week was for me always very interesting. On Monday morning I was speaking to Mr. Gwinnell about coming with me to C and Sons to warn them not to do anything that would involve legal penalties in connection with their porcelain but it was not something that he was keen to do and he said that if I can [could] find someone else it will please him better. Mr. Barr to whom I spoke later gave me proof of his friendship, saying he was ready to do what I considered right but he advised me to wait a few days for he thinks their charter will be published this week. I have been several times on this matter to my father and he has finally resolved to do nothing, as they have behaved differently from what he expected. And I am very glad about it, But

[Folios 248-253 cut out]

. . . cette imploi c'est vrai nous arrons bien perdu au commencement et peut etre je doit être étonné qu'aux lieu de gagner nous n'avons pas perdu. J'ai le dessin d'essayer un peu de pieces pour etre certain sur ce sujet — Mercredi il m'arriva un chose qui m'a beaucoup troublé. Kitchen m'apporta un epreuve de couleurs sur laquelle il y avoit de l'or. Par plusieurs circonstances je ne peu que soupçonner que cette or etoit de sa preparation mais je le trouve bon de ne rien dire. J'ai besoin de beaucoup plus de fortitude et de patience aussi bien que resignation a la volonté de Dieu. Oh mon Dieu donnez moi tout ce qu'il me manque et afin que je sois preparé pour toutes les peines de cette vie.

. . . this week. It is true we lost at first and perhaps I must have been surprised that instead of winning we have not lost. I have the plan to try a few pieces to be certain on the matter. On Wednesday something happened which troubled me. Kitchen brought me a test of colours on which there was some gold. For some reason I can only suspect that this gold was his preparation, but I find it best to say nothing. I

225

need more courage and patience as well as submission to the will of God. Oh God, give me all I am lacking so that I be ready to face all the troubles of this life.

Samedi le soir 5th 10 p.m.

Cette apres midi je preparai de l'or avec Mc Hampton ou plutôt elle la fit qu'a je n'etois pas avec elle la moitié du temps. La quantité de 2 onzes jai mis à part 2 petistes quantittées de ¹/8 onces chaque. Pour faire des epreuves combien de la Porcelaine ou peut d'orer avec cela — je crois que m'es soupçons touchant M. Kitchen ne sont pas fondé peut être je me tromp pourtant j'ai bien fait de garder secret mes pensées nous n'avons vendus que tres peu cette semaine, et j'entend que C et fils vont bien, je veut le laisser à Dieu que sait le mieux a faire.

Saturday 5th September 1789 10 p.m.

This afternoon I prepared some gold with Mrs. Hampton, or rather she did, for I was not with her half the time. The quantity was 2 ounces. I put aside 2 small amounts of ¹/8 ounce each to test how much porcelain one can gild with that. I believe my suspicions touching Mr. Kitchen have no foundation. Perhaps I am mistaken and yet I have done well to keep my thoughts to myself. We have sold only very little this week. I understand that C and sons are doing well. I leave it all in God's hands, who will know what is best to do.

Wednes. Mard at 8 Clock
16th.

Hier je leur donnais encore 2 onces de l'or excepté une quart, Que j'ai fondu pour des epreuvers touchant la quantite dont nous nous lisons — il y avait un peu de reste c'est pourquoi ils ont été plus que 19 jours en ce servant de mes 2 onces — hier Mc Hampton preparoit encore 2 onzes de l'or ici — Je vient d'entendre hier que les filles ne sont pas content des gages que nous leur donnons et que c'est bien probable que C et fils en ont besoin et qu'ils souhait de prendre le nôtre c'est une chose desagreable mais il faut faire le mieux qu'on peut —

September 16 1789

Yesterday I again gave 2 ounces of gold, less a quarter which I omitted for tests touching the quantity under discussion — there was a little left over, that is why they took more than 19 days using these 2 ounces. Yesterday Mrs Hampton prepared another 2 ounces of gold here. I just heard yesterday that the girls are not satisfied with the wages we gave them, and that it is likely C and Sons need them and that they hope to take ours; this is very disagreeable but we must do the best we can.

Sunday October 11, 1789 — 7 pm

Agreable scenes do but arise to leave an inquietude behind them. Our life is a mixture of pleasant and painfull & each affects the other. Have had the honor & pleasure of a long visit from my Dear Parents & Sisters. They arrived here Thursday Evening the 10th of Sepr I went to meet them & supd at Burlingham on the Tuesday & returned home after supper. They staid at B till Thursday — Father left us on Monday the 21st & went by the Bristol coach & from thence to Hilstone — He settled with Tallack & also bought a share in a lead mine there; returned on Saturday the 3rd of this month. Friday the 25 of Sepr Mr Whitwell arrived here. He had been a journey into Scotland & made this in his way home. On Thursday Oct 1st he & father returned to London & last Thursday the 8th Father & Mother & Sisters also left me & have since the pleasure to learn they are safe arrived at Hackney.

October 1789

I desire to esteem it a great mercy so much affection exists among our Family & is the most pleasant reflection of my life. Father coud not determine what it was best to do about Shaw. Sometimes he seemed resolved to come to an explanation fully with him but after all, thought it best to leave it for the present. So made him the usual present & only told him to do his best.

A very disagreeable circumstance turned up which we coud no way find out. The white & fine blue glaze was spoiled by some blue being put into it; at least there was every reason to believe this had been the case, but coud not find out. Have had a place enclosed tht the Glaze may always be kept locked up. I went to the Mills[1] with Mr Whitwell & examined one of the men respecting what quantity he weighted up together. There is one article which he coud not tell me what it was, but I brought a piece of it home & Kitchen thinks at is the St. Stephens Clay, the same my Father brot a sample of with him from Cornwall, & that Shaw has injured the body by putting some of this into it. I intend to take some method of examining into this. With respect to our Gilding & business have great cause for thankfullness that we have done very well. Chamberlain I believe does hurt us a little, but our Trade does not seem much diminished, if at all — I find the want of fortitude & perseverence. These are very essential requisits in such a situation as mine is. —

I go on trying Bodys & Glazes with Kitchen & begin to get a tollerable insight into the process of the Manufactory, — but I much want to do more in this myself. I must contrive some method to do it. — I am fearfull of leaving the Many & that makes me not know what is best about going to France. Have hinted to my Bror for him to go but hardly think that woud do, & it does seem of importance. Rather think shall go but purpose writing my Br again about it & determine what to do. — On Monday the 2 of Sept. I went with Mr Whitwell to Overbury to Mr Trimms, an acquaintance of his. — He has a very clever daughter whom my sisters want to recommend to me I dined with her & her sister. The rest of the family were from home. She seemed clever in the family & a tollerable share of sense but had not the je ne sais quoi. Its possible I may think different upon further acquaintance, which I shoud wish to cultivate with the Family, they having the character of an agreeable one. Mr M. and his son called here last Wednesday, to acknowledge my visit, & promised to call at least when they came to Worcester. Have reason indeed to humble myself on account of an undue attachment to the present world. How much alas its hopes & fears agitate me more than they ought; a soul whose Eternal state will befriend by his conduct in this life. —

Lords Day 18th October 1789 6 pm

I am now really & fully involved in the cares & anxieties of life & alas have reason to be ashamed that they have so distracted my mind that I cannot attend to anything

1. *The Company's Grinding Mills were on the Dick Brook at Shrawley, some 7 miles from Worcester.*

to improve my mind or for the good of my soul. To whatever I move my attention it soon returns & from schemes concerning my business this is a melancholy reflection, & oh forbid it Lord that I shoud be contented thus. Arouse thee my Soul, fly to that God who is always willing to afford grace & strength when sought unto for it. How vain & deluding are all these fancied goods, incapable of affording any satisfaction, & yet do they fascinate my mind. — Our Kiln of Bisct. ware yesterday Sevennight[1] was so bad that I determined to examine it to know the cause. On Thursday I went again to the mills. Shaw had not been there but had sent them orders not to put in any more clay till he came again. They had therefore left it out. They said they had only put it in since the mills were finished; that they had some of the same clay a year and half since but had not used it since that time; that immediately the mills were finished he sent a Barrell of it & that since then they had always weighed it up with the Best Clay. When I returned the Kiln was burning & I saw Shaw very carefully attending to it. It was when drawn much better than the last because better fired but much inferior to what the ware used to be, & also to a proof which was in of the last best clay which was received from the Mills on Tuesday, & in which by the Mens account at the mills there was none of this Clay. Upon questioning Shaw what coud be the cause, he replied he supposed the men must have made some mistake in the weighing & left out some of the Glass. I asked him how the trial was; he said not very good, but it appeared to him to be owing to its not being sufficently fired. Unless I have been deceived by the other men he is guilty of infamous duplicity. I stated all these circumstances daily to my Father who in a letter rec^d this day says he is of my opinion, but that as I think of going to France had better keep the matter to myself till my return. I purpose going to the Mills again tomorrow or Tuesday to see wether I can get further insight into this matter. — With my F^r & B^r advice have at last resolved to go to France & expect my B^r here on Tuesday to supply my absence. Have wrote Lord Harcourt for his opinion wether it is safe & intend wait his reply before I go. On Wednesday I weighed up a Fritt which Kitchen got into the Glaze Kiln for me & yesterday I weighed up a Body & also another fritt. I intend to continue to make trials & shall be glad to do it entirely myself without having Kitchen see it, as its possible, tho I ought not to entertain the thought, he may put something else to it. — Have had a midling week in London. We have lately done a great deal of business, indeed have great cause for thankfulness. The prospect of seeing my friends in London, tho' but for a day, affords me no small pleasure but cannot help being a little anxious about a Friends Journey in the present distracted state of their affairs, but in the path of duty I may commit myself to providence.

Saturday November 21 1789 10 am

In reply to my letter to Lord Harcourt, his Lordship wrote me a very friendly letter advising me by no means to go to France at present as I shoud run the hazard of being stop'd within the wall of Paris, or perhaps something more disagreable. This determined me not to go. My brother arrived here from London on Tuesday the 20th, & I determined to embrace so favorable an opportunity of paying my friends in London a visit. — Left Worcester in the hail of Saturday the 24th & breakfasted at

---

1.   *i.e. a week ago yesterday.*

Coventry Street. Next day my Sisters & Brother B were kind enough to meet me. It was very pleasant way of spending a week, indeed it coud not but be gratifying to see so many whom one holds so dear. Br B was obliged to leave London the next day. I staid till Monday the 2^d of this month & left London in the Mail that evening, emplyed myself in exam.g our stock of French goods & sent an order to that Manufact.^y to make us up a large & complete assortment against the Winter. We had a very good week while I was in London & indeed have altogether done exceeding well at Coventry St. Was much concerned on my return to hear my Brother had had one Kiln of ware entirely spoiled by sulphur, the cause of which they coud not ascertain. We fired the day of my arrival & the next & both were good kilns but on Friday had a few spoiled. The first proof we took out was a little sulphured, the second worse & but very little good ware in the Kiln. The cause still remained a secret. We tried everything we coud think of, giving the Kiln more air for drawing off our sulphur that might arise from the ware. Saturday we fired again & very good. Tuesday we had a little damaged & Thursday more. This began to make both my brother & self very uneasy & the more so as we coud not ascertain the cause. At last I resolved to try the large Kiln, which after repeated experiments does exceeding well & since that time we have gone on very well. The cause appears to me now to have been the Charcoal having no vent at top, being covered all over with fresh Charcoal forced into the Kiln. We are now carefull to keep the sides clear & also lute the cover as close as possible; however I have an idea of altering the top so as I hope to keep the Sulphur out at a certainty. This indeed was a trying business, my Brother fumed to bear it still worse than I. Last Monday he left me & returned to Town. Have also had another very important matter to engage my attention. We have been making some oblong Dishes & have had several fly [cracks] in the Glazing which has made me suspect Shaw was making further alterations in the Body. This was Kitchens opinion, with whom I have continued to make trials both of Body & Glaze. At last I resolved to talk to Shaw plainly about it, & had my Fathers orders thereto. On Wednesday the 11th, in the presence of my Bro.^r I have a very long conversation with him. He made what appeared to me very equivocal replys to what I said about the altera^s he was making, while he told me he had not made any. However I concluded by telling him I was resolved to know the composition & had my Fathers orders to demand him to weigh it up with me. He seemed greatly concerned to find Kitchen had told me the process & to question desired a month to consider an answer. After consulting again with my Father & other friends here, I again spoke to him last Monday before my Brother left Worcester & concluded by telling him I shoud expect his answer to my demand on Wednesday. Accordg^{ly} on Wednesday I talked with him again & he promised to give it me in writing as it was not convenient just yet to weigh up either body or Glaze. And on Thursday morning he gave it me signed with his name. This is a matter which I can no way account for or indeed scarcely believe what I know & yet its possible he may have deceived me, tho' hardly probable. However I shall endeavor to get more certain evidence next week by weighing up with him. These have been altogether very trying matters, but not enough to take my mind from everything else.

Mes pensées on roulées pour quelque temps sur le sujet de mariage j'ai vu avec bien de plaisir M.ᵉ G et j'en aie entendu beaucoup a son avantage asser pourtant pour m'enspirer le desir de connoitre encore plus touchant elle mercredi le 10 du courant j'allai apres diné chez son pere — je fit quelque affaire expres, je le trouvai avec sa fille et j'y restai pour une demi heur voyant asser . . .

My thoughts have revolved for some time on the subject of marriage. With much pleasure I saw Miss G and I have heard many things to her advantage enough to inspire with the desire to know even more about her. On Wednesday the 10th instant I went after dinner to her father's house on a deliberate business visit. I found him with his daughter and I stayed there for half an hour, seeing . . .

[*Folios 263-270 are cut out*]

January 1790

Je dois rejouir. Ces idées son contraire a toutes les regles de la delicatesse et ils montent clairement que la personne qui les tien et bien strange au monde. Nous avons employé nos deux meilleurs peintres la semaine passe pour faire quelques belles desseins pour le Duc de Clarence nous en avons bein fini trois assiettes et je les ait envoyé a Londres: l'un est en arabesque en or une autre la figure de l'esperance et l'autre de la Patience.

I just rejoice. These ideas are contrary to all rules of good conduct and they clearly show that the person who holds them is very different from the world. We used our two best painters last week to make some very fine designs for the Duke of Clarence, we have already completed 3 plates and I have sent them to London. One is a gold arabesque design, another the figure of Hope, the other of Patience.

Dimanche le 24 9 p.m.

Nous continuons tout ensemble de bien faire et le monde va avec moi passablement outre les deux assiettes dont jai ecrit ci dessous nous avons fait deux autres en Figures, La Paix et l'Abondance, S.A.R. le Duc de Clarence a fixé d'avoir le dessein de l'Esperance avec la decoration que nous avons mit sur l'assiette la Paix et il en a commandé une Service a Table qui se montera a plus de sept cents livres sterling il nous a donnez une an pour la faire faire — lundi derriet nour avons fait une Grand Illumination ici la jourde la naissance de la Reine, qui a fait beaucoup de bruit. Tout le monde dit que c'est la meilleure exhibition dans ce genre qu'ils on jamais vu ici. Nous avons aussi bien publier l'ordre donner et ces deux choses assiste beaucoup de faire parler le monde sur le success de cette tranᵉ. et sur notre progress. Personellement je ne suis pas asses desconcerter pour me faire du mal, deja le vient de penser d'une autre qu'en sera l'avennement je ne sais pas (mais actuellement j'en pense serieusement) . . .

Sunday 24th 9 p.m.
We are continuing we work together for the good of all, the world is passably fair to me. Apart from the two plates mentioned below [? above] we have made two others with figures — Peace and Plenty. H.R.H. Duke of Clarence has decided on the Hope design with the decoration that we put on the Peace plate, he has ordered a table service that will amount to more than £700 sterling. He has given us a year in which to complete it. Last Monday we had a grand illumination here on the day of the Queen's birthday, which made a lot of noise. Everyone says that it was the best

thing of that sort that has ever been seen here. We have also published the order that the Duke of Clarence has just given us and these two things help much in providing subject for gossip in society on the success of these transactions and our progress. Personally I am not so put out as to do myself injury. Already I have been thinking of another one, what will be the outcome I do not know (but at present I am thinking about it seriously) . . .

Dimenche le 21 10 p.m.
L'intention inconnue ci-dessus à gangé la force depuis se temps la et j'ai actuellement l'intention de declarer mes sentiments a la personne a qui elles sont interressantes les deux mois passés je me suis fait bien intime avec cette famille et je me suis servie de toute occasion particulier de parler sans langue et de ganger la coeur qio m'est cher dans une affair importante on ne peut que craindre mais je n'ai pas de raison poutant il ne faut pas ce faire certain —

Sunday the 21st 10 p.m.
My intention previously uncertain has gained in strength since that day and now I intend to declare my feelings to the person to whom they are of interest. These last two months I have become intimate with this family and I have used every private opportunity to speak their language and to win the heart that is dear to me. In an important matter we can only fear, but as yet I have no reason for so doing. We must not be too hopeful.

Avril dimanche le 11 9 a.m.
Actuellement j'ai declarai mes sentiments a M G et j'ai recu d'elle une traitement agreable. L'affaire est a present certainement en bon traine. Mais je n'ai pas à present le temps de raconter les particuliers et jamais le temps ne les efforcerais de mon coeur. Je ne pense que d'elle et je ne flutte qu'elle pense aussi de moi avec plaisir.

Sunday April the 2nd 9 a.m.
Now I have declared my feelings for M G and have received from her pleasant response. The matter is now certainly well under way but I have not time now to go into details which time will never efface from my breast. I think only of her and I flatter myself that she also thinks of me with pleasure.

Sunday 20 February 1791 6am
In May last year was honoured with a visit from my Hon[d] Parents & dear Sisters & the 16th of June My Brothers T & J also came. Was married the 17th in a few days after they returned to London & we also went there. 3 weeks after I went to France on business, was absent from Thursday till the Monday week & we returned to Worcester after an absence of about a M[o]. [month]. Mr Gillam accomp[d] us to London. This 7th Dec[r] Mrs Hunt died after a very long illness & the 23 Mrs F & I went to London again as I was very desirous of my being at our first Family meeting. We had a comfortable interview with my Dear friends & took our stock. Brother returned with us to Worcester where we finished the stock, & had great cause to be thankfull for a good year — nothing very particular has happened since that time. We have been rather uncomfortably situated with respect to Publick worship as many of us think our Minister's conduct has been inconstant with his Character. We have endeavored to induce him to resign. I have not been very active;

he has at length given in his resignation this day to go at Michaelmas. Therefore hope we have the prospect of being more comfortable in this respect. Since were married have by degrees entirely left off going to Mr Pointings meeting — On Friday Mrs Hampton was taken very ill, so I was obliged to manage the burning of the G^d Kiln: Fortunately, by the attention I have paid to this, was able to do it & I hope coud without much difficulty in case we were to loose her, but this I hope will not be the case as she is getting better. It woud however I fear put us to some inconvenience. After some months illness Shaw the Manuf^y Clerk Died last Sep^t. This event must have been attended with very different consequences had it happened a year sooner; indeed most probably woud have stopd the manufactory but I had obtained the process from him after having found it nearly out otherways by the assistance of Kitchen. Therefore was able to carry it on myself indeed had done it for some months previous to his Death. Providence seems to have interfered rather in a particular manner in this & other events that have happened since our establishment in business. By the improv^t we have made Chamberlain has been prevt^d from injuring us. At least we scarcly feel it. Soon after Shaw, Lewis died. He managed the printing. This was a sudden event, but also instead of being an injury, was the contrary, as we carry on that at less expence. I had a great deal of trouble in securing Shaw's Papers which contained the whole process, but at last secured them for Ten Guineas, paid his Father. Had expected to pay a much larger sum. How many changes! I have indeed abundant cause for gratitude. We cannot be happier than we are & daily offer our prayers to the God of all Grace to give us the wisdom & Grace that we may be increasing blessings to each other & usefull to others & that we may be fitted for every event, more humble & dependant on him & in every respect preparing for everlasting happiness.

Sunday 27 February 1791 8 a.m.

Nothing particular has happened the past week. As to business, have been pretty fully taken up as Mrs Hampton has been confined all the week. She is now rather better. On Thursday I called to see one of our Potters who has been long very ill. The poor man is now in a deplorable state, his legs full of ulcers & sores & almost offensive to come near. As he has long been a burden to the Club he belongs to they have lately stop^d the assistance he rec^d from it & he is almost in want — shall see if I can do anything to get him allowed money from it again. Have for that purpose spoke to see the Att^y who has some influence with the managers of it — how little are our minds usually affected by the distinguishing favors of providence to us — Have been much surprised nor less pleased by a Letter rec^d today from my Brother B. He says his wife is in the Family Way — this will, I am certain, afford great pleasure to all our Family — they have I think been married upwards of 7 years.

[A few months later, in July 1791, John Flight died at the early age of 25.]

Appendix IV

Extracts from the Account Books of James Ross

I give below a list of all the entries for Flight and Barr in James Ross's account books, which contain accounts for the engraving of bill heads, factory backstamps, engravings for book publications advertising the Company, engraving silver items for sale to the Company's clients. On a number of occasions James Ross was paid out of china goods. Lest it be thought that Barr Flight and Barr were long winded in paying their accounts, this was not uncommon practice in those days.

MESSRS FLIGHT AND BARR
CHINA MANUFACTURERS, WORCESTER

1792		
June 18th	Card Plate and Billhead.	£4. 4. 0d.
1793		
April 28th	2 Waiters crested.	1. 6
October 10th	Card Plate £2. 2. 0. Door Plate 6/6d	2. 8. 6
	Received J.R.	6. 14. 0
1795		
October 1st	Plate of the factory presented to Mr. Green	26. 5. 0
	750 Impressions and paper to ditto	4. 10. 0
	200 ditto for their own use.	1. 4. 0
1796		
April 23rd	Card Plate of the factory	3. 13. 6
May 23rd	Remainder of Mr. Joseph Flight's subscription to Mr. Green's book	10. 6
	Ditto to Mr. Barr's	10. 6
	Ditto Thos. Flight Esq.	1. 1. 0
	Ditto Reverend Mr. Osborne	1. 1. 0
	Ditto Edward Kitchen	1. 1. 0
	J.R. Received Aug 8th 1798	£39. 16. 6
1798		
Sept 7th	Altering front of Factory and retouching Card Plate	1. 11. 6
October 28th	View of front of Factory for Bakers Welsh Tour.	5. 5. 0
1799		
February 9th	45 Spoons cypher's 3 letters, and name on box.	1. 3. 0

May 1st	Alterations and additions to Factory Plate for framing	2.	2.	0
May 17th	16 Colour'd Prints 16/-			
	36 ditto Plain 6/- Paid Mr. Jukes	1.	2.	0
August 20th	New Card and Bill head plates	5.	5.	0
1800				
June 7th	2 Brass Plates, engraved, wax'd and polished door bell.		5.	0
1801				
April 18th	Altering Factory Plate for Bakers use	1.	1.	0
May 29th	New Plate of Factory for Bissets Directory with alterations	10.	10.	0
1802				
June 9th	Fish Knife and two Butter Knives Cypher'd	—	2.	3
1804				
January 4th	Knife and Fork cypher'd 1/- Decr. 27 Bill head plate, Barr, Flight & Barr £2. 2. 0	2.	3.	0
May 24th	2 Tongues, Cheese Knife and Thimble cypher'd		2.	3
1805				
August 21st	Altering 1 card and 2 Billhead Plates.		10.	6

£31. 2. 3

October 14th 1800 Mrs Simmonds' China £4. 9. 6			
6 Blue and White Coffee cups 15. 0	5.	4.	6

Balance £25. 17. 9
March 16th 1807 settled this account J.R.

1807				
March 23rd	Altering and retouching Factory Card Plate	1.	11.	6
April 2nd	Ditto names, etc. on large Factory Plate (Bisset)		17.	6
April 14th	Label Plate for transferring names on china		12.	6
1808				
September 12th	Umbrella 1/6 Names on two knives 2/-		3.	6
	Retouching Label Plate.		7.	6
1813				
March 25th	New Label Plate (Crown & Feathers)		15.	0
December 16th	Card Plate. (Mr. Martin Barr).		7.	6

Settled December 15th 1817 J.R. £4. 15. 0

This closing of James Ross's accounts with Barr Flight and Barr ends with a reference to the death of Martin Barr senior.
"Mr. Barr died of Appoplexy, Nov. 10th 1813, (the very same day on which Mr. Osborne died the year before) in his 57th Year, and was buried at the Angel Street Chapel (north and south) on the 18th following. J.R."

Appendix V

Chemical Analysis of Flight and Barr Porcelain

A comparative spectrometric semi-quantitive analysis of the new Flight and Barr porcelain with the earlier Davis/Flight type was done by the British Ceramic Research Association. I am fortunate in having the help of Paul Rado, the chief chemist of the Worcester Royal Porcelain Company, in putting these technical details into simple layman's terms.

The "A" piece was crescent marked of the typical soft paste type of pre-1795 and the "B" piece of the harder looking body and glaze of post-1795 with an incised B mark.

		A%	B%
Alumina	(Al_2O_3)	5.00	5.00
Lime	(CaO)	0.5	0.20
Cobalt Oxide	(Co_3O_4)	—	0.02
Cupric Oxide	(CuO)	0.01	0.01
Ferric Oxide	(Fe_2O_3)	0.20	0.20
Lead Monoxide	(PbO)	5.00	2.00
Magnesia	(MgO)	5.00	5.00
Manganous Oxide	(MnO)	0.01	—
Nickel Oxide	(NiO)	0.01	0.02
Potash	(K_2O)	2.00	2.00
Silica	(SiO_2)	Major Constituent	Major Constituent
Soda	(Na_2O)	0.50	1.00
Titania	(TiO_2)	—	0.02
Zirconia	(ZrO_2)	0.05	0.20

The analysis conclusively shows that both pieces were "Soft Porcelain" since they contained frits as indicated by the content of Lead Monoxide although "B" contains less; in addition they contained soaprock (steatite) as indicated by the Magnesia content. The alumina content of both is very low (being indicative of a "soft" soft paste), only about one fifth of the classical Hard Paste composition (50 clay, 25 feldspar, 25 Quartz). The low lime content shows that no bone ash or only very small amounts of bone ash were used. By combining two methods of strong fluxing (the glass, or frit, content and the use of soap rock) the ancient Worcester potters were able to fire at very low temperatures compared to ours; they must have been conscious of conserving fuel — we could learn something from them in this age of fuel and power crises.

At the same time as the spectrometric semi-quantitive analysis, X-ray defraction tests were carried out. These showed sample "A" as having "some Cristobalite, some Quartz, some Clino-enstatite and with a little Feldspar, sample 'B' being as sample 'A' but with less Quartz and Enstatite but more Cristobalite and also a small amount of an unidentified phase." Both samples appeared to have an appreciable amount of a glass phase present.

This X-ray diffraction test confirmed the deductions reached from the spectrometric analyses, viz the presence of enstatite which is derived from the soap rock. The quartz and cristobalite are derived from silica which according to the spectrometric analysis constituted the main constituent.

Appendix VI

The Marks of Flight and Barr

Although code marks for the year of manufacture were not used it is possible to put the production of wares within a reasonably close dating by the following marks. This is not an exhaustive list as there are a number of slight variations which are not listed. It is worth mentioning again that pattern numbers were not used by Flight and Barr but the use of gilders numbers, from 1 up to 30 or so, is found written usually in gold just inside the footrim. Most marks are onglaze, except the disguised numerals and crescents, which are in underglaze blue, as also can be the word Flight. The initials BFB and FBB under a crown are invariably impressed and the perculiar B mark is always incised. The following list of marks is put into rough chronological order.

1      *The so-called "disguised numeral marks" in underglaze blue — range from about 1776 to 1792.*

2      *Typical "square" mark runs from about 1760 to about 1795 in underglaze blue.*

3      *Typical crescent marks in underglaze blue from 1760 to 1792, the crescent tending to become very small from about 1785 to 1792.*

4   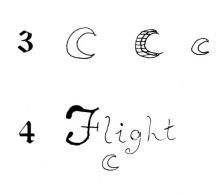   *About 1783 to 1788, in underglaze blue.*

5 *Flight* 	1783-92, in underglaze blue or purple.

6 FLIGHTS 	*Impressed in the clay, a very rare mark 1783-92.*

7 WORCESTER Manufactory FLIGHT 	*Very rare printed mark, the words enclosed in an oval and with a crown above, about 1788-92.*

8 *Flight* 	*In underglaze blue, 1788-92, used on the Duke of Clarence "Hope" service and occasionally on other ware.*

9 *Flight & Barr Worcester Manu^{rs} to their Maj^s* 	*In script, about 1792-1804.*

10 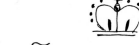 *Flight & Barr Worcester* 	*In script, about 1792-1804.*

238

11 ☾ *Flight & Barr Worcester*

A rare mark, in underglaze blue, about 1792-1800.

12 $F \& B$

A very rarely found incised initial mark, about 1792-1804.

13 B   B ×   B ⁄

Typical forms of an incised mark, commonly found on teawares, about 1792-1804 (but an example with a date 1806 is known, which could have been the using up of some old pieces.

14 BARR WORCESTER PORCELAIN MANUFACTURERS TO THE KING

A very rare printed mark, about 1800.

15

Barr Flight & Barr
Worcester
Flight & Barr
Coventry Street
London

Manufacturers to their
Majesties &
Royal Family

A typical example of a hand script written mark under a crown of about 1804-13; there are a number of variations, sometimes the London showroom details are omitted, sometimes the Flight and Barr details appear above the Barr Flight & Barr ones and these marks, written with a pen, normally occur on the best wares.

16

BFB

An impressed mark, the standard mark of 1804-13, found on all types of wares, with or without written or printed marks.

17

FLIGHT & BARR
COVENTRY STREET
LONDON

BARR FLIGHT & BARR
WORCESTER
MANUFACTURERS TO THEIR
MAJESTIES &
ROYAL FAMILY

An elaborate mark, enclosed within an oval, a variation is found having the words "Royal Porcelain Works Worcester" above the oval and the words "Established 1751" below; about 1804-7.

18

BARR FLIGHT & BARR
ROYAL PORCELAIN WORKS
WORCESTER

LONDON HOUSE
Nº 1 COVENTRY STREET

The use of the royal crown and the Prince of Wales feathers date from about 1807-13. A more elaborate form is found with the wording enclosed in an oval surrounded by the words "Manufacturers to their Majesties Prince of Wales and Royal Family Established 1751" surmounted by the crown and feathers.

19

BARR, FLIGHT & BARR
Proprietors of the
Royal Porcelain Works
WORCESTER
Established 1751

This — the most elaborate of the marks — is found enclosed in a circle, the words surmounted by the Royal coat of arms and with the Prince of Wales feathers and a ribbon below; around the outside of the circle appear the words "Manufacturers to their Majesties and the Prince Regent London Warehouse No. 1 Coventry Street". 1810-13.

20

FLIGHT BARR & BARR
Proprietors of the
ROYAL PORCELAIN WORKS
WORCESTER
Established 1751

This is the same as mark number 19, with similar surrounding wording and arms, but has the words Flight Barr and Barr instead of Barr Flight and Barr. 1813 to about 1819. A version is also seen without the circle and outside wording.

21

ROYAL PORCELAIN WORKS
FLIGHT BARR & BARR
WORCESTER
&
COVENTRY ST. LONDON

About 1813-19.

22

F B B

An impressed mark, the standard mark of 1813-40, found on all types of wares with or without printed marks.

23

Flight
Barr & Barr
Worcester

A script mark of about 1813-20.

24

Flight Barr & Barr
Royal Porcelain Works
Worcester

London House
1 Coventry Street

The main script mark about 1813-40.

Index

Ackerman style patterns, 171
Allies, George, 132, 133, 139, 199
Allies, Jabez, 133, 139, 141, 199
Amhurst, Lord, 184, 212
Amphlett, 214
Angoulême porcelain factory, 23, 27
Ardilaun, Lord, 106
Argument, pattern, 161
Armorial services, 210-216
Astles, Samuel, 32,103,104,106,199

B mark, 163
Baretti of India, 212
Barker, John, 104, 106, 183, 199
Barr, George, Groomed for factory, 48;
    Father's will, 81; New Partnership, 100;
    Visits factory each day, 101; Will of
    Joseph Flight, 115; Merger with Chamber-
    lain, 130-147; Death 147; Biography, 200
Barr, Hannah, 81
Barr, Maria, 147
Barr, Martin, junior, Groomed for factory,
    48; Made a partner, 63; Father's will, 81;
    New Partnership, 100; Visits factory each
    day, 101; Meets Michael Faraday, 111-114;
    Will of Joseph Flight, 115; Merger with
    Chamberlain, 130-147; Death, 147;
    Biography, 200
Barr, Martin, senior, Executor of John Flight,
    29; Joins factory, 30; Obtains money, 32;
    Improves quality, 42; Takes son as
    apprentice, 63; Improvement in body, 70;
    Death, 80, 234; Will, 81; Biography, 200
Barr's orange colour, 184
Bat pattern, 161
Bat printing, 170-172
Baxter, Thomas, 103, 104, 106, 109, 111,
    169, 172, 180, 183-184, 200-201
Beeley, alias of William Billingsley
Bell, Edward, 201
Bell pulls, 168
Berrow's Worcester Journal, 34, 35, 63
Berwick & Co., 132
Billingsley, Lavinia, 66, 201
Billingsley, Mrs. Sarah, 66, 201
Billingsley, Sarah, 67-68, 201
Billingsley, William, Character, 65; Starting
    at Worcester, 66; Wages, 67; Work and
    Bond, 70; Contract dispute, 72-80;
    Biography, 201
Binns, R.W., 30, 34, 70, 130, 170, 178, 189
Bishopp, Sir Cecil, 211
Blind Earl pattern, 166
Blomberg, 214
Blue grounds, 11, 185
Blue scale, 11
Bly, John, junior, 101, 202
Bly, John, senior, 101, 201
Bone china, 189
Brackenbury of Skendleby, 214
Bradley, James, 202

Bradley, Samuel, 16, 36, 39, 202
Brewer, Robert, 202
British Ceramic Research Association, 42,
    235
Broadfoot, William, 202
Brotherton, Alderman, 34
Brunswick Cup, 174-178
Buck, Adam, style patterns, 171
Buckingham, Duke of, 212
Butterfly wing handles, 186

Cale, Frederick, 202
Caradine, Thomas, 202
Carden, Henry Douglas, 133, 139, 141, 202
Caudle cups, 168
Caughley factory, 11, 160
Chaffers' Marks and Monograms, 100
Chamberlain, Humphrey, 32
Chamberlain, Robert, Rival manufactory,
    24; First orders, 25; Opens new shop, 26,
    222; Report by Green, 41; Biography,
    202
Chamberlain, Walter, 132-133, 143, 145-146,
    202
Chocolate cups, 168
Clarence, Duke of, 27, 28, 184, 212, 230;
    see also William the Fourth
Clements, painter, 202
Cole, Solomon, painter, 32, 100, 103, 183,
    202
Coney, 214
Cottages, 186
Cotterill, Joseph, 65, 103, 203
Cotton, Lady Augusta, 175
Courtown, Lord, 18, 219
Coventry, Earl of, 169, 174, 175, 183
Crested services, 210-216
Crowther, G.C., 203
Crowther, Thomas, 106, 203

Dack, Peter, 203
Dark, Peter, 203
Davis, George, "Dr.", 106, 162, 203
Davis, John, 203
Davis, William the elder, 11, 161
Davis, William the younger, 11
Day, C., 203
Desk sets, 180
Dewsbury of Derby, 223, 224
Digby, Colonel, 18
Dilwyn, Lewis of Swansea, 70, 74
Disguised numeral marks, 161
Ditton, Thomas, 203, 204
Dixon of Raneshaw, 212
Dobbs, Thomas, 203
Doe, Enoch, 203
Doe and Rogers, 203
Doe, William, 103, 106, 203
Dorset, Duke of, 219, 220
Doughty, Joseph, 203
Dovey, Jos., 203

Dovey, Richard, 203
Downes, Baron, 213
Dutton, Thomas, 203, 204
Dyer, Richard, 204

Eagle handled cup, 183
East India Company, 169, 211
Elton of London, 214
Encaustic tiles, 146
Etruscan shapes, 104
Everett, Thomas, 213

Fabulous birds, 162
Fancy birds, 162
Faraday, Michael, diary, 109, 111-114
Fern, Andrew, 204
Ferrier of Hemsby, 212
Field, Mr. H., 222-224
Figures, 188
Fisherman and cormorant pattern, 161
Flight family tree, 13
Flight, Ann, 115, 220
Flight, Bannister, 12, 29, 115, 232
Flight, Christian, 115
Flight, Hanson, 12
Flight, John, His diary, 12, 217-232; Early
    life, 14; Journey to Cornwall, 15, 217;
    Commences at factory, 16; Opens Lon-
    don shop, 22, 218; Visits France, 23, 219;
    Builds new kiln, 25, 219; Trouble with
    kiln, 22, 222; Meets future wife, 27, 230;
    Further French trip, 28; Death, 29, 232;
    Biography, 204
Flight, Joseph, Master of Carpenters Com-
    pany, 12; Obtains new painter, 27;
    Confronts Shaw, 28; New Partnership,
    100; Dies, 115; Biography, 204
Flight, Thomas, junior, 12, 115
Flight, Thomas, senior, Buys factory, 11;
    History, 11; Trip to Cornwall, 27; New
    partner, 30; Dies, 48; Biography, 204
Flight and Chamberlain merger, 130-147
Flower paintings, 174
Ford, Jeremiah, 115
Foss, Richard, 204
French style porcelain, 23, 36, 220
Frit porcelain body, 70
Fuseli, Henry, 200

Gadroon rims, 184
George the Third, Visits Worcester, 16;
    Grants Royal Warrant, 16; Visits factory,
    18, 218
Gew Graze soaprock mine, 45, 46
Gibbons, Mr., 220
Gilders' numbers, 161
Gilding processes, 100, 180, 182, 225-226
Gillam, Miss Ann, 27, 230-231
Gillam, Robert, 32
Gillam, Thomas, 30
Gillam and Barr, 30
Gloucester, Duke of, 184, 211
Godden, Geoffrey, 162
Gold preparation, 225-226
Goldworthy, Colonel, 18, 219
Gordon, Lord George, 12
Gort, Viscount, 214

Gothic style, 188
Green, Valentine, 16, 162, 204
Gresley, Sir Roger, 211
Ground colours, 185
Guinness, Sir Arthur, 106
Gwinnell, Mr., 222, 225
Gwynn, Col., 219

Haines, Henry, 204
Hamilton, Lady Emma, 200
Hamilton, Sir William, 200
Hampton, Mrs., 24, 26, 27, 204, 220, 221,
    226, 232
Harcourt, Countess of, 16, 218
Harcourt, Lord, 27, 218, 220, 228
Harlequin services, 180
Haslem, John, 66
Hastings, Marchioness of, 184
Hatchett, Charles, Visit, 46, 48
Haydon, B.R., 201
Hayton, C., 204
Hebb, C.H., surgeon, 32
Higgs, Samuel, 204
Holgate of Walden, 214
Holloway, Thomas, 204
Holloway, William, 204
Hope, H.T., 106
Hope service, 184
Hornblower, Jethro, 45
Horsehay Company of Shropshire, 48
Horse head handle, 180
Houghton, Sir Henry Bold de, 212
Hughes, William, 204
Hunt, Emma, 82, 101, 204, 231
Hunt, Dr. L.B., 182
Hyde, John Brooke, 132, 133, 139, 204

Ice pail, 174
Imari style, 169
India patterns, 169, 174
Inkwells, 180
Isaac, J.W., 145

Japan patterns, 169, 174
Jardinière, 166
Jay, Richard Suinthill, 214
Jeffs, Mrs., 220
Jewelling, 186
John, W.D., 66
Johnson, John, 205
Johnson, Joseph, 82
Johnson Matthey and Co. Ltd., 182
Jones, John, 205
Jones, Joseph, 205
Jones, Thomas, 205

Kitchen, Edward, 26-27, 205, 222, 224-225,
    229, 232
Knight, James, 30
Knight, Jonathon, 205

Lane, the traveller, 139
Lauderdale, Earl of, 213
Lead, John, 205
Lewis, a printer, 232
Liverpool wares, 160
Lilly, John, 132, 133, 139, 141, 145, 205
Lloyd, Thomas, 205

Los Angeles County Museum, 200
Lowe, Mrs., printer, 101, 205
Lowe, James, 205
Lowe, Thomas, 103, 183, 205
Lowestoft wares, 160

Maidment, Mr., 218
Maitland, Patrick Barclay, 212
Malabar, Leslie, 23
Manason, Henry, 205
Manason, William, 205
Marbling, 174
Marjoriebanks of Lees, 211
Marks, 161-164, 168, 179, 237-241
Mask jugs, 168
Mason, a painter, 205
Match case, 174-178
Meadowes, James, 205
Miller and Lund lease, 43
Minet, Hughes, 213
Miniatures, 188
Mirza, Abbas, 214
Morland, Benjamin, 175
Mortlocks, china dealers, 139
Mountmorris, Earl of, 213
Muscat, Imaum of, 189
Music candlesticks, 175-178
Music meeting, 16
Music pattern, 160

Nance, E. Morton, 72
Nankin blue and white, 11
Neal, Mr., 218
Nelson, Lord, 171, 200
Neptune and Britannia, 171
Niblett, Jos., 206

Ogle of Ogle Castle, 213
Onslow, Earl of, 211
Oude, Nabob of, 184, 213
Oxford, Countess of, 16
Oxford, Earl of, 219

Page, a painter, 206
Page, W., 184
Paine, Thomas, 206
Painting processes, 100
Parker, John, 139, 206
Parry, Mr., Visit to Cornwall, 43
Pattern Numbers, 166
Pearls applied, 180
Peat, Charles, 206
Peel, Sir Robert, 211
Pembroke, Lady, 218
Penderill-Church, John, 43
Pennings, Nicolas, 206
Pennington, James, 82, 206
Pennington, John, Comes to factory, 27,
    223; Painting subject, 104; Corporation
    Punchbowls, 168; Hope service, 184;
    Biography, 206
Pennington, Robert, 206
Peugh, Thomas, 206
Pewtress, Flight and Halliday, 12.
Piercy, George, 206
Pitman, C., 206
Pitman, John, 103, 206

Pitt, William, 212
Plaques, 169, 188
Powys, Mrs. Lybbe, 115
Price, Bill, 210
Price, H. Rokeby, 106
Price, James, 82
Prince of Wales, 184
Printing, 172
Pyne style patterns, 171

Quaker House in Worcester, 43
Queen Charlotte pattern, 166
Rackham, Arthur, 72
Rado, Paul, 235
Rawson, John, 66
Richards, Charles, 206
Richards, Thomas, 207
Richards, William, 207
Robins and Randall, 208
Rogers, Darby, 207
Rogers, Thomas, 104, 207
Ross, James, engraver, 23, 30, 63, 172, 207,
    233-234
Rous Lench Court, 200
Royal Lily pattern, 21, 160, 169
Royal Warrants, 21, 63, 161, 219
Rundall or Rundle, 213
Russia, Emperor of, 184, 213

Scale blue, 162
Sèvres factory, 182
Shah, Futte Ali, 214
Shaw, factory foreman, 27, 65, 207, 218,
    224, 227-229, 232
Shells, 172
Sherwin, Ishmael, 207
Showrooms, 166
Shuttleworth, 211
Siddons, Mrs. Sarah, 106
Silk, painter, 207
Silver Articles engraved, 24
Smith, John, 104, 207
Smith, Samuel, 207
Smith, Thomas, 207
Soaprock material from Cornwall, 43, 45,
    46, 189
Spare, William, 207
Square marks, 162
Stafford, Marquis of, 106
Stinton, Charles, 106, 207
Stinton, Henry, 104, 207
St. John, Fleming, 132-133, 139, 141,
    145-146, 207
Stones, Robert, 199
Stourhead, 184
Sulphuring of ware, 26, 160, 223, 229
Swansea, possible move to, 16, 218
Taylor, Jos., 207
Taylor, Watson, 106
Taylor, William, 208
Taylour, 212
Tebo, 208
Tennant, R.C., 106
Three Choirs Festival, 16
Tomkins, John, 208
Tomlins, ground layer, 208

Toulouse, John, 208
Transfer Prints, 160
Translucence, 11, 160
Trim, Mr., his daughters, 27
Turner, Francis, 208
Turner, George, 208
Turner, James, 208
Turner, John, 139, 208
Turner, Moses, 208
Turner, Thomas, 11, 208

Vaisseau à mats, 168
Valentia, Lord, 184
Varden, R., 208
Vases with bolts, 178
Vermiculi pattern, 174
Vernon, Thomas, 11
Vincennes factory, 182

Walker, Henry, 211
Walker, Samuel, Character, 65; Starting at
    Worcester, 66; Bond, 70; Contract
    dispute, 72-80; Biography, 208
Wall, Dr. John, 11, 208

Walmesley, Sir Thomas, 212
Warmstry House factory details, 39
Warner, R., diary, 45, 166
Warranted mark, 164
Warren-Poynton, 214
Webster, Moses, 103, 208
White House, 184
White-Jervis, Sir John, 212
Whitgrave, 214
Whitwell, T., 27, 221, 223, 226-227
Wilkinson, 214
William the Fourth, service, 103, 185-186,
    189; see also Clarence, Duke of
Willow pattern scenes, 11
Wills, Geoffrey, 24
Woods, William, 209
Worcester College, Oxford, 211
Worcester Corporation punch bowls, 22, 35,
    168
Worcester Society of Arts, 203
Wykeham of Swalcliffe, 212
Wyndham, 212

Yates, James, 132-133, 135, 146, 209